SHAKESPEARE
IN HIS OWN AGE

SHAKESPEARE
IN HIS OWN AGE

EDITED BY
ALLARDYCE NICOLL

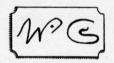

CAMBRIDGE UNIVERSITY PRESS

CAMBRIDGE

LONDON · NEW YORK · MELBOURNE

Published by the Syndics of the Cambridge University Press

The Pitt Building, Trumpington Street, Cambridge CB2 1RP

Bentley House, 200 Euston Road, London NW1 2DB

32 East 57th Street, New York, NY 10022, USA

296 Beaconsfield Parade, Middle Park, Melbourne 3206, Australia

ISBN 0 521 06430 9 hard covers
ISBN 0 521 29129 1 paperback

First published as *Shakespeare Survey 17*, 1964
Reprinted 1965 1974
First paperback edition, as *Shakespeare in his own age*, 1976

Shakespeare Survey was first published in 1948. For the first
eighteen volumes it was edited by Allardyce Nicoll under the
sponsorship of the University of Birmingham, the University
of Manchester, the Royal Shakespeare Theatre and the
Shakespeare Birthplace Trust. Kenneth Muir has edited
volume 19 onwards.

Printed in Great Britain
at the
University Printing House, Cambridge
(Euan Phillips, University Printer)

CONTENTS

LIST OF PLATES

LIST OF PLATES

EDITORIAL PREFACE

The present volume, issued in the fourth centenary year of Shakespeare's birth, does not, and could not, aim at presenting a general comprehensive survey of Elizabethan life and thought. Many aspects of the age have deliberately been omitted—some because they have been fully explored elsewhere, others because they impinge less directly on the dramatist's career. Thus, for example, there are no chapters on such important but already well-documented subjects as Elizabethan costume and pictorial art. Rather, in the planning of this book an effort has been made to select themes which have been neglected, or which have received comparatively little attention, or which, although surveyed in the past, appeared to demand reappraisal.

Naturally, throughout the book Shakespeare's genius presides, but no effort has been made to focus all attention on his writings, since it has been thought more important to reserve as much space as possible for the treatment of the environment amid which these writings took shape. With this end in view the several contributory chapters have been arranged in three main sections.

The first of these deals with the physical environment. Shakespeare was born and died in a small market town, from which he moved, during his middle years, to work in the metropolis, and it is eminently proper that a start should be made with a survey of life in town and country-side. We do not know what practical experience he had of seafaring, but no Elizabethans who passed even a small part of their time in London or reasonably close to the coasts could escape the impact of the ocean which engirdled their island, giving it safety, sustenance and strength: after city and country, therefore, the sea takes pride of place. The sea brought Englishmen of that age into contact with realms beyond their islands; many of the Folio plays have foreign settings; Othello is a Moor, and Shylock a Jew, of Venice; in *The Tempest* the newly discovered wonders of another continent find their imaginative mirroring; there is, accordingly, virtue in trying to assess in what light these insular, sea-roving subjects of Elizabeth looked upon men of other races. Like his fellows and rivals, Ben Jonson and George Chapman, Shakespeare did not attend a university, but all three certainly went to grammar school, and, if he did not seek to attain to such advanced self-made scholarship as they later sought to acquire, he shared with them the fundamental benefits which Elizabethan grammar schools so richly offered; and hence the world of sixteenth-century education becomes of prime significance for us. No Elizabethan, rich or poor, could escape daily contact with the law, so that familiarity with legal processes was widely spread over the entire population; unless we make fullest allowance for this we may be tempted to credit Shakespeare with a legal training for the existence of which there is no real justification —like most of his companions he no doubt imbibed from boyhood an awareness of the law's ways and delays. In one respect, however, he was unlike the majority of his theatrical fellows: no prison gates seem ever to have clanged behind him; yet, paradoxically, the ever-imminent threat of incarceration which confronted so many men in his time, combined with his own avoidance of such danger, makes an account of London's Clinks and Counters seem obligatory.

In the opening chapters of the second section the main themes are the prevailing thought of the period—its fundamental, and generally accepted, philosophy—and the aberrant views of nonconformist groups and individuals: the idea of the Establishment in church and society and the ideas of religious dissidents and of angry young men. While the advance of science lagged far behind that which dominates our own lives, the Elizabethan age was tentatively, gropingly, stretching out its hands to the present, and while its medical knowledge and practice may appear hopelessly primitive, some things were being learned which were destined to prove a fundamental basis for the doctors of the future—and once more, if every man was his own lawyer, every man was his own doctor and every sailor at least his own astronomer. Science and medicine, then, demand our scrutiny. In those days physicians often indulged in methods savouring of wizardry, and we need to give full weight to the almost universal belief in an enveloping universe of strangeness, of evil and of good inhabited by denizens extending from material witches to wraith-like creatures beyond the reach of human touch. Nor can we neglect that associated and elusive belief in the power of symbols which prevailingly coloured so much of the age's thought and which almost insensibly guided the lives of its men and women.

In the third section attention is given to certain selected aspects of the artistic and recreational life of the period—the theatres, naturally; the active printing presses which disseminated everything from expensive folios, handsomely bound, to cheap paperbacks; and, alongside these, that realm of song and balladry which made street and tavern, private house and country fair, ring with melody, lyric beauty and jigging rhyme. When all has been said, the true glory of the Elizabethan age must be found to rest in its strange power over words—words winged with splendour, barbed with wit, and so fashioned that, although issuing from an environment far removed from ours, they have retained all their compulsive force. Appropriately, therefore, the final chapter seeks to suggest the source from which Shakespeare and his poet-companions drew their command over language. An attempt, too, has been made to present this picture visually as well as by the printed word. All the illustrations have been selected with this end in view, and one set of plates in particular has been devised, largely with the aid of the late F. P. Wilson, to give at least a glimpse of something not dealt with in the text—the sports and games which were a solace and delight on summer days and winter's long candle-lit evenings.

A.N.

DAILY LIFE

I

LONDON AND THE COURT

'Welcome to London'

'London, the Head and Metropolis of *England*...the seat of the *British* Empire, and the Chamber of the *English* Kings.' The description is that of a foreign traveller, Paul Hentzner, in 1598. Awestruck and not a little amazed, he noted that 'The Wealth of the World is wafted to it by the Thames'.[1] More briefly he noted his companion's loss of nine crowns to the skill of the London pickpockets. This London to which Shakespeare, the provincial, came in the 1590's, was already a magnet to people of all descriptions. A riverside town, it depended for its existence on trade by sea and river, and for its greatness on that trade plus its close links with the government of the realm. The centuries had seen its gradual growth from a leading town to a capital comparable with almost any in Europe. To the provincial, faced for the first time with its size, its bustle, its close-packed houses and its rush of traffic on road and river alike, it was alarming or electric.

To those sojourning in London it had all that a great capital can offer. Gresham's Royal Exchange had achieved its object as a centre for the merchant community. Whole streets were occupied by shops, the London artisan making up the raw materials of the provinces and the London shop-keeper selling the finished product. Wealth and talent were concentrated there—all the wit and wisdom of the Elizabethan age. There men of many tongues mingled, sermons were endowed and good preachers at a premium. The great cathedral of St Paul served both as a church and as a series of 'walks'. In it journeymen stood for hire and gossip ran unrestrained. Round the cathedral and the five-score parish churches lay the narrow-fronted houses, a cellar below, a shop or workshop on the ground floor, living quarters on the first and second floors and a garret above. The gables and steep-pitched roofs covered an urban people still wedded to the country, going Maying on May Day and finding open country within a mile of its street doors. Shakespeare could find there all that he needed, audiences, characters, encouragement and competition.

When able to assess what lay around him, he could begin, as all visitors began, to bring order to his impressions. The apparently endless streets stretching in ill-ordered fashion from the palace of Westminster and Petty France on the west to Poplar on the east, and from the north bank of the Thames to Clerkenwell and Whitechapel, could then be divided into their essential components. Their central core was the original walled city, running in a rough semi-circle from the Tower to the street now known as London Wall and then south-westwards to the River Fleet. Some of that wall remains to this day though its defensive ditch has long disappeared. Shakespeare, exploring his new home, would have found the ditch deep, the walls complete, and entry possible only at guarded gates and posterns. Less than forty years before his arrival, Wyatt's rebellion had seen it standing siege and in the 1590's the citizens were still regularly exercised in arms. But growth and prosperity had gradually taken the city's limits well beyond its walls, and then, as now, they ran from the site of Temple Bar, at the western end of Fleet Street, northwards to High Holborn and then east to include Smithfield, Moorfields and The Minories. These were the liberties of the city and in them its writ ran. Beyond lay other areas in which its citizens had rights but no complete authority.

Of these, the most important was Westminster. Here Tudor power had added to the little nucleus of buildings round the palace and the abbey an increasing number of streets and houses. Magnates, spiritual and lay, had long found it wise to have mansions near to the royal courts of justice and the centre of the administration. As Tudor statutes increased and Parliament sat more often and for more of the year, officialdom grew and with it the tide of houses spreading away from the Abbey and the river frontage below Charing Cross and the Strand. The result was to create on the very doorsteps of the royal palaces of Westminster, Whitehall and St James an area in which regulation was lacking and that prop of Tudor town government, the independent merchant or craftsman householder, in danger of being swamped by its most feared alternative, the poor, suspect, tenement-dweller. The year 1585 had brought a drastic remedy, the preamble to the 'act for the good government of...Westminster' summarizing the dilemma which then faced all London, including even the city itself.

Forasmuch as [it ran] by erection and new building of divers houses, and by the parting and dividing of divers tenements within the city and borough of Westminster and the liberties of the same, the people thereof are greatly increased and, being for the most part without trade or mystery, are become poor, and many of them given wholly to vice and idleness, living in contempt of all manner of officers within the said city, for that their power to correct and reform them is not sufficient in law as in that behalf were mete and requisite.[1]

The statute's answer was authoritarian. The Dean of Westminster Abbey, or the High Steward—usually a man of weight in Court circles—yearly appointed from among the inhabitants twelve burgesses to continue in office from year to year during good behaviour, who, with twelve assistants similarly appointed, governed the city.

How effective these Westminster burgesses were, it is hard to say, but at least they tried, as their records surviving for the years 1610–15 plainly show.[2] Elsewhere on this north bank of the Thames the work fell on the Middlesex justices. On the Surrey bank, where the close-built area was smaller and poorer, the Surrey justices were in charge. There, opposite the palace of Westminster stood the palace of the archbishop of Canterbury at Lambeth, itself a flourishing village. Downstream the marshes created a gap but in Southwark the needs of port and shipping were spreading the buildings on through Bermondsey towards the royal dockyard at Deptford. Yet the south bank in general was a poor relation, and Southwark the suspect home of the Marshalsea, Queen's Bench and Clink prisons, of the stews against which the preachers and the city fathers waged common war, the malodorous trades of the tanners, the soap and sugar boilers and the brewers, and the popular, morally dubious delights of the bull-ring and the theatre.

All through Shakespeare's sojourn in London this increase in its houses was a trouble to those in authority. Stow,[3] citizen, chronicler and student of Tudor London, punctuates his descriptions with laments about alleys built and fields swallowed up, and every available record bears him out. Queen, Privy Council and City[4] were doing all they could to prevent it. The City[5] had been grumbling about it in Henry VIII's reign and Elizabeth, in July 1580, was moved to forbid both new buildings and the conversion of old houses into tenements. In 1590 she was ordering the Lord Mayor and the Master of the Rolls to report all infringements and to stay all building in progress.[1] In the intervening years the City had worked to the same end and in 1593 it was lobbying for a bill to make new houses and conversions illegal within the London area. The bill became an Act and the City instituted quarterly inquiries backed by presentments and prosecutions but the changes continued. James I followed the same policy, again with the City's active support, and with no greater success. The built-up area continued to grow. Reliable statistics do not exist, but in 1603 it contained between 200,000 and 250,000 people, perhaps four times the number of a century earlier.

The authorities' motives were sensible enough. They feared the problems of crowded alleys, the diseases they spread, the plague that was rife in them, the problems of cleanliness, sanitation and water-supply they created, the difficulty of maintaining law and order, the doubt whether food and fuel could be provided, the attraction they had for those daemons of Tudor administrators, the vagrants, the rogues and the idle and masterless men.

No sketch of Shakespearian London can afford to ignore these problems. As in every large West European town, the city fathers had both to safeguard the means which enabled the town to exist, and the standards of quality and production which protected its consumers against fraud. Water supplies, for example, were a constant and expensive anxiety. London citizens in their wills left money to the water carrier who daily brought them water tankards from the public conduits, and legacies for the maintenance of those conduits. In 1580 the City had adopted the suggestion of Peter Morris, a German engineer, for pumping supplies via tide-operated water wheels under London Bridge. In the 1590's it negotiated with Bevis Bulmer, gentleman, for engines to pump a further supply, and James I, with rare wisdom, rescued from failure Sir Hugh Myddleton's project for a supply from the springs of Hertfordshire—the New River which still helps to provide London with water.

Bread was an equally serious problem. In normal years London drew much of its corn from the valleys of the Thames and its tributaries. If harvests were good, all went well, but in a year or years of dearth, prices rose swiftly and the corn bodger became an object of execration. The problem grew as London grew and, in the 1520's, the City began to adopt a policy which by Shakespeare's day was standard. The companies governing the city's trades, the mercers, fishmongers, goldsmiths, clothworkers and others, were ordered to pay for stocks of corn to be held in the municipal granaries and sold at reasonable prices as the need arose. Six thousand quarters, for example, were demanded in the winter of 1590, one-third of it rye, and forty-nine of the companies were ordered to contribute their quotas, the merchant taylors 562 quarters, the grocers 525, the mercers 492 and so on, down the scale to the minimum assessment of 6 apiece from painter-stainers, curriers and plasterers.[2]

Fuel was also a problem, especially the coal which, as wood supplies dwindled, loomed ever more important to manufacturer and consumer alike. Here the difficulty was not dearth but combination by suppliers on the north-east coast to extract maximum prices. This the City fought with all its power, whilst continuing its normal practice of protecting the consumer against fraud and the poor against the consequences of their poverty. Stocks for sale to the latter were built up each year, with surveyors to supervise them. All supplies were measured by sworn measurers as they were unloaded, but a trade which has always suffered from the occasional fraudulent retailer produced many in Shakespearian times and dealt with them appropriately. In one fortnight in 1592 four sellers of charcoal, convicted of selling in sacks two bushels per sack short, were sentenced to two hours apiece in the pillory at Cheapside, London's greatest shopping street, their false sacks slowly burning below their noses. Half stifled by the smoke, and pelted by the passers-by, they returned to gaol until able to produce adequate sureties not to err again.

This supervision of quality and standards, which was one of the essentials of civic policy, dovetailed into that of the safeguarding of supplies. A handful of examples must typify a whole range. The aldermen annually appointed vintners to report both on the quantity of wine available in the city and the amount which was not wholesome. In 1593 that report listed 1068 tons 4 hogsheads of which two tons three hogsheads were not wholesome. Similarly, searchers of hops and of soap were appointed each year, the wardens of every trade were expected to maintain periodical searches of the shops of their members, and every trade could, in the public interest, be regulated as occasion demanded. The inn-holders in 1593 were threatened with prison if the hay they sold departed from a prescribed weight and cost, whilst the committee set to report on the number of barrels of strong and of double beer obtainable from a quarter of malt provoked such indignation, presumably from apprehensive brewers, that two of these were committed to Newgate for the abuse with which they greeted it. Yet the result was an acceptable scale of quality and prices plus a promise from the brewers that their carts would carry measures so that even the poor could be served at their doors and at the prescribed price.

Bread, both brown and white, was subjected to an almost continuous review, the weight of the penny loaf being prescribed on the basis of the price of grain with always a wary eye on the harvest reports. Thus in August 1593 the weight of the penny wheaten loaf was ordered to be 22 ounces. Five months later it was altered to 20 ounces and the City wrote to the Lord Treasurer asking that the transport of corn and grain overseas be prohibited. Twenty-five years later, when bread prices had risen alarmingly and the City and the Privy Council were successfully striving for reductions, the White Bakers' Company protested that they were being driven out of business, fortifying their complaint with not unreasonable figures for their costs.[1]

Some civic legislation was part and parcel of royal orders or Acts of Parliament. The lenten restrictions on the eating of meat are one example. Whether these were inspired by the shortage of winter keep for animals, the wish to foster the fishing fleets or the injunctions of religion, much trouble was taken to enforce them. The City required from the Fishmongers' Company reports on the stocks in hand, and people caught eating meat without licence were treated with full publicity. Nor was this a short-lived unenforced policy. In the 1590's watch was kept at the city's gates for meat consigned to unlicensed consumers and licences were still being obtained by such eaters in St Margaret, Westminster, nearly a century after the four women recorded by Unwin as being sent to the stocks for eating meat in a tavern in 1563.[2]

Leather, almost as essential as food or drink, had been regulated anew by statute in 1562-3.[3] In London the powers of search by the Curriers' Company were confirmed and the City itself given, and ordered to exercise, special supervision over made wares. This it did, sworn searchers reporting quarterly with lists of wares condemned. Shoes, girdles, girths and pillions, portmanteaux and even leather-based girdles of velvet and of gold twist appear in their lists, the makers ranging from Holborn to St Katherine's on the north bank and from Lambeth to Southwark on the south. After condemnation the wares were appraised by sworn appraisers and the searchers, bound in the high sum of £400 apiece, began again.

If the victualling and clothing trades were chief objects of statutory and civic regulation, public health and public order were a never-ending preoccupation of Crown and City alike. By all contemporary standards, London was well-provided with hospitals.[1] St Bartholomew's and St Thomas's were hospitals in the modern sense, served by physicians, barber-surgeons and the apothecaries who, in 1617, gained a charter of their own. Bethlehem Hospital provided for the lunatics—that Bethlehem whence Shakespeare drew material for *Lear* and Dekker for *The Bellman*, and Christ's Hospital received a steady stream typified by the orphan of John Fippes 'sadler' 'who died a very poor man' and whose daughter Elizabeth, aged three or thereabouts, was 'sent to Christ's Hospital there to be virtuously brought up'. The difficulty lay, not in those well-organized sectors, but in the sectors of ill-organization and of calamity. Tales of the filthy streets and sanitary horrors of Elizabethan London are only true in part and cannot compete in scale or nausea with the days either of Fielding or Chadwick. The organization of scavenger and raker worked reasonably well. The trouble came, as always, in places of uncertain jurisdiction, in Whitefriars, the Alsatia of *The Fortunes of Nigel*, and in other places where the immunities of the former monasteries were proclaimed defiantly in the tenements and back alleys built over their former precincts. The City could, at intervals, repeat its orders to the unpaid ward officers, that the streets and lanes be cleansed and swept daily and the filth and dung taken away at least thrice weekly by the raker, and the results were at least as effective as modern orders about speed limits in built-up areas. Hentzner noted that 'the streets in this City are very handsome and clean'[2] but he did not visit the Alsatias and it was with Water Lane in Whitefriars that the City was then struggling. The dock at its river end was much used by brewers' and innkeepers' drays fetching water, by barges with cargo and by woodmongers for coals. All left debris and droppings. The lane and the narrow alleys off it were full of tenement dwellers who used it as a refuse dump and a privy. Though the City was keen to introduce proper control, the difficulties were added to by the ownership of land there by a leading privy councillor, Lord Buckhurst. Inspection, a full report and an Act of Common Council produced adequate remedies, on paper, but with what actual success it is hard to tell.[3]

If sanitation was one of the normal problems of local government in London a worse problem, bubonic plague, was becoming a continuous, rather than an occasional threat. In Shakespeare's lifetime London was seldom free from it. No cure was known, and all that the Privy Council, the College of Physicians and the City itself could do was to repeat orders whose ineffectiveness had been many times proven. Private charity contributed money which the City officially distributed, but flight, the reduction of all business, and reliance on heaven were the usual recourse. Thus in July 1593 a special meeting of the court of aldermen ordered that

the summoning of all Juries as well in the Lord Mayor's Court as both the Sheriff's Courts and also the keeping of the Court of Conscience shall be forborne until it shall please Almighty God of his infinite mercy to stay the present infection of the plague within this city.[4]

This particular outbreak, it is true, stimulated the long-mooted idea for building a separate place of isolation, a pest-house, for plague victims as an alternative to forcible confinement to their own homes. Helped by a loan from the committee administering London's share in a successful privateering venture against Spain, this official pest-house was built in 1594. Some twenty years later Parliament authorized compulsory plague rates to meet expenditure on relief, but Shakespeare had been in his grave for half a century before London could be considered free from the disease.

Rogues and vagabonds, the last of the City's standing problems in matters of ordinary everyday life, were a problem affecting all Tudor England. Inevitably London attracted many of them and especially those driven out of their usual vocations. The soldiers and sailors caught up in and discharged from Elizabeth's wars or garrisons, cultivators displaced by inclosures, refugees from religious persecution in France or the Low Countries joined there with discharged servants, ne'er-do-wells, deserted women and wretched orphans. They lurked in the brick-fields near Islington, in the purlieus of the markets and in any corner where they could find cover. At their worst they formed mutinous assemblies by the Royal Exchange or on Tower Hill, driving the City to appoint provost marshals and to keep, night after night, in every ward, patrols of scores of armed men whose task it was to search all ale-houses, inns, cellars, lodging houses and any other likely harbouring place and to bring before the justices all incapable of giving a good account of themselves. At its simplest it was as with Edward Bennett and Elizabeth Randall;

who have wandered within this city...vagrantly and have otherwise been of lewd and unhonest behaviour... [as they have confessed]...shall be tied at a cart's tail and whipped out of this city as rogues and vagrants and to have a passport delivered unto them declaring their said offences according to the form of the statute in the 22nd year of Henry the eight.[1]

At its worst it was an order to provide nightly two hundred 'well and sufficiently weaponed and appointed' men and one hundred by day to safeguard the vulnerable parts of the ward of Faringdon outside the wall, the other wards providing their normal watches besides reliefs for the burden falling on that hard-pressed area.[2] When Shakespeare first arrived in the city it was striving to turn the former royal palace of Bridewell into a self-supporting workhouse in which to train vagrant children in the habits of industry. By the middle of his stay Parliament had enacted the Elizabethan poor law. But at no time, either then or in the next two hundred years was the problem completely solved. The workhouse was no cure and Dickens' Artful Dodger had his exact Elizabethan counterparts.

The government of the city, as Shakespeare knew it, followed the pattern common to most English towns, standing out by size and complexity rather than by constitutional innovations. A lord mayor, elected for a year from twenty-six aldermen elected for life by the citizens of the twenty-six wards into which the city was divided, headed the court of aldermen. That court provided the day-to-day government, the seniors being justices of the peace and each being responsible for the running of his own ward. Supplemented by some two hundred common councilmen elected annually by the wards, they formed the civic Parliament, legislating, taxing and ordering the city. Standing committees of aldermen and common councillors dealt with matters of continuing concern—for example the civic estates, London Bridge or martial affairs. Centuries of hard bargaining with the Crown had brought an autonomy it never dared to take for granted. The officers of the Crown were almost entirely excluded. It chose its own sheriffs, as it chose its mayor and aldermen. Its mayor was *ex-officio* conservator of the Thames and admiral of the port, chief magistrate, coroner, escheator and principal in the commission of felony. It administered its own law, appointed its own police, ran its own army, enrolled its own deeds and wills, determined its own citizens and looked after their orphans. Retail trade within the city was the monopoly of its citizens, and their organized authority over standards of craftsmanship extended in most cases three miles beyond the liberties, in some, for example the goldsmiths and the stationers, throughout the realm.

Yet this whole imposing structure was preserved by a balance of forces and needs. The Crown needed the loyalty and taxable capacity of the city. It needed the skill of its members for the day-to-day running of government, whether as financial advisers of the expertise of Gresham, customs farmers like William Garway and Nicholas Sutton, merchant members of the Levant or Russia or East India companies, or goldsmith venturers in the company of mineral and battery works. The city, in its collective capacity, required the assurance of a stable government, royal backing against the exactions of foreign states and the minimum of interference in its day-to-day life. Each harassed the other and each had ample opportunities for so doing. The Crown had only to yield to the importunities of some courtier, in partnership, no doubt, with a city syndicate, and grant a monopoly of starch or playing cards, for the affected parties in London to bring all possible pressure to bear to get it reversed. In turn, the citizens exported illicitly as much as they dared and opened their purse strings as grudgingly as they could. Shakespeare, the provincial, dealt comparatively little with such civic affairs, though Jonson, the Londoner, mirrors them again and again, and the records of the Crown are full of the manœuvrings of those concerned.

Perhaps monopolies and warfare produced the worst frictions and a glance at the latter shows the extent and effect of the Crown's demands in the city. The years 1591–4 saw, in 1591, the compulsory provision of six ships and one pinnace, complete, as in all these demands, with crews, stores and victuals, at a cost of £8000, and 650 men with, again as in all these demands, arms, clothes and equipment, for Brittany and France. The year 1592 required £6000 for ships and 450 men for Normandy; 1593 required 650 men for France, and 1594 six ships and two pinnaces for Brittany and 300 out of an English contingent of 1500 for the Low Countries. These were provided by means of heavy civic taxation on companies and individuals, and to an accompaniment of distraints and committals for refusal to pay, and new taxes to meet arrears of those already granted. Some men may have volunteered, but many were pressed. Masterless and idle men, caught in the civic sweeps, were kept in Bridewell as stand-by's and the general quality may be judged by the Privy Council's addition to the Queen's letter of January 1593:

And because upon occasion of like service heretofore there hath not been so good regard had to the choice of the men for their abilities of bodies, years, and condition as hath appertained, whereof hath followed that many persons levied and imprested hath either there at London, or after they were arrived at the place of their services, through fear either run from their captains or offered money to them or to their officers to be discharged and suffered to return as by experience hath often appeared though severely to be punished as an offence of dangerous example and hindrance to her Majesty's service.[1]

Before very long the Council was demanding sixteen ships and 10,000 men to meet a possible invasion by Spain, but, well before that, the aldermen were entreating one of their number 'to be the means to procure the sum of one or two thousand pounds to be taken up for the affairs of this city after the rate of £6 for the hundred by the year or at less rate if possibly he can'.[1]

Lack of space prevents any lengthy description of the Crown's relationship, via the justices, with the suburbs in Middlesex and Surrey. Poorer and less well organized, they were less suited to provide the good order, detailed regulation and men and money needed by the Crown, but, so far as they could or could be driven to, they did. The sessions rolls for Middlesex in 1598,[2] the year in which Jonson was indicted for the manslaughter in a duel in Shoreditch Fields of the quarrelsome Gabriel Spencer, are a revealing commentary on the state of affairs. Jonson acknowledged his guilt, and having plead his clergy, was branded with the Tyburn T and duly released. The city boundaries were no barrier to the faults of the age and page after page records the swift quarrels leading to death by sword or dagger, the assaults, thefts, murders and robberies, the throwing of filth into the streets, the vagrants, the illegal bowling alleys, the false measures, the occasional rape and the rarer case of poisoning, the thefts of livestock and the indictments for non-attendance at church. Other years produce prosecutions for coin clipping, following a trade without having been apprenticed, breaches of the orders against new buildings, the keeping of inmates, conversion of houses into tenements, unlawful assembly—even a burglary of St James's Palace when the Queen was in residence. Joined with the city in drives against the armed rogues who infested the metropolitan highways Middlesex showed the same reluctance to contribute money.[3] Its assessments were much lower than the city's—two horses (£60) for Ireland and 100 recruits for the Low Countries instead of ten (£300) and 600 recruits. Its slowness to comply brought a stinging rebuke from the Council and orders, similar to those given by the Lord Mayor, to commit defaulters to prison. Though in almost all matters of government the Crown looked to the City first, in anything of general concern the Home Counties were necessarily ordered to play their part. Shakespeare, living for the most part in the suburbs, was less affected than the tradesmen of Cheapside or the Royal Exchange but he could not fail to be aware of these demands.

Such concentration on the town must not obscure the Court. True, in Elizabeth's reign and to a lesser extent in James', the Court spent long periods outside London, yet present or absent it was an important component of the town. Four royal palaces were situated there, Westminster, Whitehall, St James's and The Tower. Hampton Court, Richmond and Greenwich were hard by, linked to it by the ease of water transport. Elizabeth, in the summer heat and in the early autumn, might spend much of her time outside London, but London was her principal residence and James gave even more of his time to it.

The organization of the Court was important. It included the household, the main departments of the central government, and that core of society which surrounded, served and derived its living from the throne. All three shaded into each other. In the household of Shakespeare's day, the masters of the horse were the Earls of Essex (1587–97) and of Worcester (1597–1616). They dealt with the outdoor organization of the household, as the lord steward dealt with that downstairs and the lord chamberlain with that upstairs. Outside the household, but within the Court, lay, at least in part, most of the organs of the central administration—in attendance on the Sovereign, the Privy Council; in the palace of Westminster, the law courts and the exchequer; in the City the wardrobe, and in the Tower the mint. The army and the navy were still in that transition from the *ad hoc* to the regular which was ended by Cromwell and Charles II, but the needs of continental wars ensured that London and its port were always to the fore in both services.

More important, the Court was the magnet which drew to London from all over England the politically and the socially active members of the governing class. The sessions of Parliament, the activities of the law courts, and London's monopoly of law schools, helped, but the Court was the major factor. 'By wide distribution of favour the Crown and its ministers sought to link to themselves the interests and the hopes of the great majority of the English governing class.'[1] That class was small, and service in the household of a social superior had long been regarded as a training and an education. It was applauded in print by the author of *A Health to the Gentlemanly Profession of Serving-Men*, whilst Valentine, the courtier and city dweller, in *Cyvile and uncyvile life*, set out to show that it was best done in the town house of a courtier:

For the young man of good birth, poor estate and average talents a political career was the obvious choice. He viewed entrance into the Queen's service not as a bold bid for fame and fortune but as a prosaic and workaday matter of making a living.[2]

Hence the importance of a patron and of service in a household of standing. When Sir Christopher Hatton wrote to the father of Peter Dutton after that youth had served in Hatton's household, that the Queen judged 'that he will prove a man meete to be hereafter employed in service, to the benefitte of his countrye' and promised that, should he like to look to royal service and 'to followe the leif of a courtier, for a time, he shall have my best furtheraunce for his preferment'[3]—then the youngster was indeed launched. The Court, in fact and not just in theory, was the fountainhead of preferment, and every important office-holder was surrounded by a swarm of suitors, clerks, ushers and attendants alert for favours and fees for themselves and for those who, in their turn, looked for access to the great man. The size of the swarm helped to show the importance of that great man: any decline in his influence was quickly registered in the numbers attending him.

Inevitably Court and city were closely linked. The fine clothes, the jewels and plate, the wines and the luxuries, required by Queen and courtier alike, could seldom come from any but the London tradesmen. Essex's horseman's coat of black velvet embroidered with pearls and valued at £800,[4] could only be provided by a man of substance; and the fortunes left by the great London merchants ensured that their sons and daughters could make acceptable matches anywhere in the realm. The city was the chief source, on terms, of credit and mortgages, and the popular plays of the day, being written for London audiences, were naturally full of city allusions. Jonson freely satirized the alliance of the courtier and the citizens alert for mutual profit. Fynes Moryson, the traveller, showed the London tradesmen feeding on the Court's appetite for rich clothes:

All manners of attire came first into the City and the Country from the Court, which being once received by the common people...the Courtiers justly cast off, and take new fashions.[5]

Equally he reports the commonplace that the gentry 'daily sell their patrimonies, and the buyers (excepting lawyers) are for the most part Citizens'.[6] But Jonson the playwright looked more deeply and saw master Cymbal's news monopoly[7] and Meercraft the great projector and inventor of the new office of 'Master of the Dependencies' working with Thomas Gilthead the goldsmith and city usurer and the Lady Tailbush who intrigued at Court for monopolies. There was no love lost in this alliance of Court and City. As Gilthead said

> Wee must deale
> With Courtiers, boy, as Courtiers deale with vs.
> If I haue a Business there, with any of them,
> Why, I must wait, I'am sure on't, Son: and though
> My Lord dispatch me, yet his worshipfull man—
> Will keepe me for his sport, a moneth, or two,
> To shew mee with my fellow Citizens.
> I must make his traine long, and full, one quarter;
> And helpe the spectacle of his greatnesse. There,
> Nothing is done at once, but iniuries, boy.[1]

But the partnership was necessary. The monarch was the great source of patronage.[2] By direct appointment or by letters recommending, by the leasing or selling of royal lands, by grants of monopoly or other privileges Elizabeth, and later James, held the keys to fortune or favour. Those keys her entourage sought to use. Within reason such use was not unpopular in the city. A grant of citizenship at the request of some courtier was permissible and the city's records are punctuated by them. But the intervention in a civic office of importance was not easily excused and, still less so, any reduction through royal favour of the duties owed by prominent citizens to the city.

This working partnership weakened as Elizabeth's control weakened, and grew more precarious after James's accession. London continued to thrive and to grow. The citizens who had helped to finance Raleigh's expedition which captured the great Portuguese carrack in 1592 were prepared to finance later expeditions and even to invest in the Virginia Company. But privateering was less fruitful than legitimate trade and the success of the East India Company was a revelation to all parties. James had none of Elizabeth's instinctive skill and political dexterity. The struggle at Court for influence and the competition for lucrative concessions intensified. The careers of Robert Cecil and Sir Arthur Ingram and the records of the farming of the various London customs duties amply demonstrate this. For the successful the rewards were enormous, if usually precarious. Shakespeare, writing nationally, might ignore this. Jonson, the Londoner, drew rich material from it. While James sought to convert the half-timbered houses of his capital into brick, while Inigo Jones was building the Banqueting House as the finest modern stone building in London, the shrewder citizens were accumulating vast fortunes and obtaining high honour. Alderman Baptist Hicks became Viscount Camden and alderman William Cocayne, whose widow married the Earl of Dover and whose son became Viscount Cullen, left only one of his five marriageable daughters so lowly estated as to be content to be married to one of James' new race of baronets. At the top at least, the Court and the city were more closely intermingled than ever before, and by the time of Shakespeare's departure, London itself had become the capital of an even larger realm.

2

PROVINCIAL LIFE

'Our country manners'

The little town in which William Shakespeare opened his eyes in the spring of the year 1564 consisted of only six or seven streets, housing about two hundred families in all—probably fewer than a thousand people.[1] Less then twenty miles away, a day's journey through Warwick and Kenilworth, lay the populous city of Coventry, with between seven and eight thousand people, one of the half dozen largest towns in all England. The city of Canterbury, in which Christopher Marlowe saw the light of day a few weeks before Shakespeare, in a shoemaker's house, comprised about seven hundred families, round about three thousand people in all.

Birmingham, a day's journey to the north of Stratford, was little bigger than Stratford: a return made in 1563 gives it about two hundred families. And up and down England were many ancient borough-towns even smaller than this: towns like Banbury, Burford, or Chipping Norton counted their populations in hundreds, certainly not above eight hundred each. Liverpool at this date had seven streets and about seven hundred inhabitants. The largest city in England, outside London, was Norwich, the capital city of a rich province, but even here there were fewer than fifteen thousand people: about the size of Truro or Dorchester today. Probably only half a dozen other towns in England had as many as ten thousand people. Cities as important as Gloucester may have had five thousand, Worcester about seven thousand. Everything was on a very small scale: even in the biggest towns one could see the green countryside at the end of the streets and could walk into it within five or ten minutes.

In the whole of England there were only three million people, fewer than there had been before the Black Death two hundred years earlier, though the country was just beginning to fill up again and all around, in towns and villages alike, old men would have noticed more children playing about in the streets. More children were being born, and, what was more important, more were surviving the perils of infancy and growing up to manhood and marriage. William Shakespeare himself was one of eight children (four sons and four daughters), of whom however three died in infancy or childhood. This was a not untypical picture of an early Elizabethan family. How far the Shakespeare family of William's generation was typical in its longevity we do not know since we are only just beginning to study such questions in the sixteenth century. Of the eight children who were born, two died in infancy (before the age of one), another (Anne) died at the age of eight. Among the adults, Edmund died at twenty-eight, Richard at thirty-nine, Gilbert at forty-six, and William at fifty-two. This gives an average age at death for the four Shakespeare brothers of only forty-one, again a fairly typical figure so far as we yet know. The females of the same generation showed a much greater divergence: two died in infancy, one at eight years, and Joan—the only one who survived the perils of childhood—lived to be seventy-seven, before dying in 1646. But again the average age at death was only forty-two. William Shakespeare's only son, Hamnet, died at the age of eleven, in 1596; but his two daughters reached

13

respectable ages, Susanna (who married John Hall) died in 1649 aged sixty-six, and Judith, who married Thomas Quiney, lived on to see Charles II's restoration, dying in 1662 at the age of seventy-seven. Again this is fairly typical. Once past the early perils of life, women tended to live a good deal longer than men (as they do today). Widows were a numerous class in sixteenth- and seventeenth-century England as anyone knows who has studied local records in detail.

Whether or not the Shakespeare family was completely typical of its age in its pattern of births and deaths, it was certainly quite typical in its ancestry, above all in its country connections. In the England of the 1560's nine people out of ten were country born and bred; and of those living in towns big enough to be considered urban in their way of living, a high proportion had been born in villages round about and had come into town to seek employment or to build up a business. Shakespeare's father and grandfather—and many generations before them—were of Midland farming stock, and above the average country level to judge by John Shakespeare's marriage to Mary Arden. He moved into the town of Stratford from Snitterfield, some three miles to the north, just about the middle of the century,[1] and was at first described as a glover or a whit-tawer (one who cured skins for glovers). But at various dates he is described as a butcher, and a dealer in wool, malt and timber. All this is very characteristic of the sixteenth century. The labouring class were specialized workers for the most part, but, in the towns particularly, an up-and-coming man might have two, three, or four different occupations and might be variously described. Within ten to fifteen years John Shakespeare had prospered sufficiently to reach the governing class of the borough, being chosen bailiff of the town in 1568. William Shakespeare, then, was born into a very respectable *bourgeois* family, one of the handful of local families who ran the town of Stratford, as all the Elizabethan towns were run, as a petty oligarchy.

The focus of the local countryside everywhere in England was the market-town, of which there were rather more than eight hundred altogether. These were the centres of trade and of social intercourse, once a week in the smallest towns, two or three times a week in the larger. It is difficult to recapture their overwhelming importance in the social life and the economic life of sixteenth-century England, partly because we are so intensely urbanized today and the weekly market, even where it is still lively and busy, no longer meets the social needs of lonely country-dwellers. The markets of the country-towns were the great mechanism for the exchange of commodities, many of them being highly specialized, like the big corn markets of Eastern England, such as Swaffham in Norfolk, and the cattle and sheep markets of the Midlands in particular. Market-towns were thick on the ground in Hertfordshire above all, no fewer than twenty in this one small county. At the other extreme, the vast county of Northumberland had only eight, and the north of England generally was poorly served. Indeed, in Shakespeare's England the north was generally poor altogether: a harsh climate, much wild upland and poor soil, thinly peopled, its industries only just beginning to make their mark on the country as a whole. It was the east and south-east of England that was thickly peopled, best farmed, with most towns and most money—though the south-west had shot up spectacularly during the first half of the sixteenth century with its mining and cloth industries, its fishing and shipbuilding, and its successful farming of all kinds.

Shakespeare and his farmer forebears were born in a kind of landscape which has all but dis-appeared from England today, a landscape in which villages, and indeed most towns also, were surrounded by huge hedgeless 'open' fields. Each Midland village at any rate had three of these great fields, running to several hundred acres each, divided into a multitude of small strips. Considerable areas of common pastures remained, though far less in the Midlands than anywhere else in England. But the old English woods were fast disappearing during Shakespeare's lifetime. How much of the ancient Forest of Arden really remained at this date is hard to say. Much of it had been felled and converted into farm-land as early as the twelfth and thirteenth centuries, but Saxton's map of Warwickshire (1576) shows the northern half of the county—the Arden country—still well-tree'd and there can be little doubt that considerable stretches of old woodland survived, probably mostly enclosed within the hunting parks and chases. But the southern half of Warwickshire was very treeless, the so-called Felden country between Stratford and the Oxfordshire and Northamptonshire borders. Some of the villages in this part of the county remained 'open' until well into the nineteenth century, and Shakespeare would undoubtedly have recognized not a few unchanged features— little groves and woods, patches of scrub and rough pasture, and long rolling slopes of arable disappearing over the horizon.

The Midlands were, by and large, the most highly cultivated part of England, though there were still plenty of places for boys to play in and work off their energies. But as one went westwards or northwards, the country landscapes changed their character. Villages became fewer. The hamlet and the isolated farmstead became more characteristic. The large open fields tended to disappear, and the small enclosed fields of the modern pattern to predominate, with big old hedges, more extended stretches of woodland, and certainly more upland wastes. But around London, too, the open fields were disappearing at an early date for obvious reasons. Thus the beautiful collection of maps in All Souls College shows the manor of Edgeware in the 1590's as completely enclosed into small hedged fields. Only on the south side of London did vast tracts of rough commons still survive, mainly because of the poor sandy soils. Fragments of these old commons remain to this day, notably at Wimbledon and Putney, with rather miserable fragments in such places as Clapham and Wandsworth.

Though there were only about three million people in the whole country, about a fifteenth of the number today, the countryside would have seemed much more populated and 'busy' than it is in our time. For one thing far fewer people lived in the towns. And for another thing, the open fields, where they were the characteristic pattern of farming, employed a greater number of people at the multifarious tasks that had to be performed by hand in the total absence of machinery. One can see this busy rural landscape still in southern Germany—where, indeed, we can get a perfect idea of how Elizabethan England looked in its time: the unbroken miles of corn, the oxen pulling the loaded wagons and carts into the villages along green tracks between the cornlands, the multitude of women and children all bending over their necessary tasks, the little shady groves where the peasants took their noon-time ease. Shakespeare would look upon the Bavarian countryside with affectionate recognition, while the English countryside would puzzle him with its emptiness and its ugly intersections of low hedges cutting the landscape into small squares and rectangles.

Another notable feature of Shakespeare's lifetime was the great spate of building of country-houses throughout the English countryside. A few were being built as early as the 1520's, such as Sutton Place in Surrey or the beautiful Compton Wynyates, completed by the time of Sir William Compton's death in 1528. The dissolution of the monasteries in 1536–9 gave a great impetus to the building of large and stately houses, partly by enriching a new class who desired to build in keeping with their new status but also in providing beautiful sites and masses of building material in the form of masonry, lead, and timber from the pillaged monastic buildings. The Elizabethan peerage were a very small class—only some sixty families—but in addition to these there were numerous high State officials of whom Burghley and Hatton were the most outstanding, and a class of rich gentry who did well out of the Dissolution, all of whom were engaged during Shakespeare's lifetime in putting up their stately houses and creating new parks to set them off, or enlarging old parks. A new civilization was being created in these years, taking the place of the monastic civilization that had been destroyed; a civilization which in turn is being slowly destroyed in our own day after four hundred years of opulence. Many of the great Elizabethan houses have perished, such as the largest of all—Holdenby in Northampton-shire and Theobalds in Hertfordshire—but so much remains still in a country unharmed by wars, houses such as Hardwick and Longleat, Montacute and Burghley, and hundreds of others from this age of ostentatious and competitive building.

The monasteries were swept away. Church-building practically ceased for sixty years or more, except for necessary repairs. But on the secular side the building industry was busy all the time, not only with the great country houses that took twenty or thirty years to build but with thousands of lesser houses, from the manor-house down to the farmhouse and the cottage, and the merchants' and artisans' houses in the towns. Apart from the houses of the rich and the great, there was between about 1570 and 1640 a widespread rebuilding of ordinary houses in every town, village, and parish throughout England, except perhaps in the extreme north where money was not so plentiful and cultural reactions not so swift.

Shakespeare lived in an age of rapid inflation. The price-level multiplied by some three and a half times between 1500 and 1600, most of this great rise taking place after about 1545. But the upper half of the population benefited from this state of affairs. With relatively fixed costs, and rising selling-prices, the large farming class, in whom one must include most of the gentry, with all their own household needs met off their own lands, put more and more money away in their coffers, and used a good deal of it in the last quarter of the century to rebuild their old houses or to enlarge and improve them out of all recognition. In general, too, town merchants prospered and built themselves new houses. Towns like Worcester, Bristol and Totnes had whole new streets of good houses, many of which remain to this day. We also hear of the multitudes of new cottages being built, in the 1580's especially, to accommodate the rising population of these years. In Shakespeare's generation, England must have been a country very largely com-posed of new houses. Only the urban poor, a very numerous class indeed, suffered from this long-continued inflation, and town authorities became increasingly preoccupied with various devices to keep them fed in times of scarcity and abnormally high prices. Even so, their real wages fell drastically by the end of the century and it is a wonder that there were no more disturbances than there were. A great deal of this new poverty was relieved by private charity, to which merchant wealth contributed to an outstanding degree.

For the more comfortably-off half of the population there were not only new houses with the latest amenities such as chimneys and glazed windows, giving warmer, cleaner, and lighter houses, but also a remarkable rise in the standard and quantity of domestic furnishings and furniture of all kinds. Probate inventories show that in the first half of the century the majority of people lived in houses with the barest furniture and the very minimum of comforts; by the end of the century there is a complete change in this respect: better furniture, more of it, curtains and cushions, feather-beds, wainscoted rooms, all sorts of small luxuries appear for the first time in the ordinary English home.

The working-class—though that was not a description known to Elizabethans—formed the majority of the population of England in the latter part of the sixteenth century. In the towns they probably constituted at least a half of the total population, more than a half in London; and in the countryside at least one man in three was a wage-earner. To Shakespeare as a successful middle-class man they were unknown except as the ignorant, bawling mass in some of his plays, referred to, if at all, in contemptuous terms. Either that or they are simple, clownish characters good for a laugh, a tradition that still lingers on in some English writing.

This mass of people worked incredibly long hours for low wages, even if we take account of the altered purchasing-power of money between say 1564 and 1964. In Nicholas Breton's *Fantastickes*, published in 1626, we get a picture of the Elizabethan day, hour by hour. As early as three o'clock in the morning, in the summer at any rate, 'the cock calls the servants to their day's work...the milk-maids begin to look toward their dairy, and the good housewife begins to look about the house...the ploughman falls to harness his horses...and the labourer by great[1] will be walking toward his work'.

By four o'clock the servants were at breakfast, the milk-maid gone off to the cows, the spinner already at the wheel. 'Now the beggars', says Breton, 'rouse themselves out of the hedges and begin their morning craft...the thresher begins to stretch his long arms, and the thriving labourer will fall hard to his work.' By five o'clock on a summer morning 'the streets are full of people and the highways are stored with travellers: the scholars are up and going to school, and the rods are ready for the truants' correction: the maids are at milking and the servants at plough, and the wheel goes merrily while the mistress is by...the herd [i.e. herdsman] begins to blow his horn through the town...and the alehouse door is unlocked for good fellows...'. Shops in the larger towns—there were few or none in small towns and villages before the early seventeenth century—open up and set out their wares at six o'clock. The school-boy is hard at his Latin or his Greek 'and whosoever cannot say his lesson must presently look for absolution'. By seven the whole scene is a busy one. By eight the working world is stopping for breakfast: and so the long day goes on, hour by hour.

This is an idyllic picture of a long working day in summer, and there must have been such days when the sun shone and all went well. But there were cold, dark, wet mornings too and taken all round it was a hard life. For workers by the day, probably the great majority of the wage-earning class, the hours were 65 a week for the darker half of the year, and a 75-hour week during the rest of the year. This was in London in 1538, when the city authorities fixed the hours of work and rates of wages. From 25 March to 8 September (the Nativity of the Blessed Virgin Mary) men started work at five o'clock in the morning. At eight there was a fifteen-minute pause for breakfast, then on again from 8.15 until 12 noon. An hour off for lunch, and then a long six-hour spell until seven in the evening with only fifteen minutes off for 'drinking time' at four o'clock. This was a fourteen-hour day, less 1½ hours for meal-breaks, or 75 hours a week if the full six-day week was worked. All this for eightpence a day. In the autumn and winter half of the year, the working day was 6 a.m. to 6 p.m. with the same breaks for food and drink, but a reduced wage of sevenpence a day.

At Coventry the cappers, one of the most lucrative trades of the town in the early sixteenth century, seem to have worked rather longer hours. From Michaelmas to Easter it was 6 a.m. to 7 p.m.—a 13-hour day less meal-breaks; from Easter to Michaelmas it was 5 a.m. to 7 p.m.—a 14-hour day less mealtimes. In point of fact the pace of work was probably a leisurely one; and it is highly likely that on an average men worked for only half the possible number of days in the year. These long hours were lightened also by the sensible custom of a sleep-break at mid-day. This was an old custom, perhaps going back to the beginnings of human labour. At any rate it was recognized and enshrined in an Act of 1495 fixing hours of work by statute. This allowed half an hour for breakfast and $1\frac{1}{2}$ hours for dinner and a sleep. But the sleep-time was limited to the days between mid-May and mid-August. These hours of work, and the hour for sleep, were re-enacted in the Statute of Artificers in 1563, so the custom continued all through Shakespeare's lifetime.

In the provinces—for example at Exeter—a labourer could earn sixpence a day, or three shillings a week if he were lucky enough to be fully employed, in the year in which Shakespeare was born. By the time of Shakespeare's death he could earn a shilling a day: but whereas his money-wages had doubled the cost of living had practically quadrupled in the same time. In the 1560's in the same city, a journeyman could earn eightpence a day, and a master-craftsman tenpence a day. Farm-labourers in Devon got the same as town-labourers (sixpence a day) but an extra twopence a day for the very long hours worked between March and September.

Whether such long days, mostly spent in hard physical labour, and for most men out in the open air, yielded more satisfaction to more people than the wage-earner's life in the middle decades of the twentieth century is an impossible question to answer. Even today there is a world of difference between the life of a man employed by say a small Devonshire builder and that of a worker at say Ford's factory at Dagenham: and which is typical of today's wage-earner? The range of difference was not so extreme in the sixteenth century: working conditions were more uniform altogether. And there were more holidays in the year, though the modern five-day week is putting us on a level again with our Elizabethan ancestors and their numerous days off to celebrate this, that, and the other. Probably more people were happier as a whole then than now, for a variety of good reasons. It is impossible to measure these things; but certainly suicide seems to have been exceedingly rare in Elizabethan England, judging by the various records we have. Suicide was regarded as a felony, and a suicide's goods were forfeit to the Crown. Hence we get the occasional record of such an event: but it is so very rare as to be memorable. And parish registers of this period very rarely record a suicide.

How many holidays were there in the Elizabethan year? Since the Reformation the number of 'holy days' had consistently been under attack. In 1536 Bishop Latimer preached against the excessive number which, he said, led to idleness and drunkenness. There has never been any lack of comfortably placed men in authority to deplore other people's slackness. But in August of the same year Thomas Cromwell issued his injunctions to the clergy, telling them *inter alia* to urge people not to observe the 'superstitious holidays' now abrogated. Finally the matter was dealt with by Parliament which in the Act of 1552 specified the number of holidays as every

Sunday, plus twenty-three named feast days, plus Monday and Tuesday in Easter week and Whitsun week, a total of twenty-seven days' holiday a year, in addition to Sundays. At Easter and Whitsun there were breaks of three days, at Christmas four days.

If this represented a reduction on the Catholic year of an older generation, the original number must have been high. Theoretically there were fifty or more holy days in the Catholic year, but not every one was taken, as it meant a loss of pay which few could afford. But Walter of Henley had reckoned in the thirteenth century that the working year was only forty-four weeks long after taking out 'holy days and other hindrances'. In Shakespeare's time, then, the long hours of the wage-earner were considerably mitigated by holidays at fairly frequent intervals. It seems likely that most people took their authorized twenty-seven days a year, even though it all meant a loss of pay; but as the century went on, and the cost of living rose decade after decade, it is also likely that more and more holidays were sacrificed to make the extra shilling or so, until by the nineteenth century the working-class were reduced to no holidays at all except Sundays and such days, if on piecework, as they chose to spend drinking in the public-house.

The mass of Elizabethan people had what the sociologists now call a 'high leisure preference', a state of mind characteristic of under-developed countries where low wages, under-employment, and a lack of consumer-goods are features of economic life. But more significant than all that, they were linked with their localities, with their parishes and their little towns, and with the rhythm of Nature in a profound tie that we have broken long ago and tend now to deride or to sentimentalize. It was fundamentally a peasant world for four people out of five, perhaps nine out of ten, a world in which a couple of bad harvests could starve one to death, or of plagues that took most of one's children in a few days or killed parents and left small children; but also a world of equally intense satisfactions and enjoyments, of regular feasts and celebrations. Perhaps of all these outbursts of vitality, defying a world that could be harsh and cruel for most people, the Lord of Misrule's day was the most therapeutic. Here is an extreme Puritan's view, that of Philip Stubbes in *The Anatomie of Abuses* written in 1583:

First, all the wilde-heds of the Parish, conuenting togither, chuse them a Graund-Captain (of all mischeefe) whome they innoble with the title of 'my Lord of Mis-rule', and him they crowne with great solemnitie, and adopt for their king. This king anointed chuseth forth twentie, fortie, threescore or a hundred lustie Guttes, like to him self, to waighte vppon his lordly Maiestie, and to guarde his noble person. Then, euerie one of these his men, he inuesteth with his liueries of green, yellow, or some other light wanton colour; And as though that were not (baudie) gaudie enough, I should say, they bedecke them selues with scarfs, ribons & laces hanged all ouer with golde rings, precious stones, & other iewels: this doon, they tye about either leg xx. or xl. bels, with rich handkercheifs in their hands, and sometimes laid a crosse ouer their shoulders & necks, borrowed for the moste parte of their pretie Mopsies & loouing Besses, for bussing them in the dark.

In this way, he says, they start their 'devils' dance': these 'terrestrial furies' thus make a mockery of the Sabbath, invading the churches themselves with their clamorous buffoonery.

He proceeds:

They haue also certain papers, wherin is painted some babblerie or other of Imagery woork, & these they call 'my Lord of mis-rules badges': these they giue to euery one that wil giue money for them to maintaine them in their hethenrie, diuelrie, whordome, drunkennes, pride, and what not. And who will not be buxom to them, and giue them money for these their deuil[i]sh cognizances, they are all mocked & flouted at not a little. And so assoted are some, that they not only giue them monie to maintain their abhomination withall, but also weare their badges & cognizances in their hats or caps openly. But let them take heede; for these are badges, seales, brands & cognizances, of the deuil, whereby he knoweth his Seruants and Clyents from the Children of God; And so long as they weare them, *Sub vexillo diaboli militant contra Dominum et legem suam*: they fight vnder the banner and standerd of the deuil against Christ Iesus, and all his lawes. Another sorte of fantasticall fooles bring to these hel-hounds (the Lord of misrule and his complices) some bread, some good-ale, some new-cheese, some olde, some custards, & fine cakes; some one thing, some another....[1]

There were these wild outbursts, and besides that more sober celebrations such as May Day, or Rogation Monday, Plough Monday, and many another day that linked men and women with an antique world. One must not exaggerate the harshness of life. There are glimpses of leisure and comfortable living among the farming class certainly, the largest single class in sixteenth-century England. Across the centuries I recognize my own direct ancestor, George Hoskins, born a year before Shakespeare, a successful yeoman farmer during all the years that Shakespeare was famous, and dying in the last days of the year 1625 at the age of sixty-two. In his big East Devon farmhouse, as described in his probate inventory, I read—besides all the usual furniture, and the farming gear and corn and livestock—of 'a treble viall' and of five hogshead wine barrels (a noble stock to leave behind), of a bible in English, and some armour from his younger days. The plentiful wine, the home-made music, the reading (for there were other books besides the bible), the larders and pantries filled to satisfaction with bacon, butter, cheese, beef, and pork, the large-scale brewing, the large family successfully brought to adult life—five sons and five daughters—despite the hazards and misfortunes of a comparatively long life: here is the authentic picture, from a prosaic and matter-of-fact record, of one kind of man who spanned the whole of Shakespeare's life.

Most people certainly did not enjoy this comfort and degree of culture, but they belonged nevertheless to a more satisfying world—despite its physical hazards and high mortalities—than that which we inhabit. It was far from being an Affluent Society. But they had three abiding satisfactions that have, for most people, disappeared from the modern world. Work: for many more than today there was work that satisfied some at least of their creative instincts, even the labourer in the fields. Place: for many more than today lived in a place in which they had roots, that had deep meaning for them though they could not have expressed it in words. They moved about more than we sometimes think, but almost always within sight of familiar hills and horizons. They frequented the same market-town even if they changed villages, and saw the same friends all their lives. Family: families retained a sense of identity, for they maintained a permanent home, a permanent gathering-place of the whole clan. Mumford wrote, 'Men are attached to places as they are attached to families and friends. When these loyalties come together, one has the most tenacious cement possible for human society.' Elizabethan society, away from the restless strivings of London, in the deep countryside and its provincial towns, was built with this tenacious cement. It was wholly fitting and in keeping with Man's nature that William Shakespeare should have returned to his native place at the age of forty-seven, to spend his last five years busy with the social and civic affairs of Stratford-upon-Avon, surrounded by the people with whom he had grown up in the half dozen little streets he had known as a boy.

3

SAILORS AND THE SEA

'The portly sail of ships'

I

The ship was the all-purpose transporter to those who lived along the coasts or on the estuaries of Tudor and Stuart England. Movement by water along rivers and by coastal navigation was, at most seasons, easier than by land. The Thames was the main highway of London and of its environs, crowded with boats and lined with ships. The Thames fairway led not only to France, Spain and the Low Countries, to Muscovy and the Indies, but to Harwich and Hull, Newcastle and Leith, to Dover, Portsmouth, Exeter, Plymouth and Bristol. Ships and sea travel were taken for granted by those who lived on the coast and estuaries. And these people formed the larger portion of the population at the time.

Coastal trade was carried on, for the most part, in small ships of some 20 to 80 tons burden. Some were little more than sailing barges or boats under sail. Others were more seaworthy and stouter. There were a few larger coasters, of 100 to something over 200 tons, attached to the larger ports.[1] Some of these were old merchantmen, too slow or uncertain for longer voyages, others were specialized transports, like the Newcastle coalmen. The common rig of two masts for the smaller and three for the larger gave most of the coastal shipping a stereotyped look, but the knowing eye could spot local variations in build and sail plan which brought variety to the picture.

The number of ships in them is what is most striking about the ports of the late sixteenth century. Coasters were small, distribution took many individual vessels, and the merchantmen which carried on the overseas trade of England were themselves of no great size. The majority of them were of 80 tons or less and it took a great many ships of this size to supply the needs of even this country's three million or four million people. Mainly three-masters, they, too, had a characteristic outline, with square stern, a somewhat beaked bow and rather high upper works aft, and similar works, though much lower, forward. The Levant Company employed bigger ships, ranging from 250 to 400 tons in late Elizabethan times and up to 500 tons under the first Stuart. The East India Company did so also.

The queen's or king's ships were still some way between a great personal squadron and a permanent institutionalized fleet. A part-time navy of merchantmen, temporarily converted, was still an essential part of the country's maritime defence. Perhaps the professionalism of the Elizabethan navy board can be said to have provided the bureaucratic structure of a navy proper, but the fleet depended very much for its continuance and growth on the whims of the sovereign rather than on the expertise of officials. A rebuilding and refitting programme, such as was carried out by Hawkins in the years before the Armada, was still exceptional, although there had been something like it in Henry VIII's reign. Ships were kept on the strength for decades, even a generation or more, in case they should come in useful—as some old stagers did in the Armada year—but there was also some systematic attention to new design: the employment of expert ship designers, Matthew Baker, Peter Pett, and his son Phineas, brought a measure of continuity and progress. The new galleons of the pre-Armada years, longer, lower, more beaked, more systematically and heavily gunned, were formidable ships of 400 to 800 tons (there were even two ships of 1000 and 1100 tons, respectively, in the Armada campaign). The lesser vessels differed scarcely at all, except in armament, from merchant vessels. The small pinnaces, independent vessels of 25 to 50 tons, showed more variation in design, while the still smaller pinnaces carried or towed by the larger ships were little more than large boats fitted with one or two masts, with fore-and-aft or square sail rig.[1]

The public image of the royal navy was well conveyed by Sir Jerome Horsey in his dialogue with the Tsar, Ivan IV, in 1576:[2]

Ivan. Yt is reported your Quen, my sister, hathe the best navie of shipps in the world.

Horsey. Yt is true, and please your Majesty...For strength and greatnes to breake and cutt thorow the great occean, turbulent seas.

Ivan. How framed so?

Horsey. For art, sharpe-kielled, not flat-bottomed; so thicke and strong-sided that a cannon shott can scarse pearse thorow.

Ivan. What ells?

Horsey. Everie shipe caries cannon and fortie brass peces of great ordinance, bulletts, musketts, powder, cheyne-shott, piekes, and armor of defence, wild fier worckes, stancions for fights, a thowsand marriners and men at arms, souldiers, captaines, and officers of all sortts to guide and govern; discipline and dailie devine preyers; bear, bread, bieff, fish, bakon, pease, butter, chese, vineger, oatmeall, aquavita, wood, water and all other provicion, plentifull, fitt and necessarie for foode and maintenance of men; ancers, cabells, takells, masts, five or six great salls spread, aunctients, fleggs, costly silke banners displayed with the Quens ensignes and arms, wherat all other kings shipps bend and bowe; dromes, trompetts, taber, pipe, and other instruments of warlicke designes and defiance to the enymie; abell to assault and batter the strongest mariten towns and castells that ar; most tirrable and warrlicke for the aied, conduction and defence, of her Majestys alyance and frends.

Queen Elizabeth's navy-royal was never quite like this, but this spirited propaganda picture, perhaps, most vividly calls it to mind.

Ships' names,[3] too, bring home some of the sea flavour of the time. Many of the Queen's ships of the Armada period had names which stuck for centuries in the Royal Navy—*Dreadnought*, *Rainbow*, *Revenge*, *Tiger* (also a popular merchant ship name), *Triumph*, *Victory*, *Vanguard*, but *Bull* would soon seem undignified for a royal ship and *Ark Royal* would not be revived until the twentieth century. The *Virgin God Save Her* was one of Sir Richard Grenville's prizes, in her name cocking an irreverent snook at the Spaniards. The *Golden Hind*, the *Mayflower*, the *Delight* are good merchant ship names, as are the more intimate family names like *Margaret and John*, *Susan Parnell*, *Pansy*, *Hearty Anne*. Others seem a little odd, or frivolous, to us—the *Bark Buggins*, the *Makeshift*, the *Black Dog*, the *Rat*, the *Heathen*, while *Three Half Moons* sounds more like an inn than a ship. Some of the privateering vessels had deliberately bizarre names like Sir Robert Dudley's *Earwig* and *Frisking*, and John Chidley's pair, *Wildman* (alias *Susan*) and *Wildmans Club* (alias *Susan's Handmaid*).

Just as the ports—and the roads nearby—and the estuaries held many ships so did the coastal towns breed and keep many sailors.[1] The boatmen and lightermen of the Thames were a numerous tribe, and a quarrelsome one as well. The thickest population of merchant seamen was in the Thames-side parishes east of London Bridge, St Katherine's, Wapping, Ratcliffe, Limehouse, and Rotherhithe, and besides merchantmen they supplied privateers (largely financed by London merchants) and the royal ships (often by impressment) as well. The quality of the seamen engaged in the coastal trade (and the ships they used) seems to have been lowest of all—apart from a specialized group, those in the coal trade—but it was an hereditary craft and families might remain in one branch of it for generations. For a substantial part of the population, the sea, we may remind ourselves, offered the natural way of earning a living. The dull or the conservative stayed where they were born and sailed to no great distance; the more venturesome, ambitious and unruly moved on to other branches. On the shorter merchant shipping routes the life was not a bad one. These ships were not overmanned, the pace was slow, the turn-round at foreign ports was leisurely (and there were foreign drinks, and women and even sights to entertain the seamen, even if they were often short of money), while the dangers from weather, though the Channel was always treacherous, were not excessive. English waters and those of the adjacent shores were mostly charted, if by no means always adequately. The merchants trading to the Low Countries, France and Ireland, at least in years of peace or comparative peace, do not seem to have had trouble in getting crews. For the longer voyages, to Spain, Portugal and the Atlantic Islands, the Baltic, Russia by the northern route, the case was rather different. If the ships were somewhat bigger, the danger from weather was greater too. Cooped up in inadequate quarters in bad weather for considerable periods, the seamen cannot have been too comfortable. In northern waters, especially, they were often unable to keep warm or to get hot food, the seas being too rough for them to light fires. But conditions would not always be so bad; voyages to the Straits, that is to Morocco, North Africa, the Mediterranean generally, seem to have been popular enough. The merchant seaman's pay was normally rather poor: the somewhat longer voyages, when his pay piled up, were probably the more profitable.

The toughest of the merchant seamen were the fishermen. The North Sea herring fishing vessels might not go far but the men worked hard, under heavy pressure and in inferior boats (hence the pressure at the end of the sixteenth century that they copy the Dutch herring buss). The east coast too had a long tradition of deep-sea fishing off Norway and Iceland, while in the south-west the Devon and Cornish fishermen gathered in pilchards when they came and then pushed out to fish off the Atlantic coasts of Ireland in competition with French and Spaniards and Portuguese. They went also, increasingly, to Newfoundland, often in ships of no more than 80 tons, sometimes less, but with some larger ships engaging in the trade in the new century. The Newfoundland run was a risky one: if the weather held westwards it could occasionally be easy, but it usually meant adverse winds at some stage, while riding home with the westerlies might also mean having to cope with storm and tempest. At the fishing grounds, the labour of taking cod by hook and line from boats was considerable, as was the shore-drying of the bulk of it on wooden stages. The ships tended to be overmanned to make the lading as short as possible, which in turn made living conditions poorer on board. On the other hand, if the season was a good one, cod fishing was profitable for all concerned, as the appetite for cod in meat-starved Europe seemed insatiable.

Apart from the Newfoundland fishery, voyages outside European waters were still, in late Elizabethan times, unusual: Russia and the Mediterranean were only just within the normal range of English shipping. The beginning of the privateering war in 1585 saw a change. From 1585, down to 1602 at least, ships—perhaps 200 each year—went off both singly and in packs to hunt and rob the Spaniards in the West Indies and on the high seas. The sailors saw in the Caribbean new significant parts of the non-European world and learnt to adapt themselves in some measure to tropical conditions for the first time. It is true that there had been trade with Guinea since the 1550's and, intermittently, with Brazil since earlier still, but the number of ships employed was small and the mortality of the seamen engaged, at least for Guinea, excessive, so that it had not become a 'normal' commercial route. Yet Guinea in the East and the West Indies in the West became the foci for expanding exploration. The Roanoke voyages to what is now North Carolina and Virginia between 1584 and 1590 were extensions merely of the West Indies privateering run, just as Gilbert's voyage of 1583, the St Lawrence voyages of 1593–7 and the expeditions to the later New England from 1602 onwards were all extensions of the old Newfoundland passage. The same might be said of the North-west Passage exploration from 1576. The Guinea and Brazil routes again acted as leads into the South Atlantic, both East and West, and helped to make possible the circumnavigation, and the would-be and actual East Indian voyages that, from 1601, made the Cape route one of only comparative novelty. The real breaks with the older shipping routines had come with Drake's passage of the Pacific and Cavendish's successful imitation of his feat. To the seaman, to sail out into the unknown or the imperfectly known was an adventure, but it is doubtful if it affected him as anything more than another job, one with more danger than usual perhaps, with, at the same time, a little more reward. The fact that Drake's men came back rich in 1580 had a great influence in making far-ranging voyages of exploration attractive to the seaman.

The seamen, on long voyages, had much to endure. Accommodation for the men was limited and poor: on privateering voyages ships were overmanned to provide fighting men and prize crews, while ships going to the tropics also took extra personnel on account of the high mortality there. Rough weather meant that fires could not be lit for cooking or warmth, and on northern voyages this meant that the men suffered much from cold. In the tropics beer went sour, dried fish rotten, and biscuits mouldy. North or South, the men became more lousy as the voyage continued. Luke Fox summed up in 1635 the seaman's lot[1] as 'but to endure and suffer; as a hard Cabbin, cold and salt Meate, broken sleepes, mould[y] bread, dead beere, wet Cloathes, want of fire'. There were some demands from the seamen for more space for themselves, and some degree of privacy, but Raleigh did not think it was possible to satisfy it:[2] he said, 'Man may not expect the Ease of many Cabbins and Safety at once in Sea-service.... And Albeit the Mariners do covet Store of Cabinns, yet indeed they are but sluttish Dens that breed Sickness.' The Armada campaign showed how deadly bad food alone could prove. Hundreds died from virulent food-poisoning as the hastily-gathered stores interacted on the crowded press-ganged crews. On board ship hygiene was poor at any time, and especially so in these circumstances. On long runs, shortage of water, and the bad quality of what there was, was a serious matter. The foods carried, salt beef and pork, wet-salted or dried cod, biscuit, beans, peas, with beer, wine and a little oil, were nutritious enough while they were new and could be cooked, if they could be supplemented by even a little fresh fruit and vegetable.

On long voyages the diet produced scurvy, which could decimate a crew if it were neglected for too long, and as the food deteriorated, wet beri-beri and food-poisoning followed.[1] An enlightened commander such as Richard Hawkins tried to curb scurvy with citrus fruits (oranges and lemons), but his example was not widely followed. Physicians advocated various decoctions of scurvy-grass and water-cress which might in sufficient quantity have been effective enough had not, as one suspects, too much of their vitamin C been boiled out of them. Plague might well be picked up in temperate latitudes; typhus was a commonplace of nautical life; in tropical waters, malaria more deadly than that endemic in the Thames basin or even yellow fever might be had from mosquitoes. Dysentery, always associated with infected food, might in tropical varieties prove mortal so that the 'bloody flux' was specially feared at sea. The men could rarely change their clothes even if they had a change of clothing. This increased the risks of infection in low latitudes and the impact of chills and pneumonia in high. The run of accidents on a sailing vessel was often great; wounds from shot, sword or splinters were widespread after an action. Surgeons were carried by many ships on long voyages or on sea-campaigns. They were expected to have served their apprenticeship and to have satisfied the Barber-Surgeons' Company of London of their qualifications. There were a few outstanding surgeons, like William Clowes, who learnt much of their craft at sea, but the quality was often low, and many surgeons at sea had little or no training. Expected to treat only the outer man, they left disease largely to the captains. On important expeditions a physician might be carried; more often there was an apothecary with some knowledge of herbs and nostrums. So captains had to do what they could from the book. George Wateson's *The cures of the diseased in remote regions* (1598)[2] was the first working text-book of tropical diseases and did not help very greatly with its simple programme of bleeding, diet and elementary medication.

Sir Francis Drake was most interested in the problems of keeping food and water at sea. He knew the versatile inventor Sir Hugh Plat,[3] who produced for him 'a certain victual in the form of hollow pipes', a form of *pasta*, which was reckoned to retain its qualities for up to three years at sea. It may have been used as early as the Drake circumnavigation, though this is not certain, and it was undoubtedly employed in the Drake–Hawkins expedition of 1595. Plat maintained that he found also that the mixing of a certain amount of vinegar with the water made it keep better and longer: this notion too Drake took up. Whatever the effects of such experiments, it is noteworthy that Drake kept the *Golden Hind* a healthy ship on her three years' voyage, which was unprecedented and ranks as one of his most outstanding achievements.

Danger at sea was not confined to the elements and to poor food and disease. Coastal piracy was endemic on the coasts of Europe at this time and it flourished especially in the west, Devon and Cornwall, South Wales, South and South-west Ireland. Coasters were continually being robbed when they were not taking their turn to rob. In the English Channel there were not only English pirates but French and Flemish ones as well. Piracy usually involved a certain amount of violence, though sometimes the pirates found intimidation enough, and it is possible at times to suspect collusion between seaman and pirate at the expense of the shippers of the cargoes. Merchant ships on voyages outside home waters usually carried arms and were able to put up some resistance to attacks in which seamen were sometimes killed or more often hurt. From 1585 onwards the comparatively mild dangers of piracy gave place to a militant free-for-all at sea.[1] Dutch, Flemish, French (royalist or Catholic League) ships, as well as English vessels, had licence to take enemy ships at sea which they almost always interpreted as generously as possible. English 'ships of reprisal' were first released in quantity in 1585 and were supposed to restrict their attacks to Spanish and Portuguese vessels, but in fact they attacked every vessel going to or coming from Iberian ports, or even thought to be doing so, French, Flemish, Dutch, Hanseatic, Scottish, Danish, all with the utmost impartiality. Moreover, hostility between English ships and those from the Catholic League ports in France provided fresh excuses for mutual violence in European and North American waters, English attacks in Newfoundland on foreign shipping having an almost continuous history in the twenty years from 1582. Which ships belonged to pro-Spanish Flemings and to anti-Spanish Dutch remained most obscure, and neither side allowed their final allegiance to stand in the way of a chance of booty. The voyage of the *Brave* and the *Roe*,[2] two small English pinnaces, which were supposed to go to North America but got only to the Azores, is an astonishing record of violence at sea in the Armada year, every ship's weapons being turned against all others, Scots, French, English, Hansards, Flemings, each attacking and being attacked indiscriminately. It is remarkable that, with so much lawlessness current at sea, so many ships could still carry on with their ordinary tasks. Queen Elizabeth and Henri IV, however, spent the last years of the old century and the first of the new in trying to wipe the slate clean of old injuries between their subjects and to render the Channel safer, if not safe. This process was then taken up between James I and Philip III when the Treaty of London had brought peace again, in European waters at least, between Great Britain, Spain and Portugal. The Iberian trade soon settled into its peacetime channels. But the privateering tradition died hard. James I was not wholly able to cope with sea robbery, though greater English control in Ireland was of some assistance in limiting its range, and the sea-rovers were, in part at least, driven to seek bases as far away as Algiers, Morocco, and even Newfoundland. The continuance of the struggle of Dutch and Spaniards until the truce of 1609, however, meant that excuses for sea-fighting and robbery, under flags of convenience where necessary, continued in western European waters.[3]

The activities of the East India Company from 1601, the enhanced activity of the Guinea merchants after the peace and the regular Virginia voyages after 1607, together with the continued West Indies venturing which came to concentrate on illicit trade with the Spanish settlers rather than on plunder, all turned the exceptional runs of the Elizabethan seaman into more or less routine voyages for his Jacobean successors, but up to 1623, in the Far East at least, there were fresh probings of distant seas still to be made, with the chance of clashes with Portuguese and Dutch which might well be deadly, while the Southern Pacific was still outside their bounds. The expanding sailors' world had not yet quite reached its limits.

Joseph Hall was among those who wondered if all this sea enterprise for commercial gain was worth while, writing[4] of 'the greedy Merchant that for gaine Sailes to both Poles, & sounds both Indian seas'. In the end, it is true, 'his long beaten bark from forth the maine Unlades her weary fraight', but only that he 'shall as he please, Raise by excessive rate his private store, And to enrich himselfe make thousands poore'. Such doubt about the virtues of capitalistic maritime enterprise seems to have been rare, the prerogative, perhaps, of the satirists alone.

The common sailor was bred to the sea, following in his father's wake at a tender age, but if he was tough, intelligent, ambitious and lucky he could move fast enough up the long ladder of promotion from ship's boy to master. If he was no more than a competent craftsman he might rise no higher than master of a coaster, or master's mate on a merchantman, but if he was capable of picking up some degree of technical skill in navigation as well as of commanding men, he might, quite early, become master of one of the bigger and farther-ranging merchantmen, mounting, with good fortune, to command her as captain. If he were to go farther he would need to show some capacity for trading or managing his ship's affairs so as to make himself indispensable to a merchant or a mercantile partnership, since many merchants were also shipowners. He could then expect to buy the part-ownership of a vessel: he might even be encouraged or helped to do so by the merchants in order to give him a stake in their enterprises. From there he could pick up shares in other ships until he could, perhaps, set up as a shipowner, going ashore to run his vessels from Thames-side or Bristol, and even build his own ships, qualify for state subsidies, take on government contracts and die rich. Such a career seems to have been that of Peter Hill, mariner, of Rotherhithe.[1] Born in 1535, he evidently worked his way up to owning a fleet of merchant ships trading to Hamburg, Spain and Newfoundland by the time he was in his fifties and became master of Trinity House in 1589. He could then afford to speculate by sponsoring walrus and whale fishing ventures in the St Lawrence, get bounties for the ships he built at Rotherhithe, contract to bring soldiers from the Low Countries to Ireland, and die, at 80, in 1615, the eldest brother of Trinity House, founding a school for the children of poor sailors in his will. Or there was Christopher Newport of Limehouse, another Thames-side sailor.[2] K. R. Andrews has traced him from his first appearance as a common seaman in 1581 to his death in 1617 as a shipowner and probably rich, but still at sea, in command of East Indian Company and Virginia Company squadrons, until the year of his death. Privateering ventures in the West Indies gave him, as it gave other seamen, their chance of advancement. Master of a privateer in 1587, he became captain of the *Little John* in 1590 and, though losing an arm in a fight with the Spaniards, did well enough to go out in command of a squadron of four privateers on a cruise in 1592. This made his fortune and from then he scarcely looked back, investing in shipping from 1596 onwards and taking a rich haul of silver from the town of Tabasco in Mexico in 1599. He presented James I with a gift of crocodiles in 1605, and was chosen to transport the first English colonists to found Jamestown and Virginia in 1607. His last ten years at sea saw him win much distinction in western and eastern seas alike: he was one who was not prepared to stay on shore to spend his profits. William Borough is yet another example.[3] Sailing before the mast on Richard Chancellor's epoch-making voyage to Russia in 1553, he taught himself everything he could about navigation and chart-making so that he rose rapidly to be master, captain and finally a chief pilot of the Muscovy Company in the 1570's. He had a clear scientific mind, as is shown in his writings, and turned his attention fruitfully to problems of educating pilots, the assessment of compass variation and the building up of the navy. He transferred to the royal service as Clerk of the Ships in 1582 and in that and other offices had, with Hawkins, much to do with improving the naval administration between then and his death in 1599.

A significant problem in Elizabethan England was to adapt the traditional training and lore of the seaman to new responsibilities and techniques. Ocean sailing required quite different handling from coast-wise and short-haul navigation. English seamen were slow to adapt themselves to new circumstances. 'English masters and pilots', E. G. R. Taylor has written,[1] 'remained of the old-fashioned sort.... That is not to deny that the Englishman was a good sailor, he was. But his ideal of a good sailor was a good coaster, a man who knew the tides, the landmarks, the shoals, currents and "dangers", who could box the compass, tell the time by sun and star, and take his ship into every harbour by soundings of depth and "ground". Such a seaman had a deep distrust of instrumental navigation, clinging obstinately to "the old ancient rules" which had become quite insufficient once ocean enterprise was seriously engaged on.' The story of how techniques of navigation developed, through the reorganization of Trinity House at Deptford, the training of new-style masters in the navy, the translation of foreign navigation manuals, beginning with that of Martin Cortés in 1561, and the ultimate growth of a native navigation literature, has been told in detail by Lieutenant-Commander D. W. Waters.[2]

Dr John Dee attempted to put Euclidean geometry at the service of the seamen, yet most navigation techniques remained dependent on continental teaching until the 1580's. In the last twenty years of the sixteenth century Englishmen began to make valuable independent contributions both to the theory and the practice of navigation. Much attention was given to the problem of the variation of the compass and its dip (the latter being first established by Robert Norman in 1580).[3] The theoretical work of Borough, Norman and William Bourne was greatly facilitated by the combination of good sea charts and improved tables from Dutch sources in *The mariners mirrour* (1588).[4] Thomas Hariot has left us much information on how he taught Sir Walter Raleigh's pilots to work out problems of compass variation and the estimation of latitude by Pole Star and Sun by new, refined methods which reduced errors to a minimum. He did not, unfortunately, publish them.[5] Both he and Edward Wright worked on the problem of the construction of a sea chart which would record direction correctly on a plane surface. Mercator's map in 1569 provided an academic solution of the problem by showing how the necessary distortions of latitude and longitude could be related to one another. Wright, in his *Certaine errors in navigation* (1599)[6] showed how the practical seaman could, using a chart on the Mercator-Wright projection, construct a nautical triangle which showed latitude and longitude, direction and course correctly.[7] The famous map of 1599 ('the new map with the augmentation of the Indies', *Twelfth Night*, III, ii, 85–6), added to the second edition of Richard Hakluyt's *Principal navigations*,[8] was a demonstration of the new seaman's view of the world. Already Wright, with Emery Molyneux, had produced an improved view of the earth in the round in the globe published in 1592, of which the sole surviving specimen is in Lord Leconfield's possession at Petworth, while the second edition is represented by the globe in the Middle Temple (1603).[9] Robert Hues, who had sailed the world round with Cavendish, expounded, in his *Tractatus de globis* (1594), how the globes were constructed. The globe and book alike were honoured by being adopted on the continent.[10] William Gilbert, also, was incited to experiment on magnetism by the issues raised by the practical navigators. His *De magnete* (1600)[11] is mainly a discussion of his thesis that the earth is a magnet and that planetary motions can be explained by magnetism, but it is also concerned with practical navigation problems of magnetic declination and dip. By 1603 the up-to-date navigator had to know a little trigonometry in order to employ the detailed and reliable tables which were by then available. He was still incapable of establishing his longitude at sea by instrumental means, so that the errors of dead-reckoning sailing still held him back from knowing his precise position, but with his 'true' chart and effective instruments and tables for finding latitude, the Jacobean sailor was well enough equipped for world-wide voyaging.

The captain of a ship of war, whether one of the Queen's ships or a privateer, was, more often than not, a soldier, not a sailor. He was chosen to lead men, not ships, so that, in sea campaigns and privateering, seamanship was the business of the master and his mate—fighting that of the captain. But masters, as we saw, could become captains, and soldiers turned captains, too, could become expert at sea, some of them being willing to learn navigation and chart-making in order to have the more effective direction of their ships, especially on long voyages of exploration. Drake was an expert seaman; Hawkins never lost his skill at sea even if for so many years he sat in government office. Raleigh felt so strongly about the matter that he put himself to school under the mathematician Thomas Hariot and sent his captains and masters to pick up the new science from him also. Even the wild, unstable Cavendish became a first-rate cartographer. On the other hand some sea adventurers appear to have known and cared little about the way in which their ships were sailed. Martin Frobisher, it is probable, was, for all his experience, a poor navigator.[1] Even on Drake's West Indian expedition in 1586, it was possible, through errors in navigation and disregard of the cumulative effect of compass variation, for the fleet to set out from Cartagena for Havana and end up at Cartagena again sixteen days later.[2]

At the other end of the scale impressment brought into the navy many useless landsmen. Raleigh was to complain in James' reign[3]—'For many of these poor Fishermen and Idlers, that are commonly presented to his Majesty's Ships are so ignorant in Sea-service as that they know not the Name of a Rope and [are] therefor insufficient for such Labour.' Privateering, with its high profits for sailors, paid by shares from the richer prizes, attracted landsmen too, some of them men of good education, others of poor character. Some scarcely adapted themselves to a sailor's life. Most privateersmen had a reputation for rough, pirate-like behaviour. Discipline was poor; the men were frequently drunk, especially after taking a prize, and were liable to fight each other brutally over the pillage which they were allowed to pick up. Masters and captains frequently quarrelled and sometimes fought. K. R. Andrews has given many instances of this sort of behaviour.[4] Thus Captain Barnestrawe, a Dutchman, of the *Tiger* of London, 'was not regarded by the Englishe men but greatlye reviled and called copernose and...he was fitter to drincke ale than to be a Captaine'. On one of the Queen's ships such conduct would have been punished very severely.

It is possible, just, to get a picture of what the Elizabethan seaman looked like: it is also possible to get an impression of the smell of 'a tipe of Thames-street stinking of Pitch and Poor-John'.[5] The London Museum has a seaman among its models, whose blouse and breeches turned up in an old collection of theatrical costume, and which are quite probably the original tar-stained garments of a sailor, run up by a sailmaker at sea before 1600.[6] That this was a common way for seamen to get their clothes is shown by a case against the Breton pilot of an English ship at Newfoundland in 1536 who cut up new sail-canvas to make a jerkin and a pair of slops for a seaman.[7] The knitted coif with its hanging ear-flaps, the knitted and felted Tudor bonnet worn above it, and the piece of knitted material worn like a scarf, are all Tudor, but not specifically seamanlike, though close to those worn by seamen shown in engravings of the time. Thomas

Churchyard, in 'A Pirates Tragedie'[1] has left us a verse which fits in well enough with this picture:

> With horie beard and scorched face,
> With poudred hede, and heare unshorne,
> With hackes and hewes, in every place,
> He seemed like, a man forlorne....
>
> A Sea mans cappe, on hedde he ware,
> A slidyng sloppe of Friers graie:
> A checker Kaep, both thinne and bare,
> To furnish up, his quaint araie.
>
> A cables end, his girdle made,
> His shirt besmerde, with Pitch and Tarre:
> Close by his side, a rustie blade,
> This carle in youth, a man of warre.
>
> A Pilotes compass, he did holde,
> To showe what science he profest.
> The skill whereof, had made him bolde,
> To saile the seas, both East and West.

This casual figure did not differ much in appearance from the men of the Queen's ships. Admiralty contractors had concessions to sell clothes to these seamen and this must have produced some degree of uniformity in dress. But there was no uniform except for those few men whom it pleased the captains to deck out in the Queen's, or their own, liveries.

At sea the sailors sang and played instruments, listened and danced to them. Sir Richard Grenville could serve a banquet to the Spanish officials in Hispaniola in 1585[2] 'with the sound of trumpets, and consort of musick', while Luke Warde tells of a similar celebration in Brazil, with Fenton[3] 'in his Pinnesse with his musike, and trumpets, and I in my skiffe with trumpets, drum and fife, and tabor, and pipe, accompanied them'. Though primarily for the disciplining and encouragement of the men in battle and for entertaining the captain and his associates at meals, the consort of music (or ship's band) brought a taste of relaxation to the men on long voyages which was very valuable for morale.

How far were the seamen literate? It is surprising, perhaps, how many of the thousands of witnesses in sixteenth-century cases in the High Court of Admiralty, the great majority of them common seamen, could and did sign their names rather than make a mark. This does not prove much, but it is probable that among the privateersmen at least, though not necessarily among those engaged in the coastal trade, the level of literacy and intellectual capacity was moderately high, so affecting the records of sea travel they have left us. The master of a merchantman was expected to keep a log of his position by dead-reckoning, checked for latitude and position by celestial observation, with some written indication of weather and a note, very much at his discretion, of 'occurrences'. The latter might easily expand into some sort of journal of the voyage. The Muscovy Company seems to have insisted on a journal being kept, though this was not usually done by the captain or master, but by someone assigned to the task of recorder, like the purser, cape merchant, or chaplain, if there was one. Using the data in the ship's log as a basis,[1] the official journal might be brief or discursive as the writer thought fit or had time for: he might even have so much time on his hands that he kept a private diary as well as his official narrative. And of course, on an exploring voyage, there were always likely to be a few other unofficial journals kept as well. On a short merchant voyage the log was only a document to record for the owners or charterers the actual performance of the ship. When the expedition's object was exploration or the exploitation of a new and distant branch of commerce, the detailed journals became of great importance as the primary records of what occurred and was observed. These journals became in turn the basis of published accounts of completed voyages.

II

There is a thin trickle of narrative about the English overseas voyages of the sixteenth century from the time Richard Eden in 1555 included with his translation of Peter Martyr's *Decades* accounts of the first two Guinea expeditions of the 1550's.[2] Other voyages tended to be celebrated in ephemeral ballads, very many of which have been lost. It took some time, certainly, to find an acceptable vehicle for the voyage narrative. When Richard Chancellor wrote a narrative of his voyage to Russia in 1553, Clement Adams turned it into Latin and published it in 1555.[3] Robert Baker, however, took a different route to publication and threw his narrative of the Guinea voyage of 1562–3 directly into English verse, afterwards carrying on with this method for his journeys elsewhere.[4] John Hawkins, on the other hand, set down a plain prose narrative in English of what had happened to him on his fateful third voyage to the Caribbean[5] and this became the more usual pattern for the sea narrative of the period. George Turberville was one of the few Elizabethan poets to spend some time overseas. He was evidently much affected by his experiences which he retailed in a series of verse epistles and other poems to his friends, many of them about the sea, but they were not published until they appeared, appended to his *Tragical tales*, in 1587.[6] Already in his *Epitaphes* (1570),[7] probably written before he went to Russia, he has several sea verses. The Frobisher voyages called out a number of published narratives: that of Dionyse Settle was not, he told his readers, that of a seaman;[8] but George Best's was and it was literate enough, almost prolix at times.[9] Thomas Ellis too, wrote a narrative of the third voyage (1578), *A true report of the third and last voyage into Meta Incognita*,[10] and in his epistle apologized in would-be flowery language for being a mere sailor: 'I being a Sailer, more studied and used in my Charde and Compasse, and other thinges belonging to Navigation, than trayned up in *Minervas* Court, or taught by the sage Philosophers the fathers of eloquence, whose sweets and sacred sappe I never sucked. But yet, because I knowe, that the best part of men, will weigh my good will, rather then finde fault with my simple skill.' How genuine this ingenuousness was on his part does not appear, but he too tells a plain tale well enough. Much less plain was that told by David Ingram in the autumn of 1582 to Sir Francis Walsingham and other worthies and then published in 1583.[11] One of Hawkins' men left on shore in 1568, he claimed to have walked, with two others (conveniently dead when he gave his story) from the Gulf of Mexico to Cape Breton from which he was rescued by a French ship in 1569. The elephants and red sheep and other unusual features of North America are, one feels, the end product of a long run of tavern tales where the original story has been eventually overlaid by the 'truth' of fiction. There is no doubt he believed his own story, and was prepared to go with Sir Humphrey Gilbert in 1583 almost to Cape Breton to prove it. Thomas Church-yard managed to celebrate in verse and prose in 1578 the expeditions of both Sir Humphrey Gilbert and Sir Martin Frobisher without leaving English shores himself,[1] though this led it to be rumoured facetiously that he was going to sea in the Virginia voyage of 1585.[2] Job Hortop, whose 'voyage',[3] with various imprisonments interspersed, lasted from 1568 to 1590, did much better as a seaman author in 1591 than Ingram had done, making a plain tale exciting and conveying his own bravery and resourcefulness without boasting. Arthur Barlowe was a soldier before he became a sea captain in 1584, but his narrative of the 1584 reconnaissance voyage[4] up the American coast is a polished one, though perhaps the polish was applied by Raleigh who seems to have circulated it in manuscript to would-be subscribers to the 1585 Virginia voyage. Other sailors' narratives that got into print were taken down by non-seamen from the lips of seamen who could tell but not write them. Indeed there is a tendency in the later Elizabethan years for the overseas narratives to be written by men who are not primarily sailors! *A summarie and true discourse of Sir Frances Drakes West Indian voyage* (1589),[5] on Drake's 1585–6 expedition, was by at least three hands, none of them seamen's; the account of the last fight of the *Revenge* by Raleigh, no ordinary seaman; the Guiana voyages written up by him or by Lawrence Keymis, sea-captain, but again no common seaman.[6] It was Richard Hakluyt, however, who, in the first edition of *The principall navigations, voyages and discoveries of the English nation* in 1589,[7] spread out a feast of sea narration. Every type of sea and land journal, with much of the correspondence associated with the voyages, appears for the Muscovy Company expeditions from 1553 to 1588. There is Drake and there are Cavendish, Hawkins, Frobisher, Gilbert, and much besides on the Levant and Guinea ventures. The nautical element in the narratives varies greatly, but a great deal was written by the sailors themselves. Some of the finest northern voyage journals—Christopher Hall for the 1576 Frobisher voyage, those of Hugh Smith and Nicholas Chancellor for the North-east Passage voyage of 1580—give extended and vivid impressions of the rigours and monotonies of northern sailing, and contrast with Luke Warde's account of the leisurely cruise in tropical waters which, for most of the time, Edward Fenton's voyage was. Those mentioned, too, were never to appear in print again unpruned. An encyclopaedia of the sea and distant lands, written for the most part by travellers, many of them sailors, was from 1590 onwards at the disposal of all those interested in overseas matters or in seafaring. In the decade between the preparation of the first and the appearance of the second edition of *The principal navigations*,[8] which in three, smaller, volumes more than doubled the material made availabel, Hakluyt was able to add much that was notable—'The booke of the great and mighty Emperor of Russia', by Richard Chancellor; Andrew Barker's narrative (1576), Pretty's account of Cavendish's circumnavigation, reprints of Best and Bigges, and, of course, much excellent material, a good deal of it reprinted, for the 1590's. Moreover, nearly a fifth of the bulk was made up of 'foreign voyages', narratives of non-English explorers put in to cover areas hitherto inadequately covered by Englishmen. By 1600 there was thus an extensive library of the sea. Thereafter the contribution of the seaman himself to English overseas sea-narratives survived in, for example, the first East Indian Company pamphlets *A true and large discourse of the voyage…set forth the 28 of April 1601* (1603) and *A letter…to the…East Indian merchants in London* (1603), and in *The last East-Indian voyage* (1606).[9] But James Rosier's account of George

Waymouth's American voyage in 1605, *A true relation of the most prosperous voyage...in the discovery of Virginia* (1605),[1] if close to the log, is not a seaman's narrative, nor are John Smith's *A true relation of such occurrences as hath hapned in Virginia* (1608) and *A map of Virginia* (1612),[2] though both have a soldierly directness. John Nicholl, *An houre glasse of Indian newes* (1607),[3] on a Guiana voyage, and Silvester Jourdan, *A discovery of the Bermudas*[4] (1610), have a nautical touch—and are probable *Tempest* sources.[5] It seems to be generally agreed that Shakespeare had seen, before he wrote *The Tempest*, a manuscript copy of William Strachey's 'A true reportory of the wracke, and redemption of Sir Thomas Gates Knight; upon, and from the Ilands of the Bermudas', unprinted until 1625. This was written in the summer of 1610 and brought to England in the autumn.[6] With it Shakespeare may have seen two Virginia Company pamphlets, *A true and sincere declaration of the purpose of the plantation begun in Virginia* (1610), and *A true declaration of the estate of the colonie in Virginia*[7] (1610). Robert Harcourt's *A relation of a voyage to Guiana*[8] (1613) is mainly a record of land travel, as indeed are the major Jacobean travel books by William Lithgow, George Sandys and Fynes Moryson. And if Samuel Purchas indicated in successive editions of his *Pilgrimage* (1613, 1614, 1617)[9] that he had many sailors' narratives in his hands and may thus have opened them to judicious or persistent inquirers, it was not until 1625 that he released in his *Pilgrimes* a whole new fleet of sea narratives. By then Shakespeare was dead and the Elizabethan sea-tradition was becoming a part of history, not of life.

The sailor's image in the popular mind passed through several stages in the Elizabethan and Jacobean periods. For the most part, he was regarded simply as the conveyor of goods and passengers, little more animate than his ship. As a frequenter of taverns he was known as a man with time on his hands, between voyages, in which to flaunt his trophies (if his voyages were the sort from which parrots or silks derived) and his tales (long-winded and exaggerated no doubt, if also exciting and disturbing). He was, also, the smelly, independent, drunken, loud-singing and quarrelsome individual encountered by the quays and in and out of drinking places and brothels. From time to time the ventures he had taken part in would strike the imagination of the individual or the crowd, would lead to ballads or poems, or even to popular enthusiasm for his kind of exploit, and so, by transference, for his manner of life. But it is doubtful if this happened at all until Drake's return from his world-circling voyage in 1580. It is likely to have become general in 1585. In that year the seafaring man came into his own, or at least into all the headlines. The London ship, the *Primrose*, escaped from the hands of Spanish officials when an embargo was clamped down suddenly on English shipping in May, and soon Humphrey Mote had written up and had published *The Primrose of London with her valiant adventure on the Spanish coast*,[10] inaugurating, with the government action at the time the pamphlet appeared, nearly twenty years of unremitting sea-warfare against Spain. The letters of reprisal issued by the Privy Council released several hundred privateers to recover the value, and more, of ships and goods impounded in Spain. The rash of privateers which was spread out over western European waters—almost all of them converted merchantmen—gave a new prestige, a national one, to the sailor and a new interest to the sea itself. The privateersman too became a more colourful figure for a material reason: if he now appeared in tavern or brothel it was, likely as not, with some pillage, silver, jewellery, fine clothes, or ornaments to peddle or give away as gifts. The favourable popular image which the sailor gained was enhanced and magnified as the Queen's ships came into action, first against Cadiz in 1587 and later in the Armada campaign. But the privateering seaman found his chronicler in Henry Roberts, the journalist in whom, Louis B. Wright says,[1] 'the spirit of the seagoing commoner, of the Elizabethan citizen adventurer, speaks at first hand'. The first prose tract of his to survive is probably the anonymous *The seamans triumph*[2]—though the ascription to him is by no means certain—a gloating tribute to the men who took the great carrack, *Madre de Díos*, in 1592. His hastily written, and carelessly printed, report of another capture of the same year was the fruit, it appears, of a casual visit to Clovelly. In *Our Ladys retorne to England, accompanied with saint Frances and the good Jesus of Viana*,[3] the religious names of the ships lent a blasphemous jibe to the title. He celebrated the Mediterranean voyages of Edward Glenham in *The honorable actions of Edward Glemham [sic]* and *News from the Levant seas*,[4] even if these expeditions involved piracy against Venetian shipping as well as legitimate prize-taking from Spaniards. Next, he turned to narrate and extol James Lancaster's experiences in Brazil in *Lancaster his allarmes*.[5] The series of pamphlets, with their racy titles, helped to build up the privateering sailor and his commanders as popular figures.

Newes out of the coast of Spaine (1587), by Henry Haslop,[6] is the first of the popular news-pamphlets to help establish the image of the Queen's ships and their personnel, although armed merchantmen also took part. The Cadiz action which it celebrated was a mere curtain-raiser to the Armada campaign. This brought out not only such morale-maintaining calls as Anthony Marten's *An exhortation, to stirre up the mindes of all her majesties faithfull subjects to defend their countrey*,[7] but also news reports of the effects of the campaign on the retiring Spanish fleet like *Certaine advertisements out of Ireland* (1588),[8] and polemical tracts on the respective achieve-ments of the fleets such as *A packe of Spanish lyes* and *The copie of a letter to Don Bernardin Mendoza*.[9] It had to await a detailed narrative until Petruccio Ubaldini's *A discourse con-cerninge the Spanish fleetes*[10] appeared in 1590, which, however, paid its due, if tardy, tribute to the seamen. The sailor could scarcely look back after this, and so for the Lisbon expedition of 1589 we have *A true coppie of a discourse written by a gentleman, employed in the late voyage of Spaine and Portingale* (1589).[11] The purely naval events of the 1590's, after the epic story of the *Revenge*, were not all favourable subjects for publicity. Henry Roberts' verse[12] on the 'outset' of the Drake expedition in 1595, *The trumpet of fame*, could be followed only by Henry Savile's *A libell of Spanish lies* (1596),[13] a defensive retort to Spanish claims on their great victory over Hawkins and Drake in 1595–6, which had revealed the weaknesses of the Elizabethan war fleet. An official declaration of the fleet's objectives prefaced the Cadiz action of 1596,[14] but the not unmixed result led to the suppression of all the accounts, even the version published by Hakluyt in 1598 and afterwards withdrawn.[15] A few small naval-privateering actions were celebrated between 1600 and 1602: *A true credible report of a great fight at sea between certain ships of England and five ships of warre of the king of Spaines* (1600),[16] the sailor, Richard Mansell's *A true report of the service done upon certain gallies* (1601),[17] and the recently recovered account of Sir Thomas Shirley's Mediterranean action, 1601,[18] *A true discourse, of the late voyage made by...Sir Thomas Sherley...on the coast of Spaine* (1602), all of them keeping alive the reputation of the men of the Queen's ships.

But the days of the sailor as hero were rapidly passing. Already, in 1598, Henry IV of France and Queen Elizabeth tried to cut down the Channel sea-war, and a proclamation on 8 February 1599[19] for peace at sea was the first move to end the chaotic state of affairs which existed in the

English Channel. The effect, only partial it is true, was to turn the tide still further against piracy, as was shown by the proclamation of 20 March 1602,[1] restricting the activities of privateers so as to limit piracy especially in the Mediterranean. The privateers, after the pirates proper, became a nuisance rather than a national asset, and a very early result of James I's accession was the annulment of all letters of marque against Spain on 23 June 1603.[2] This marked the end of the long semi-official sea-war begun in 1585. It meant that all hostile English maritime activity in European waters was henceforth purely piratical, though it did not clarify the situation outside Europe in the same way. The positive side was the restoration of peaceful trade, signalized for example by *A proclamation or edict touching the opening of the trafficque of Spaine with these countries* (1603[–4]),[3] which meant a different, non-dramatic role for the privateersman. The sailor was again, with few exceptions, the common carrier only of the sea.

If, in the years after 1604, the sailor did something new in the non-European seas, he stood, as we saw, some chance of being celebrated in print, even when the emphasis in travel literature had shifted decisively to land travel. If he engaged in piracy in spite of all the proclamations against it, he might win mention in a newsletter or even possibly a pamphlet, but if he returned openly to England he was quite likely to adorn a gallows in the end.

The seamen on the royal ships too had a thin, uneasy time. The better and more vigorous of them drifted off into the merchant service. Nathaniel Butler, writing in 1634,[4] is looking back over the past thirty years when he speaks of 'that loathness or rather loathing which of late days hath so possessed this kind of people [the common mariner] against all service in his Majesty's ships and fleets'. The officers, officials and naval suppliers all combined in graft, corruption and neglect to leave the navy successively weaker as James I's reign went on. There was little for the ships to do; intermittent reports on the bad state of the navy in 1608 and 1618 did bring a little improvement (and the construction of a few fine ships), but this improvement was not persisted in, and the decay continued. In these post-war years the prestige of sea service in the royal ships was at its lowest ebb. The Elizabethan navy-royal was out of date, out of fashion and, almost, out of mind. Pride in its past and the effective reshaping of it as a service had to await a new generation. The merchant fleet was, by contrast, active, growing in numbers and in tonnage, against stiff Dutch competition, and penetrating in some strength the routes pioneered by the Elizabethan seaman.

III

The modern Londoner need scarcely be aware of the maritime life of London and its river. In Elizabethan and Jacobean times it was impossible to ignore it. Shakespeare's assimilation of the atmosphere of the sea and of the talk of sailors was largely unconscious. But it was not wholly so: he learnt more than he would have taken in without some conscious effort. That he did so partly by listening to sailors is evident from the ease and range of his sailors' talk. His swearing boatman in *The Tempest* appears to have been a real figure. He gained many of his impressions of the sea from the seamen he heard, although it is unlikely that he did not make at least coastal voyages himself. R. R. Cawley concluded[5] that 'When all his references to matters of the Sea are gathered together and carefully considered, Shakespeare shows himself to have been, not merely interested in, but tolerably familiar with conditions aboard'. He remembered too a number of the outstanding events in maritime history and gained appreciably from his reading.

It is reasonably clear that he followed the news pamphlets which accompanied, as we have seen, most major actions at sea, while he knew something of Hakluyt.[1] Just how far he explored the travel literature of his time it is difficult to say. Cawley doubted whether he shows the kind of knowledge of what happened overseas such 'as could be gathered from a close reading of the very considerable voyage literature which had been written by his time'.[2] The reading which undoubtedly lies behind *The Tempest* may have been exceptional in its range.

Shakespeare was concerned with sailors and sea matters only in so far as he could transmute them for dramatic or poetic ends. His storm scene in *The Tempest* would be impossible if he had not had an ear for sea-language and some knowledge of how a ship was handled. That his sea-knowledge was second-rate[3] may prove the negative that Shakespeare was no seaman or connoisseur of seamanship, but this is no reflection on the scene as drama. He needed knowledge of the theatre, which he had superbly by 1611, not expertise in the fine points of sailing, to bring it off. At a deeper level, the sea, its restlessness, its storms, its analogies in its course to human passions and destinies, was frequently in his mind and in his words. Wilson Knight sees a whole world of allusion in *The Shakespearean Tempest*.[4] He concludes:

From the beginning to the end of Shakespeare's work all 'projects' are associated with sea-adventures; adverse fortune with tempests, but happiness with calm seas and the 'gentle breath' of loving winds.... We have seen tempests become wedded to the plot, closely entwined therewith, and expanding their significance symbolically throughout the drama. [In the final plays] the poetic image tends not only to blend with, but actually to become the plot.

For him *The Tempest* becomes the culmination of a trend of thought which kept the sea and the sailor, the storm and the sea-adventure, subordinate to the demands of plot and imagery until they were at last allowed full rein in surface story and in underlying meanings in the late great play. Whether the historian and the critic can go all the way with Wilson Knight or not, his exposition of the kind of assimilation involved in the poetic and dramatic process enables us to see in what ways Shakespeare employed his knowledge of the sea, as one only of many instruments to illuminate human actions.

4

ELIZABETHANS AND FOREIGNERS

'The three corners of the world'

The impact of foreigners on a community or a culture is affected, obviously enough, both by the opportunities for contact and knowledge that exist, and by the framework of assumptions within which information about foreign lands and customs is presented and received. The period with which we are concerned here—let us say the sixteenth and early seventeenth centuries—is well known as one in which the amount of scientific information about the world increased dramatically. In the Renaissance period England, like the rest of Europe, acquired modern-style maps; trade-contacts with Turkey[1] and Russia[2] became a commonplace feature of economic life; visitations of Red Indians, Eskimos, and Negroes,[3] an influx of refugees from Europe, plantations in the New World, and knowledge of other European ventures of a similar kind—all this might seem to give the average Englishman of the early seventeenth century almost as much expertise in physical geography as is possessed by his modern counterpart. But this is to reckon without the 'framework of assumptions'. It is probably true to say that by the early decades of the seventeenth century more scientific information was available than could be digested within the terms in which the world was traditionally conceived; and it is certainly true that the facts of physical geography which were accepted by sailors as useful in practice were very difficult to accommodate within the sophisticated and complex traditions that form the natural background to literature.

What was the framework of assumptions concerning foreigners? When we look at medieval writings seeking for information that bears on the question, 'what attitudes to foreigners were traditional in English literature?' we find little evidence; and this very absence must be our starting-point. Most medieval literature is located in a dimension that cares little for the compass. It is true that Chaucer's Knight had been

> At Alisaundre...in Pruce.
> In Lettow hadde he reysed and in Ruce,
> No Cristen man so ofte of his degree.
> In Gernade at the sege eek hadde he be
> Of Algezir, and riden in Belmarye.
> At Lyeys was he, and at Satalye,
> Whan they were wonne; and in the Grete See.[4]

And of his Wyf of Bath he tells us,

> thryes hadde she been at Jerusalem;
> She hadde passed many a straunge streem;
> At Rome she hadde been, and at Boloigne,
> In Galice at seint Jame, and at Coloigne.[5]

But the interest of these journeys is not geographical; the points mentioned are only important as points of connection with the Divine.[1] The typical travellers of the Middle Ages—the pilgrim and the crusader—often brought back information which the modern geographer sees to be of scientific value, but this information was only a by-product (and they saw it as a by-product) of movement on quite another plane. There is no point in complaining that the sixth-century monk Cosmas, 'should have known better'[2] (a phrase we shall often meet in this study) than create a *Christian Topography*[3] which Sir Raymond Beazley has stigmatized as 'systematic nonsense',[4] as a marvel of 'scientific supernaturalism'.[5] It is true that Cosmas Indicopleustes ('he who has sailed to India') was a notable traveller: he had travelled to Malabar and Ceylon, and then back again to Egypt before he settled to write his account of the world. And it is equally true that he did not use this geographical experience to influence his Bible-centred model of the world. But why should he? If the Bible gives the most important information about the world, then it is proper to avoid the snares of mere sense impression, by clinging (so far as is possible) to biblical texts and intentions. It may be proper to remember here the famous scholastic exercise on the word Jerusalem:

Literally, it is the city of that name; allegorically it represents Holy Church; tropologically, it signifies the faithful soul of whosoever aspires to the vision of eternal peace; anagogically, it denotes the life of the dwellers in Heaven who see God revealed in Zion.[6]

What is, on a map, only a physical position (neither more nor less important than any other) acquires intensity of meaning by the superimposing of spiritual senses over the physical one; the undifferentiated physical fact has to aspire to spiritual meaning in order to become important. The medieval *mappa mundi* is an excellent demonstration of this view of geography. It details an image of the world as Christendom, centred on Jerusalem, not only because Ezekiel v. 5 reads, 'Thus saith the Lord God; This is Jerusalem: I have set it in the midst of the nations and countries that are round about her', but because the Holy Land represents the natural hub of Christian experience, which spreads out from this centre to the fringe of circumambient waters (for 'God said, Let there be a firmament in the midst of the waters' [Gen. i. 6]) where Pagans live, close to Leviathan (both whale and Devil), together with Negroes, apes, semi-homines and others whose distance from full humanity could be measured by their geographical distance from that area where humanity had been most fully realized in the life of Christ.

Other aspects of medieval geography and ethnography bear witness to the same basic assumptions.[7] That primitive view of the Ptolemaic 'threefold world'[8] which saw the continents as populated by the sons of Noah—Africa by the descendants of Ham, Asia by those of Shem, Europe by those of Japhet—*could* have been used as the starting point for a science of ethnography. But the interest of the medieval mind was less in exploring the racial differences than in categorizing theological statuses. And to some extent we ought to be able to understand the force of this preference, even today. That explanation of the black skin of the Negro which sees it as a mark of God's disfavour, visited on the descendants of Ham, remains potently attractive, even in an allegedly scientific world. In the medieval world, it was the scientific fact that was the sport, present but useless. The *mappa mundi* in Hereford cathedral categorizes Europe and Africa by these names; but the words *Europa* and *Affrica* are interchanged—'an "error"', remarks Denys Hay, 'which could scarcely have occurred if the words had meant anything'.[9]

The *mappa mundi* survived for longer than might have been expected.[1] Competent *portolani* or coastal charts exist from the end of the thirteenth century, and probably existed even earlier;[2] but though these might be useful to mariners, it did not follow that the learned would consent to take notice of them.[3] Indeed if we see the *mappæ mundi* as primarily 'emblems of man's spiritual world', there is no good reason why the two kinds of knowledge should conflict. As in the parallel case of Ptolemy and Copernicus, the two maps showed remarkable powers of co-existence, even though they were (seen on a single plane of 'truth') mutually exclusive.

The capacity of the individual mind to remain quite happy in the possession of incompatibles is a source of endless fascination when we read the Tudor voyagers and their propagandists. Dr John Dee, scientific colleague of Ortelius and Mercator, was at the same time a myth-bound and credulous charlatan.[4] Sir Walter Raleigh was a competent navigator and explorer; and yet he asserted his belief that there were headless people on the Caora river, 'with their eyes in their shoulders, and their mouthes in the middle of their breasts', giving as one reason for the belief that 'such a nation was written of by Mandeville'.[5] Sir John Mandeville's *Travels* was the most popular of all the travel books; Josephine Waters Bennett records twenty-five English editions before 1750.[6] Richard Hakluyt, a hero of modern geography, included Mandeville's *Travels* in the first edition of his *Principall Navigations* (1589), alongside more modern travellers and observers whose standards were quite different from his. John Stow, the painstaking and accurate antiquary, recorded in the margin of his copy of Norden's *Description of Hertfordshire* (1598), his opinion that Mandeville's 'travayles in forraine regions and rare reportes are at this time admired through the world'.[7] In the same way, when Stephen Batman in 1582 reissued Trevisa's medieval translation of Bartholomaeus Anglicus' *De Proprietatibus Rerum*, he included additional material from such painstaking modern observers as Sir Humphrey Gilbert, Stow, Gesner and Ortelius, seeming not to notice that the new patches tore away the substance of the old, fabulous material.[8] The result is a hotch-potch, neither entirely spiritual nor scientific, but in a Limbo somewhere between. Geoffroy Atkinson, in his survey of the French geographical literature of the Renaissance, has noted:

La survivance des idées de l'ancienne géographie et des 'Images du Monde' côte à côte avec les vérités nouvelles est responsable d'une partie de la confusion qui caractérise ce domain littéraire, surtout avant 1560. Mais jusqu'en 1609 les ouvrages 'géographiques' présentent, à nos yeux d'aujourd'hui, un mélange du croyable et de l'incroyable.[9]

If anything, the confusion in France is more obvious than that in England, though not different in kind. No English figure focused as sharply the contradictions of the age as did André Thevet, 'grand voyageur' and Cosmographer Royal. Thevet's *Cosmographie Universelle, illustrée de diverses figures des choses plus remarquables veuës par l'auteur* (1575) is a wilderness of marvels. The work was criticized by the geographers of the day, but the author won the acclaim of Ronsard, Jodelle, and de Baif.[10]

The learned did not come clearly to the aid of the practical traveller, by establishing rational boundaries to assumptions about foreigners; neither did the practical man use his experience to correct his frame of reference about what might be expected. The travellers, as Wittkower has told us:

from the Dominican and Franciscan monks of the thirteenth century to Columbus and Fernão de Magellan, went out to distant countries with a preconceived idea of what they would find. Many of the travellers were learned; they had a knowledge of classical authors, they knew their Christian encyclopaedias, their treatises on natural science, their romances, they had seen on their maps the wondrous nations in those parts of the world to which they were travelling—in short, their imagination was fed from childhood with stories of marvels and miracles which they found because they believed in them.[1]

Writers on early geography tend to be disdainful of this 'frame of reference', to be implacably progressivistic in their viewpoint. Penrose never tires of castigating Columbus for the 'curious medievalism' of his thought—elsewhere his 'perverse medievalism' or his 'warped medieval-ism'[2]—but the interest of our period would seem to lie precisely in this overlap between the medieval world and the modern one, an overlap which allowed development and smooth progression rather than jarring disruption.

The new information which the English voyages of the sixteenth century brought to the national culture had to be fitted, as best it could, into a received image of what was important. This means that the facts were not received in quite the same way as they would have been in the nineteenth century. Historians of the last century were much taken with the idea of the Elizabethan imagination liberated by the voyagers. But there is little evidence of this outside the unhistorical supposition, 'that's how I would have reacted'. The voyages certainly did expand the physical horizon, but it is not clear that they expanded the cultural horizon at the same time. Englishmen became aware of India, Brazil, and the Spice Islands as possibly exploit-able sources of wealth; to some they suggested possible avenues of imperial expansion (this we may take to be the master impulse in Hakluyt);[3] there was a small but influential circle interested in the technical (map-making, economic, astronomical) arrangements that had to be involved. But none of these were close to the traditional areas of culture; and to many of those who were close, it seemed that the new activities offered only new opportunities for baseness. George Buchanan spoke for many of the wisest minds when he declared that it was Avarice that had discovered America.[4] The image of man in his theological, political and social aspects could not be much affected by the discovery of empty or primitive lands; the aim of travel in this period is usually stated to be the observation of courts, universities and other sophisticated societies; and America could not offer anything of this kind. Atkinson has shown how small a proportion of French geographical literature in the period 1480–1609 was actually concerned with the New World.[5] In France in this period there were twice as many books published about the Turks[6] as there were about both the Americas, and four times as many about Asia in general. What is more, the proportion of books devoted to America actually drops as the period advances. The same balance seems to exist in Italian and Spanish literature also,[7] and there is no reason to suppose that the English figures are very different; the 'framework of assumptions' made the facts of physical geography seem uninteresting to the average cultured man of the period, a source neither of instruction nor of illumination.

Geographical exactitude was no part of the literary tradition, and even those writers who 'should have known better' show astonishing carelessness about place-names and modes of transport, using them for their associations, not for their reality. It may be that we can now 'exonerate' Shakespeare for shipwrecking Perdita on the sea-coast of Bohemia,[1] but it remains hard to find Helena a reasonable route from Rousillon to Compostella which goes via Florence,[2] or explain Proteus' sea-journey from Verona to Milan.[3] But Shakespeare is not exceptional, this is only common form in the period. Barnaby Rich's Don Simonides sails from Venice to Genoa (possible, I admit) and only a few hours from Venice is shipwrecked 'in a wilde deserte...onely inhabited with brute and savage beastes'; there he wanders for seven days before he meets another human being.[4] And yet Rich had served abroad in Holland and France and had been at sea as a privateer.[5] Henry Roberts was an author who spent most of his energies recording voyages and singing the praises of seamen. He was a sea-captain himself, and had been to Algiers, to Brazil and the Canaries.[6] But when he comes to write a romance, such as *A Defiance to Fortune* (1590) he makes his hero take ship from Siena,[7] while his *Haigh for Devonshire* (1600) describes a journey from Bordeaux to Rouen via the forest of Ardenne.[8] Thomas Lodge wrote his *A Margarite of America* (1596) while at sea with Cavendish:

Touching the place where I wrote this, it was in those straits christned by *Magelan*; in which place to the southward many wonderous Isles, many strange fishes, many monstrous Patagones withdrew my senses...so that as there was great wonder in the place wherein I writ this, so likewise might it be marvelled....

It is obvious enough from the tone of this description that it is the legendary strangeness of the place rather than its factual existence that, for Lodge, makes it worth literary mention. The *America* of his romance has nothing to do with geography. The Empire of Cusco is no more Peruvian than that of Mosco is Russian; both (as C. S. Lewis has remarked) 'are conceived as high pagan civilizations in some undefined period of the past'.[9]

Marlowe is well known to have had a map.[10] He seems to have written *Tamburlaine* with Ortelius' *Theatrum Orbis Terrarum* open in front of him.[11] It was a trait of scholarship to use the most scientific atlas for his thesaurus of names; but he used it as a poet, not as a geographer, arbitrarily selecting quite unimportant towns to stand for the regions he intended.[12] There is little or no sense of reality in the places where Tamburlaine operates. Babylon, Natolia, Zanzibar, the Terrene and the Euxene seas—these, the last enchantments of the atlas, fitly convey the magic of 'the sweet fruition of an earthly crown'; but it adds nothing to imagine the physical reality of such places.

Sometimes, however, the new facts did cohere with assumptions already existing, and already prepared for in terms of emotional impact. The search for a Terrestrial Paradise was one of the motifs which the early voyagers caught easily from their fabulous predecessors.[13] And even the facts of American life could not wholly disabuse the imagination of the dream of an ideal natural civilization:

the people most gentle, loving and faithfull, voide of all guile and treason, and such as live after the maner of the golden age.[14]

...soo that (as wee have sayde before) they seeme to lyve in the goulden worlde, without toyle... without lawes, without bookes, and without Judges.[15]

The history of the New World seemed to give body and reality to this old dream, especially where (as in England and France) it provided a nationalistically attractive contrast between the ideal innocence of the exploited Indians and the corruption of the 'civilizing' Spaniards, who in stead of spreading Christian religion by good life, committed such terrible inhumanities, as gave those that lived under nature manifest occasion to abhor the devily character of so tyrannical a deity.[1]

To be fair to the Spaniards, one must note that the *History of the Indies* by Las Casas is one of the most eloquent documents in the whole of this literature; but Las Casas can hardly be taken as representative of the Spanish colonizers; and it is to the countries excluded from conquest that we must look for further development of this theme. Sir Thomas More's *Utopia*, Montaigne's *Essays* (especially that on the Cannibals) and Shakespeare's *The Tempest* all show a view of the 'savage' which is powerful, because they see him in relation to European sophistication, as an implicit criticism of European ways of life. In this respect the figure of the exotic foreigner is very like that of the pastoral shepherd; Gilbert Chinard has made this point in respect of Ronsard's *Isles Fortunées* (of 1553):

ses sauvages ne ressemblent pas plus aux vrais sauvages que les bergers de tout le XVIe siècle ne ressemblent aux pastours de l'Ile-de-France ou ceux de Sannazar aux pâtres italiens. Si la vie et l'observation avaient fourni quelques traits, un point de départ assez difficile à situer, l'imagination poétique n'avait pas tardé à tout embellir et à tout magnifier.[2]

The foreigner could only 'mean' something important, and so be effective as a literary figure, when the qualities observed in him were seen to involve a simple and significant relationship to real life at home. Without this relationship, mere observation, however exact, could hardly make an impact on men caught up in their own problems and their own destiny.

The image of the world as a Christian entity centred on Jerusalem, and awareness of foreignness only in the sense of devil-prompted infidelity—this was, it is true, a vision which bore little relation to the general hatred of 'strangers'—even Christian strangers[3]—and the mass persecution of them, which went on all through the Middle Ages. But it is equally true that these eruptions of man's base nature were not canonized by theory, and so did not emerge in literary expressions. Europe retained a strong common culture well into the seventeenth century. Chaucer was widely read in at least three European literatures, but he shows little awareness of cultural distinctions, and he is probably right enough in failing to do so. Erasmus and More do not seem to have thought of one another as 'foreigners', and even such later humanists as the Scaligers, or Lipsius, or Casaubon knew 'the foreigner' only in the sense of 'the boor', the man whose Latinity fell below an international standard of excellence, such as today applies only to hotel cuisine.

But this common culture seems to exist in the seventeenth century largely as a hang-over from the period of a common faith; the fragmentation of faiths in the period of the Reformation had its eventual result in the fragmentation of national cultures. The career which carried Isaac Casaubon (1559–1614) from international scholarship to Anglican apologetics[4] may serve as a model of the whole drift of interests. The national claim to represent a separate (and better) religious tradition—the development of 'God's Englishman' to set against Popish wickedness—made the old organization of the West as Christendom, centred on Jerusalem, seem unsuitable, even in theory. When Jerusalem is set

In England's green and pleasant land

it becomes obviously desirable to create another, England-centred, intellectual pattern of European races. But we should beware of supposing that a pattern of races emerged readily from the Europe that Christendom had become, a pattern capable of supplying moral discriminations rich and complex enough for literary use. There were, of course, intellectual patterns by which the main European nations could be related to one another. There was the ancient climatic contrast[1] which set Northern phlegm against Southern blood, and which was much invoked to contrast the grossness of the Teutons with the passionate conduct of the Latins. But this does not take one very far; more detailed relationships of place and temperament, such as John Davies of Hereford's 'never yet was fool a Florentine'[2] have the air of being climatic glosses on an existing cultural image. Surveys of the time are fond of making lists of French, English, Spanish, etc., national characteristics, such as we find in Portia's review of her suitors,[3] or at the end of Fynes Moryson's *Itinerary*,[4] as a mode of rhetoric in Thomas Wilson's *Art of Rhetoric*,[5] or as a poem in Turler's *The Traveller*.[6] But such lists hardly go beyond journalistic generalizations about superficial mannerisms (e.g. clothing, or eating habits):

> The Dutchman for a drunkard
> The Dane for golden locks,
> The Irishman for usquebaugh
> The Frenchman for the [pox].[7]

Here is material for caricature, but hardly for character.

Modern authors sometimes create profoundly revealing conflicts out of the clash of racial *mores*; for a modern author may see civilizations as representative of possible lines of development in human consciousness: Godbole, Aziz and Fielding in Forster's *A Passage to India* or Lambert Strether and Mme de Vionnet in Henry James' *The Ambassadors* provide obvious examples of this. But the complexity of valuation and the withholding of immediate judgement that these works require is a rare gift at any time; the Elizabethan urge to moralize was normally served most easily by presenting the foreigner in terms derived from simple nationalism. The European foreigner appears in post-Reformation English literature, in fact, as part of a process of vulgarization (in both senses of the word). He comes into literary focus caught between the xenophobic poles of Fear and Derision, which had always operated where Englishmen and Foreigners came into contact, but which was new as a literary image. And this applies not only to plays like *Jack Straw* (> 1593) and *Sir Thomas More* (*c.* 1596) which take anti-foreign feelings as their subject-matter, but is inescapable in any work showing the foreigner living in England; in such a context the 'stranger' could be shown to be a villain or a clown, but little else.

William Haughton's run-of-the-mill comedy *Englishmen for my money: or, a woman will have her will*, which he seems to have written for Henslowe about 1598, may be taken as a fair example of stock attitudes (of the more genial kind) to foreigners who tried to live in England. It tells the story of Pisaro, a 'Portingale' usurer-merchant resident in London,[8] whose three daughters are (illogically enough) totally English in outlook. They are wooed on one side by three English gallants, and on the other by three foreigners, a Frenchman, a Dutchman and an Italian. The daughters prefer the English suitors, the father promotes the foreigners; and the plot thus consists of the usual New Comedy type of intrigue and counter-intrigue. In the end the Englishmen (of course) win the girls and the foreigners accept this proof of superiority. What is interesting about this play in the context of a general consideration of foreigners is the super-ficiality of the colouring that their nationalities provide. We can recognize the plot of the usurer's fair daughter as a recurring stereotype. Usually the father's choice is rich and old, and ridiculous for these reasons; Haughton has added foreignness to the list of disqualifications, but it does not appear really different in kind from the other qualities of a standard pantaloon. Foreignness is no part of the moral structure, but is only an intriguing local colour.

Sometimes, though less frequently (as is understandable in any literature that aims to be entertaining rather than disruptive) the foreigner living in England is shown as more malignant than comic. In such cases he is seen (as always) to be dangerously 'cleverer than us', as slick, devious and lacking in integrity. In Robert Wilson's *Three Ladies of London* we meet Artifex, an honest English tradesman, who cannot sell his honestly made wares, 'for there be such a sort of strangers in this country | That work fine to please the eye, though it be deceitfully'.[1] When Artifex has been brought near enough to starvation he succumbs to these foreign wiles and is instructed by the Franco–Scottish Fraud how to make trashy goods look attractive. In the sequel-play, Wilson's *Three Lords and Ladies of London* Fraud reappears, this time (dressed as 'an old French artificer') deceiving the honest English clown Simplicity.[2] The moral structure of these plays derives from a very different convention from that of *Englishmen for my money*, but the 'foreignness' of Fraud is as incidental as that of the suitors in Haughton's play. He is not wicked because he is foreign but foreign because he is wicked.

At the same time, however, as these prejudices were invading literature from the market-place, increased national separateness was making foreign culture *more* attractive. The sense that foreigners are 'cleverer than us' can also be taken to mean that we must learn from them; rustic integrity can also be seen as provincial backwardness. 'Home-keeping youth have ever homely wits', says Shakespeare,[3] and the vision of courtly culture that he gives us in his high comedies is always set abroad. The New Learning substituted classical for biblical Holy Places as points of pilgrimage (geography was only taught in the period as ancillary to classical History and Litera-ture).[4] But the cultural image of Rome could not obliterate its politico-religious significance sufficiently to turn it into a second Jerusalem. Throughout the period there is a strong ambi-valence in the attitude to travel. The obvious educational advantages are seen; yet (as S. C. Chew has remarked) 'It is difficult to discover in the literature of the period any whole-hearted and unqualified commendation of travel'.[5] The power of European and especially Popish corruption to mar the youth of England was much mulled over by moralists; and travel itself (even in the abstract) is seen as of doubtful spiritual utility;[6] it was dangerously close to *curiositas*—that spending of effort on matters no way essential to salvation. The bottom panel of the engraved title-page of Samuel Purchas' *Pilgrimes* (1625)[7] seems to provide a useful emblem of this ambivalence. Purchas was, of course, a clergyman as well as a propagandist for the voyagers, and the two roles were not entirely coherent. On one side the title-page tells us that 'soldiers and Marchants [are] the worlds two eyes to see it selfe'; in the middle it shows us Purchas reading verses from Psalm xxxix, 'for I am a stranger with thee, and a sojourner, as all my fathers were', and 'verily every man at his best state is altogether vanity', and from Hebrews xi, 'they were strangers and pilgrims on the earth'. We are still close to the medieval attitude, even here among the documents of the new geography.

I have suggested that the clear emergence of the foreigner in post-Reformation English literature was part of a process of *vulgarization*. Vernacular and popular prejudices invaded literature, to deprive those who were known from close contact with English life of any status save that of failed Englishmen. And the more intimately these strangers are known, the less their *strangeness* seemed intriguing, the more it seemed despicable. The Irish, the Welsh and the Scots were normally seen as absurd deviations from an English norm; and the better known Europeans acquired the same status.

The inhabitants of the Low Countries ('Dutch' and 'Flemings')[1] were the best-known strangers in Elizabethan England. In the census of 1567 there were 2030 Dutch in London out of a total of 2730 aliens in all;[2] in Norwich at the same time there were about 4000 Flemings[3] and there were considerable numbers distributed throughout East Anglia and the southern counties. In 1573 there were said to be 60,000 Flemings in England.[4] But neither the Low Countries nor their inhabitants appear to have much significance in the literature of the time. Of course there are plenty of 'butter-box' fat Dutchmen in the drama, characters with names like Hans van Belch,[5] usually drunk, and unable to speak English even when sober; but these waterfront humours do not add up to anything like a serious image of what it is like to be Dutch. With the exception of Marston's 'Dutch Curtezan'[6] I know of no seriously used character in the period alleged to be Dutch; and I cannot think of a single play or romance which is set in contemporary Holland or Belgium.

It seems as if the Dutch were too close to the eyes of the English beholders for anything more than detailed idiosyncrasies to be observable. France, whose Huguenot refugees soon began to rival the Dutch and Flemings in numbers, was not in very different case. In so far as the French fitted into the Southern climatic stereotype of hot-blooded, fiery-tempered, subtle, dandified, smooth-tongued and Roman Catholic, their role duplicated that of the Italians (see below); but France as a country was too well known to be complex and divided in itself to provide a fitting background for the full development of these characteristics. The Elizabethans seem to have been aware of France as a great and complex polity, working out in its history approximately the same problems as beset England. Marlowe's *The Massacre at Paris* (1593) and Chapman's political plays are set in France, but are not 'foreign' in the sense that they are self-consciously un-English. France is in these cases a convenient locale for the pursuit of political and religious conflicts that could not be safely dealt with in an English setting. The locale and the history are real and so avoid the escapist emphasis of Ruritanian settings, but French national characteristics play little part in the effect. The casts of such plays have little or nothing in common with characters like Dr Caius (in *The Merry Wives of Windsor*) or the Dauphin in *Henry V*, who appear in contrast to the English and whose national characteristics are as superficial as those of the Dutchmen we have already discussed.

It seems to be the great virtue of Italy as a setting for literature of this period that everyday experience (and prejudice) supplied so little check and limitation to imaginative rendering. The number of Italians living in London was very small. In the census of 1567 there were only 140 Italians recorded;[7] and by 1580 the number had dropped to 116.[8] There was no traditional relationship between the countries, not even the relationship of war (as with France and Spain), and no strong economic links (as with the Low Countries and the Hanseatic ports). Italians are rarely mentioned in the petitions in which London merchants regularly complain of the unfair competition of aliens and strangers; and when Hand D (commonly supposed to be

Shakespeare's) in the play of *Sir Thomas More* makes Sir Thomas speak of possible reprisals against English merchants abroad, he does not even mention Italy as a possible scene of such activity:

> go you to ffraunc or flaunders to any Iarman
> *prouince* [to] spane or portigall nay any where.[1]

The absence of these varieties of knowledge gave all the greater strength to the cultural image of Italy as the land of wit (in all the variety of meanings that the word contained), of pleasure and of refinement, the home of Petrarch and Bembo and Castiglione and Ariosto, of Machiavelli and Guicciardini. It was an image which could be turned various ways (like the word *wit* itself), towards romance or towards diabolism, for use in comedy as well as in tragedy. The absence of a clearly defined central government in Italy further increased the malleability of the image, for it was only in a cultural sense that Italy was a 'country' at all. There, the high life of courts could be portrayed without intruding questions of responsibility (as they could hardly be in France or Spain, let alone England), whether in a mood of elegant idleness (the Milan of Shakespeare's *Two Gentlemen*) or in one of criminal selfishness (the Venice of Marston's *Antonio and Mellida*). And in the conflicts between these states there was no question of aligning one side or another with the English way of life. Italy as an image was sufficiently remote from England not to enforce immediate and invidious comparisons of national detail; but its way of life was (especially in tragedy) strange enough to force comparison with English life at a general moral and social level. The ambivalence of which I have already spoken in relation to travel, the simultaneously held desire to know, and fear of knowing, operated at maximum pressure in relation to Italy. For here there was a plethora of imaginative material and very little of that practical experience which might have limited its use.

I have elsewhere[2] developed the view that the 'Italy' of Elizabethan and Jacobean tragedy is related to England in the same way as the abstract world of the Morality play (say Skelton's *Magnificence*) is related to real life (say the court of Henry VIII). I have suggested that just as the Renaissance search for 'reality' led Bishop Bale to substitute Stephen Langton and Pandulphus for Sedition and Private Wealth,[3] just so the developing sense of geographical 'fact' led from the 'Gargaphie' of *Cynthia's Revels* to the 'Italy' of *The Revenger's Tragedy*—though both should be seen as providing basically only the physical name for an abstract idea (in this like the medieval 'Jerusalem'). That argument was concerned principally with the corrupt Italian courts which are so common a feature of Jacobean tragedy; I do not wish to repeat here the interpretations essayed there; but there is a parallel line of argument centred on the mercantile world of Venice which should make the relationship between England and the image of Italy sufficiently clear.

Robert Wilson's late morality, *The Three Ladies of London* (c. 1581), focuses neatly the observed relationship between Venice and London. This play shows the gradual domination of London by the Lady called Lucre (who may be taken to stand for the acquisitive instinct) and the exiling of her virtuous sisters, Love and Conscience. Among the new servants who flock to serve Lucre is one called Usury, and in conversation with him she reveals her genealogy:

Lucre. But, Usury, didst thou never know my grandmother, the old Lady Lucre of Venice?
Usury. Yes, madam; I was servant unto her and lived there in bliss.

Lucre. But why camest thou into England, seeing Venice is a city
Where Usury by Lucre may live in great glory?
  Usury. I have often heard your good grandmother tell,
That she had in England a daughter, which her far did excel.[1]

The point is then made that what Venice has been in the past London is now becoming; and nowadays, Lucre concludes,

> I doubt not but that you shall live here as pleasantly,
>   Ay and pleasanter too, if it may be.

It is clear enough that Venice is here a type-name for 'the commercial society' and represents an ethos which could create a 'Venice' in London, by the same route as might establish 'Jerusalem' in England's 'green and pleasant land'.

It is the dynamism of this threat to life as it is that gives force and propriety to the most rigorous development of this morality image—to the Venice of Jonson's *Volpone*. Jonson has painstakingly documented the topography of a real Venice; but, as often with Jonson, the texture of physical reality is only a surface. The social habit on which the plot turns (legacy hunting) belongs to the Roman Empire, not at all to the Venetian Republic. But it matches the Venetian background, for it turns the acquisitive instinct into the sole dominating force of social existence. Obsessed by their mania for money, these characters achieve their Venice by losing their humanity. At the level of achievement they are Magnificos, Avvocatori, etc.; but beneath the Venetian robes lie the predatory fur and feather and membrane of fox and flesh-fly, raven, gor-crow and vulture. The merchant as predator today holds Venice in fee; but tomorrow (the moral seems to run) it may be called London. As if to drive home this point Jonson throws into his animal city an English innocent abroad and his resolute tourist wife. This pair, Sir Politic and Lady Would-be, measure not only the distance of Venice from London, but also the ease with which it could be traversed. Their virtue is protected by nothing but their ignorance, not even by their will to be virtuous, for what they 'would be' is Politic, that is, Italianate, that is, amoral.

Shakespeare's *The Merchant of Venice* is clearly less rigorous in the use of the Italian setting to focus the meaning of the play. The Venetian world is here self-sufficient and does not ask to be brought into relation to London. But the setting is not without propriety for all that. What we have here (and in this the play is comparable to *Volpone*) is a world of Finance, where lovers, Christian gentlemen, friends, enemies, servants, daughters, Dukes, fathers, Jewish usurers, all express themselves in terms of financial relationship; and where the differences between love and hate, bounty and selfishness, Mercy and Justice, Christianity and Jewry are all treated in terms of money and how to handle it. Shakespeare focuses his Venice, however, not by pointing it back to England, but by pointing it out to the remoter world of 'blaspheming Jews',[2] whose non-Christianity, like that of pagans, infidels, Moors and Turks gave depth of meaning to 'foreignness' that mere difference of European race could hardly do.

I have suggested that the Elizabethan awareness of foreigners was closely conditioned by a traditional religious outlook on the world; and that much 'new knowledge' lay fallow or was treated in a merely superficial manner because of this. The European nations were inexorably emerging from the matrix of Christendom; but they did not yet stand distinct enough from one another to allow simple dramatic opposition. Even Italy supplied a distinct moral image only in the small areas of power-politics or commercial practice. These were hardly to be seen as the fruits of a deeper level of national wickedness; an Italian on the stage had to do more than announce his racial identity before his moral status was known. For such large-scale contrast the Elizabethan author had to go beyond Europe, and draw on oppositions that were older than ethnographic differences, on the conflict between God and the devil, between Christian and anti-Christian.

Shakespeare's *Merchant of Venice* treats its Italians as Christians (though merchants) and therefore 'like us'. For the opposition is with a figure who stands outside Christianity altogether, and whose commercial practice is seen as a part of his religious attitude—legalistic, obdurate, revengeful. In sixteenth-century England the threat of the infidel outsider still had the general effect of stilling internal European oppositions and stressing the unity of Christendom. When the Turks attacked Malta in 1565 the English dioceses appointed prayers to be read 'every Wednesday and Friday' 'to excite all godly people to pray unto God for the delivery of those Christians that are now invaded by the Turk';

Forasmuch as the Isle of Malta...is presently [*at the moment*] invaded with a great Army and navy of Turks, infidels and sworn enemies of Christian religion...it is our parts, which for distance of place cannot succour them with temporal relief, to assist them with spiritual aid...desiring Almighty God... to repress the rage and violence of Infidels who by all cruelty and tyranny labour utterly to root out not only true Religion, but also the very name and memory of Christ our only Saviour, and all Christianity.[1]

When Don John of Austria (Philip of Spain's half-brother) defeated the Turks at the battle of Lepanto, England was in the middle of a life-and-death struggle with Spain and the Pope (this was the year of the Ridolfi Plot); Elizabeth might treat the news with the wry awareness that the balance had been tilted against France;[2] but the popular reaction was one of rejoicing:

The ninth of November a sermon was preached in Paules Church at London, by maister William Foulks of Cambridge, to give thanks to almightie God for the victorie, which of his mercifull clemencie it had pleased him to grant to the christians in the Levant seas, against the common enimies of our faith, the Turks.[3]

Present at this service were the Lord Mayor with the aldermen and the craftsmen in their liveries:

And in the evening there were bonefiers made through the citie, with banketting and great rejoising, as good cause there was, for a victorie of so great importance unto the whole state of the christian common-wealth.[4]

Foulkes's sermon took as its text, Psalm xvi, verse 4: 'Their sorrows shall be multiplied that hasten after another god.' The force of the old conception of the world is too obvious on such an occasion to require comment. And throughout the period, the glory of Lepanto did not fade. James I wrote a famous poem on the subject. In 1593 Gabriel Harvey can ask the very rhetorical question,

Who honoureth not the glorious memory and the very name of Lepanto: the monument of Don John of Austria, the security of the Venetian state, the Halleluia of Christendome, and the welaway of Turky?[1]

And Thomas Randolph can sum up for us the general nostalgia for Lepanto when he says (well into the next century), 'The last valour show'd in Christendom | Was in Lepanto'.[2]

Shakespeare in *The Merchant of Venice* uses the figure of the Jew rather than the Turk to represent the pressure of infidel forces on the Christian dispensation. This was necessary if the play was to turn to interpretations of a mode of conduct, not on the tragical arbitrament of war. But the point of infidelity is the same. Congreve's Lady Pliant was picking up an old tradition when she pursued her husband with the string of names, 'heathen...Turk, Saracen...Jew'.[3] In medieval representations the Jew swears by Mahomet, and he does so as late as in Wilson's *Three Ladies of London*;[4] in Marlowe's *Jew of Malta* Barabas and Ithimore make a point of the common Jewish-Turkish interests:

> we are villaines both
> Both circumcized, we hate the Christians both.[5]

The two catch phrases, 'to turn Turk' and 'I am a Jew if...' were making precisely the same point—of betraying one's baptism, or selling one's soul to the devil.

Modern scholars often labour to document the exact racial background of Shylock (or Othello); and certainly we can say that Shakespeare *could* have learned many true facts about these remote races. But the evidence of the plays suggests that the old framework of assumptions about Jews, Turks and Moors—and this means theological assumptions—provided the controlling image in his mind.

It is clear that few Elizabethans had met a Jew (or a Turk, or a Moor); Jews provided no economic threat to the country. And so a modern historian can legitimately wonder at the residual prejudice through which 'Shakespeare could stir the blood of his audience by the spectacle of a Jewish usurer, three hundred years after there had been Jews in the land'.[6] This is only a difficulty, however, if we ignore the point made by Dr Michelson:

the New Testament and nothing but the New Testament is to be blamed for the peculiar psychology of the Jew in literature...down to and inclusive of Shylock this psychology was never based on observation, but simply taken over from the New Testament.[7]

To the Bible-readers and sermon-attenders of the Elizabethan age there was no difficulty in recalling the nature of the Jewish threat, a threat which was never-ceasing, for as Christ himself had remarked of the Jews, 'Ye are of your father, the devil',[8] and between the devil and the godly no peace could be imagined. In the medieval English *Play of the Sacrament* the Jew Jonathas is depicted as a rich man; but his wealth is not directly involved in his sin, which is simply the ritual re-enactment (with a consecrated wafer) of the central and never-to-be-forgotten sin of Jewry—the betrayal and murder of Christ.

When in 1594 Dr Lopez was arraigned for attempting to murder the Queen, Sir Edward Coke did not fail to raise his Jewishness in the argument against him: 'This Lopez, a perjured traitor and Jewish doctor, worse than Judas himself, undertook the poisoning.'[1] But it is the biblical sin that is still the key to the attitude. Again, when Lopez was at the gallows he 'declared that he loved the Queen as well as he loved Jesus Christ, which coming from one of the Jewish profession [= confession] moved no small laughter in the standers-by'.[2] What the audience could not forget was the relationship between the Jew and Christ; his activities in the world of the present could only be understood in the light of this. Shakespeare in *The Merchant of Venice* hardly mentions religion; but the contrast between the man who gives his life for his friend and the self-justifying legalist is squarely based on Scripture, however glossed with economic and psychological probability. And Jewish usury itself was seen by Shakespeare's contemporaries as more than an economic fact. It was an anti-Christian practice only proper to Jews, not because they were forced to live by it, but because Judas their eponym had sold Christ for thirty pieces of silver. And a usurer is a Jew whether he is racially (confessionally) Judaic or not. Bacon uses the verb 'to Judaize' of usury in general.[3] 'Lombard-Jew' is a typical conflation of appropriate nationalities, since (as Langland tells us)

Lumbards of Lukes...lyven by lone as Iewes[4]

and in the Elizabethan period we find the same compound in Nashe,[5] and in Beaumont and Fletcher's *The Laws of Candy*—'an usurer or Lumbard-Jew'.[6]

The acceptance of the idea 'Jew' as a fairly blank norm of villainy[7] gave authors an opportunity to play an effective theatrical trick on the audience's expectations, dramatizing the idea 'worse than a Jew'. In Wilson's *Three Ladies of London* we meet Mercatore, a Christian merchant from Italy who undermines English sturdiness by importing knick-knacks, 'Musk, amber, sweet powders, fine odours, pleasant perfumes, and many such toys, Wherein I perceive consisteth that country gentlewomen's joys'.[8] Mercatore cheats Gerontus, a Jew, of the money for these imports, and when Gerontus meets up with him in Turkey, and asks for his money, the Christian threatens to 'turn Turk' (quite literally) and so (in spite of Turkish abhorrence) escape the debt. Gerontus, rather than see such a shocking breach of Christian faith, cancels the debt. This is wildly unrealistic, of course; but it is a good indication of the extent to which the Jew in this period is an idea or a norm rather than a person.

Another sophisticated use of the Jew figure can be seen in Marlowe's *The Jew of Malta*, where Jew and Christian once again (as in *Three Ladies*) face one another under pressure from the Turks. This time, however, everyone is much more realistic, meaning much more unpleasant. The Jew has all the wickedness that was traditionally associated with his nation; but the Christian is almost without his expected virtue. The author again uses the expected opposition only as a ground plan or *canto fermo*, over which he works sophisticated inversions and variations.[9] Marlowe's play treats racial prejudice of a quite distinct kind from anything we know in the modern world; for the prejudice is not so much based on observation of what Jews actually do, as on assumptions about what kind of things people with this theological status are expected to do. This kind of unobserved *a priori* assumption obviously lends itself to dramatic inversion.

A pamphlet of the seventeenth century bears the curious title, *The blessed Jew of Marocco, or a blackamoor turned white*.[10] The two paradoxes in the title are obviously seen as parallel; and what I have said already about the attitude to Jews can be (in large) applied to 'Moors' also. Indeed I wish to go farther and point to *Othello* as the most magnificent specimen of the dramatic 'inversion of expected racial values' which I have discussed above in relation to 'Jew' plays. In order to make this point one must first note that in Elizabethan drama before *Othello* there are no Moor figures who are not either foolish or wicked. Eleazer in *Lust's Dominion* (c. 1600), Aaron in *Titus Andronicus*, Muly Hamet in *The Battle of Alcazar* (c. 1589) supply the norm of dramatic expectation—of a man whose colour reveals his villainy as (quite literally) of the deepest dye. We can have no doubt, of course, that Shakespeare's Othello, like the 'Moors' I have already mentioned, is not conceived of as a 'sheikh of Araby' type of coloured man, but as 'the thick-lips', 'the devil', with 'collied' complexion—in short, as a coal-black Negro.[1] The word 'Moor' was very vague ethnographically, and very often seems to have meant little more than 'black-skinned outsider', but it was not vague in its antithetical relationship to the European norm of the civilized white Christian. Elizabethan authors describe Moors as existing in many parts of the globe: we hear of the 'Mores of Malabar' from Spenser,[2] of Moors in Malacca from James Lancaster,[3] of Moors in Guinea from Eden,[4] of Moors in Ethiopia from Lodge,[5] of Moors in Fukien from Willes,[6] of Moors in America from Marlowe[7] and sundry others. There seem, in fact, to be Moors everywhere, but only everywhere in that outer circuit of non-Christian lands where, in the *mappæ mundi*, they appear with the other aberrations— 'salvage' men, satyrs, apes, skiapods, and the creatures that Othello knew of old:

> The Anthropophagi, and men whose heads
> Do grow beneath their shoulders.

Throughout the Elizabethan period, indeed, there seems to be a considerable confusion whether the Moor is a human being or a monster. In the 'plat' of *Tamar Cam* (1592) we are told of an entry of 'Tartars, Geates, Amozins, Nagars, ollive cullord moores, Canniballs, Hermophrodites, Pigmies' etc.[8] a characteristic medley; in *Volpone* we have a list of undesirables that Volpone has coupled with to produce his Fool, Dwarf and Hermaphrodite; the suppositious parents are

> beggers,
> *Gipseys* and *Jewes*, and black-*moores*.[9]

In the street-pageants and processions of the time, Moors played a considerable part—but again a part that was often interchangeable with that of the Devils, Greenmen, etc. As Withington has remarked:

The relation between wild-men, green-men, foresters, Robin Hood, the Moors, and the devil is very difficult to clear up. A great many cross-influences must exist; and it seems obvious that all these figures are connected.[10]

Finally we have the evidence of the English folk-play. In this, the enemy of St George is variously called 'The Turkish Knight, Black Morocco Dog, Morocco King, Black Prince of Darkness, Black and American Dog'.[11] Such confusions are obviously parallel to those which surround the Jew figure; and the reason, I would suggest, is the same in both cases. The Moor, like the Jew (but with less obvious justification), is seen in primarily religious terms. The epithets that Jonson and Shakespeare apply ('superstitious Moor' and 'irreligious Moor')[12] seem to me the basic ones. And the Moor had a very obvious advantage for the presentation of *a priori* wickedness; however large was the 'bottle nose' that Henslowe used to present the Jew of Malta on the stage,[13] it could not have been as impressive as the total sable of the Moor; which was seen as an emblem of Hell, of damnation, as the natural livery of the devil. Thomas Heywood may be taken to represent the general view when he speaks of

> a Moor,
> Of all that bears mans shape, likest a divell.[1]

Indeed we may remove the *like* qualification; the devil himself appeared to many in the body of a Moor. Reginald Scott in his *Discovery of Witchcraft* (1584) tells us that 'A damned soule may and dooth take the shape of a blacke moore',[2] and that Bodin 'alloweth the divell the shape of a blacke Moore, and as he saith he used to appear to Mawd Cruse, Kate Darey, and Jone Harviller'.[3] St Birgitta (of the fourteenth century) tells us in her *Revelations* that she saw the devil in the form of 'an Ethiope, ferefull in syght and beryng'.[4] St Margaret had the same experience.[5] In Shakespeare's own day the Enemy was still using this form. Sara Williams, one of the possessed women described in Harsnet's *Popish Impostures* (well known as a source of diabolical names in *King Lear*) was said to have seen 'a blacke man standing at the doore, and beckning at her to come away';[6] this was a demon, of course. Later, another black figure tempted her to break her neck down the stairs, and (at another time) to cut her throat.[7] Samuel Butler, with characteristic acidity, summed up the whole belief in a couple of lines:

> Some with the devil himself in league grow
> By's representative, a Negro.[8]

If this is a fair summary of received expectations about black men, we can see how Shakespeare is using this background in his *Othello*. Iago presents the civilized, white, Christian viewpoint in just these terms. But, as in the parallel case of Gerontus in *The Three Ladies of London*, the supposed outcast turns out to be the true Christian, while the nominal Christian with the white skin appears as the devil's representative. And again, as in Wilson's play, the Turks provide a pressure that sharpens the moral issues. Othello appears not only as noble, gracious, courtly, Christian, loving, but he is even the leader of Christendom in the last sense in which Christendom had any meaning—in the Crusade against the Turks, 'hellish horseleaches of Christian blood'.[9] The play thus may stand as one of the latest (as it is the supreme example) of representations of foreigners, using the old assumption that foreigners are meaningful because of their status in God's Providence. The play does not assent to this proposition; but Shakespeare accepts what the older geography could give him—a freedom to concentrate on essential moral problems—where the new geography could only give him facts. There is enough 'Moorish' and 'Venetian' colouring to prevent us losing our sense of the here-and-now in place and character; but this is only a starting-point for an exploration of what such characteristics imply. The 'overlap' in Renaissance geography of which I have already spoken, the co-existence of radically different and scientifically incompatible views of the world, allows Shakespeare to explore, swiftly and coherently, the image of the foreigner, the stranger, the outsider in a dimension which is at once terrestrial and spiritual.

5

EDUCATION AND APPRENTICESHIP

'Degrees in schools and brotherhoods in cities'

Forasmuch as God's glory, his honour, and the wealth public is advanced and maintained by no means more than by virtuous education and bringing up of youth under such as be learned and virtuous schoolmasters, whose good examples may as well instruct them to live well as their doctrine and learning may furnish their minds with knowledge and cunning, [I] have thought it good,...to erect the said Free Grammar School and to provide a reasonable and competent stipend for the schoolmaster of the same....   Preamble to the Statutes of Witton (Chester) Grammar School (1558)

For what maketh a nation to be a glorious nation, but that the people are a wise and an understanding people? What is it whereby we come so near unto the Highest, or to that blessed estate from which by our first parents we are so fallen, and to which we must be renewed and restored, if ever we shall inherit again the tree of life, as by true understanding and knowledge, especially if the same be sanctified unto us? Yea, what is it else whereby we excell the beasts, but by this divine reason, with which the more we are enlightened by the spirit of the Lord, through the means of learning, the more we differ, the more we do excel?   John Brinsley, *A Consolation for our Grammar Schools* (1622)

I

Few peoples have possessed more faith in learning than Englishmen of Shakespeare's age. One of the ironies of history is that the term 'enlightenment' has become associated with an age when this enthusiasm—at least in England—burned less brightly than it had a century and more earlier. Evidence of this devotion to learning exists in profusion. State papers, sermons, letters, account books, works of social and religious criticism, and handbooks for self-improvement all testify to its prevalence. Statements coming from the early sixteenth century and others framed amid the turmoil of civil war show that over the years this ideal maintained a strong hold on the minds of Englishmen. An outpouring of bequests and donations prove, moreover, its power to move men to unselfish acts. To be short, in Shakespeare's England the sentiments expressed in the epigraphs at the head of this chapter were not fleeting fancies, but widespread, perduring, efficacious beliefs that ordered men's lives and unloosed their purse strings.

To the Tudor humanists—Colet, More, Elyot, Cheke, and Ascham, to name the most important—must go the first tribute for nurturing love and respect for learning. They succeeded in passing on to their countrymen not only their own delight in letters, but also their deep faith in the power of learning to transform men and society. In their generous urge to remedy the abuses and evils they saw around them they confidently exhorted their contemporaries to adopt the study of *bonae literae* as the means to engender wisdom and virtue and to eradicate greed and indolence, the taproots of injustice and social disorder. Good learning, once implanted in

England, would, they predicted, bring about the rise of a well-constituted commonwealth equal to those of the Greeks and Romans.

Not far behind the humanists came the religious reformers. To the enthusiasm for learning wakened by the humanists they added the passion of religious conviction. They argued in part that the usurped authority of the Pope had persisted so long because ignorance bred superstition. One of the reforming preachers of Edward VI's time deplored the past in these words: 'we were so overwhelmed with the clouds of blind ignorance and ignorant blindness that we neither knew God nor ourselves aright, neither did we understand what the will of God is, nor what we ought to do to please him, nor how to walk in his holy and blessed ways.'[1] The reformers therefore looked on learning as a chief means for religious change. On the one hand they pleaded for the establishment of schools and increased support of the universities to educate a preaching clergy; on the other they upbraided the nobles and gentlemen of England for being so backward in learning that they could not man the offices of the king and relieve clergymen of their secular duties.

The doctrines that the humanists and the Protestant reformers preached had much in common. An assumption that underlay them all was the deep conviction that learning was an indispens-able salve to heal the sores of both Church and Commonwealth. The humanists, advocating primarily education for the gentlemen of England, expected the good that would spring from learning to work in society from the top down. If the 'governours' were learned, wisdom and justice would reign not only at Westminster but in the seats of authority in the counties and towns. They were not explicit in outlining what measures would comprise wise and just policy. To their way of thinking these details were not necessary. The knowledge of the good would be sufficient. Learned men in the councils of the government would so order things that the sources of injustice, exploitation, and other abuses would be checked and the normal relations between the various degrees of men would then assure peace and righteousness. The Protestant reformers had in this respect a somewhat broader view than the humanists. Spurred by a sense of urgency about the state of the Church, especially the lack of adequately trained clergymen, they felt that relatively wide educational opportunities were needed to right matters. Set in Bishop Latimer's impassioned words, their plea ran:

For if ye bring it to pass that the yeomanry be not able to put their sons to school...I say, ye pluck salvation from the people, and utterly destroy the realm. For by yeomen's sons the faith of Christ is and hath been mantained chiefly. Is this realm taught by rich men's sons? No, no; read the chronicles; ye shall find sometime noblemen's sons which have been unpreaching bishops and prelates, but ye shall find none of them learned men.[2]

Beyond this particular professional reason for making education an open rather than a closed matter, the reformers insisted that the maintenance of true religion depended in large part upon that degree of intellectual nurture which would permit the faithful to be readers as well as hearers of the word of God. The more the people—under the guidance of the clergy to be sure—could search the Scriptures for themselves, the farther would England be from the superstitions of Rome and the safer would she be from threats to the purity of the faith.

The arguments of both the humanists and the religious reformers had a cogency that appealed to practical administrators and statesmen, not just to humanitarians. Through most of the sixteenth century, Englishmen were deeply disturbed by the problem of poverty and its attendant evils—mendicancy, prostitution, vagabondage, brigandage and thievery, general social disorder, and riots and rebellion. Guided by scholars and preachers, they analysed this problem in terms that did not stop with remarks on the perversity of the human will or the incomprehensibility of God's ways but thrust on to describe the apparent increase in poverty and the rise of bands of masterless men as abnormal developments whose underlying causes were—at least in part—social and therefore remedial. Some like Sir Thomas More pointed to rich men's pride and greed as the chief source of these conditions. Others, without underestimating the role of these factors, looked beyond the faults of the few to the shortcomings of the many. To almost all of them ignorance was the root cause of most of the social diseases of the times. Learning was therefore their cure. An Elizabethan schoolmaster, writing on the 'Vtilitie of Schooling' put the point in these words:

Knowest thou not what profit and commodity learning bringeth to the children of Adam? Look upon the barbarous nations, which are without it; compare their estate with ours; and thou shalt see what it is to be learned, and what to be unlearned. They for want of learning can have no laws, no civil policy, no honest means to live by, no knowledge of God's mercy and favour, and consequently no salvation nor hope of comfort. We by the means of learning have and may have all these things. Therefore in that thou dost enjoy thy lands and livings, in that thou mayst procure such things as thou wantest, it is the benefit of learning. In that thou sleepest quietly in thy bed, in that thou travelest safely on the way, in that thieves and enemies do not spoil thine house and household, kill thy children, take away thy life, it is the benefit of learning. Nay, go further. In that thou thyself runnest not to the like excess of iniquity—art no thief, no murderer, no adulterer, it is the benefit of learning. Dost thou not here see what a plentiful harvest of all good fruits learning bringeth forth?[1]

To men with this point of view, legislation that would curb the greed of enclosing landlords, repress riots among the lower classes, provide labour for unemployed men, and relieve the necessities of the destitute was not enough. Only if educational opportunities were expanded might all baptized Christian subjects be 'virtuously brought up from their childhood, and taught good arts' so that each of them according to his station might serve God and the good of the realm.[2]

One of the earliest and most enduring examples of men acting in accord with such principles can be seen in the founding of Christ's Hospital in 1552. The corporation of London, responding more quickly than the rest of the country to the abuses of the time—perhaps because they were aggravated within the narrow limits of the city—sought to deal in a systematic way with the problem of the poor homeless men, women, and children, not merely to remove them from the streets but to make them where possible 'profitable members in the common wealth'. They appointed a committee of aldermen and prominent citizens to advise them on the problem. Education was one of the measures recommended. Consequently, as a contemporary chronicler of their good works wrote, 'first they devised to take out of the streets all the fatherless children and other poor men's children that were not able to keep them and to bring them to the late dissolved house of the Greyfriars which they devised to be an hospital for them where they should have meat, drink, and clothes, lodging and learning and officers to attend upon them'.[3] From the beginning Christ's Hospital was not only an orphanage but both a petty and a grammar school. Its staff consisted of a schoolmaster and usher for the grammar school and a writing master and two schoolmasters for the petties.

In the context of such thought and deeds, a provision of the Statute of Artificers (1563), which is frequently overlooked, gives clear evidence of the great importance that the practical men of the Tudor age placed on education. This law, mercantilist in nature, had among its objectives the maintenance of a strong agrarian economy and the prevention of vagabondage and social disorder. Both sections four and five were strong measures to guarantee an adequate supply of agricultural labourers. Section five provided that all persons between the ages of 12 and 60 who were not otherwise employed or who did not belong to certain excepted groups could be 'compelled to be retained to serve in husbandry by the year, with any person that keepeth husbandry, and will require any such person so to serve within the same shire where he shall be required'. The exceptions included apprentices and 'a student or scholar in any of the universities, or in any school'.[1] Although other sections of the act placed property qualifications on many classifications of apprenticeship, no similar restriction was put upon enrolment in schools or universities. The inclusion of such a proviso in legislation of this nature is therefore weighty testimony to the wide acceptance that the educational ideas taught by the humanists and reformers had gained.

Indeed so general was the endorsement given these ideas that some genuine friends and supporters of learning felt it necessary to warn men of Shakespeare's day that training in the liberal arts might not be suitable for all children in society and that it might not be an infallible cure for social ills. These men believed that broad educational opportunities would produce problems as well as benefits for the community. While accepting the view that England needed learned men to serve in Church and State, they feared that too generous provision for education would create an idle and dissatisfied class. Thus Richard Mulcaster, the first headmaster of Merchant Taylors' School, realizing that the number of places requiring grammar school learning was limited, warned in the 1580's that unregulated schooling for boys might be a source of trouble: 'To have so many gaping for preferment, as no gulf hath store enough to suffice, and to let them roam helpless, whom nothing else can help, how can it be but that such shifters must needs shake the very strongest pillar in that state where they live, and loiter without living?'[2] Thirty years later Sir Francis Bacon, whose interests in the advancement of learning are beyond question, gave his outspoken opinion on this subject. Commenting to James I on the advisability of carrying out the will of Thomas Sutton, the founder of Charterhouse, he wrote:

Concerning the advancement of learning, I do subscribe to the opinion of one of the wisest and greatest men of your kingdom: That for grammar schools there are already too many, and therefore no providence to add where there is excess: for the great number of schools...doth cause a want, and doth cause likewise an overflow; both of them inconvenient and one of them dangerous. For by means thereof they find want in the country and towns both of servants for husbandry, and apprentices for trade: and on the other side, there being more scholars bred than the state can prefer and employ; and the active part of that life not bearing a proportion to the preparative, it must needs fall out, that many persons will be bred unfit for vocations and unprofitable for that in which they were brought up; which fills the realm full of indigent, idle, and wanton people, which are but *materia rerum novarum*.[3]

Bacon concluded his argument with a plea that Sutton's bequest be diverted from the endowment of another grammar school to the use of the universities.

Mulcaster, Bacon, Ellesmere (perhaps the great man to whom Bacon referred), and a few others touched on a danger spot in Shakespeare's England: in early Stuart times a class of clerical and lay alienated intellectuals contributed to social, religious, and political unrest.[1] Yet their warnings went unheeded. Leaders of the time unfortunately did not make a substantial increase in the supply of livings for learned men. But neither did they lose their enthusiasm for learning as a general good. Shakespeare's works demonstrate this point. *Love's Labour's Lost*, for all its lampooning of those who had drunk too much ink, is a window into the times that allows us to see a playwright and an audience who felt assured enough of the value of learning to be amused at the foibles and excesses of its less balanced admirers. Even by portraying pretenders to erudition and pedants as men who were seeking recognition by paying homage to the social idea that they thought would readily win them approval, Shakespeare reveals how much stock his England put on learning. It was a society in which the school and schoolmaster—pedantic, verbose, and thin-skinned as he might be—had a secure and indeed still expanding role. It was a community in which grammar schools were still being founded, in which university enrolments were still mounting, in which knowledge of letters was leavening the trades and arts, and in which the metropolis, as became a bustling centre of industry, business, and international trade, was experimenting with new and applied branches of learning.[2]

II

No phenomenon of the sixteenth century better illustrates the English preoccupation with education than the development of grammar schools. It underlines two points that have already been noticed: the widespread concern for education as a matter both good in itself and essential to social reform; and the conviction that learning in the classical humane letters was not only the groundwork but the better part of all education. The first of these manifested itself concretely in an amazing increase in the number of grammar schools offering opportunities for learning; the second in the evolution and standardization of the curriculum within these schools.

Anyone who will even casually leaf through John Venn's *Biographical History of Gonville and Caius College, Cambridge* will quickly discover that Shakespeare's England was well supplied with grammar schools. For the five years from 1600/1 to 1604/5, for instance, 132 matriculants in Cambridge from Caius prepared for the university at 64 different schools; only four received their training from private tutors at home. Most of these schools were in East Anglia and fully half of them were schools whose existence cannot be ascertained from any other easily accessible records. Some of these may have been private schools in the sense that they did not possess any endowment and were not chartered by public authority. They depended on tuition fees for their entire support. The Rev. William Smyth, rector of Elsing, Norfolk, for example, kept a school where he educated four boys who entered Caius in these years, including two sons of his own. Of the public grammar schools that sent students to Caius, some were in cities like London and Norwich, some in boroughs like Bury St Edmunds and Cambridge, and many in market towns and parishes like Aylsham, Cheverly, Earl's Colne, and Stradbrooke.[3]

W. K. Jordan's recent studies of philanthropy in England amply demonstrate that not only in East Anglia but throughout the realm Englishmen of Shakespeare's day were being richly supplied with grammar schools. His study has indeed been a good antidote to the impression left by A. F. Leach that Tudor Englishmen destroyed more schools than they established. Not only were famous institutions like Westminster, Merchant Taylors', Harrow, and Charterhouse founded in these years, but literally hundreds of others similar to Shakespeare's own grammar school at Stratford first came into being during his lifetime. In London and the ten counties investigated by Jordan the number of schools increased nearly tenfold between the years 1480 and 1660, and the period of greatest growth and heaviest giving to this cause came, after a steady rise in Elizabeth's reign, in the first two decades of the seventeenth century. Almost invariably donors made their gifts in the form of capital endowments so that the institutions thus established became enduring and permanent features of English life. It was a veritable outpouring of private wealth for long-range public purposes and went far toward remodelling the contemporary and later character of English society. Describing the situation in 1660, a date somewhat after Shakespeare's lifetime to be sure but still reflecting the results of developments that largely occurred before his death, Jordan writes:

In only two counties could a boy have lived at a distance of more than twelve miles from an available grammar school in which he might have found free tuition under the terms of the founder's deed or gift. No city and no market town in all the ten counties lacked a school, while there were few really large villages without some place of instruction. Or to put it another way, there was by 1660 an endowed grammar school for something like each 6000 of the estimated population of this great area, one for each 4400 of population if the unendowed schools be added as well.'[1]

Before the Education Act of 1870 there was in England only one to every 23,750 persons. Truly then the philanthropists of Shakespearian England had here as in many other areas of English life done mighty works and by their efforts laid the foundations of a national system of education.

The term 'national system of education' is the only proper one to apply to the network of schools that sprang up in these years. Although the financial support for these new institutions came overwhelmingly from private sources, the principles guiding the founders in the drafting of statutes and thus determining the curriculum had been formulated by national authorities. Ecclesiastical canons, royal injunctions, and parliamentary statutes spoke with one voice from 1529 to 1604 to set the basic essentials for grammar school education. The spirit of all these regulations appeared in the earliest of them, a canon passed by the Convocation of Canterbury in 1529. After specifying that teachers should be orthodox and of good reputation and that they should first teach boys good conduct and a summary of the faith, this ordinance provided for a uniform pattern of instruction so that boys who might migrate from one school to another would not be penalized. 'No author of grammar rules or precepts', so it read, 'shall be put before boys being taught grammar except the one which the archbishop of Canterbury with four bishops of the province, four abbots, and four archdeacons...shall next year prescribe for boys to read.'[2] A royal injunction of a few years later, ordering that William Lily's *Introduction of the Eyght Partes of Speche* be the grammar taught throughout the realm, repeated and reinforced these sentiments: 'Among the manifold business and most weighty affairs appertaining to our regal authority and office,' ran Henry VIII's decree:

we forget not the tender babes and the youth of our realm whose good education and godly bringing up is a great furniture to the same and cause of much goodness. And to the intent that hereafter they may the more readily and easily attain the rudiments of the Latin tongue without the great hindrance, which heretofore hath been through the diversity of grammars and teachings, we will and command, and straightly charge all you schoolmasters and teachers of grammar within this our realm...as ye intend to avoid our displeasure and have our favour to teach and learn your scholars this English introduction here ensuing and the Latin grammar annexed to the same, and none other....[1]

Elizabeth I confirmed her father's regulation by enjoining all schoolmasters to teach 'the grammar set forth by King Henry VIII of noble memory, and continued in the time of King Edward VI and none other'.[2] The Constitutions and Canons of 1604, after the change in dynasties, renewed the force of this injunction and instructed all ecclesiastical visitors to enforce it within the arch-deaconries and bishoprics of the realm.[3]

Such measures did much to assure that a boy in Newcastle had much the same education as his contemporaries in Stratford and Exeter. Even though, as noted in the introduction to Lily's grammar, 'the variety of teaching is divers yet, and always will be, for that every schoolmaster liketh that he knoweth, and seeth not the use of that he knoweth not',[4] all English grammar school pupils entered the precincts of learning through the same gateway. The influence of the humanists and the compelling example of famous and successful institutions like Winchester, Eton, and St Paul's guaranteed that the rest of their schooling would be essentially uniform. Almost without exception Englishmen of the time believed that learning in classical letters opened a vast treasure of wisdom and knowledge. Hence all grammar schools not only used the same introductory text but also substantially the same curriculum in the later stages of their work. T. W. Baldwin, after his monumental and exhaustive survey of grammar school educa-tion in Shakespeare's day, puts the point in these words:

the sixteenth-century grammar school curriculum was highly organized and had by the middle of the century been standardized into essential uniformity....Grammar, vulgars and Latins, and parsing and construction are its uniform tools for attaining Latinity, and these are used according to a definite and systematic scheme. Whether there was to be one master or many, a few pupils or a large school, three forms or six or eight, the curriculum and its methods remained fundamentally the same.[5]

A typical schoolboy of Shakespeare's England would have begun his education at the age of four or five.[6] His work in these tender years would not have been in the studies of the grammar school but in reading and writing English, the subjects taught in the petty schools. His primary aids to acquiring such elementary knowledge would have been the horn-book—a wooden tablet covered with a parchment on which was printed the alphabet, basic syllables for English words, and the Paternoster in English, all of which would be protected by a transparent sheet of horn; the *ABC with Catechism*—a volume combining the Paternoster, the Creed, the Ten Command-ments, and short catechistical exercises on the fundamentals of the Christian faith; and finally the *Primer*—a devotional book usually containing prayers and metrical versions of the psalms. At this stage of learning, a boy probably had the company of his sisters or other little girls, although the latter rarely if ever went on to grammar school. For two or three years he and his school-mates learned reading and writing, the rudiments of spelling according to the fashion favoured by his master, and the fundamentals of the authorized religious beliefs. In his final year in petty school he might have been introduced, depending upon his own capacities and the time and ability of his teacher, to the parts of speech in Latin and even to the accidence. In villages or small market towns the petty school was frequently joined to the grammar school and was taught either by the usher (undermaster) or by older boys or even by some elderly man or woman. More usually, however, the two kinds of schools were kept separate.

Upon leaving petty school at the age of seven or eight the schoolboy began his serious training. The purpose of the grammar school was clear, precise, and widely understood and accepted in Shakespeare's day. Briefly it was to teach a mastery of Latin grammar and to introduce a boy to the riches of learning and wisdom contained in Latin literature. Greek and even Hebrew were added to the curriculum of some schools in Elizabeth's reign, but they supplemented and did not replace the basic studies in Latin. Only occasionally did grammar schools give instruction in other subjects like arithmetic and penmanship. Christ's Hospital, for instance, had a writing master on its staff from the beginning. And some schoolmasters like Richard Mulcaster saw much good in mathematical studies. Yet the dominance of Latin and the belief that one needed to learn classical languages before being qualified to study arithmetic and geometry prevented any significant dilution of the curriculum.

A boy's work was divided into forms, either three, six, or eight according to the custom followed by his school. Within this structure there was an even more fundamental division between the lower and upper school. If the school had a multiple staff, the usher had charge of the lower forms and the headmaster of the upper. The usher would first teach the parts of speech, if the boy had not learned them in petty school, and the accidence, that is, the declension and conjugation of Latin nouns and verbs. Instruction to this point was in English, but thereafter it was expected to be in Latin. Still under the tutelage of the usher, the boy would begin his daily tasks of memorizing grammar, parsing sentences, and practising composition. His earliest exercises were called 'vulgars' because they consisted of turning English phrases and short sentences into Latin. To aid him in writing passable Latin he would have at hand some books written just for his use: the vulgaria containing English sentences with appropriate Latin translations and colloquies giving samples of simple but good Latin discourse. The most famous of the latter was a work prepared by Erasmus himself. He would also be reading at this stage works like Cato's *Puerilis*, Aesop's *Fables*, and dialogues by Mathurin Cordier, whose connection with Calvin in Geneva gave his book special favour. In time he would progress to 'Latins' or short themes of his own composing. He was expected to follow the style illustrated in his texts and in addition he would probably make generous use of English–Latin dictionaries such as Lewis Evans' *A Short Dictionary Most Profitable for Young Beginners*, first printed in 1553.

In the upper forms the boy came under the instruction of the master himself. Here he continued his efforts to learn the style and form of good written and spoken Latin. He would now be well advanced in the incessant practice of preparing themes and would be given more difficult assignments like composing letters and orations in the style of the great master of Latinity—Cicero. Whether his master followed the traditional method of allowing boys to turn their own English compositions into Latin or whether he was a disciple of Ascham who advocated an elaborate method of 'imitation' based in large part on double translations of the best ancient authors from Latin into English and then, without book, back into Latin, the boy learned by these exercises much about writing English as well as Latin. As he progressed through his studies he was also introduced to the principles of rhetoric. He was thus taught to recognize the rhetorical forms and devices used by ancient authors, to know which ones were appropriate for each kind of discourse, to appreciate the skill required for clear and effective expression, and to discriminate between good and bad styles for himself. But his work would not stop there. Since grammar and rhetoric in Tudor days included what today would be found in courses in literature, such studies also involved the interpretation and understanding of all kinds of writing: poetry and drama, history and biography, moral essays and orations, to name the most important. Authors whom he would read, at least in part, were Terence, Virgil, Ovid, Plautus, and Horace; Sallust, Cicero, Caesar, Martial, Juvenal, and Livy; and among the moderns Erasmus and Baptista Mantuanus. Before the end of his career he would have delivered several declamations and perhaps have participated in Latin plays, especially those of Terence. If his school was among the better ones, he would also have begun to master Greek grammar.

The life of a schoolboy in Shakespeare's day was untouched by any modern sentimentality about childhood. Still less was it affected by any theories that separated social adjustment from learning. Indeed, if a boy were to become a civilized creature, well-adjusted to his fellows, education and the discipline by which it was accompanied would be chiefly responsible for achieving that result. Although Ascham and some others at the time did not believe that corporal punishment contributed to the learning process, few schoolmasters put his precepts into practice and hence spared the rod. Beside severe discipline the Tudor schoolboy had to put up with long hours. Usually school began at six or seven in the morning and lasted until five or six in the evening. There would usually be a recess from eleven to twelve or one and some schools also gave breaks both morning and afternoon. School kept for six days a week and also for most weeks in the year. Shorter vacations were allowed than today, although there were more frequent single holidays. On many of these, however, he would probably have to attend church with his schoolmates as he regularly had to do on Sundays. It was a severe life, but one which most boys of the time seemed to survive without serious damage to their spirits or their health.

The network of grammar schools in England was national in number and distribution, and the course of study pursued within them was determined by national standards. But did they also have a national effect in terms of the children who attended them? Were they, in other words, institutions that made the opportunities and social benefits of learning available to a relatively large number of boys, or rather did they affect only the lives of the privileged few?

The answer to this question, largely because of a lack of statistical information, must be pieced together from scraps of evidence. It is not, however, ambiguous or indistinct. Much that is known reveals that this system of schooling, while it was not inspired by a modern concept of mass or democratic education, was a broad rather than an exclusive or an aristocratic one. For instance, Shakespeare's 'whining schoolboy, with his satchel | And shining morning-face, creeping like snail | Unwillingly to school' is part of melancholy Jaques' portrayal of the universal experience of man from the cradle to the grave. Could this picture have had the intended effect had it not been rooted in reality and did it not therefore reflect the boyhood of both many persons in the pit and their betters?

Perhaps the best way to get an impression of the breadth of opportunity offered by the free grammar schools is to determine not which boys may have attended, but which boys probably could not have attended. The chief limiting factors on enrolment in grammar schools were first the need of most poor parents for the labour of their sons and secondly a national fear that too much education would start a flight of agricultural labourers from the land and bring on a decay in husbandry and an increase in vagabondage. Hence lads from the lowest ranks of society, whose strong backs and sturdy arms were economic assets to their families and landlords and whose presence on the land was seen as a guarantee of social stability, were generally denied schooling. They may have numbered one-half of the boys of England. Still these restrictions were not rigidly enforced, no more than were the precise and definite property qualifications for apprenticeship.[1] And since they fell oppressively only on the boys from the very lowest ranks of society, they allowed a broad representation from the other groups to enjoy the advantages of education. In the country, sons of leaseholders and yeomen as well as gentlemen; in the villages, market towns, and cities, sons of artisans and shopkeepers as well as merchants and professional men could acquire learning.

To consider this question from another angle, not only did the grammar schools enrol boys from a broad segment of English society but they also sent them out to take places in all the respectable callings and occupations of the realm. They were not intended only for scholarship or the professions. Shakespeare's England did not have an eleven-plus examination. On the contrary, the statutes of many grammar schools give evidence that their founders expected a large number of boys upon leaving to become apprentices. Certainly some schoolmasters did so. John Brinsley, for instance, recognizing that not all boys were able to be scholars, still believed that grammar school learning would stand them in good stead and that they in return would bring credit to their schools: all so trained would be useful, 'some to store the universities, others to adorn all other places and conditions of life; that thereby might be had men expert in each kind, as necessity should require, for the common benefit and good of all'.[2]

The motives that inspired the great benefactors of education in Shakespeare's England, especially the merchants of London, reveal the social importance of these institutions perhaps better than any other evidence. To these men, as Jordan has so well said, the founding of a free grammar school was, among other important considerations,

an instrument of social rehabilitation which they were creating with their great generosity. They were determined that no boy with native ability infused with ambition should be denied opportunity and they sensed, certainly correctly, that education alone could break the shackles which bound whole classes of men. The testimony to this impulse...is often moving and as often intensely personal. Thus scores of London merchants of humble provincial birth, who had won great wealth, when they came to set their wordly affairs in order, bethought themselves of the poverty and ignorance which had all but overwhelmed them. This explains...why so many of them ordered the founding of a free school or a great scholarship fund in the home parish with which they had had few if any ties for a full generation. They remembered their own youthful hardships, the narrowness of the margin of their own emancipation, as they set out in poignant personal terms the motives which impelled them to make their foundation...in that particular parish, as if to ensure for ever opportunity for boys not unlike themselves in this remembered corner of England.[3]

The position of the grammar schools was, therefore, a key one in Shakespeare's England. Boys attended them between the ages of seven or eight and fifteen or sixteen. Upon leaving, a few like Ben Jonson, who had caught at Camden's Westminster the spirit and love of letters, became scholars without additional formal education; others, not necessarily less talented, pursued further studies at the universities; and still more became apprentices in London or elsewhere. Whatever their later careers, the grammar schools had been for all a common beginning. And they provided them all, as they went their separate ways, a measure of common culture, instilled by exposure to Latin grammar and letters as well as by respect for the master's rod. Not least among the examples of what such culture might mean was Shakespeare himself.

III

The universities of Shakespeare's day, even though not all the scholars and men of letters received training there, were vigorous institutions.[1] They had recovered since the early sixteenth century from the sterile intellectualism that had beset them for more than a hundred years. Logic, under the criticism of the humanists, had been enriched with rhetoric; metaphysics with moral philosophy; and the statutory curriculum as a whole with extra-statutory readings and instruction by tutors and college lecturers who were in large part supplanting the regent masters, the ancient teachers in Oxford and Cambridge. Thus the course of studies, especially for the bachelor's degree, had become a mental diet fit for the nurture not only of clerkly scholars preparing themselves for professional degrees in law, medicine, and divinity but also for gentlemen seeking the arts of civility and the pathway to preferment in the service of the prince.

In *The Two Gentlemen of Verona* Shakespeare himself showed the new repute that the universities had won because of these changes. Panthino, confidential servant to Antonio, reveals some of the matter in reporting the misgivings of Antonio's brother over the idleness of his nephew Proteus:

> He wond'red that your lordship
> Would suffer him to spend his youth at home
> While other men, of slender reputation,
> Put forth their sons to seek preferment out:
> Some to the wars, to try their fortunes there;
> Some to discover islands far away;
> Some to the studious universities.[2]

Antonio, who shared his brother's apprehensions, tells the rest in his reply:

> I have consider'd well his loss of time,
> And how he cannot be a perfect man,
> Not being tried and tutor'd in the world.[3]

For a young man of the times, then, the journey from grammar school to the university was, as it still is in large part today, his first adventure into the world—his initiation into the estate of manhood. Even though university students of the sixteenth century usually matriculated a year or two younger than now, they still were expected to put aside childish things and change from schoolboys into men. At the universities the eyes of the world were upon them and their reputations first began to grow.

The psychological break between school and university was probably greater than the intellectual one. In many respects the university curriculum overlapped that of the grammar schools. Indeed, if a boy had gone to one of the better schools—Westminster under Camden or Merchant Taylors' under Mulcaster for example—he might already have been well read in texts that would be his chief studies during his early terms at Oxford or Cambridge. To Elizabethans, however, repetition was not necessarily a fault. They still believed that most of what man needed to know was to be found in ancient letters, and that the process of learning was deepening one's understanding, not broadening one's mastery of facts.

The statutes of both universities called for a student to be in residence for sixteen terms or four years, though by the end of the sixteenth century it had become usual to dispense with one year of residence. In Shakespeare's days an Oxford scholar should have heard lectures in grammar, rhetoric, dialectics or logic, arithmetic, and music: grammar for two terms, using Linacre's *Rudiments* and readings from Virgil, Horace, or Cicero's *Epistles*; rhetoric for four terms using Aristotle's *Rhetoric*, Cicero's *Praeceptiones*, or Cicero's *Orations*; logic for five terms using Porphyry's *Institutions* or Aristotle's *Dialectics*; arithmetic for three terms using texts by Boethius and Gemma Frisius; and music for two. A Cambridge undergraduate had a slightly different schedule. The Cambridge statutes forbade the teaching of grammar within the university except to the choristers of Trinity and King's Colleges. No arithmetic or music was prescribed; philosophy was substituted for them. Thus a Cambridge scholar heard lectures in rhetoric his first year and others in logic his second and third years. He concluded his course with the study of philosophy. Throughout their residence students at both universities were expected to participate in scholastic disputations: first by attendance and observation; then by acting as a first opponent to another man's argument; later still by being the respondent or the propounder of answers to the question under discussion; then by participating *pro termino* to provide disputants for the exercises of other scholars; and finally by taking part as a respondent at least twice in the formal Lenten disputations for determining bachelors, at which time he demonstrated his qualifications for a degree.

The curriculum described here, traditional as it may appear, reflected important changes from the medieval course of studies and even more important changes in views on the purpose and nature of university education. The undergraduate studies of medieval Oxford and Cambridge were concentrated in logic and were based almost entirely on Aristotle's organon, the parts of which a student should have had read to him with commentary at least twice. Even studies of grammar and rhetoric, the latter of which was restricted to bachelors of arts pursuing work for the M.A. degree, were mere adjuncts to logic and as such suffered from dialectical speculation. The whole undergraduate course, in other words, was technical education, subordinated to the use to be made of it in the higher studies of scholastic philosophy and theology. In the sixteenth century, concessions made to humanist criticism of the medieval universities had readjusted the emphasis placed within the curriculum upon the various subjects of the trivium. These reforms, by transferring rhetoric from the advanced part of the arts course to preparation for the B.A. and by expanding work in both grammar and rhetoric to include readings from the *literae humaniores*, gave the undergraduate curriculum more content, ended its subservience to metaphysics and theology, and made it into a self-justifying enterprise. As a consequence changes also occurred in the purposes for which one pursued the B.A. course. It came to be viewed as a programme of studies which would give a young man the breadth of knowledge and wisdom to pursue a career in both Church and State without further formal education. He was henceforth prepared to finish his education by independent study. Even the authorities at Cambridge acknowledged this point in 1608 when they excused all candidates for the M.A. from residence requirements on the grounds 'that a man once grounded so far in learning as to deserve a Bachelorship in Arts is sufficiently furnished to proceed in study himself'.[1]

It has long been the custom to deplore the intellectual sterility of Tudor Oxford and Cambridge. Contemporary evidence seemed to support such an attitude: again and again the governing bodies of the two universities passed statutes lamenting the emptiness of the lecture halls and the inattention to duty of the lecturers and levying higher and higher fines to enforce obedience to university regulations; just as repeatedly the moralists of the time, noting the neglect of lectures and exercises, bemoaned the time-serving of both students and dons. What most contemporary critics overlooked then, and what historians of the universities have also disregarded, was that the ancient methods of education at Oxford and Cambridge were being displaced by better and more efficient ones. The lectures of regent masters in the public schools of the universities were being supplanted, even as endowed professorships were being founded to supplement them, by lectures given within the colleges and supported by college revenues of various kinds. Furthermore, printing had made both textbooks and commentaries easily accessible to students so that they were no longer dependent on cursory and ordinary lectures for their basic knowledge. And finally a new kind of teacher, who could give personal attention to the needs and capacities of his students, had appeared on the scene. By the end of the sixteenth century the college tutor had become the most important influence on an undergraduate's education.

In the late sixteenth and early seventeenth centuries, as these changes became generally accepted and as university enrolments, especially of men drawn from the ranks of the gentry, rapidly rose, Oxford and Cambridge continued to undergo significant developments. Most noteworthy among these was the growth of an extra-statutory curriculum that supplemented, and even for some students who were not seeking degrees replaced, the statutory studies. Behind this new departure lay in part a concern for the needs of the young gentlemen who were flocking to the universities. Many tutors shared Gabriel Harvey's view that they should take pains to have 'gentlemen to be conversant and occupied in those books especially, whereof they may have most use and practice, either for writing or speaking, eloquently or wittily, now or hereafter'.[2] The subjects that made up the extra-statutory curriculum varied, to be sure, according to the interests of the students and the educational ideas of the tutors. Most commonly tutors would supplement readings prescribed by statute with others that would bring learning in a traditional field up-to-date. Thus, without changing the subject-matter of the curriculum materially, considerable new material was brought to the attention of students, and university education was kept abreast of current thought. The introduction of Ramus' logic and rhetoric is the most notable example of this kind of extra-statutory development. Closely akin to such a change of emphasis was the use of Machiavelli and Bodin in moral philosophy and Copernicus and Kepler in astronomy and natural philosophy. A greater divergence from the statutory curriculum came with the introduction of entirely new fields of study such as the history of modern states with readings from Comines, Guicciardini, and English authors such as Camden,

Speed, and Martyn, cosmography and navigation, and modern languages like French and Italian. All these interests could be and were cultivated in Oxford and Cambridge in Shakespeare's day.

Shortly after Shakespeare's death some of these studies were formally recognized by the establishment of professorships to teach them. Thus Sir Henry Savile, by endowing two chairs in geometry and astronomy, did notable work in modernizing mathematical studies at Oxford. The Savilian professor of geometry was to teach not only Euclid but also Apollonius' *Conics* and Archimedes and thus provide fundamental understanding for further advancement in pure mathematics. The professor of astronomy was, to be sure, still to base his lectures on Ptolemy, but he was to interpret Ptolemy's works in the light of the findings of Copernicus and other recent authorities. Both were to teach practical applications of their theoretical fields, including land measurement, practical geometry, geography, and the mathematical parts of navigation. Other professorships in new fields were also founded in these years: the Camden and Lord Brooke chairs in history and the Laudian in Arabic. Yet the most important pioneering was still left to the tutors and students themselves, for whom the statutory requirements were really a light load. They did not 'scruple of diverting from the common road of studies...to any part of useful learning'.[1]

The ultimate effect of all these changes was to transform Oxford and Cambridge into institutions whose primary purpose was undergraduate education. The universities ceased to be merely seminaries for the training of the clergy and became places to prepare young Englishmen for service to the State as well as the Church. Measured either by enrolments, the number of degrees granted, or by importance of the course of studies to society, the higher faculties, except for divinity, fell in status throughout Shakespeare's lifetime. Civil law, jealously watched by the practitioners of the common law, had never recovered from the setback it had suffered with the demise of its twin, canon law, at the Reformation. The study of medicine remained in these years conservative and tradition bound. The most eminent physicians of England got their professional training abroad. Only the study of divinity gained ground. But though the universities continued to serve the community well by turning out a good supply of learned divines, they no longer performed this function as their sole mission.

The universities of Shakespeare's England were, then, contrary to long accepted opinion, vigorous institutions. They had been revivified by the effects of the humanist movement and other social and intellectual developments of the Tudor period. Their function had been transformed so that they prepared both clergymen and laymen for high and honourable service to the community. The undergraduate course, kept up-to-date by extra-statutory additions to the curriculum, provided an education that gave men a breadth of understanding useful in the councils of the nation, an ability to express themselves in cogent, well-reasoned and sometimes eloquent arguments and speeches, and a familiarity and respect for things of the mind, both old and new.

IV

Apprenticeship, the means of entry into 'brotherhoods in cities', and also into humbler trades like those of the thatcher and tiler in villages, was in itself an essential part of education in Shakespeare's England. It would probably be going too far to compare apprenticeship with the training in present-day technical colleges in Britain or in colleges of engineering, business administration, and applied arts in the United States. Yet apprenticeship had much in common with these modern institutions and supplied for Shakespeare's society more than training in manual skills. An apprentice carpenter or mason would learn, in addition to the basic elements of his trade, much that was to be known about design, structural engineering, and architecture; an apprentice barber-surgeon something about anatomy; and an apprentice grocer, draper, or clothier a good deal about conditions of trade, commercial law, foreign exchange, and shipping. All of them should also have received the moral guidance needed to make them good citizens as well as special instruction in the ethical principles of their trade or 'mystery'. Finally, to the extent that many young men only became apprentices after leaving grammar school, this kind of education came at the same stage in life that formal technical learning still does today.

The regulations governing apprenticeship had been laid down by Parliament in 1563 in the great Statute of Artificers. Perhaps the first point to note about them is that under the provisions of the statute, as Margaret Davies has said, 'apprenticeship in Elizabethan and Stuart England was the rule and not the exception in economic and social life except in certain well-defined employments at both ends of the industrial scale: those using unskilled labour in mining, quarrying, or transport; and at the other end, those in which the place of the independent master craftsman was taken by the entrepreneur managing the investment of capital'.[1] The second significant matter to remember is that this statute in one respect made the term of apprenticeship uniform. It was to be a minimum of seven years for all trades. It might, of course be longer; for it was not to expire before the apprentice had attained the age of 24 years.[2] Thirdly this act established property qualifications for apprenticeship to some of the more desirable trades or crafts, such as those of the merchants, mercers, drapers, goldsmiths, ironmongers, embroiderers, clothiers, and woollen cloth weavers. Such a restriction, however, did not apply to craftsmen in more than a score of trades, including smiths, carpenters, bricklayers, rough masons, millers, line weavers, and coopers. They could take as apprentices children of persons who had no lands.[3] In all its provisions it showed an anxiety to exclude from apprenticeship, except to agricultural pursuits, all persons who were agricultural labourers or who occupied husbandry.

As one might expect, London occupied a special position in the system of apprenticeship. The statute of 1563, for instance, contained exemptions for London and Norwich from such of its provisions as were contrary to their customs. Such legal privileges reflect the esteem and reputation in which the London crafts and trades and the tradition surrounding them were held. London was a bustling rapidly growing metropolis; it had use for more trades than other towns and cities and provided a greater scope for craftsmen in the practice of their mystery than did even the largest provincial centres. As a consequence apprenticeship in London seems not only to have set an example for country practices, but it probably was widely sought as an experience that gave a young man a special mark of distinction and perhaps an economic advantage over his home-trained competitors. Some very interesting statistics on London apprenticeship strongly suggest that a high proportion of the persons bound to London masters sought the prestige of London training, not membership in London companies. Of the apprentices to London carpenters and masons in the seventeenth century only 40 per cent of the former and 44 per cent of the latter became freemen of their companies.[4] On the other hand, of the apprentices to printers between the years 1605 and 1640, nearly 70 per cent took up their freedom.[1] The explanation of this discrepancy does not lie in differences in opportunity or in differences in conditions of work in the varying occupations, but rather in differences in the laws regulating them. A Star Chamber decree of 1586 strictly controlled printing and made the Stationers' Company the enforcing agency. It outlawed presses set up beyond the boundaries of London and its suburbs, except for one each in the universities of Oxford and Cambridge.[2] Therefore a printer could not practise his trade in the country; he had to stay in London, even if he were to work as a journeyman. Carpenters and masons, on the other hand, were free to return to the places whence they came, and a high percentage of those who completed their apprenticeship apparently did so. Another piece of statistical information tends to confirm this inference. Although an unusually high percentage of apprentices to printers became freemen of the Stationers' Company, a far smaller percentage of apprentices to stationers who were not printers did so. The Star Chamber decree did not restrict non-printers to the environs of London. Indeed the number of men freed by service within the Stationers' Company between the years 1605 and 1640 was only 47 per cent of the total number of apprentices to stationers, both printers and non-printers.[3]

The kind of training provided apprentices is a subject that cannot be handled concretely without getting into almost endless detail. A few generalizations, based primarily on practice in London, may help nonetheless to give it some substance.

The indenture by which a young man was bound apprentice was a contract of mutual benefit to the two parties concerned. As a contemporary apologist for apprenticeship explained, it was an arrangement by which the master provided the apprentice 'with instruction and universal conformation or molding of him to his art' and the apprentice in turn served his master 'with obedience, faith, and industry'.[4] This kind of agreement was enforceable by either party on the other, usually by action brought before the officers of the company to which they belonged. Surviving records give evidence of both kinds of cases. Court books of the various companies frequently contain records that apprentices, who had in one way or another failed to abide by the terms of their apprenticeship, were discharged and would never again be allowed to become apprentices. Occasionally they have entries showing actions taken against masters for neglecting to instruct their apprentices, not only in their trade but in 'learning'.

What was meant by the term 'learning' in this context is not entirely a matter of conjecture. Words that cast light on this question are to be found in Edmund Coote's *The English Schoolemaister*. Explaining his purpose in writing the book, Coote remarked:

The learneder sort are able to understand my purpose and to teach this treatise without further direction. I am now therefore to direct my speech to the unskilful, which desire to make use of it, for their own private benefit; and to such men and women of trade, as tailors, weavers, shop-keepers, seamsters, and to such other, as have undertaken the charge of teaching others.[5]

Likewise Thomas Masterson, in his 'plain and brief arithmetical speculative manner', expounded 'needful questions applied to paying, receiving, buying, selling, bartering, mixtions, exchanges, companies, interests, etc., with the artificial order of working to find the things in them required' so that his readers might 'make an entrance to learn the true, brief, and orderly assoiling of questions arithmetical, daily happening among merchants and other'.[6] Or again, James Peele showed that he too wrote for a similar group of readers by entitling his book *The Pathe Waye to Perfectnes, in the accomptes of Debitour, and Creditour: in manner of a Dialogue, very pleasaunte and proffitable for Marchauntes and all other that minde to frequente the same: once agayne set forthe, and verie muche enlarged* (1569). These authors, whose works are only a sampling of a vast number of textbooks and handbooks on similar and allied subjects, were obviously writing for a need. Coote believed his book would be used by artisans and tradesmen who had 'undertaken the charge of teaching others', most likely apprentices; and Peele indeed made the merchant in his dialogue say that he would set his servant to school to learn the new system of bookkeeping.[1] All of these books, and others like them, went through multiple editions. Some works, especially ones of penmanship, received such hard usage that no copies are now extant.

The indenture of apprenticeship established, of course, an intimate relationship between a young man and his master. Both the Statute of Artificers and the regulations of the various companies and trades limited the number of apprentices any master might have at one time. Rarely could he keep more than three. Apprentices lived in the master's household and usually learned the principles and techniques of their chosen trade under the direct supervision of the master in workroom, warehouse, shop, or counting house. They usually became apprentices at the ages of 15 to 17 and their terms of training did not expire, unless they were put out for good cause or unless they could prove mistreatment by the master, until they had attained the age of twenty-four and had served for a minimum of seven years. A programme could therefore be adjusted from week to week or from month to month to suit individual needs and capacities as well as the convenience of the master. At the end of their terms some proof of their acquired skills was usually imposed before they could be admitted to the freedom of their companies. The Society of Apothecaries, for example, required an examination by the Master, Wardens, and examiners nominated by the President of the Royal College of Physicians to test apprentices' 'knowledge and election of simples' and their expertness in 'the preparing, dispensing, handling, commixing and compounding of medicines'.[2] A set of satirical verses was not, perhaps, so much a judgement on the adequacy of these tests as on the competence of the medical profession as a whole when they lampooned an apothecary become doctor in these words:

> He kill'd by others warrant formerly,
> He kills now by his own authority.[3]

Apprenticeship in Shakespeare's England was still very much a part of the system by which young men were trained to serve themselves and their fellow men. Made uniform throughout the realm by the Act of Artificers, it still brought into the trades, commercial enterprises, and minor professions of the realm lads from all ranks in society. Apprentices had in those times pride in their status and were spirited young men. They must not therefore be confused with parish apprentices who only appeared in great numbers at a later date. The dress of apprentices was distinctive. A contemporary of Shakespeare's described their appearance in these terms: an apprentice wears a 'flat round cap, hair close-cut, narrow falling band, coarse side coat, close hose, cloth stockings, and the rest of that severe habit [which] was in antiquity, not more for thrift and usefulness, than for distinction and grace, and were originally arguments or tokens of vocation or calling'.[4] In order to govern this body of energetic, proud, and some-what restless young men, especially in London where there were great numbers of them, all masters were charged with responsibilities like those imposed on masters of the Clothworkers Company:

masters shall charge and give in commandment unto their prentices that on holidays they shall truly wait upon their master or masters to the church and there to serve God. And after to wait upon their master or masters at dinner and supper.

And in no wise to go from their master's house or door without the license of their master. And their masters shall give no license to no prentice to go forth to no place without he know whither he goeth, and in what company he goeth in.[1]

They were particularly warned to keep their apprentices from haunting taverns, alehouses, bowling alleys, and other suspicious places and from consorting with prostitutes and enjoying unlawful games. It was therefore a training that in its best forms provided moral as well as technical education and was thought to prepare for such an estate in life that gentlemen could 'put their children who are not rather inclining to arms or letters to apprenticeship, that is to say, to the discipline and art of honest gain, giving them a title of being somewhat in our country'.[2]

V

A discussion of education in Shakespeare's England would not be complete without mention of the unique contribution that London was making to English intellectual life. Aside from its outstanding grammar schools and its superior training for apprentices, London offered remarkable opportunities for self-education to the thousands who came from the countryside to seek their fortunes within its precincts. To appreciate this fact should not of course make one blind to the seamy side of this teeming metropolis with its cony-catchers and cutpurses, its overcrowded tenements and smelly streets, its false hopes and soul-searing frustrations. Rather one must note that amidst these unpleasant by-products of a city rapidly outgrowing both its boundaries and its old ways of dealing with social problems there were also creative forces at work. To be short London developed in these years what might be called a system of adult education. It was rooted in the urge to self-improvement of a mobile population, partially freed from the restraints of custom; it was nurtured by a cheap press turning out, profitably to be sure, a stream of publications including both handbooks of practical value and English texts on professional and theoretical subjects; and it was supported at its highest level by endowments of generous citizens and gentlemen.

Sir George Buck, struck by this development, called early seventeenth-century London 'the third university of England'. In justifying his use of this term, he wrote:

I saw that not only those arts which are called liberal, but also all or the most part of all other arts and sciences proper and fit for ingenuous and liberal persons were and are in this city professed, taught, and studied: which is (adding but *cum privilegio*) as much as can be said for the name and authority of any university, and which can be rightly said of very few other universities in Christendom.[3]

Included in his list of subjects 'proper and fit for ingenuous and liberal persons' were some that would surprise even the most ardent empire builder among present-day educational administrators. In his enthusiasm he named not only the traditional disciplines such as the seven liberal arts, philosophy, metaphysics, law, medicine, and theology, but a variety of newer and usually practical studies such as surgery, hydrography, navigation, cosmography, various foreign languages, calligraphy, brachygraphy (shorthand), stenography, military arts, dancing, printing, heraldry, art of revels, art of memory, and alchemy.

The stock to be put in the literal accuracy of Buck's report is perhaps best suggested by the list of languages purportedly taught in London. It starts with the usual classical languages, runs through Chaldean, Syriac, and Arabic, and concludes with Italian, Spanish, French, Dutch, Polish, Persian, 'Morisco', Turkish, 'Muscovian', and 'Slavonian'. Yet many, if not all, these languages, 'fit for ambassadors and orators, and agents for merchants, and for travellers, and necessary for all commerce and negotiations whatsoever', could be learned in the city.[1] What is more, for Arabic at least, listed by Buck probably out of enthusiasm rather than full understanding of the extent to which it was taught, the interest of Londoners may well have contributed to the movement that won it widespread attention and finally acceptance at Oxford.

In other words, behind Buck's statements, despite their exaggeration, stands much to justify his name for London. Apart from the Inns of Court, which are described elsewhere in this volume, lectureships, established by various benefactors, oftentimes under the auspices of one or another of the corporate bodies of the city, provided instruction at an advanced level in both applied and theoretical aspects of knowledge. Most were given in English, though some were also delivered in Latin for the benefit of foreigners in the realm. Under the Royal College of Physicians there were the Lumleian lecture in surgery (established 1583), lectures in anatomy, and later, shortly after Shakespeare's death, the Goulstonian lecture in pathology.[2] In 1582 Sir Thomas Smith left a bequest for a lectureship in mathematics, first held by the Elizabethan mathematician and navigator, Thomas Hood. Most famous and most influential were, of course, the professorships of Gresham College, founded on revenues given by Sir Thomas Gresham and derived from the rent of shops in the Royal Exchange. The first Gresham professors, seven in number—one each for four of the liberal arts (rhetoric, music, geometry and astronomy) and one each for the three higher faculties (law, medicine and divinity), were elected in 1597 from a list of men nominated by Oxford and Cambridge. Three of the professors finally chosen were Oxford men; three Cambridge men; and one held degrees from both universities.[3]

The establishment of these lectureships in the bustling commercial, literary, and political capital of the realm is eloquent testimony to the vigorous concern for learning possessed by Shakespeare's England. They were also significant contributions to the advancement of learning then and later. Long before the precursor of the Royal Society was meeting in Gresham College these London lectureships were becoming notable. It was, for instance, as Lumleian lecturer that William Harvey first propounded his findings on the heart and the circulation of the blood.[4] It was as Gresham professor of geometry that Henry Briggs, probably one of the most neglected figures in English intellectual history, worked out aids to navigation such as tables to determine latitude from the declination of the sun and the North Star. Even more important, Briggs immediately perceived the value of Napier's invention of logarithms and almost single-handedly began to explain their use and to provide tables of logarithms for navigators, surveyors, and others for whom such a method of simplifying complicated computations would be helpful.

After he became Savilian professor of geometry at Oxford, his work was carried on by a brilliant successor, Edmund Gunter, who had been educated at Westminster and Christ Church, Oxford.[1]

The London lectures in medicine provided physicians with what can be called post-graduate studies in their profession. They offered a type of training badly needed to supplement the conservative, literary curriculum in medicine characteristic of the universities. The Gresham professorships made perhaps their most important contribution in encouraging a marriage between the theoretical learning of university trained men and the practical knowledge of London artisans, merchants, and navigators. Both needed the other, and though the universities were not so backward in mathematics and natural philosophy as their statutory curriculum would lead one to believe, they did not offer such fruitful opportunities for a union between theory and practice as did London.

In short a system of adult education, as well as the number of excellent grammar schools like Westminster, St Paul's, and Merchant Taylors' and other societies like the Inns of Court, made Shakespearian London a unique educational and intellectual centre in the land. To make this statement does not concede, with reference to a question currently in dispute, that Oxford and Cambridge were failing to keep abreast of contemporary thought, nor does it acknowledge that the 'university' of London was more important to the intellectual advancement of England than the two ancient universities.[2] Such a statement merely says that a full picture of education in Shakespeare's England must include the London scene. It also suggests that the atmosphere in which the university-trained lecturers found themselves in London gave their efforts a character and an effect that was perhaps different from teaching in the same subjects at Oxford and Cambridge. One would perhaps be not too far from the truth if one said that university training and adult education in London were complementary and that both were essential ingredients in the intellectual ferment of the times.

VI

The system of education which has been here described was in very important respects the creation of the sixteenth century. Of course it had medieval beginnings. The grammar schools, universities, and apprenticeship were all inheritances passed on to Shakespeare and his contemporaries by the generations that came before them. Yet Englishmen of the Tudor period did not receive these institutions passively. They adapted them to suit in large measure their own aspirations and purposes. In the process they remodelled them, then spread great numbers of new schools throughout the countryside, and finally welded the whole network into a coherent, well-articulated system. Their work, despite its shortcomings, was a praiseworthy effort, infused and inspired by the genius of the age. They built for their own purposes, but like the art of Shakespeare their purposes had a universal character. As a consequence they left not only a durable monument but a living heritage to their descendants on both sides of the Atlantic and around the world.

6

THE LAW AND THE LAWYERS

'The terms for common justice'

I

In the England of Elizabeth II, few people have any close contact with the law. The householder is liable to jury service, a witness may give evidence, the purchaser of property may consult a solicitor and for the motorist there are numerous legal hazards. These incidents apart, few become embroiled with the law and the number which engages in litigation is small indeed. It was far otherwise in Shakespeare's day. The English were then noted litigants, surpassed only by the Welsh, and lawsuits abounded.[1] The old axiom—that sooner or later every Elizabethan turns up in the records of one court or another—has much truth in it; indeed, but for this, we should know less about Elizabethan dramatists, Shakespeare not excluded.

That Elizabethans were 'law conscious' to an extreme degree does not, however, imply that they were unduly quarrelsome folk. Such, of course, there were—peppery characters like Sir Thomas Tresham[2] whose son betrayed the Gunpowder Plot, and notorious scoundrels like William Gardiner, J.P.,[3] the enemy of the London actors—but for most of the subjects of Elizabeth I, appeal to the courts was a natural step. In the first place, they were less insulated from the law than are their descendants. Jury service was a regular, not an exceptional duty, and in a large county could involve over a thousand jurymen a year. Techniques of property dealing and family settlement produced familiarity with the law also; one of the favourite assurances, the fine, was no less than a collusive lawsuit in a royal court. With titles dependent on legal devices and jury service a pressing obligation, it is small wonder that law came directly into the lives of Elizabethan Englishmen.

But the Queen's subjects were influenced by law in another way. In Elizabethan society, the law entered into many concerns from which it is now excluded. Estate administration was a matter, not of farming, but of court-keeping. How the craftsmen of the towns worked and what the peasants of the villages grew was controlled by the gild and the manor court. Those who escaped supervision, the workers in domestic industry and the occupiers of enclosed farms, were regulated nevertheless in the courts of Quarter Sessions. Law dominated public administration.[4] The Quarter Sessions performed the work now carried out by local governnment officers, supervising highways and bridges, tolls and markets, public assistance and employment. The same jury reported the names of criminals as the details of defective bridges, and the justices dealt equally with the village ruffian and the shrewd dealer. The same was true at a national level. Departments of state included the Court of the Exchequer and the Court of Wards, and the principal political institution was the High Court of Parliament. Even belief and behaviour were subject to a court, for the church had its own judicial system which supervised faith and morals. Ben Jonson suffered in an ecclesiastical court for his faith[5] and several of Shakespeare's other associates fell foul of the bishops for their morals.[6]

73

All in all, it is not surprising that the Elizabethans were law conscious; from cradle to grave, every part of life was the business of one court or another. Legal skill was no mystery. Everyman needed enough knowledge to defend his rights and the law was the gateway to many a career. For country gentlemen legal expertise was essential.

It is necessary that noble men and gentlemen should learne to be able to put their owne Case in law and to haue some Iudgment in the office of a *Iustice of peace and Sheriffe*; for thorough the want thereof the beste are oftentymes subiecte to the direction of farre their *Inferiors*.[1]

An important justice like Robert Shallow had to know his law.

II

The law student who came to London at the end of the century must have found the multitude of courts confusing. If he turned to the most recent handbook for law students—*A Direction or Preparative to the Study of the Law*, by William Fulbecke[2] he discovered that the law had no fewer than eight branches, the laws of nature and of nations, civil law, common law, statute law, customary law, the *jus merum* and the *jus aequum et bonum*. A less pedantic analysis would have substituted three categories, common law, civil law and canon law. Common law had at first been no more than 'the custom of the King's courts', but by the sixteenth century it was a body of case law, modified by statute and interpreted by reason, and it was supreme throughout the land; its principal concern was with real property and written obligations. Common law records were kept in Latin and procedure was conducted in a mixture of English and debased Norman-French. The classic way of beginning a civil action was by purchasing a writ and the defendant was then compelled, by distraint on his goods and ultimately outlawry, to appear in court; trial was by a jury of twelve, never by a judge alone. In criminal cases, the characteristic common law procedure was by indictment and, again, jury trial.

Civil, or less ambiguously, Roman law, had influenced the embryonic common law, but in the sixteenth century it appeared as an import from Europe where it was enjoying a great revival. Continental fashion had a considerable influence on the newer English courts; civil law doctrines took no root, but civil law 'written' procedure did. This was conducted, and records kept, in the vernacular. A case began with the recital in writing of the plaintiff's wrongs to which the defendant was compelled by a *sub poena* to make a reply, also in writing. The interchange continued and witnesses were examined until the judges could decide the case. A similar procedure was used by the church courts which administered canon law; business was conducted in Latin but the stages of complaint, reply and investigation were repeated. Canon law was, indeed, Roman law adapted to ecclesiastical matters. It had suffered a serious reverse during the Reformation when appeals to the Papal courts were abolished and it ceased to be a separate university discipline. Gradually, too, it had lost its traditional jurisdiction over first offences committed by literate persons—the so-called 'benefit of clergy'. Notwithstanding, canon law continued to be administered in the church courts, machinery for hearing appeals in England was invented and civil lawyers took over from the canonists.

III

To discover where these various systems were administered, the student might be able to consult one of the manuscripts then in circulation which described the different courts, for example, Richard Robinson's 'Briefe Collection of the Queenes Majesties Most High and Most Honourable Courtes of Recordes':

Six therbe servinge for Administracion of Justice, Viz. The most high and most Honorable Court of Parliament. The high and Honorable Courts of Chauncery: Kinges bench: Common Pleas: Starrechamber; and of Requestes to the Kinges Maiestie: And three other Courts beinge for his Maiesties revennues are theis—The Honorable Court of the Exchequer: of the Wards, and Lyveryes: And of the Dutchy or Countye Pallatine of Lancaster.[1]

The functioning of Parliament as a court of justice was of intermittent interest only, but the other courts in Robinson's list could be observed by the new student during term time in and around Westminster Hall.[2] The three most ancient sat in the body of the Hall itself, on the right of the north door was the Common Pleas, on the southern dais sat, at the right, the Chancery and at the left the Queen's Bench. Queen's Bench and Common Pleas each administered common law. Theoretically the former was confined to 'pleas of the crowne'—principally criminal cases —and the latter to 'civill matters...specially such as touch landes or contractes',[3] but as civil litigation was obviously the more lucrative business, the Queen's Bench was continually poaching on the preserves of the Common Pleas. By the end of the sixteenth century the two were exercising a concurrent jurisdiction over most civil suits. The Queen's Bench, in fact, took few criminal cases in the first instance. The great majority of crimes were dealt with locally at the Quarter Sessions and Assizes, and state trials were usually taken by special commission.

The Court of Chancery stood in marked contrast to its neighbours: indeed, it existed to supply their deficiencies. Litigants for whom the common law provided no remedy could petition the Chancellor to exercise discretion on their behalf. Theorists applied to this discretion the continental term 'equity' and gradually the distinction between the *jus aequum* and the *jus merum* became sharper.[4] Yet William Fulbecke was premature to inform students that equity and law were separate systems. Despite a strong tendency towards strict interpretation in the common law courts, decisions '*ex aequo* and *bono* and according to conscience' were often given. Conversely, Chancery always exercised its equity in the light of common law principles. The suggestion that Chancery was primarily a court of the civil law is unfounded. The Chancery used only the forms of Roman law; it administered an equitable construction of the common law.[5]

The other courts listed by Robinson were held in rooms adjoining Westminster Hall. On the right of the entrance a staircase led to the Court of the Exchequer. The Exchequer was 'a place of account for the reuenewes of the Crowne' and Richard Robinson duly mentioned among the officers of the court 'Mintmasters [and] Monyers', but it also possessed special judicial machinery, the Exchequer of Pleas. In theory, this common law court only considered revenue matters, but since anyone who represented himself as indebted to the crown could bring a suit in the court, with a little ingenuity most civil litigation could be brought into the Exchequer. In this way the court had become, by the middle of Elizabeth's reign, the equal of Queen's Bench and Common Pleas.

From the stair on the left of the entrance to Westminster Hall, the visitor could make his way to the Court of Star Chamber. The Star Chamber was the most famous of the so-called 'prerogative' courts which had been developed under the Tudors to supplement the existing legal system. It was in essence the Privy Council meeting in the Star Chamber (the ceiling was 'decked with the likenes of Stars guilt')[1] to deal with complaints of criminal behaviour. It could not impose the death penalty or confiscate property, so the trial of felony was confined to common law courts, but Star Chamber could act where they were powerless in suppressing riots, libel, and other conduct endangering order, interference with justice and disobedience to royal injunctions. Only a very small proportion of the court's work consisted of government prosecutions although these have ensured for the Star Chamber an unpleasant reputation. In truth it was a popular institution which could deal effectively with strong-arm tactics, jobbery and sophisticated roguery. Common law was administered but process was according to Roman law and equitable pleadings were allowed. The Star Chamber was in criminal law what the Chancery was in civil, a court administering common law in an equitable fashion by modern continental methods.

A staircase opening into Westminster Hall near to the Queen's Bench led to the White Hall where sat another prerogative court, the Requests. This administered equity in civil cases to litigants whose poverty prevented their suing elsewhere and procedure was according to the Chancery pattern. Sharing the White Hall was the Court of Wards and Liveries. Primarily a revenue court, this was responsible for the enforcement of royal rights over the estates of minors, but, because litigation often arose, the Wards possessed judicial machinery conducted also on the Chancery pattern. The last of the nine courts was the Court of the Duchy of Lancaster. This legal curiosity, a development of the private council of a medieval noble, enjoyed an equity jurisdiction over civil suits arising on or about Duchy land. It sat in the Duchy Chamber, near the Wards, and procedure was again on the Roman law model.

Westminster was a hive of legal activity, but the new law student may well have echoed in seriousness Sir Thomas Smith's rhetorical question: 'How all Englande (being so long and so large, and having so many shyres and provinces therein) can be answered of justice in one place?'[2] In fact there were opportunities of obtaining justice outside Westminster. Two prerogative courts dealt with the problems of the more remote areas, the Council of the North and the Council in the Marches of Wales. Each possessed criminal jurisdiction similar to that of Star Chamber and an equity business akin to Chancery, and under royal commission they were able to act according to common law in felonies. Every borough possessed a court which administered an amalgam of merchant custom, common law and local by-laws. The jurisdiction of many small towns was insignificant, but others, especially London, had complete judicial systems of their own, criminal as well as civil. Foreign and commercial suits were brought in the special Court of Admiralty which administered a maritime and mercantile law common to the trading community of Western Europe. A judicial system which existed throughout England was provided by the Quarter Sessions. These were held by the justices of the peace for each county and handled a wide variety of legal cases as well as the business of county administration. All criminal offences, from petty misdemeanours to serious felonies, could be tried before the justices and a jury. They could not hear civil suits as such, but a multitude of torts were considered because they infringed public policy or good order. More solemn and dramatic than the sessions were the visits, in the lent and summer of each year, of her Majesty's Commission of Gaol Delivery and *Nisi Prius*, better known as the Assize. The chosen town was crowded with J.P.'s and other prominent men of the shire, jurymen and local officials, lawyers and suitors, constables and prisoners. On arrival, the Justices were feted by the corporation while the sheriff and the local notables sent presents of venison, game, fish and sweetmeats. The assize opened with due pomp in the 'towne house' where the first item was a speech by one of the Justices which 'telleth the cause of their comming and giveth a good lesson to the people'.[1] This covered political and administrative as well as judicial matters, for the assize commission served to link central and local government.[2] The court then proceeded to 'deliver' or empty the gaol of criminals awaiting trial, generally serious offenders specially remanded from the Quarter Sessions. This criminal business was followed by suits at *nisi prius*, civil cases from Westminster which had reached the stage of trial. Rather than drag a local jury to London, the justices took the case at assize time and certified the results to Westminster.

With a description of this *nisi prius* procedure Richard Robinson concluded his discourse on the courts of the realm; '*Deo Laus, Regina Vivat, Valeantque Comuniter Leges*'. What of the remaining variety of law, canon law? To administer this, the church had a hierarchy of courts from the archdeacon to the archbishop and in addition there were many special franchises or 'peculiars' which had courts of their own. The jurisdiction of church courts was extensive. It embraced all ecclesiastical questions—'Causes belonging to benefices' and 'Causes concerninge the Church and devine service'—'Causes matrimoniall' touching 'Marriage and [the] solempnisacon thereof' and 'Testamentarye causes',[3] for which at Canterbury and York there were special probate courts. But the courts christian had also a responsibility for the 'Correccon of crimes in generall' which involved the prosecution of every sin not already proscribed by statute or common law—sexual immorality, irreligious opinions and behaviour, witchcraft, heresy and drunkenness. The wide competence of the spiritual courts was, however, qualified by a serious weakness: they lacked coercive power. Obedience could only be enforced by excommunication, which was irritating rather than effective, and during the early part of Elizabeth's reign in some dioceses clerical jurisdiction showed signs of collapse.[4] Nevertheless, church courts did manage to survive—although how effective this activity was is an unsolved problem—and remain active until the Long Parliament.[5] The difficulties they experienced were increased by the withdrawal of the lay support to which they were entitled, as common lawyers increasingly regarded the ecclesiastical law as a rival to be frustrated. What could have been accomplished is illustrated by two tribunals which were in an exceptional position and enjoyed strong royal support, the courts of High Commission at London and York. Entirely separate from the traditional pattern of clerical jurisdiction, they were the ecclesiastical counterparts of the Star Chamber and the Council of the North. They had power to fine and imprison and could turn with confidence to the prerogative courts for assistance. Unlike the regular church courts, the High Commission was popular—except with common lawyers jealous of it or religious individualists restrained by it; where other courts christian could not enforce their edicts or were hampered by a common law which offered no alternative redress, the commissions at London and York offered effective remedies.

IV

Hostility towards ecclesiastical courts was the more intense because the civil lawyers who staffed them had no community with the common lawyers of the royal courts. The leading ecclesiastical lawyers had been organized since 1511 in the 'Association of doctors of law', better known as Doctor's Commons. The society was not responsible for teaching—this was undertaken at the universities where Henry VIII had established regius professors of civil law—but its members had a monopoly of appearance in church courts and in the court of Admiralty. Doctor's Commons, as the name implies, also provided residential accommodation and some corporate life for the civilians. Important civil lawyers were never very numerous,[1] but their influence was considerable, for knowledge of continental law was the qualification of the diplomat; Sir Thomas Smith, the first regius professor of civil law at Cambridge, was a distinguished envoy and secretary of state, and so too was Dr Thomas Wilson, better known today for his books on rhetoric and usury.

In the light of the scholastic reputation and European fame of some civilians, Elizabethan common lawyers appear insular and only remarkable for numbers. The profession was large, and growing ever larger. In 1574 it totalled 1400, and in 1586, 1700, an increase of 20 per cent in twelve years.[2] Pressure of this sort put the Inns of Court and Chancery, the professional societies of the common lawyers, under a continual need to increase accommodation. In 1574 the Middle Temple reported that it had 92 chambers but by 1586 it had contrived to find a further 46.[3] It is not surprising that a critic declared it 'one of the greatest inconveniences in the land that the number of the Lawyers be so great'; he estimated the profession at about 4000 plus 'an infinite number' of smaller fry.[4] But numbers—real or imagined—are deceptive, for the majority of those scrambling for admission were not attracted by the legal training which the Inns, unlike Doctors' Commons, offered. Some, of course, aspired to become lawyers and others to a career, such as estate management, where legal training was an advantage, but most Englishmen of Shakespeare's day saw the Inns as finishing schools for gentlemen. Their attitude was typified by Arthur Hall when in 1558 he wrote to his guardian, Sir William Cecil, for permission to go abroad, or if war prevented the grand tour, then to an Inn of Court.[5] Men like Hall were in a majority; returns for the four Inns of Court show that of 761 members present in May 1574, 176 were lawyers and 585 were 'gentlemen'.[6] The view that the Inns were centres of polite as well as practical education was not a new one, but it became extremely popular in the second half of the sixteenth century. In the reign of Henry VII the Inns took only 40 new students a year, by 1540 the number had doubled and in the 1560's it reached 160.[7] Thereafter admissions snowballed—in 1580 nearly 250 were enrolled.

Emphasis on the social function of the Inns led naturally to a weakening in their educational system.[8] Every student should have gone through a series of exercises in pleading under the supervision of his seniors and have attended a number of readings, the lecture courses given by one of the chief lawyers in the society each Easter and Michaelmas. Absence incurred a fine, but an increasing number of men who were not serious students were prepared to pay and avoid their studies. Those who should have taught them often took the same way out; time was valuable and, with books readily available, oral instruction seemed anachronistic. Exercises became irregular, and readings occasions for the reader to display his brilliance and subtlety.

Social life, conversely, was more important. Christmas and the great occasions of the professional year had always been celebrated, but by the turn of the century there was plenty of more informal entertainment as well; the conversion a few years later of one Inn library into a gambling saloon was symptomatic.[2] The Inns were thriving centres of literary enterprise and were noted for an interest in drama, both play-going and play-acting; the members of the Inns regularly entertained the sovereign on important occasions, such as the marriage of Princess Elizabeth to the Elector Palatine, which was celebrated in 1613 by two Inn masques, one, presented by Lincoln's Inn and the Middle Temple, by George Chapman, and the other, from Grays Inn and the Inner Temple, by Francis Beaumont.[2] The Inns also sponsored professional plays; the gala performance of *Twelfth Night* before Elizabeth I in 1602 in the Middle Temple Hall is only the best known of a number of occasions. And there were as well the less reputable pleasures of London, the sort that Robert Shallow remembered.[3]

Amid social events of Inn life, a minority of professional lawyers and law students—perhaps 30 per cent of the whole—continued on their way. The legal profession was divided, then as now, into the barristers who plead in court and the attorneys who conduct litigation, but sharp cleavage between the two was of recent growth. Many barristers and attorneys traditionally began their studies together in the Inns of Chancery and although the would-be barrister had soon to transfer to one of the four Inns of Court which alone had the right to call men to the bar, he was not forbidden to work as an attorney while training there nor even compelled to complete his studies for the bar. The Inns of Court were also always ready to welcome the prosperous attorney who wished to join as a sign of his increased social and professional standing. But during the reign of Elizabeth a change was taking place. The Inns of Court tried to force members who were attorneys to study for the bar in the hope that the decline in 'learning' could thus be arrested.[4] The Privy Council, concerned to regulate the increasing numbers in the legal quarter of London, attempted to confine attorneys to the Inns of Chancery.[5] These efforts, coupled with the 'polite' reputation of the Inns of Court, led to a growing separation between the barristers and attorneys and in 1614 to a declaration by the greater Inns that, while a barrister was a 'principal person...in administration of Justice', attorneys were 'but ministerial persons and of an inferiour nature';[6] henceforth no attorney was to be suffered in their societies, the Inns of Chancery were the proper place for such lesser men.

Suspicion of the junior branch of the profession was increased by the appearance at this same time of a new figure, the solicitor. Most attorneys were attached to either the Queen's Bench or the Common Pleas and were supposed to restrict their activities to the one court; there were perennial complaints about the multitude of attorneys, but it seems unlikely that there were more than a few hundred at Westminster.[7] The new prerogative courts, however, limited very severely the number they would allow to practise[8] and the Chancery excluded attorneys altogether by giving their work to the clerks of the court. But the officers provided could barely keep up with necessary formal procedure; someone was still needed to prepare and direct a case, in Tudor parlance 'to solicit the suit'. The need was clear but the solicitor was distinctly not popular. His qualifications and behaviour were nobody's responsibility and the prospects for crime were excellent. Nor was it any comfort that many solicitors were also attorneys of the Queen's Bench or Common Pleas, for the control which these courts could exercise was slight. It is no accident that dramatists who portray a rascally lawyer, a character such as Throat in

Barrey's *Ram Alley* (1611), generally depict him as an attorney or solicitor. The statute of 1605 which attempted to limit soliciting to those who 'are known to be Men of sufficient and honest Disposition' was a pious hope and a dead letter.[1]

Unlike the attorneys and solicitors, Elizabethan barristers had a long formal training before being allowed to practise, and throughout their career remained under the discipline of the Inns. Ten years' study in all was the ideal of the royal judges, seven before call to the bar and a further three years before taking cases alone, but this was more a desired standard than a requirement; some students waited for only five years and others for nearly ten. Of the lions of the profession, Edward Coke studied law for seven and a quarter years after coming down from Cambridge, and was called at the Inner Temple when twenty-six; Francis Bacon squeezed Cambridge, thirty months abroad and his bar studies into just over nine years to become a barrister at the age of twenty-one.

Training over, the next problem was the building of a practice, a task as unpredictable in the sixteenth century as in the twentieth. Generally, however, barristers received some assistance from their social connections; two out of three came from gentry families and it was to the society of his home area that each, by custom, looked for his first clients. It is no accident that Coke first appeared for a Norfolk parson or that after four years he was advising Ipswich corporation. Most barristers also had useful connections within the profession and many belonged to 'legal dynasties'. Francis Gawdy from 1588 to 1607 Justice, and later Chief Justice of the Common Pleas, was the son and grandson of a lawyer, his brother was a Justice of the Queen's Bench, his wife came from a family of judges and his only child married the nephew of a Lord Chancellor. Half the barristers, Coke again included, enjoyed the additional advantage of being eldest sons, able to rely on expectations during the lean early years and finally on a private income. But younger brothers who received 'thatt which the catt left on the malt heape'[2] took to the law with an equal or superior zest. Success there was one of the best means for the portionless gentleman to acquire capital and so set up as a landed squire. And although James I tried to restrict the bar to gentlemen born,[3] the gentility of some invited incredulity. The censorious Sir George Buck might assert 'It is an error to thinke that the sonnes of Graziers, Farmers, Marchants, Tradesmen and artificers can be made Gentlemen, by their admittance... [to an] Inne of court',[4] but these sons knew that, in reality, 'whosoever studieth the lawes of the realme...shall be taken for a gentleman'.[5]

Among the assertive groups in the community, the common lawyers were consequently notorious, competing with ubiquity and pertinacity for land, wealthy widows and heiresses, and for profitable matches for their offspring. Social rewards varied, of course, with the measure of professional success. The fifty benchers who governed the Inns of Court and the thirty or so younger barristers of the front rank[6] enjoyed considerable wealth. A competent barrister could net £600 a year,[7] equivalent then to the income from a well-run farm of 1000 acres,[8] and during his career could accumulate enough capital to buy an estate. Financial and social opportunities were even greater for those who were advanced to the next stage in the legal hierarchy, the rank of serjeant-at-law. This conferred the exclusive right to plead in the Court of Common Pleas and in time led to the even more glittering prize of a seat on the bench. Judicial salaries were small, but the income from fees was substantial. A puisne judge might make £1000 net per annum[9] and the chief justices were notoriously wealthy; it is no surprise that of the dozen chief justices in the reigns of Elizabeth and James I, six founded families which joined the peerage and the rest county families. The most spectacular rewards of all went to the law officers of the Crown. Gossip put Coke's earnings as attorney-general at £12,000 or £14,000 per annum[1] and Bacon, when attorney-general, valued the post at £6000 a year.[2] On either valuation the holder was well into the peerage category:[3] the three men who held the office while Shakespeare lived in London each endowed an earldom.[4]

V

The courts in which Elizabethan lawyers practised were similar in plan to the modern law court. In Westminster Hall,[5] the judges sat on benches against the walls raised high off the floor; over them were canopies and the arms of the sovereign were blazoned on the walls behind. Immediately below each bench was a green baize table for the clerks and opposite, behind a wooden barrier (the bar of the Court), stood the parties and a multitude of counsel, attorneys and observers; a jury was rarely required but could be accommodated on the right of the clerks' table. At the assizes the royal justice sat on a raised bench accompanied by the more important justices of the peace; the rest of the county magistrates occupied a bench in front on a lower level. In the well of the court stood a table at which the clerks and the county officials sat and beyond that was the bar of the court. The jury apparently sat behind the accused or the parties involved and at the back of the room a space was reserved for the gaoler and his prisoners.

The prosecution of a criminal could commence in two ways.[6] His victim could complain to a justice of the peace who would then issue a warrant for the arrest of the accused. If, however, the criminal were caught red-handed, he could be detained by any citizen and committed to the local constable. Whether taken summarily or on a warrant, the accused was immediately brought before a J.P. The justice questioned the prisoner and his captors 'of the fact and circumstances' and made a report of 'as much thereof as shall be material to prove the felony' to the court which was to try the case. Inquiry following arrest was twice parodied by Shakespeare,[7] but it was an effective method of constructing a case. Before the next sessions or assizes, the accusation was drawn up as a formal indictment, and as soon as the court met, this was tested by a grand jury to determine whether a prima facie case for trial existed. If unconvinced, this jury would reject the indictment with the endorsement 'ignoramus' but far more often the indictment was 'found' and noted 'billa vera'. The court then proceeded to arraign the prisoners. The clerk addressed them by name:

A.B. come to the barre, hold up thy hand.

A.B. thou by the name of A.B. of such a towne, in such a countie, art endicted, that such a day, in such a place, thou hast stolen with force and armes an horse, which was such ones, of such a colour, to such a valor, and carried him away feloniouslie, and contrarie to the peace of our soveraigne Ladie the Queene. What sayest thou to it, art thou guiltie or not guiltie?

If, as was usual, the reply was 'not guilty' the clerk asked 'how wilt thou be tryed' to which the only permitted answer was 'by God and the Countrie', that is by a jury.[8] The sheriff already had jurymen in attendance and these were called into court one by one to take the oath. As a defence against bias, the accused could challenge up to twenty jurymen and the empanelling

81

continued until twelve had been sworn unchallenged. The cryer of the court then proclaimed: 'If any can give evidence, or can saie any thing against the prisoner let him come nowe, for he standeth upon his deliverance'. In response to this, the witnesses entered the court and the deposition which the examining justice had taken was read out. The witnesses were sworn, gave their evidence and an argument between the accused and his accusers developed. Prosecuting counsel were only employed in important trials, but the supposed impartiality of the judge did not prevent him from examining witnesses and prisoner as he wished and even the jury might join in the debate. Counsel was also denied to the prisoner unless a question of law arose. The logic of this was as good as the result was bad; a prisoner could only be convicted upon clear evidence and if the burden of proof was on the prosecution, then the accused had no need to conduct any defence. What made matters worse for the prisoner was that he was denied any opportunity to make a statement or give evidence on oath and he received no copy of the indictment or notice of the evidence against him. By the end of the century he sometimes had a grudging permission to call witnesses on his own behalf but even when admitted, his witnesses could not give evidence on oath and there was no provision for compelling their attendance. Faced with a barrage of accusation and open to an inquisition by the judge, the accused had to make the best defence he could alone.

When the debate in court could get no further, the judge turned to the jury:

Good men, ye of the enquest, ye have heard what these men say against the prisoner, ye have also heard what the prisoner can say for himselfe, have an eye to your othe and to your duetie, and doe that which God shall put in your mindes to the discharge of your consciences and marke well what is saide.

The jury might then retire to agree upon a verdict although commonly the same jury listened to one or two further cases first and discussed them altogether. While considering their decisions jurymen were confined without food, drink or firing so, as Smith said, 'it is no marvell, though they made expedition'; the knowledge that, at the same time, the judges had retired to dine helped to sharpen their wits. When the jury returned to court, the prisoner was again called to the bar, his indictment rehearsed and the jury asked for their verdict:

'"What say you? Is he guiltie or not guiltie?" The foreman maketh aunswere in one worde, guiltie, or in two, not guiltie: the one is deadlie, the other acquiteth the prisoner.'

For crimes under the degree of felony, the penalty was imprisonment, flogging, a fine, forfeiture of goods or more than one of these, in the case of felony, death and forfeiture. The condemned felon, however, had still a chance of saving life, but not property, through the custom of benefit of clergy. Before sentence began, the prisoner claimed that he was a clergyman and only subject to ecclesiastical penalties. A psalter was given to him and if he could stumble through the 'neck verse' the Bishop's representative, specially present for this purpose, would acknowledge his claim. The successful 'cleric' was branded on his hand to prevent his enjoying the privilege twice and he might be gaoled for one year; the farce of handing him over to the bishop had been abolished in 1576.[1] The identification of literacy with holy orders had been false for generations and it was unfair that a man's life should depend upon his ability to read.[2] Nevertheless, the anachronism of 'benefit of clergy' did mitigate the severity of the law and the standard of literacy demanded was not high. But all felonies were not 'clergyable'. Parliament had specifically withdrawn the privilege from the graver crimes, and where new felonies were created, benefit was generally barred. Notwithstanding, the list of felonies without clergy was still comparatively short; the savagery of the Waltham Black Act belonged to the eighteenth century.[1] There was also a regular procedure for pardoning offenders who had been able to plead mitigating circumstances. Those found guilty of causing death by misadventure or in self-defence had no sentence passed on them but were remanded in custody until pardoned.

On the felon who could not read or who had been previously convicted, and on the felon guilty of a crime without benefit of clergy and with no mitigating evidence to put forward, the court pronounced sentence:

Thou shalt first returne to the place from whence thou camest, from thence thou shalt goe to the place of execution, there thou shalt hang till thou be dead...Sherife doe execution.

The formality of a criminal trial was in marked contrast to the haphazard fortune of the prisoner after conviction. By a 'Ko-Ko-like' logic he was 'as good as dead' and the law worried very little further about him; Coke wrote in *The Institutes*—'because the judgement is the guide and direction of the execution, we shall treat principally of the judgement and incidentally of execution'.[2] The sheriff was responsible for seeing that 'the sentence is straight put in execution' but he was apt to wait until enough prisoners had been collected to justify the expense and trouble of a hanging. And with delay came hope. A reprieve was the only way of grading the punishment of felonies and it was often granted. Of course, money and influence (as always in sixteenth-century England) were helpful in dodging the gallows, and a friendless pauper stood much less chance of a reprieve than a convict with aristocratic connections.[3] Shakespeare's description of the condemned prisoners in Vienna, one of whom had escaped for nine years because 'His friends still wrought reprieves for him', is an accurate comment on the fate of felons in Elizabethan England.[4]

When all has been said and done, how many criminals were ultimately sent to the scaffold? Commentators agreed that the number of executions was very great and Sir Edward Coke lamented

to see so many Christian men and women strangled on that cursed tree of the gallows, insomuch as if in a large field a man might see together all the Christians, that but in one year throughout England, come to that untimely and ignominious death...it would make his heart to bleed for pity and compassion.[5]

But it is difficult to translate these assertions into statistics. In the county of Devon, out of 387 persons indicted in 1598, capital sentences, not necessarily all performed, were passed on 74.[6] However, in Middlesex in the last ten years of Shakespeare's life, about 70 persons a year were executed.[7] That county probably had a high rate of crime, but if only twenty persons per annum were executed in rural shires, upwards of a thousand hangings took place in England and Wales each year.[8] It seems that more criminals went to the gallows annually than under the much harsher code of George III.[9] The number of capital crimes was smaller but the tenderness of late-eighteenth-century judges towards the accused was missing, and although transportation was first proposed in 1611 as an alternative to the death sentence, it did not come into regular use until after the Restoration.[10]

VI

Crime and punishment in past centuries naturally draw the attention. But for lawyers of every age, and not least the Elizabethans, the main concern is with civil actions; criminal prosecutions provide an interruption of drama, not always welcomed and seldom very profitable.

Any contemporary of Shakespeare determined to go to law had first to decide where to bring his action. The choice between common law and equity was simple, for Chancery could only deal with cases not provided for elsewhere. But if restricted to common law, the suitor had then to select between the Queen's Bench, the Common Pleas and the Exchequer. Since there was little distinction between their jurisdictions, each was driven to compete for business by devising fictions which would evade the dilatory and costly traditional process for bringing a defendant to court. The victor in this commercial battle was the Queen's Bench, the means, the notorious bill of Middlesex. By this subterfuge a plaintiff secured the arrest of his opponent for a supposed offence committed in the county where the court was sitting, that is, Middlesex, and then proceeded with the real action.[1] Competition between benches also allowed plaintiffs to sue in several courts simultaneously and defendants in one court to begin a counter suit elsewhere. The result was friction between the courts; the Queen's Bench exploited its power of redressing errors in the Common Pleas and the judges there retaliated when they sat in the Exchequer Chamber to revise errors in the Queen's Bench. Bickering lasted until late in the seventeenth century.

Once the court had been chosen and defendant compelled to answer, the next stage was the pleading.[2] Pleadings were written statements of the case for each side, and continued until both arrived at a single issue upon which the case could be decided. Issues were of two kinds, law and fact. In the first, called demurrers, the parties agreed upon the facts but each claimed 'that by lawe he ought to have it'. Counsel then argued this before the court and the decision of the judges on the point of law ended the suit. An issue of fact arose when one party 'traversed', that is

to denie any deede as not doone, not his writing, that the man by whome the adversarie claimeth was not the adversaries auncestor, or the evidence which his adversarie bringeth is not true...and the other [party] joyneth in the affirmative and will averre and prove the same.

The case was then taken before a jury of twelve at *nisi prius*. Counsel put the case for their clients, each producing witnesses and documents in support (although the parties themselves could not give evidence) and cross-examining opposing witnesses to drive 'them out of countenance'. The judge summed up, the jury retired and returned with their verdict; the only reward they received was a dinner provided by the winning side.

Proceedings at equity, which began with the plaintiff's bill of complaint, the defendant's answer and the interchange of replication and rejoinder, rebuttal and surrebuttal, depended not upon pleading to an issue but upon the balance of the evidence and the rights of the case. At common law an action often turned upon a technicality of pleading, and especially on the choice of the correct issue. In a Chancery suit, the parties were able to submit everything which they imagined would help their case, relevant and irrelevant. Chancery documents thus grew prolix, and Chancery draftsmen rich; by order of Chancellor Ellesmere one was paraded round Westminster Hall with his head stuck through a 120-page replication which ought to have been no longer than sixteen.[1] When the parties had exhausted their memories, the court drew up a list of interrogatories, and these were put on oath to the witnessses for each side. With the stories of plaintiff and defendant and the written evidence of the witnesses before them, the court determined the case. The scope of Chancery jurisdiction was wide. Actions which were not admissible in common law but had to be taken in equity included the working of trusts and partnerships, mortgages, the administration of the estates of deceased persons, and the granting of injunctions to prevent injury. Contracts could be enforced in Chancery, whereas common law could only penalize breaches of contract.

But whether in law or equity, the way of the Elizabethan litigant was proverbially hard. Although law suits multiplied, few, according to popular opinion, resulted in justice; 'whoso liveth in the court shall die in the straw', 'a little gould in law wyll make thy matter better speede', 'the law is not the same at morning and at night'. Jeremiahs and satirists united in support of this lore.

> In Court of Wards, Kings Bench, & Common place
> Thou follow'd hast one sute, this seu'n yeeres space.
> Ah wretched man, in mothers wombe accurst,
> That could'st not rather lose thy sute at furst.[2]

Much of this abuse was well deserved. Large sections of the common law were obsolete and litigation was slow, expensive and bedevilled with technicalities. Judges and lawyers were not always disinterested. Edward Hake of Barnard's Inn attacked colleagues who 'arsiuersie turne eche thing' for 'the sugred sappe that Justice yieldes'.[3] Sir Roger Manwood, Lord Chief Baron of the Exchequer, had a particularly unsavoury reputation. Chancery also had its share of faults. Inadequate staffing caused delay, procedure became complex and expensive and corruption notorious; in 1621, Francis Bacon, the Lord Chancellor, was himself disgraced for accepting bribes.

Yet all was not black. The common law judges, notably Sir Edward Coke, gradually put their house in order. They began to devise remedies against sophisticated injuries such as slander, to take notice of parole evidence and to develop a more modern approach to commerce and to contract, liability and personal property. The Chancellors, especially Thomas Egerton, Lord Ellesmere, tried hard to improve equity. An important advance transformed the mortgage from a barely disguised sale into a form of security. The very limitations upon the scope of equity which followed reforms in the common law helped to produce a more regular and dependable form of judicial discretion. Equity, also, was constantly in use to assist the common law where its procedure was deficient; when, for example, a litigant could not begin his suit without access to documents held by his opponents, Chancery would 'discover' them. The court would do everything possible to facilitate proper trial and discourage mere litigiousness.

VII

To critics obsessed with the sufferings of the righteous poor, improvements in the English legal system meant, of course, little. In 1646 the radical John Lilburne could still write of 'the tedious, unknowne and impossible-to-be-understood common law practice in Westminster Hall',[4] while the Chancery was stigmatized in 1653 as 'a mystery of wickedness, and a standing cheat'.[5] But by this time the legal system had become the centre of political controversy. There had always been controversy between courts which offered remedies for the same distress. Personality, too, produced friction, most notoriously when the Lord Chief Justice, Sir Edward Coke, attempted to indict Ellesmere, the Lord Chancellor. Yet in the reign of James I, business rivalry and issues of 'flesh and blood' took on a wider significance as part of the quarrel between the crown and Parliament over the nature and extent of royal initiative in government. Since prerogative courts existed by this initiative, Star Chamber, Requests and the rest became natural targets in any attack on government by will and discretion. Soon it was being argued that equity had no justification apart from the prerogative. Aristotle's maxim *Melius est civitatem a viro optimo quam a lege optima gubernari*[1] was anathema to common lawyers. Equity was an alien system; as John Selden said, 'Equity is A Roguish thing, for Law wee have a measure know what to trust too'.[2] Even Chancery, whose antiquity and usefulness Coke and his fellows admitted, came to be included among the prerogative courts. During Shakespeare's lifetime the common law was held in check and, in November 1616, Coke was sacked, the first of a number of judges dismissed over the next twenty years for political reasons. But Parliament made common cause with the lawyers and eventually, in 1641, all the prerogative courts were abolished. Chancery, vital to the working of common law, escaped.

Whether the rumblings of these storms ever reached Shakespeare in his retirement we shall never learn, but the legal world for which he and his fellow dramatists had often written was coming to an end. Yet was Shakespeare closely concerned with the law? His appearances in lawsuits have been earnestly scrutinized but they are not distinguished from thousands of others. His plays disclose a familiarity with legal jargon, but no more than could have been picked up from his father's litigation or acquired incidentally. The ravings of Lear and references to 'the law's delay' or 'the breath of an unfee'd lawyer' show that he was familiar with current cynicism about the law, yet he ignores the problems of the system. The only sustained attack on the profession (*2 Henry VI*, IV, ii and vii) derives from his sources and the only lengthy parody is the speech of the grave-digger in *Hamlet* (v, i) and the prince's reflections which follow. Trial scenes have importance only as spectacles and convenient dramatic devices and they are not localized; an English jury-trial is never depicted and the courts of Venice or Vienna do not represent civil law at work. The only exceptions to this are the activities in several plays of J.P.'s, constables and gaolers, but Shakespeare is again not concerned with them as cogs in the legal system but rather as figures of authority. He never employs the popular stock character, the bad lawyer or the conventionally unjust judge. In fact, Shakespeare seems little concerned with lawyers or with litigation; the legal world was a source of patronage and little more.

This lack of interest is nothing remarkable. Shakespeare was burningly concerned with the metaphysical problem of justice. To someone with such preoccupations, the complex legalisms of sixteenth-century England were irrelevant. *Summum jus, summa injuria.*

7

LONDON'S PRISONS[1]

'The prison gates'

I

1. *The Tower*

In *London* and within a mile, I weene,
There are of Iayles or Prisons full eighteene,
And sixty Whipping-posts, and Stocks and Cages,
Where sin with shame and sorrow hath due wages.
For though the Tower be a Castle Royall,
Yet ther's a Prison in't for men disloyall...
And last it is a *Prison* unto those
That doe their Soveraigne or his lawes oppose.

2. *The Gatehouse*

The Gatehouse for a prison was ordain'd,
When in this land the third king *Edward* reignd:
Good lodging roomes, and diet it affoords...

3. *The Fleet*

Since *Richards* reigne the first, the Fleet hath beene
A Prison, as upon records is seene,
For lodgings and for bowling, there's large space...

4. *Newgate*

Old Newgate I perceive a theevish den,
But yet there's lodging for good honest men...

5. *Ludgate*

...No Iayle for theeves, though some perhaps as bad,
That breake in policie, may there be had.

6. *Poultry Counter*

The *Counter* in the Powltry is so old,
That it in History is not enrold.

7. *Wood-street*

And Woodstreet Counters age we may derive,
Since Anno fifteene hundred fifty five...

8. *Bridewell*

Bridewell unto my memorie comes next;
Where idlenesse and lechery is vext:
              ...for Vagabonds and Runnagates,
For Whores, and idle knaves, and such like mates,
'Tis littell better than a Iayle to those,
Where they chop chalke, for meat and drinke and blowes...

13. *White Lion, Kings Bench, Marshalsea, Counter, and Clinke*

Five Iayles or Prisons are in Southwarke plac'd,
The *Counter* (once *S. Margrets* Church defac'd)
The Marshalsea, the *Kings Bench*, and *White Lion*,
Where some like *Tantalus*, or like *Ixion*,
The pinching paine of hunger daily feele...

And some doe willingly make there abode,
Because they cannot live so well abroad.
Then ther's the *Clinke*, where handsome lodgings be...

14. *The hole at S. Katherines*	Crosse but the Thames unto *S. Katherins* then, There is another hole or den for men
15. *East Smithfield Prison*	Another in East-Smithfield little better, Will serve to hold a theefe or paltry debter.
16. *New Prison*	Then neere three Cranes a Iayle for *Hereticks*, For *Brownists, Familists*, and *Schismaticks*.
17. *The Lord Went- worths*	Lord *Wentworths* Iayle within White Chappel stands,
18. *Finsbury*	And *Finsbury*, God blesse me from their hands. These eighteene Iayles so neere the City bounded, Are founded and maintain'd by men confounded: As one mans meat may be anothers bane, The keepers full, springs from the prisners wane.

This exhaustive list of London prisons is condensed from one of the lesser publications of 1623, John Taylor the Water Poet's pamphlet *The Praise and Vertue of a Jayle and Jaylers*.[1] It includes all the London prisons of Shakespeare's day, and its brief comments are most pertinent. There will be no need for us to concern ourselves with the lesser gaols, nos. 14–18 in Taylor's catalogue and the White Lion and the Counter in Southwark remain little more than names even after thorough research. And as Taylor remarked, the Tower of London and Bridewell were only incidentally prisons, having their own particular functions. It is worth noting, however, that it was probably in Finsbury Prison that Christopher Marlowe and Thomas Watson passed the night of 18–19 September 1589, after William Bradley's death, not Newgate as Mark Eccles conjectures.[2]

Taylor's account is accessible to any student of minor Jacobean writing and many references to prisons are scattered throughout the popular literature of Shakespeare's times. Yet once we try to pass beyond these superficial comments and oft-repeated details it soon appears difficult to learn much about the history of English prisons at any period before the eighteenth century. Yet to Shakespeare's contemporaries imprisonment was an aspect of everyday life which any man could easily experience. There were indeed particular hazards for the professional writer. One need only recall Thomas Dekker's two imprisonments, in the Poultry Counter in 1598[3] and in the King's Bench for debt from 1613 to 1620, and Ben Jonson's three imprisonments, in 1579 for his share in *The Isle of Dogs* episode, in the following year for killing Gabriel Spencer in a duel, and in 1605 for his collaboration in *Eastward Ho!*[4]

Of the prisons in Taylor's list nine are of special importance—Newgate, Ludgate, the two Counters in the Poultry and Wood Street, the Fleet, the Gatehouse Westminster, and in Southwark the Marshalsea, the Clink and the King's Bench.

The first four of these were under the government of the City of London. Newgate was before all else the principal criminal prison of London, holding all those who were to be tried for petty treason, felony or misdemeanour at the Gaol Deliveries of London or Middlesex, whose alleged crimes had been committed within the area of jurisdiction of those Courts. Ludgate was the prison for all freemen and freewomen of the City of London, committed for any cause except treason or felony. In practice it became almost exclusively a debtor's prison. The Counters were directly under the jurisdiction of the two Sheriffs of London, who held their respective courts there. They were intended for persons who offended against the City laws; all others committed there were supposed to be transferred as early as possible to the appropriate prison elsewhere. They remained open all night to receive persons arrested by the watch for disturbing the peace. Of the two, the Counter in Wood Street was easily the larger and therefore it is not surprising that there are far more literary references to it than to the Poultry Counter; both the debtor and the brawler were far more likely to be taken there.

The other five prisons were all under the direct jurisdiction of the Crown. The Fleet and the Marshalsea can be properly considered together for they were both closely connected with the administration of the royal justice at the highest level and were the chief prisons in England for all offences except high treason. During medieval times the Fleet had become the recognized prison for Common Pleas, Chancery, Star Chamber and the King's debtors.[1] The Privy Council committed far more persons there than to the Marshalsea, and the Warden was prepared to receive anyone from a duke or an archbishop downwards. Under Elizabeth and the early Stuarts many recusants were imprisoned there and the prison also received persons committed by the monarch's personal decree. The abolition of the Star Chamber in 1641 led to a deterioration in the status of the Fleet which finally made it a debtor's prison only. This change has confused many Shakespearian commentators concerning the significance of Falstaff's committal there.[2]

The Marshalsea was always considered the second prison in England. An unknown Marshal (i.e. the Keeper) tried to remedy this inferiority by a memorandum entitled 'Reasons to prove that prisoners from the Councell bourd Committed, should be sent to the marshalsey',[3] but his arguments apparently failed to produce the desired effect. Yet the Marshal was always in attendance on the Court and his prison received those who offended against the great ones there. The Marshalsea seems also to have been particularly appropriated to religious offenders, Protestants under Mary, Catholics under succeeding regimes. Though all the main London prisons received their share of recusants, yet the large number of famous or notorious Catholics from Bishop Bonner onwards who passed through the Marshalsea seems to indicate a special function, perhaps related to ecclesiastical courts. Pirates and all other persons connected with maritime offences or disputes, including the Thames watermen, were committed there. Possibly this was due to its close proximity to the Admiralty Court held in the former St Margaret's Church.[4]

Although Taylor refers simply to 'The Gatehouse', as indeed do almost all contemporary documents and therefore later writers, yet it appears that during an undetermined period there were *two* prisons at Westminster. In 1603 Stow wrote:

The Gate-house is so called of two Gates, the one out of the Colledge court toward the North, on the East side whereof was the Bishop of Londons prison for Clearkes convict, and the other gate, adioyning to the first but towards the west, is a Gaile or prison for offenders thither committed.[5]

Stow writes of the Bishop's prison in the past tense, yet during 1614 the Privy Council made a number of orders in which 'the Gatehouse' and 'the convict prison' in Westminster were distinguished.[6]

The Gatehouse was owned by the Dean and Chapter of St Peter's Westminster from Elizabeth's accession until its demolition in 1776.[1] Like the Fleet and the Marshalsea it was much used for state prisoners, presumably because of its nearness to the centre of government. The controlling authorities were the Privy Council, the Bishop of London and the High Commission.[2] The prisoners always included a noteworthy proportion of recusants, both lay and clerical, and it also seems to have been used for local, non-political delinquents. 'Good lodging roomes, and diet it affoords', wrote Taylor, and these may be studied in some detail in the bills of charges for state prisoners submitted to the Privy Council by successive Keepers between 1592 and 1610.[3]

The prison for the Clink Liberty within the Borough of Southwark had been used for the detention of local breakers of the peace since the early fifteenth century, and probably first acquired its familiar name between 1498 and 1509.[4] Lexicographers of slang assume, a little dubiously I feel, that the clink of a prisoner's fetters had something to do with the fact that 'clink' became a slang synonym for 'prison'. In Shakespeare's day this prison assumed a specialized function in connection with religious offenders, probably because of its proximity to the Bishop of Winchester's residence. In John Selden's 'old story of the Keeper of the Clink' the Keeper receives in turn 'a Priest of the Church of *Rome*', 'A silens'd Minister' and 'A Minister of the Church of *England*'.[5] The two last-named would be for trial before the High Commission, which committed a number of persons there but probably more, because of convenience, to the Gatehouse Westminster. At the end of the sixteenth century lay recusants were imprisoned in the Clink, but with the turn of the century records show an increasing number of priests detained there. From 1608 onwards some priests, who had taken the oath of allegiance and advocated this compromise to alleviate the sufferings of English Catholics, were lodged in it for safe custody, protected by the King and the Anglican Church from the over-zealous attentions of both papists and puritans. These priests were very comfortably settled in their sets of chambers and lived there for many years.[6]

Lastly, we come to the King's Bench Prison, often so called even in Elizabeth's reign. Though some state prisoners were on occasion committed there it received a much smaller proportion than most of the other principal prisons outside the City; the bulk of the prisoners were persons brought before the Judges of the King's Bench, of whom the majority were debtors. Under Elizabeth commissions were appointed to mediate and arbitrate between creditor and debtor, deriving their ultimate authority from the Privy Council.[7] After her death these Commissions were unfortunately allowed to lapse for fifteen years.

II

It will be noticed that of all these prisons only Newgate was intended to accommodate those charged with criminal offences. Men and women were imprisoned for many reasons of which criminal charges covered only a part of the whole. In very few cases are there any signs that a term of imprisonment was regarded as a punishment as in later times. Prisons were thought of simply as places where persons were kept in safe custody because it was considered too dangerous to leave them at large. This might be because of their crimes, for reasons of state, or because in civil cases such as debt they might evade the execution of the law. In none of these instances was a person imprisoned for a specified length of time. Those suspected of treason or disaffection against the Crown were held until their offences could be proved; if proof was lacking but it was thought perilous to release them they might be held indefinitely. Although a writ of *habeas corpus* could be claimed, the position was clearly set forth by the judges in 1591:

We think that if any person shall be committed by Her Majesty's special commandment or by order from the Council-Board, or for treason touching Her Majesty's person, any of which causes being generally entered into any court it is good cause for the same court to leave the person committed in custody.[1]

The position of suspected felons was simple enough. They were held until trial and if convicted until the execution of the sentence—a summary one in which imprisonment had no part. (There were conditions which could postpone the execution of sentence, even for a considerable time, but they did not usually operate.)

However, sometimes a prisoner accused of felony or petty treason refused to plead either guilty or not guilty. Thus he evaded trial and a conviction which carried with it the confiscation of all the criminal's property by the Crown. The penalty for this refusal was *la peine forte et dure*, the legal name for the process popularly known as 'pressing to death', in which the victim was stretched upon the ground and weights heaped upon his body until he died. Legally this could be made such a lingering process that the victim broke down and agreed to plead, and so apparently it was practised in the eighteenth century.[2] But in Elizabethan and early Stuart times it seems to have been recognized that if a person chose to die in this way his courage ought to be respected. Consequently, death was hastened by placing a sharp stone or piece of wood under the person's back.[3] George Wither attacked those

> Who beeing brought to triall by the Lawes
> For their offence are obstinately mute.
> To these forsooth, the commons do impute
> A manly resolution[4]

and it is a fact that during the first eighteen years of James' reign at least forty-one men and three women were pressed to death in Middlesex alone. In the years 1609–18 the Middlesex Sessions records show thirty-two persons pressed to death and 704 hung.[5] This sentence was carried out in the prison where the person was held, and thus part of Newgate became known as the Press Yard.

I have dealt with this practice, only incidentally connected with the prisons themselves, because the comparative frequency of these executions was reflected in allusions by important authors, Dekker, Nashe, Milton (the second epitaph on Hobson, the University carrier) and Shakespeare himself. Three of Shakespeare's allusions clearly associate it with standing mute:

Richard II, III, iv, 72 (1597):

> *Queene.* Oh I am prest to death through want of speaking.

Troilus and Cressida, III, ii, 215–18 (1609):

> *Pan*[darus]...Whereupon I will shew you a Chamber with a bed, which bed because it shall not speake of your prety encounters presse it to death; away.

91

Sonnet 140, lines 1–2 (1609):

> Be wise as thou art cruell, do not presse
> My toung tide patience with too much disdaine.

Other plain allusions are found in

Much Ado about Nothing, III, i, 75–6 (1600):

> *Hero.* ...O she would laugh me
> Out of my selfe, presse me to death with wit.

and *Measure for Measure*, V, i, 528–9 (1623):

> *Luc*[io]. Marrying a punke my Lord is pressing to death, whipping and hanging [i.e. the three sentences passed at Newgate Sessions].[1]

From these allusions we can deduce that Shakespeare felt no horror concerning this practice, rather he accepted it as a normal basis for a joke or an exercise of wit; only in the first example quoted is a real physical violence felt.[2]

A few cases can be found in which a person was specifically imprisoned for a few days only.[3] Here, quite clearly, the intention was to teach a sharp lesson, the chief penalty being the payment of the numerous fees involved in entering and leaving prison for however short a period. In other coercive imprisonments, for recusancy for example, it was the heavy expenses involved and the difficulty of attending to one's affairs from prison which constituted the punishment, or rather the pressure exerted to obtain conformity. When a person was imprisoned for offending some great personage, for an overreadiness with tongue or pen, he was likely to remain until he could obtain pardon by petitioning either the person offended or some other important person who would intercede on his behalf. This was far more likely to be efficacious than embarking on the troubled seas of the law, even if the offence was not against the monarch.

The arrest of debtors by the sergeants and their yeomen attached to the Counters, who had been feed by the creditor, is a recurring situation in the drama (cf. *Com. of Errors*, IV, i). We cannot here examine the rules and traditions under which these officers operated[4] or recount the malpractices of which they were accused or the evasions thought up by those arrested. Once imprisoned the debtor had to settle somehow with his creditor or remain there indefinitely. The grave anomaly existing in the law was that once a creditor had obtained a court sentence of execution against his debtor no further action could be taken to compel payment. Consequently two special kinds of debtors could be found in the London prisons. First, there were the 'politic bankrupts', persons who had obtained large sums or amounts of goods on credit and then feigned bankruptcy. When they were arrested they lived comfortably in prison on the proceeds. This practice was denounced by various writers of whom Dekker was the most eloquent. These debtors were often able to force a settlement on their creditors, paying only a proportion of their actual debt.[5] Such sharp practices naturally made creditors suspicious of any bankruptcy, and so there are complaints about hard-hearted creditors. A second kind of debtors were those who had elected to remain in prison for life, thus preserving their possessions for their heirs, for debts were entirely personal and death cancelled the obligation. There was a strong feeling that this was morally justifiable if the creditor was an unjust one such as a usurer:

In these cases, I thinke a man may embrace the prison in the case of his children, and give his liberty in portion to his little ones...on the contrarye for deintinesse of liberty...to sell that which hee might lawfully hold, I account for an open disgrace, and as much in effect as to cast his Children to starve in prison for his desired pleasure.[1]

Such imprisonment for debt was a continual hazard, especially in London. The extravagance of court life, accelerating in James' reign, spread in widening circles; there was continual business speculation at home and abroad—the case of Antonio in *The Merchant of Venice* was only unusual in its happy conclusion; and, most to our purpose here, the livelihood of the professional writer was always precarious. It was as a sharer in the playhouse, not as a playwright, that Shakespeare made his money. With characteristic hyperbole Nashe wrote of the Counter:

a Gentleman is never throughly enterd into credit till he hath beene there; that Poet or novice, be hee what he will, ought to suspect his wit, and remaine halfe in a doubt that it is not authenticall, till it hath beene seene and allowd in unthrifts consistory.

...I protest I should never have writ passion well, or beene a peece of a Poet, if I had not arriv'd in those quarters.

Trace the gallantest youthes and bravest revellers about Towne in all the by-paths of their expence, & you shall unfallibly finde, that once in their life time they have visited that melancholy habitation.

...there is no place of the earth like it, to make a man wise...

I vow if I had a sonne, I would sooner send him to one of the Counters to learne lawe, than to the Innes of Court or Chauncery.[2]

III

Any attempt to describe the life of the prisoner is obviously difficult, for conditions varied widely between prisons, within prisons, and even from prisoner to prisoner. As in other spheres of official administration, uniformity, efficiency and impartiality between persons or social classes were notably lacking. In each prison, too, a wide range of influences was at work, physical and human, the condition and adequacy of the buildings, the behaviour of the prison keepers from the highest to the lowest and of the prisoners themselves.

The character of the head keeper could make a great difference in a prisoner's life, for he was the absolute master in his house unless the controlling authority intervened, and any intervention took a long time to become effective. It was of the greatest importance that the Keeper should keep a firm grip on the administration of the prison; otherwise all kinds of disorders amongst the under-keepers, whom he appointed, and the prisoners soon flourished. It was preferable therefore that he should reside in the prison himself; the City authorities managed to enforce this rule at Newgate and two Keepers were dismissed, in 1595 and 1636, who did not comply with it.[3] (But in the two Counters it appears that there were commonly deputies in charge.) In 1639 a Keeper of Newgate, Richard Johnson, was reported to be

too often overtaken with drinke and att such tymes mightily predominating and disturbing the prisoners without any iust cause...[and] very unchast incontinent and intemperate and that in such a high manner as is not fitt to recite the same.

But it was not until two years later that he was dismissed from office because of the continual escapes and disorders resulting from his neglect.[1] Generally speaking there was probably a lot in Hornet's remark: 'I will...be surly and dogged, and proud like the Keeper of a prison.'[2]

However a Keeper behaved when he was in office he certainly had not taken on the job out of a sense of duty but in order to make a profit. In all prisons the income of the Keeper came not from any salary but from the charges he made for bed and board and the fees exacted from the prisoners. Indeed because the prisons were essentially business enterprises the office of Keeper was transferable or inheritable like any other property or else granted for the life of the incumbent. The keeperships of Ludgate, Newgate and the two Counters, like all City offices at the time, were bargained for and sold; or rather, it was the *reversion* of the office which was granted, and more than one grant at a time might be awaiting fulfilment. Considerable sums were involved; William Day, who died in 1615 after having been Keeper of Newgate for only 18 weeks, 'joyneinge with others in the buyinge of the Keeper of Newgate his place, disbursed... 496 *l.*, being his whole estate, for the same'. After Day's death, it was said, the Lord Mayor and Sheriffs 'receaved great summes of money from others for the said place of keeper'.[3]

Normally, the fees which head keepers were legally entitled to exact from their prisoners were for committal and discharge and for exemption from fetters—the last being usually a formality in prisons other than Newgate, where the Keeper retained this ultimate sanction against the dangerous criminal. These legal charges were regulated by the appropriate authorities; in the Fleet Prison charges of all kinds were on a sliding scale adjusted to the prisoners' social rank; these had been ratified by a commission appointed in 1561 and remained in force well into the following century.[4] The entry fees there ranged from £10 for an archbishop, duke or duchess down to 13*s.* 4*d.* for a yeoman and nothing for a poor man; the discharge fees from £3. 5*s.* down to 7*s.* 4*d.* for a yeoman or a poor man. But there was a host of other fees, 'The Clarkes ffee for makeing the Obligacion', 'The ffee for entring the name and cause', 'The Porters ffee', 'The Iaylors ffee', and 'The Chamberlins ffee', all graduated.

In the City prisons, the only other ones for which we have detailed orders, fees were not so steep. At Newgate the felon or suspected felon had to pay 14*d.* on entry; discharge fees were more complicated: for those acquitted by proclamation the fee was 4*s.* 8*d.*, for those acquitted by verdict 8*s.* 8*d.*, and those committed upon commandment and then released were to pay only 14*d.* If a prisoner remained 20 days after acquittal unable to pay his fees he was to be released, the City Chamberlain paying £20 a year in composition of such fees.[5] At the Counters there seems to have been no entry fee, only a charge of 4*d.* for lights, at Ludgate a fee of 14*d.* only; at the Counters the discharge fees were 6*d.* or 4*d.* and at Ludgate 2*s.*[6] But of course there were abuses—the detailed orders would lead us to suspect them even if actual complaints were not on record.

The Gatehouse Westminster is the only other prison for which particular record of fees has survived, included in the bills submitted to the Privy Council.[7] In 1595 there occur two instances of 10*s.* charged as 'fees of commitment', but in all later bills, from 1597 onwards, only a 10*s.* fee on discharge is noted; by 1602 this had become simply 'for fees', so probably this was regarded as an inclusive charge.

But official fees were only a part of what a new prisoner had to pay; there were many other exactions, mostly comprehended under the word 'garnish', which the *Oxford English Dictionary* defines as: 'Money extorted from a new prisoner, either as a jailer's fee, or as drink-money for the other prisoners.'[1] Garnish appears to have been a universal prison custom; at any rate I have found evidence of it in Newgate, the two Counters, Ludgate, the Fleet and the King's Bench. The City authorities forbade the keepers to exact garnish from the prisoners[2] and also ordered the suppression of 'a drunken manner of garnish in wine or other strong drincke, [used] by all such prisoners as goe to the Maisters side at their first commitment to Newgate'.[3] But it flourished without interruption amongst the prisoners themselves, particularly in the Counters.

Detailed information concerning the various exactions which went under this name are given by William Fennor in his account of Wood St Counter in 1616.[4] On entering the Master's Side, the best lodgings there as elsewhere, he was charged 'a garnish' of 2s. by the chamberlain for the privilege.[5] On the following day at dinner his fellow prisoners exacted a garnish of a pottle, that is, half a gallon, of claret, and he was next charged a garnish of 6d. for a quart of claret for the under-keepers so that he might have the liberty of the prison.[6] Some weeks later his poverty compelled him to remove to the cheaper Knight's Side and the steward there tried to extort a garnish of 1s. 6d. from him. When Fennor refused to pay he was lodged in a room unpleasantly near a privy.

All in all, any person 'arrested into one of the counters' was likely to find himself about an angel, that is, 10s., out of pocket from the various fees and exactions; both Robert Greene, in 1592, and Fennor named the same sum.[7]

Accommodation thus varied according to the ability of a prisoner to pay for it. In some prisons, perhaps the majority, it was possible for a prisoner to have a chamber to himself, but everywhere the sharing of chambers and even beds was usual; the Orders for the Fleet Prison include the phrase 'lyinge lyke prisoners two in a bedd together'.[8] Geoffrey Mynshul wrote of the inconvenience of 'an ill bed-fellow', especially a snorer, and also of 'three men...forced to lye thrusting in one bed'.[9] Dekker, his fellow-prisoner in the King's Bench, gives good advice on the subject:

Call therefore him not thy Bedfellow, who is familiar with thee in thy Chamber, and scornes to looke upon thee in the Parlor: part sheetes with such a man: the earthie smell of such dead familiaritie turnes thy Bed into a Grave wherein thou art buried alive.[10]

In 1606 it was enacted that in the Counters and Ludgate no prisoner should be charged more for a bedd with Blankettes sheetes and Coverlettes then ijd a man for a night and though there shalbe three or more in one bedd, not above iiijd for the bedd for a night Nor for a couche more then after the rate of a pennye by the weeke...if anye honest person shall require to lye alone in a bedd, of the best sort then he shall pay for everye such bedd no more then foure pence a night.

Ludgate prisoners who so wished were allowed to provide their own bedding paying only 'for his or her beddes roome iijd a weeke'.[11]

But these are regulations aimed to protect prisoners able to pay for at least a minimum of comfort. In the Common Gaol of Newgate, the Holes of the two Counters and similar places elsewhere penniless unfortunates lay closely packed on the floor with little or no covering.

I lye me down on boords as hard as chennell:
No bed, nor boulster, may affoord reliefe,
For worse then Dogs, lye we in that foule kennell.[12]

The Hole in the Poultry Counter before the Great Fire

was not, nor could not be twenty Foot square, for sometimes forty, sometimes fifty Prisoners, to be and lie constantly in, dress and eat their Meat in, and for all other necessary Occasions and Offices....

Neither was, nor could there be a particular separate Apartment or Ward for women to be, and lodge in, but were necessitated to be and lie in the mens Ward promiscuously together....[1]

Prisoners' food was subject to as wide a variety, dependent on comparative affluence, as accommodation. In the Fleet the grandest could eat alone if they so wished. Elsewhere prisoners tried to cut down expenses by catering for themselves and Dekker describes their activities vividly:

But the time of munching being come, all the sport was to see, how the prisoners...ranne up and downe, to arme themselves against that battaile of hunger....Some ambling downe staires for Bread and Beere, meeting another comming up stayres, carrying a platter...proudly aloft full of powder Beefe and Brewis....Every chamber shewing like a Cookes shop, where provant was stirring.[2]

These prisoners were buying commons in the prison or having food cooked for them in the prison kitchen. Both were liable to be expensive, and indeed in 1620 there was a mutiny in this prison, the King's Bench, after which the prisoners complained to the Privy Council

of a windowe shutt up by Sir George Reinell [the Marshal] whereby they were debarred from takeinge in their victuall out of the streete and consequently compelled to take their victuall from Sir George Reinells servaunts to their great charge and inconvenience as beinge farr deerer then that which they could buy abroade.

Sir George replied

that the windowe was shutt up for the safe keepeinge of the prisonners, and for their meate, though it were true that at his comeinge to the prison there was taken 2*d.* upon every joynt as in other places, yet that was now leaft of and had not been used for theis 7 years past.[3]

The Marshal's excuse sounds a weak one. It is interesting that 'theis 7 years past' largely coincides with Dekker's imprisonment in the King's Bench. His fellow-prisoner Mynshul had a good deal to say about excessive charges for food, the peculations of the head cook and charges for cooking (the prisoner 'payes eightpence in the kitchen for dressing a groat's worth of fish').[4]

In general, however, prisoners ate together in messes of various kinds. In certain prisons they ate at the Keeper's table. In the summer of 1621 Edmund Cannon, a priest imprisoned at the Clink, went with the Keeper Davison to his country house at Upminster in Essex

to beare Davison and his wife company who remayned in that place for diverse weekes, and in as much as [Cannon]...did bord with his keeper hee held it fitt to go thither where the table was kept.[5]

The 1574 Orders for Newgate mention prisoners who are 'allowed to goo downe to the Mr kepers table'; maybe this alludes to the same provision as the mention in 1612 of prisoners eating together in the Master's Side.[6]

But probably the two Counters had the most typical kind of arrangement. In 1606 it was ordered that the Keepers there shall keepe twoe tables or ordynaryes, And that no keeper...shall take of anye prisoner...for his or their diettes...at his first or highest table...not above ixd. a meale Nor at his second table...above vd. a meale.[1]

These charges were presumably for prisoners in the Master's Side and the Knight's Side respectively, which Fennor, as we have seen above, experienced in 1616. It is interesting that these orders also noted that

there hath bene great abuse in eatinge and drinkinge in excess within both ye said Compters by the prisoners...whereby they wast and spend not onlie their owne subtaunce but other mens also.

It was ordered that in future any prisoner who should 'inordinatelye or excessivelye eate or drinke' should be sent off to Newgate. There was published in 1621 (at least, this is the date of the earliest edition extant) *The Counter scuffle*, an account in verse of a supper in Wood St Counter, which on internal evidence can be dated sometime between 1612 and 1621. At this meal, at which 'a score Of madcap Gentlemen or more' were present, a quarrel arose between two of the prisoners. Lacking other weapons they used pots, platters and food, other prisoners became involved, and a battle royal ensued. A copper-plate engraving on the title-page gives a vivid impression of the brawl at its height (see Plate XIV). Though the anonymous author disclaims any pedantic accuracy, yet if his lengthy and detailed account of

> The goodnesse of their Lenten fare,
> Which is in prisons very rare,

is anywhere near the truth it would certainly have been thought excessive by the City authorities.

For an authentic account of what prisoners ate we must go back to 1592 when the Privy Council sent lists of 'the diet that is set down in the Fleet' Prison to the keepers in charge of recusants imprisoned at Broughton in Oxfordshire, Ely and Wisbech Castle. Here is an extract, dealing with one category of prisoners only:

An Es-quire, a Gentleman or wealthy Yeamon [sic]	Bone of meat with brothe Bone beef a pece Veale roasted a loyne or a brest or els one capon Bread asmuch as they will eat, small beare and wine clared, a quart	paieth weekely every manne } x[s].
Fish daies, this is the proporcion for viij or ix at a table of Gentle-men or Yeomen	Butter 2 disshes Ling a joull and of seafishe or fresh fishe iij good dishes or iiij[or] as the markett will serve	And so ratablie according to the receipt of a Noble-manne or Knight.[2]

The poor prisoners on the other hand fed as best they could, and for the destitute there were various sources of food, none particularly reliable. The best known was the alms-basket, the deep, open pannier strapped on the back of a 'basket-man', who walked the streets appealing for charitable gifts of food which were then carried back in a confused heap. The basket-man and his cry, 'Bread and meat for the poore prisoners, bread and meat', were familiar to all Londoners.[1] In John Cooke's comedy *Greene's Tu quoque* (1614), Gatherscrap, the basket-man, enters and his haul is divided up amongst the prisoners by Fox, an under-keeper; a hungry prisoner complains of his share: 'whats this to a Gargantua stomack?' Afterwards Spendall, his fastidiousness leading perhaps to exaggeration, soliloquizes:

> To such a one as these are, must I come...
> To fight and scramble for unsaverie Scraps,
> That come from unknowne hands, perhaps unwasht:
> And would that were the worst; for I have noted,
> That nought goes to the Prisoners, but such food
> As either by the weather has been tainted,
> Or Children, nay sometimes full paunched Dogges,
> Have overlickt...[2]

Other defects of this system were that the basket-men had to be paid out of alms collected for the prisoners and sometimes such money was lacking, and also that other circumstances might interrupt the collection. In time of plague, in 1625, Dekker asked, if the rich fled from London,

Where shall the wretched prisoners have their Baskets filled every night and morning with your broken bread? These must pine and perish.

The distressed in *Ludgate*, the miserable soules in the Holes of the two *Counters*, the afflicted in the *Marshall-seas*, the Cryers-out for Bread in the *Kings Bench*, and *White Lyon*, how shall these be sustayned?[3]

This is the best known of the expedients devised or evolved for the feeding of destitute prisoners. There were many others: charities instituted for purchasing food, regular gifts from the Lord Mayor, the Sheriffs and City companies, the sending of confiscated food (short weight bread, meat offered for sale on fast days) to the prisons. And money gathered from casual donations, bequests and other sources was applied to the purchase of food. Yet the more one examines the evidence available the stronger the impression that these well-intentioned charities were inadequate, and that, especially in the largest accumulation of such prisoners, the Common Gaol at Newgate, there must have been many deaths simply from prolonged food shortages allied to all the other inimical circumstances such as overcrowding, lack of exercise, disrepair of buildings,[4] bad sanitation and the like.

The glimpses we get of the habits and behaviour of the lower order of prisoners are of an irregular, unhealthy existence. The gaolers, interested only in producing their prisoners when required (if still alive), mostly thought their general or moral welfare no concern of theirs. On the other hand the City government, increasingly as it became more Puritan, tried to do something for the prisoners, legislating against the admission of unauthorized female visitors, irregular behaviour in divine services,[5] gambling and excessive drinking.[6] They tried particularly hard to prevent the sale of the strongest beer and ale to them. Here, of course, they were fighting against a well-established business, for in each prison some under-keeper or other person had the concession for selling drink to the prisoners, and a very profitable business it must have been where some would drink to drown care whilst a penny, or a garment which could be pawned, remained in their possession. As usual Dekker painted a vivid picture from personal experience:

locking up being come, that every Cocke must goe to his roost...nothing could bee heard, but keyes Iyngling, doores rapping, bolts and locks barring in, Iaylors hoarsely and harshly bawling for prisoners to their bed, and prisoners reviling and cursing Iaylors for making such a hellish din. Then to heare some in their chambers singing and dancing being halfe drunke; others breaking open dores to get more drinke to be whole drunke. Some roaring for *Tobacco*; others raging, and bidding hels plague on all *Tobacco*, because it has so dryed up their mouthes, with as many other franticke passions, as there bee severall men...[1]

Such was the framework into which individual prisoners had to fit their lives. If they were sufficiently resilient mentally and physically to make the necessary adjustments they might live many years in these surroundings. This was less likely in the cramped, unhealthy conditions of the City prisons with only a small yard for the exercise of far too many persons. But in some prisons it was possible to live a comparatively comfortable, equable life. Once he had the liberty of the prison, the right to move about freely during the daytime, a prisoner could live a life of social intercourse there. We know little of the Clink beyond the 'handsome lodgings'—it was probably closely hemmed in amongst the Bankside buildings—but there were gardens at the Gatehouse Westminster,[2] at the Fleet, the King's Bench and the Marshalsea. Of course the prison keepers made a profit from these amenities. Mynshul remarked that '(Pothearbe) the Gardiner...will have *unguentum aurem*, for the narrow path thou hast to walke in'[3] and in 1639 the deputy keeper of the Marshalsea presented a bill to a prisoner, Sir William Essex, which included 'for the benefitt of the walking in the Garden' the charge of 2s.[4] Playing at bowls seems to have been an established pastime at the Fleet.[5] At two prisons at least, the Fleet and the King's Bench, the liberty of the prison included the 'Rules', ordinary houses adjacent to the prison which had been absorbed into it because of overcrowding. In the 1630's the Rule of the Fleet included most of the houses in Fleet Lane, the majority of women prisoners being accommodated there. One prisoner, Thomas Cranley, wrote a lengthy account of an intrigue he conducted with a woman living in Fleet Lane (not a prisoner), who turned out to be a courtesan.[6]

Lastly, some mention must be made of the ways in which prisoners might leave the prison for varying periods of time. The commonest of these was leave during one day only, known as 'going abroad'. A natural outcome of the non-penal nature of most of prison life was that the chief emphasis fell on security and the prisoner was usually accompanied by a prison officer, an under-keeper from the Fleet or the King's Bench, a sergeant from a City counter. Naturally this privilege had to be paid for, and fees were accordingly laid down. At the Fleet the prisoner had to pay the Warden 10d. for a half day, 20d. for a full day's leave.[7] This was comparatively reasonable; at the King's Bench the charge was '4 shillings *per diem cum Cere, et Baccho*'.[8] Around 1620 Alexander Harris, the Warden of the Fleet, maintained that he was losing money because he had to keep 'almost 20 servants for that service onely' and the £80 or so a year which he received from fees did not cover their wages.

This custom was capable of almost indefinite extension. Some prison keepers seem to have allowed prisoners to stay out overnight (but this was probably illegal). Prisoners were sometimes allowed out of prison and even out of London if they would give sufficient security (i.e. bail) for their return, and this might be for periods of a year or more. It was of course dependent on the goodwill of the authority which had committed the individual prisoner, not the organization at any particular prison.

Felons were naturally not allowed such privileges and information was laid against one Keeper of Newgate, William Crowther, in 1580 that amongst many other abuses a woman cut-purse 'went with her keper...and Cut purses, and Spent her monye in the Gayole And being taken with the manner, her keper Rane awaye...'.[1] Nor were those prisoners who had the misfortune to be classed as 'close prisoners'. Almost always these were political prisoners thought too dangerous to enjoy the normal privileges of freedom within the prison. They were confined in a room apart from other prisoners and only allowed visitors under stringent controls. The usual intention was that they should not be allowed to communicate freely with their associates or friends before their examination or whilst the preparation of their indictment was in progress. Afterwards the rigour of their confinement might be relaxed and such prisoners, committed by the Privy Council, might be merely prevented from going abroad as were some prisoners committed by the Court of High Commission: 'Which is all the close Imprisonment which I ever knew that Court to use', wrote Archbishop Laud.[2]

When a close prisoner was allowed to receive visitors (generally specified) the Keeper or a trustworthy representative was usually supposed to be present to prevent treasonable conversation. Since prisoners sometimes tried to evade the spirit of this regulation by speaking foreign languages or Latin, it was laid down in 1618 that 'the conference [was] to bee in a language that the keeper should bee able to understand, as had beene ordered sometime heretofore in the raigne of Queene Elizabeth'.[3] Communication by writing was naturally restricted also and a close prisoner was usually denied writing materials, or else allowed to write only to the Privy Council.[4] However, it has always proved most difficult to prevent prisoners from doing this, even in modern times, and the extensive writings of some close prisoners, particularly those detained on religious grounds, probably shows that inefficiency and bribery made matters considerably easier at this period.

There is no doubt that many literate prisoners wrote a great deal. There are extant petitions and letters to important personages, in the prisoners' own or professional hands, letters to relations or friends (some smuggled out of prison), and whole books composed in prison, from *Bulleyn's Bulwarke of defence against all sickness, soreness and woundes* by William Bullein (1562) to Thomas Bayly's allegorical romance *Herba Parietis* (1650), written in Newgate, not to mention a host of miscellaneous pamphlets, poems,[5] and other literary and sub-literary works. A certain Welshman, John Jones of Gelli Lyfdy, a notable calligrapher, who spent many years in prisons in the provinces and London, particularly the Fleet, between 1611 and 1658, made many transcripts of Welsh and other manuscripts there.[6]

Prison life in Shakespeare's day was a microcosm of the world outside, a life of sharp contrasts, wealth and the direst poverty, disorder and calm, the dangers of life sharpened by disease, intrigue, suspicion, litigiousness, pride, the turn of Fortune's wheel.

It is only with an effort that we realize how normal a part it was of Elizabethan and Jacobean life.

PHILOSOPHY
AND
FANCY

8

THE COMMONWEALTH

'Degree, priority and place'

I

The Lent Sword of the City of Bristol, which is still carried before the judges at the Assizes, bears upon its scabbard the date 1594, the arms of the Queen and of the city and the first four verses of the thirteenth chapter of Romans:

1. LET EVERY SOVLE BE SUBIECT TO THE HIGHER POWER FOR THERE IS NO POWER BVT OF GOD AND THE POWERS THAT BE ARE OF GOD.

2. WHOSOEVER THEREFORE RESISETH THE POWER RESISTETH THE ORDINANC OF GOD: AND THEY THAT RESIST SHAL RECEVE CONDEMNATION.

3. FOR MAGISTRATES ARE NOT TO BE FERE FOR GOOD WORKES BVT FOR EVIL WILT THOU BE WITH OVT FEARE DO WEL SO SHALT THOW HAUE PRAIS FOR THE SAME.

4. FOR HE IS THE MINISTER OF GOD FOR THY WELTH BUT IF THOV DO EVIL FEARE FOR HE BERETH NOT THE SWORD FOR NOVGHT.[1]

It is thus an apt symbol of the political outlook of Shakespeare's age; of the basic belief, abundantly fortified by scriptural precedent, in the divine sanction behind all established authority and of the conception of the administration of justice as the primary function of the State. It reminds us, too, of the numerous ways in which these principles were proclaimed and made part of the popular consciousness and of the pattern of everyday life.

The doctrine of Divine Right is much the most important element in Tudor political thought. It was expounded in treatises and sermons with unwearying reiteration and no text was more often quoted in support of it than this of St Paul. The passage (Rom. xiii. 1–7) continues as follows in the Authorized Version:

5. Wherefore ye must needs be subject, not only for wrath, but also for conscience sake.

6. For this cause pay ye tribute also: for they are God's ministers attending continually upon this very thing.

7. Render therefore to all their dues: tribute to whom tribute is due; custom to whom custom; fear to whom fear; honour to whom honour.

St Paul was exhorting the Christians of Rome to obedience to Nero, a tyrant and a persecutor of the Faith. The duty of obedience is therefore absolute, allowing of no exception, however wicked and ungodly the ruler may be. Indeed, since all kings derive their power from God, the evil, no less than the good, are appointed by Him, as part of His divine plan. 'We need not labour', said Calvin, 'to prove that an impious king is a mark of the Lord's anger, since I presume no one will deny it, and that this is not less true of a king than of a robber who plunders your goods, an adulterer who defiles your bed, and an assassin who aims at your life, since all such calamities are classed by Scripture among the curses of God.'[2] It is, in fact, a doctrine not of absolute power so much as of obedience as a Christian duty. It applies to all forms of government, whether monarchical or not, and has not yet been narrowed down, as it was to be during the seventeenth century, to the Divine Right of Kings or the divine hereditary right of the House of Stuart. Moreover, since St Paul was not concerned with the origin of government, it is even compatible with the belief that political power derives ultimately from the people. So, for instance, it was interpreted by Hooker, in the posthumous eighth book of the *Ecclesiastical Polity* which provoked the resentment of Charles I.

Sometimes it pleaseth God himself by special appointment to choose out and nominate such as to whom dominion shall be given, which thing he did often in the commonwealth of Israel. They who in this sort receive power have it immediately from God, by mere divine right; they by human, on whom the same is bestowed according unto men's discretion, when they are left free by God to make choice of their own governor. By which of these means soever it happen that kings or governors be advanced unto their states, we must acknowledge both their lawful choice to be approved of God, and themselves to be God's lieutenants, and confess their power his.

That the Christian world should be ordered by kingly regiment, the law of God doth not anywhere command: and yet the law of God doth give them right, which once are exalted to that estate, to exact at the hands of their subjects general obedience in whatsoever affairs their powers may serve to command. So God doth ratify the works of that sovereign authority which kings have received by men.[1]

Certainly no one in the sixteenth century believed that Christian rulers could do as they pleased. Their office was a trust, to the discharge of which they were bound, no less than their subjects, by the law of God 'that they should not rule their subjects by will, and to their own commodity and pleasure only; but that they should govern their subjects by good and godly laws'. They must 'think themselves to be God's officers, ordained by God to be his ministers unto the people, for their salvation, common quietness and wealth, to punish malefactors, to defend innocents, and to cherish well doers'.[2] Their responsibility to God was something more awful and commanding than could ever be owed merely to men: and, as of kings, so also, in their degree of inferior magistrates and of the rich towards the poor. This aspect of the matter is very clearly illustrated in that interesting body of 'Commonwealth' literature which was inspired by the social unrest of Edward VI's reign, culminating in the risings of 1549—the sermons of Hugh Latimer and the works of other, less famous, men. Typical of them is Robert Crowley, a London printer, who became Archdeacon of Hereford in 1559 and whose *Way to Wealth* was published in 1550. He has no doubt at all that the causes of the troubles—inclosures, rack-renting and the rise in prices—are due to the covetousness of the rich:

the great fermares, the grasiers, the riche buchares, the men of lawe, the marchauntes, the gentlemen, the knightes, the lordes and I cannot tell who.... Men without conscience. Men utterly voide of Goddes feare. Yea, men that live as thoughe there were no God at all.... Cormerauntes, gredy gulles; yea, men that would eate up menne, women and chyldren, are the causes of Sedition.

But all this provocation did not in any way excuse the unfortunate rebels:

the devell shoulde never have persuaded the that thou myghtest revenge thyne owne wronge! The false prophetes shoulde never have caused the to beleve that thou shouldeste prevale against them with the swerde, under whose gouernaunce God hath apointed the to be. He would have told the that to revenge Wronges is, in a subiect, to take and usurpe the office of a kinge, and, consequently, the office of God. For the kinge is Goddes minister to revenge the wronges done unto the innocent.

Nor did it mitigate their just punishment, both here and hereafter: '...if everye one of them were able and shoulde sustaine as much punishment as thei al were able to sustaine, yet could thei not sustaine the plages that thei have deserved'.[1] Society was organized in terms not of rights but of duties, and all duties, whether of ruler and subject or rich and poor, were owed not to man but to God. If government rested on human ordinance alone it would have no moral basis at all. It would be a mere tyranny. Only God can create a moral obligation to obedience. It was the difficulty of translating these grand conceptions into practical, constitutional terms that was to produce the Stuart Revolution.

The resort of the oppressed lay not in resistance but in repentance and in prayer that God would move the heart of the ruler, as Latimer exhorts his congregation 'not to judge them that be in authority, but to pray for them'.[2] There was, however, one acknowledged limit to obedience, when the command of the sovereign conflicted with the will of God; cases, that is to say, not of oppression, but of conscience. When this happened, it was the subject's duty to disobey the law, and equally his duty patiently to suffer whatever penalty the law inflicted.

And here is but one exception [says Latimer], that is, against God. When laws are made against God and his word, then I ought more to obey God than man. Then I may refuse to obey with a good conscience: yet for all that I may not rise up against the magistrates, nor make any uproar; for if I do so I sin damnably. I must be content to suffer whatsoever God shall lay upon me, yet I may not obey their wicked laws to do them.[3]

Official apologists were naturally not much concerned to define such cases. In England, at least, ruled by a godly prince who was also supreme head of the Church, they might be dismissed as hypothetical. Yet the exception is historically important, for it was the plea of 'tender consciences' that led the Puritans eventually from passive resistance to armed rebellion.

This was the central doctrine of English political thought throughout the century and a half between the Reformation and the Revolution. But during that period the emphasis of it is significantly transformed. By the end of the seventeenth century, belief in divine right and non-resistance had become the distinctive tenet of the High Tories, Jacobites and Non-Jurors, the extreme Right in the political conflicts of the time. But under the earlier Tudors it found some of its most strenuous advocates among the men of the Left, as we might call them, the advanced Protestants and Reformers. One of the most uncompromising assertions of the power of the prince is in William Tyndale's *Obedience of a Christian Man*, a work of very considerable influence in the first phase of the Reformation. 'Hereby seest thou', he says, 'that the king is, in this world, without Law; and may at his lust do right or wrong, and shall give accounts but to God only': and again, 'though he be the greatest tyrant in the world, yet is he unto thee a great benefit of God, and a thing wherefore thou oughtest to thank God highly'. 'Few of us would think', he remarks in another passage, 'if we were under the Turk, that it were sin to rise against him, and to rid ourselves under his dominion, so sore have our bishops robbed us of the true doctrine of Christ.'¹ Hooper, who has been called 'the Father of the English Puritans' and who, like Tyndale, was put to death as a heretic, is equally clear about the duties of the subject in his *Annotations on Romans XIII*:

For no man can come to the office of a magistrate but by the permission and sufferance of God. Many times some persons come into the place of a ruler by false and preposterous means; as those do that for a private lucre, or private hatred to other, put up themselves, and pull down those that God hath appointed. But such ungodly coming to honour God suffereth, and appointeth for the sins of the people such evil and dissembling hypocrites to reign. But let the king and magistrate be as wicked as can be devised and thought, yet is his office and place the ordinance and appointment of God, and therefore to be obeyed.²

What was forged as a theological weapon against the claims of Rome became, in the process of time, a political weapon in the party strife of Whig and Tory.

There were many reasons why a doctrine as old as Christianity itself should have a special appeal to the Reformers of the sixteenth century. In the Middle Ages, belief in the divine authority of the temporal power was quite compatible with belief in the right and even the duty of resisting tyrants, in the name of the spiritual power, which was acknowledged by all Christendom and which could, by excommunication or deposition, chastise the sins of princes no less than of ordinary men. But to Protestants, who acknowledged no head of the Universal Church save Christ himself, who believed that salvation comes through suffering and were always deeply conscious of the corruption of man's will, which makes him incapable of judging those set in authority over him, the exaltation of the power even of wicked rulers followed as a matter of course. Moreover, the revolutionary outbreaks which attended the Reformation in Germany —the Peasants' War and the Anabaptist rising in Munster—made them especially anxious to refute the charge that they were not only heretical but socially and politically subversive. The memory of these events helps to explain the violence with which men like Robert Crowley denounced the English rebels of 1549. But here they were able to retort upon their enemies. That the Bishop of Rome had always been a menace to the civil power, and hence to peace and order, is one of the recurrent themes of Protestant polemics. 'But, O immortal God!' says Jewel in his *Apology of the Church of England*, the official defence of the Elizabethan settlement, 'and will the bishop of Rome accuse us of treason? Will he teach the people to obey and follow their magistrates? Or hath he any regard at all of the majesty of princes?...Why hath he and his complices (like Anabaptists and Libertines, to the end they might run on more licentiously and carelessly) shaken off the yoke, and exempted themselves from being under all civil power?'³ Thomas Bilson's *True Difference between Christian Subjection and Unchristian Rebellion* (1585), which is the fullest Elizabethan treatise on the royal supremacy, expounds the accusation at length, citing the examples of Hildebrand and the Emperor Henry IV, Innocent III and Frederick II and, in English history, Henry II and Becket and, of course, King John. To the Elizabethans, the Interdict of 1208 and the baronial opposition organized by Stephen Langton were simply tricks of 'Romish policie to get the subjects to murmur at the Magistrate'.⁴ 'Would Englishmen have brought their sovereign lord and natural country into this thraldom and subjection to a false foreign usurper', asks the author of the *Homily against Disobedience and Wilful*

Rebellion, 'had they known and had any understanding in God's word at all?'[1] This was the 'true doctrine of Christ' of which Tyndale complains that the popish bishops had robbed their flocks. Shakespeare's representation of John, not as the tyrant from whom Magna Carta was extorted but as the victim of the overweening pretensions of the Pope and his 'greedy Romish wolves' is thus in line with the traditions of his age. The story, incidentally, allows him to express anti-papal sentiments not only through the patriot Faulconbridge, but through the invading French. When, at the end of the play, the legate Pandulph announces that the king has been reconciled to the Church and therefore orders the Dauphin to withdraw his forces, the latter answers in defiant words which would have appealed strongly to his audience:

> And come ye now to tell me John hath made
> His peace with Rome? What is that peace to me?
> I, by the honour of my marriage-bed,
> After young Arthur, claim this land for mine;
> And, now it is half-conquer'd, must I back
> Because that John hath made his peace with Rome?
> Am I Rome's slave? What penny hath Rome borne,
> What men provided, what munition sent
> To underprop this action?   (*King John* v, ii, 91)

But as the makers of the Reformation were concerned first of all with religion, perhaps the main reason why they so much emphasized the power of the civil magistrate was that they saw in him the only means of attaining their grand object—a return to the purity and simplicity of the primitive church. To expect the Renaissance Papacy to reform itself was clearly futile. Whatever hopes there were of effecting anything by a General Council gradually faded: and, in any case, had not the Councils of the Early Church been summoned by Emperors? Scripture and History could be made to furnish abundant precedents for the authority of the civil power over the church. As Moses had rebuked Aaron for erecting the golden calf, as Solomon had built the temple, so Henry VIII and Elizabeth might lawfully lead England back to true religion: and, in the last resort, they alone could do so. The maintenance of the Faith, the ordering of the church and the correction of the faults of the clergy were not only the right, but the first duty of the godly prince. This *potestas jurisdictionis* in the spiritual sphere invested the office of kingship with still further attributes of divinity: and in actual fact, the growth in the power of the Crown under the Tudors owed much more to the accretion of ecclesiastical supremacy than to any other single factor.

Much has been written about Shakespeare's idea of kingship and the profound influence on his generation of the history of the Wars of the Roses: and we are apt to forget that these Wars were not to them a living memory, as the Civil War was to the contemporaries of the Popish Plot or as the Jacobin Terror in France cast its shadow over the Reform movements of the early nineteenth century. Very few, even, of the grandfathers of the Elizabethans could have fought at Towton or Barnet or witnessed the social conditions portrayed in the Paston letters. It was a literary reconstruction, derived from Shakespeare's main historical sources, Hall and Holinshed. Hall's pattern of fifteenth-century history, by which the Houses, first of Lancaster and then of York, paid the penalty of their original treason by coming to an end with the third monarch of the line was a topical lesson on the wickedness of rebellion. Nor was Tudor England ever quite secure from the danger of a relapse into the conditions of Henry VI's reign,

> Whose state so many had the managing,
> That they lost France and made his England bleed:
> Which oft our stage hath shown. *(Henry V, Epilogue)*

Nevertheless, we may doubt whether the strife of York and Lancaster bulked quite so large in the general consciousness as it does in the literature of Shakespeare's age. More important in propagating and reinforcing the official political doctrine was the translation of the Bible, in itself one of the most far-reaching results of the English Reformation. The pulpit, in the sixteenth and seventeenth centuries, was a more powerful means of forming opinion than either the press or the stage. Through the Scriptures, read at home and expounded in church, the great mass of the Queen's subjects, who may never have seen a play or read a chronicle, were constantly reminded of their political duties. Submission to authority was urged, not only in the exhortations of St Peter and St Paul but by the example of Christ himself. 'Render unto Caesar the things that are Caesar's' was one of the favourite texts of the time. In refusing the role of the Messiah as the Jews traditionally understood it Christ had set the pattern of obedience for all his followers. So, too, had the Virgin Mary in journeying, at the command of a heathen ruler, from Nazareth to Bethlehem to be taxed. The Jewish history, in the Old Testament and the Apocrypha, was full of such lessons. While the reign of Henry VI might be a warning, the story of David and Saul, a classic example of non-resistance, had all the force of a divine command.

The standard popular exposition of these ideas in Elizabeth's reign is the Homily 'Against Disobedience and Wilful Rebellion' which was added to the Book of Homilies in 1571, after the rising of the Northern Earls.[1] It is an impressive piece of writing: and, as the Homilies were appointed to be read in churches throughout the country, it may be assumed to have reached a far wider public than any literary, dramatic or historical work. It is divided into six parts, so that it would have taken three consecutive Sundays to deliver, and it concludes with a prayer of thanksgiving for the suppression of the recent revolt in the North. 'A rebel', the congregation was told, 'is worse than the worst prince and rebellion worse than the worst government of the worst prince that hitherto hath been.' Rebellion was the first of all sins, for it began with Adam himself. It is the root of all the others and it comprehends them all:

For he that nameth rebellion, nameth not a singular or one only sin, as is theft, robbery, murder, and such like; but he nameth the whole puddle and sink of all sins against God and man, against his prince, his country, his countrymen, his parents, his children, his kinsfolks, his friends, and against all men universally; all sins, I say, against God and all men heaped together, nameth he, that nameth rebellion. ...Thus all sins, by all names that sins may be named, and by all means that all sins may be committed and wrought, do all wholly and upon heaps follow rebellion, and are to be found altogether amongst rebels.[2]

Rebellion would only be committed, in fact, by men naturally capable of every other crime. The preacher is even made to commit himself to the dubious assertion that rebellion has never prospered and the final prayer, somewhat inconsistently, refers to the miseries following on the Northern Rising and gives thanks to God that it has been suppressed 'with so little, or rather no effusion of Christian blood'.

The Homily was only saying more emphatically what had many times been said before and was often to be said again. Its terrible denunciations are in marked contrast with the incompetent rebellion, inspired as much by fear as by hope, that largely provoked them. But they are a sign of the change that comes over the whole climate of political thought during the reign of Elizabeth. The principles of divine right and non-resistance were accepted, indeed assumed, as fundamental throughout the sixteenth century. But side by side with them in the earlier Tudor period there was a vigorous tradition of political and social criticism. It is difficult to imagine an Elizabethan speaking of the State in the famous words of Sir Thomas More: 'When I consider and way in my mind all these commonwealthes, which now a dayes any where do florish, so god helpe me, I can perceave nothing but a certein conspiracy of riche men procuringe theire owne commodities under the name and title of the common wealth.'[1] There is much else in the *Utopia*—the attack on the warlike propensities of Kings and on the savagery of the English criminal law, the ideal communism and, indeed, the whole conception of the book—that breathes a spirit very different from that of the Elizabethan age. Thomas Starkey's *Dialogue between Pole and Lupset*, which was presented in manuscript to Henry VIII between 1533 and 1536, is a comprehensive indictment of the economic and social ills of early Tudor England. Starkey believed that tyrants could be deposed and preferred an elective to an hereditary monarchy; 'if we will that the heirs of the prince shall ever succeed, whatsoever he be, then to him mbeust joined a counsel, by common authority—not such as he will, but such as by the most part of the parliament shall be judged to be wise and meet thereunto'.[2] Bold words from a royal chaplain at the crisis of the Reformation! But Henry VIII was always less sensitive to criticism than Elizabeth, provided it did not involve open disobedience. When in 1513 Dean Colet, in a sermon in the Chapel Royal, denounced the invasion of France, he was merely summoned to discuss with the king the justification of War. Perhaps the most radical of all the thinkers of the time is John Ponet, bishop of Winchester under Edward VI, whose *Short Treatise of Politique Power*, published when he was in exile at Strasbourg in 1556, is mainly concerned with emphasizing the limitations on royal power, even, like Knox, to the extent of advocating tyrannicide.[3] Most typical of all the literature of protest during the period are the constant denunciations of inclosures and the sufferings they caused to the poor which poured forth from press and pulpit, from Catholic and Protestant alike.

The Elizabeth scene is very different. The sky has darkened and the horizons of thought have contracted. The liberal humanism of More, Colet and Starkey died with the Reformation.[4] Where Latimer had blamed the covetousness of the rich as the cause of rebellion, the Homily of 1571 finds the 'principal and most usual causes' in the ambition of the leaders and the ignorance of their followers, the ignorance of those misled by the false doctrine of Rome. Sir Francis Walsingham might safely remind James VI of Scotland 'That as subjects are bound to obey dutifully so were princes bound to command justly' and quote the example of Edward II.[5] But in the England of Elizabeth far less is heard than in her father's time of this aspect of the divine right theory and even the passage already quoted from the Homily of Obedience of 1547 on the responsibilities of princes[6] was omitted from later editions. The preachers no longer sound the note of the Old Testament prophets. The Puritans, however vigorous in the ecclesiastical field, become more and more quiescent in their attitude to social problems, and Cartwright, in his controversies with Whitgift, was always anxious to repudiate the political implications of his doctrine. There is, altogether, an evident decline, in the later as compared with the earlier sixteenth century, of interest in the fundamental problems of government and a reluctance to criticize the existing institutions of society. The content of Elizabethan political thought is very largely summed up in the Homily of 1571, with its exclusive concentration on the duty of non-resistance. There is, of course, the one great exception of Richard Hooker; but even Hooker is, of all the major English political theorists, the most wholly orthodox. We always think of the Elizabethan age as the true English Renaissance, a time of widening horizons, of a flowering of the imagination, of growth and achievement in many different spheres. But in this, at least, it was not so. There is probably no period of English history during the last five hundred years when political speculation was less active or more discouraged.

The reasons for this change lie, of course, in the international situation. England under Elizabeth was in a more or less permanent state of siege. The menace of a hostile combination of the Catholic powers of Europe with the blessing of the Pope had first loomed up in the 1530's and the net seemed to have been drawn very much closer by the time of the Queen's accession. The Rebellion of 1569 was followed by the papal bull of excommunication of 1570, which is in many ways the turning point of the reign, though Elizabeth managed for another fifteen years to stave off the conflict which, as many of her subjects realized, was bound eventually to come. Moreover, it seemed highly probable at any time down to the execution of Mary Stuart in 1587 that foreign invasion or the death of the Queen would precipitate a Civil War which 'exceedeth all wars in all naughtiness, in all mischief and in all abomination'.[1] In such circumstances the violent language of the Homily against Disobedience and Wilful Rebellion is understandable. The rising of the Northern Earls, the only armed outbreak of the reign, was, as it happened, easily dealt with. But the danger of rebellion has to be measured, not only by the strength and determination of the rebels, but by the resources of the government to meet it. In the sixteenth century the arm of the State was short and the crust of order on the surface of society perilously thin. Any study of Elizabethan Quarter Sessions records, for instance, will reveal a readiness to resort to violence which might, if the spark fell, be kindled into a serious revolt. There is, therefore, something more positive than a spirit of blind repression in all these exhortations to passive obedience. The doctrine was as much religious as political, as we have seen: and amid the dangers of the time it was the cause of true religion, no less than of national independence and social order that was felt to be at stake. The Elizabethan ideal of the state was never more finely or more aptly put than by John Foxe, the martyrologist:

God has so placed us Englishmen here in one commonwealth, also in one church, as in one ship together; let us not mangle or divide the ship, which being divided perishes; but let every man serve with diligence and discretion in his order, wherein he is called; let those that sit at the helm keep well the point of the needle, to know how and whither the ship goes; whatever weather betides, the needle, well touched with the stone of God's word, will never fail; let such as labour at the oars, start for no tempest, but do what they can to keep from the rocks; likewise let those who are in inferior stations take heed that they move no sedition nor disturbance against the rowers and mariners. No storm is so dangerous to a ship on the sea, as discord and disorder in a commonwealth; the countries, nations, kingdoms, empires, cities, towns, and houses, that have been dissolved by discord is so manifest in history, that I need not spend time in rehearsing examples.[2]

The metaphor of the ship of state was never more appropriate than in this, the first age of English overseas discovery. Drake, on his voyage round the world, and the early East India captains took with them the Bible and Prayer Book and the *Acts and Monuments* as reading for their crews.[1] The parallel between the vast forces of nature against which the explorers contended in their tiny ships and the political dangers that threatened to overwhelm the commonwealth at home, the contrast, in each case, of the rigid hierarchy and order of a small community and the wide and perilous fields for expansion in which it acted must have struck them, as they strike us in surveying the complexities and the achievement of Shakespeare's England.

II

Very few Elizabethans can have been in any doubt that rebellion was a sin. But the nature and purpose of society are not described simply by defining the duties of its members: and, however unchallengeable its authority might be, government was thought of, not in terms of will, but of law. The conception of law is still largely derived from the Middle Ages and receives its classic sixteenth-century exposition from Hooker, in the Preface and Book 1 of the *Ecclesiastical Polity*. Ultimately, it is the means of giving expression to the moral order of the universe. In this widest sense, therefore, it is anterior to the State, since it embodies the will of God himself. It is merely declared and not made by human authority. But Hooker believed, unlike the Puritans, that man, 'being made according to the likeness of his Maker', could attain to some knowledge of God by the right use of reason, independently of revelation or Scripture: and thus the laws of civil society could be made to conform to the eternal law. Moreover, since God had left men free to choose under what form of government they preferred to live, the laws regulating things indifferent, such as the descent of property, would naturally vary from one community to another, according to custom and convenience. 'Generally', he says, 'all laws human, which are made for the ordering of politic societies, be either such as establish some duty whereunto all men by the law of reason did before stand bound; or else such as make that a duty now which before was none. The one sort we may for distinction's sake call "mixedly" and the other "merely" human.'[2] Here Hooker seems to be approaching the post-Hobbesian idea of law as command, as a means of effecting change. But neither he nor any other Elizabethan really thought in those terms. Even the great Reformation statutes, revolutionary as in fact they were, were in form Acts of Resumption, merely restoring to the king the supremacy over the Church which had always rightfully been his. The famous Statute of Artificers of 1563, which embodies a comprehensive economic and industrial code, was enacted, in the words of its preamble, simply because the existing laws 'cannot conveniently, without the greate greefe and burden of the poore Labourer and hired man, bee put in good and due execution'.[3] Similarly, the purpose of the Vagrancy and Poor Relief Act of 1572 was stated to be 'for avoydinge Confusion by reason of numbers of Lawes concerninge the premises standing in force togeather'.[4] The professed object of all Tudor legislation was to remedy particular abuses in the body politic, to bring back the existing law into conformity with the law of reason or with ancient custom and not to establish any new system, even though, sometimes, this was virtually what it did. It follows that the healthier the state of the commonwealth, the fewer laws would need to be passed. The main business of government, certainly the aspect of it with which the subject was most concerned, was the enforcement of law. Thus, when the Duke, in *Measure for Measure*, gives his commission to Angelo it is with the words

> In our remove be thou at full ourself;
> Mortality and mercy in Vienna
> Live in thy tongue and heart,   (I, i, 44)

and a little later he assures him that

> Your scope is as mine own,
> So to enforce or qualify the laws
> As to your soul seems good.   (I, i, 65)

The same conception of the State appears, as we might expect, in many passages of the Anglican liturgy, as, for example, in the prayer for the Church militant in the communion service.

We beseech thee also to save and defend all Christian Kings, Princes and Governors; and specially thy servant Elizabeth our Queen; that under her we may be godly and quietly governed; And grant unto her whole Council, and to all that are put in authority under her, that they may truly and indifferently minister justice, to the punishment of wickednes and vice, and to the maintenance of thy true religion and virtue.

When Sir Thomas Smith sets out, in his *Commonwealth of England*, to describe the workings of government he quite naturally devotes most of his attention to the judicature, to legal procedure and the organization of courts, rather than to those constitutional relationships which especially interest a modern historian. The political, as distinct from the feudal prerogatives of the crown were, by their very nature, undefined. 'For, as Kings are God's Images', as Salisbury reminded a conference of Lords and Commons in 1610, 'soe he that wrestleth with them may retorne home lame with Jacob'.[1] The sovereign admittedly enjoyed discretionary powers to enable him to fulfil his duty of protecting his subjects. He might, for instance, in certain circumstances, raise money without consent of Parliament or commit a man to prison without showing cause or legislate by proclamation. Of none of these things, which became great issues between King and Parliament in the following century, does Smith make mention. They were 'material matter of state and ought to be ruled by the rules of policy'.[2] It was no time, amid the dangers that beset the throne of Elizabeth, to pry into such *arcana imperii*. Yet it was not forgotten, even when the prerogative was at its highest, that the prince exercised it, not for his own but for the common good; or that, though not accountable to his subjects, he was, like them, bound by the law. Bracton's old adage *rex non debet esse sub homine sed sub deo et lege* still remained true for the sixteenth century. It is quoted by Hooker,[3] as it was to be by Coke against James I. Even so orthodox a writer as Thomas Bilson ventures to say that

if a Prince shoulde goe about to subiect his kingdome to a forraine Realme, or change the forme of the commonwealth, from imperie to tyrannie: or neglect the Lawes established by common consent of Prince and people, to execute his owne pleasure: In these and other cases, which might be named, if the Nobles and commons ioyne togither to defend their auncient and accustomed libertie, regiment and lawes, they may not well be counted rebels.

Such an extreme remedy lies, not with 'every, nor any private man' but only where 'the lawes of the land appoint the nobles as next to the king to assist him in doing right, and withhold him from doing wrong'.[1] We can imagine that if the Queen ever read this passage it was with some displeasure, for she could be extremely sensitive about dangerous historical precedents; as witness her remark to William Lambarde at the time of Essex's rebellion, 'I am Richard II; know ye not that'.[2] But Bilson was certainly not thinking of any situation that might conceivably arise under Elizabeth. It has been suggested, with great probability, that he was intending to justify the revolt of the Netherlands against Philip II.[3] Nevertheless his assertion, confused and hedged about as it is, does illustrate that vague yet strong belief in the supremacy of law, sanctioned by the will of God and attested by antiquity and custom, which made England, in the eyes of the Elizabethans, not an absolute monarchy but a commonwealth.

'Commonwealth' was the term most generally used to describe the body politic throughout the greater part of the sixteenth century. The more impersonal word 'state' was only becoming common during Shakespeare's lifetime and the development of its modern sense can be traced through the plays.[4] 'A Commonwealth', says Sir Thomas Smith, 'is called a society or common doing of a multitude of freemen collected together and united by common accord and covenauntes among themselves, for the conservation of themselves as well in peace as in warre.' It is distinguished from other forms of association by its permanence and by the common purpose which binds together the head and the members. Thus 'an host of men', as Smith goes on to say, is not a commonwealth 'because they are collected but for a time and for a fact: which done, ech divideth himselfe from others as they were before'. Nor is a community of slaves, even under the most benevolent master, 'for the bondman hath no communion with his master, the wealth of the Lord is onely sought for, and not the profit of the slave or bondman'. The Turkish Empire, therefore, where only the Sultan and his sons are freemen, is not a commonwealth but a kingdom.[5] If we ask in what sense the subjects of Elizabeth might regard themselves as free, the answer is that they were subject, not to the arbitrary will of their prince but to the law which, in theory at least, guaranteed the security and the property and personal liberty even of the poorest. As freemen, also, they had the right—and the duty—of carrying out, in their varying social stations, the tasks of government. Smith distinguishes three classes by whom 'the commonwealth, or policie of Englande...is governed, administered, and manured'; the prince, the gentlemen, including both nobles and commoners, and the yeomanry or freeholders. 'Each of these', he says, 'hath his part and administration in judgementes, corrections of defaultes, in election of offices in appointing and collection of tributes and subsidies, or in making lawes.' Thus active membership of the commonwealth is limited to the possession of freehold land, which was, indeed, the only form of tenure to which the common law, as distinct from Equity, gave any protection. But beneath all these, in Smith's analysis, there is another class, probably the most numerous of all, 'the fourth sort of men which doe not rule'. They include day labourers and poor husbandmen, copyholders, even merchants, if they have no freehold, and artificers and craftsmen. 'These', he says, 'have no voice nor authoritie in our commonwealth, and no account is made of them, but onelie to be ruled, and not to rule other, and yet they be not altogether neglected.'[6] They may be impanelled on juries, if sufficient freeholders are not available, and serve as churchwardens, ale-tasters and petty constables. England in Tudor and early Stuart times was a much-governed country and the chain of authority stretched down from the monarch and his Council, with its constant vigilance and overriding powers of supervision, to lords lieutenant, sheriffs and justices of peace, to mayors of boroughs and to officers of the manorial court and the country parish. At every stage power involved burdens, financial liability and perhaps physical danger. Office at the lowest level, though elective, was often an obligation to be evaded rather than an honour to be sought; and often very inadequately performed. Yet even the fourth sort of men might, like Dogberry, be very conscious of bearing the prince's warrant.

The conception of the commonwealth as a hierarchy, as a reflection, or, rather, a part of that 'great chain of being', linking God himself with the soul and body of every individual, which was the design of the universe, is frequent enough in Elizabethan literature and has often been expounded. The words of St Paul apply to all established authority, whether supreme or subordinate. Nor is it a hierarchy of political obligation only for, as Christopher Morris has said, 'It is the whole social order, not merely monarchy, which God has ordained'.[1] As kings were the vice-gerents of God on earth, as human law was a manifestation of His law, so the maintenance of the due ranks and degrees of society is part of the divine plan to which the whole of nature must conform. It is the only safeguard against moral chaos. Should that delicate balance be disturbed,

> Force should be right; or rather, right and wrong—
> Between whose endless jar justice resides—
> Should lose their names, and so should justice too.
> Then every thing includes itself in power,
> Power into will, will into appetite:
> And appetite, an universal wolf,
> So doubly seconded with will and power,
> Must make perforce an universal prey,
> And last eat up himself.   (*Troilus & Cressida*, I, iii, 116)

A Commonwealth, if these theories are strictly interpreted, is thus essentially a static society and its ideal state is one of harmony, with all ranks and classes inspired by a common purpose, each man recognizing his duties to those above him and his responsibilities to those below. Not all Elizabethans, indeed, held that stability was incompatible with change. Sir Thomas Smith, for example, remarks that 'never in all points one Common-wealth doth agree with another, no nor long time any one with itselfe. For all changeth continually to more or lesse, and still to divers and divers orders, as the diversitie of times doe present occasion, and the suitabilitie of mens wits doth invent and assay new wayes to reforme and amend that wherein they doe find fault'.[2] But he does not explain how the process takes place and to most men 'mutability' suggested rather Spenser's Titaness:

> Ne shee the lawes of Nature onely brake,
> But eke of Justice, and of Policie;
> And wrong of right, and bad of good did make,
> And death for life exchanged foolishlie:
> Since which, all living wights have learn'd to die,
> And all this world is woxen daily worse.

O pittious worke of MUTABILITIE!
By which, we all are subiect to that curse,
And death in stead of life have sucked from our Nurse.[1]

This backward-looking view is so contrary to much that we know was happening in the Elizabethan age and to the picture that many later historians have formed of it that it seems worth while inquiring how far the ideal of the commonwealth was ever realized or had any basis in the political and social structure. The belief that all change is for the worse underlies the outspoken social criticism of the Protestant preachers of Edward VI's time, as in the following passage from a sermon of Thomas Lever in 1550:

Therefore the devull poysoninge all hys with greedye Covetousenes, wyll cause them ever to trust to theire owne provision, and never to be content wyth their owne vocacion, but beynge called of God to be marchaunt, gentleman, lawer or courtear, yet to be readye at a Becke of their father the devyl, besides this their godly vocacion, devyllyshlie to proule for, seke and purchase farmes, parsonages, and benefices, to discourage housbandemenne from tyllinge of the grounde, and ministers from preachynge of Goddes woords: that therebye maye come a grevouse honger and dearth, and lacke both of naturall substaunce for the bodye and also of heavenly foode for the soule.[2]

Here we have the germ of the Puritan idea of 'the calling', that it was the Christian's duty not to shun the world but to overcome it by Faith and to sanctify his daily life by labouring diligently in his vocation; an idea which was developed to the point of caricature during the seventeenth century into the belief that Faith, thus manifested in good works, would be rewarded with worldly success. If only the good were prosperous it might easily seem to follow that only the prosperous were good. But to Lever and his contemporaries the emphasis was still on society and not on the individual, on the duty of accepting one's divinely appointed station in life rather than on the opportunities of spiritual or material benefit to be realized in doing so. The same concern for preserving the ancient landmarks of the Commonwealth appears also in the 'Considerations delivered to the Parliament' of 1559, a draft of a legislative programme which is generally attributed to Cecil. Limits are to be set to the annual value of land of inheritance which members of different classes may be allowed to purchase, of £5 for husbandmen, yeomen and artificers, of £10 for clothiers, tanners and common butchers, 'save in cities, towns, and boroughs for their better repair,' and of £50 for merchants, 'except aldermen and sheriffs of London who, because they approach to the degree of knighthood, may purchase to the value of £200'. Apprenticeship is to be confined to the sons of freeholders of 40s. a year and upwards and for merchants' apprentices the minimum is to be £10 a year, unless they are descended from a merchant or a gentleman. The declared purpose of these restrictions throws an interesting light both on the closely knit structure of the Commonwealth and on the social mobility which was threatening to dissolve it: 'Through the idleness of those professions so many embrace them that they are only a cloak for vagabonds and thieves, and there is such a decay of husbandry that masters cannot get skilful servants to till the ground without unreasonable wages.' In order to maintain the universities and grammar schools, only the nobility are to be allowed to keep private schoolmasters. Education at an English or foreign university from the ages of twelve to eighteen is to be made compulsory for the sons of noblemen, so that they may be qualified for the prince's service: and a third of the scholarships in the universities are to be reserved for 'the poorer sort of gentlemen's sons'. Finally, the study of the laws, whether of the civil law at the universities or the common law at the inns of court, is to be the preserve of those immediately descended from a nobleman or a gentleman, 'for they are the entries to rule and government, and generation is the chiefest foundation of inclination'.[1]

This rigid scheme never became law. But the spirit of it can be traced in many aspects of government policy during the reign, particularly in the economic field. Thus, the principle of regulating apprenticeship according to social rank was embodied in the Statute of Artificers. Only the sons of freeholders who were not husbandmen or day-labourers might be apprenticed in cities. Apprenticeship to merchants was limited to the sons of gentlemen or £10 freeholders in cities and to those of £3 freeholders in market towns. Single persons, not being freeholders, were obliged to follow the crafts in which they were brought up. All unemployed persons between twelve and sixty were to become servants in agriculture and the justices or petty constables might 'cause all such artificers and persons as be meet to labour' to work by the day at haymaking or harvest. But if the lower classes were kept in their place it was because theirs was the work most necessary to the Commonwealth and other clauses of the Act provided that contracts of service should be for not less than a year and empowered justices of peace to fix wages according to 'the plenty or scarcity of the time'. The long series of Acts of Tillage, going back to 1489 and designed to check the conversion of arable to pasture, continued in force until 1593 and were renewed in the great depression of 1597. It marks the beginning of a new era when they were finally repealed in 1624 and governments after 1640 abandoned the attempt to resist the process of enclosure. Much of Tudor economic policy has the appearance of rowing against the tide and this is especially so in the special circumstances of the reign of Elizabeth— the depression of the cloth trade after the currency crisis of the 1550's and the later closing of the Antwerp market because of the political troubles in the Netherlands; the bad harvests of the war years and the constantly increasing burden of the poor. The demands of a war economy, while stimulating industrial growth, further intensified that paternal state control which characterized every part of the national life. But if government policy was often restrictive in an age of expansion, this was because its object was rather social than purely economic. Peace and order were more important than prosperity. It was never forgotten by Elizabethan statesmen that 'there is nothing that will soner move the people unto sedicion then the derthe of victuall'.[2]

The contradictions within this system which led eventually to its breakdown are beyond our present scope. But it would be a great mistake to regard it merely as something imposed from above. The hierarchy of order and degree is at the very root of the idea of the Commonwealth and it is a hierarchy based, not on any of the categories applicable to a modern industrial society but on the broad distinction of Gentle and Simple; a distinction, not of wealth, nor, essentially, of rank, but of birth and one not created though it might be modified, by the State. The Heralds' Visitations, which are such an important feature of the social history of the time, were even more concerned with the unwarranted assumption of gentility than with the grant and certification of coats of arms. They had behind them the sanctions of the Earl Marshal's Court and offenders could be fined £10 for ignoring the Heralds' summons and made to suffer the indignity of having their pretensions publicly exposed. In the Shropshire Visitation of 1584, for example, the names of 96 persons who had been found 'most presumptuously to usurpe the name, title and Dignitie of Esquires and Gentlemen' were read out at the market cross at Shrewsbury. The proclamation goes on to 'command all Sherrifes, Commissioners, Archdeacons, Officialls, Scriveners, Clarkes, writers, or other whatsoever not to call, name, or write in any Assize, Sessions, Court, or other open place or places, any one of these persons by the addition of Esquier or Gentleman'.[1]

Such ceremonies must have been performed, from time to time, in most county towns and we can regard them as a practical application of Ulysses' famous speech,

> Degree being vizarded,
> The unworthiest shows as fairly in the mask.

But there is also another side to the picture—painted both by contemporaries and by later historians—which represents the reign of Elizabeth as the golden age of the aspiring *nouveaux riches*. The ultimate test of gentility lay not in any decision of the heralds but in popular acceptance.

For as for gentlemen [in the often quoted words of Sir Thomas Smith], they be made good cheape in England. For whosoever studieth the lawes of the realme, who studieth in the universities, who professeth liberall sciences, and to be shorte, who can live idly and without manuall labour and will beare the port, charge and countenance of a gentleman, he shall be...taken for a gentleman...(and if neede be) a king of Heraulds shal also give him for mony, armes newly made and invented, the title whereof shall pretende to have beene found by the sayd Herauld in perusing and viewing of olde registers, where his auncestors in times past had bin recorded to beare the same.

He concludes that, on the whole, such a manner of making gentlemen is 'not amisse'.[2] The corruption and rapacity of the Heralds' College were never-failing subjects for satire and their learning was often suspect in an age when many of the gentry were themselves no mean antiquaries. But so far from seeking to impose a rigid pattern on society, they were fulfilling a demand. The passion for genealogy which possessed the landed classes—and out of which, incidentally, English medieval scholarship was born—testifies to the vitality of these distinctions and even the relative ease with which the barrier might sometimes be passed is less significant than the general eagerness to pass it. The grounds cited by Clarenceux Cooke for his grant of arms to John Shakespeare in 1596 illustrate very well how flexible the dividing lines of the hierarchy might be; that he had been Bailiff and a Justice of Peace of Stratford. 'That he hath landes & tenementes of good wealth & substance 500 li. That he maried a daughter and heyre of Arden, a gent. of worship.'[3] But a century later, though the College of Arms was by then a much more reputable institution and the Visitations were far better organized, it was the indifference of men like John Shakespeare, on the margin of gentility, that helped to bring the whole system to an end.[4]

The main difference between the social structure of Tudor England and that of the period which followed the Revolution is the relation, in the former, between status and function. The idea of a Commonwealth was to this extent a reality in the sixteenth century as it no longer was in the eighteenth. The greatest nobles in the kingdom and the poorest and most ignorant of country squires were alike gentlemen and there is not yet evident in Elizabethan society any of that jealousy of the peerage which animated Squire Western and his kind and was to be a significant factor in eighteenth-century politics. The nobility were a small and exclusive class, for the Queen was very sparing of new creations and there were only 59 temporal peers at her death. They might be very dangerous to the Crown and to the country if they were allowed to get out of control, as in the fifteenth century and as nearly happened again under Edward VI. But their wealth and social and territorial influence made them still as necessary for the effective exercise of royal power as they had been under even the strongest medieval kings: and so, going down the social scale of the greater and the lesser gentry, members of each rank derived some of their importance from their dependence on members of the rank above. The whole chain of affinity led up to the coveted prizes of court favour which were dispensed, if the system worked smoothly, by the Queen herself. But it was a system, at each stage, of mutual dependence and responsibility. Essex's fear that the loss of the Queen's favour might mean the ruin of his followers or the loss of their support, reveals the forces and influences that held it together. In the absence of a standing army and a strong, centralized bureaucracy or of any element of popular control, it was the only means by which government could be carried on.

The ideal harmony of the different orders of the Commonwealth was exemplified at the highest political level in the harmony between Crown and Parliament. The great Tudors, though they all encountered opposition, yet continued to deal with their Parliaments as one and to preserve the ideal relationship of the head and the members. This tradition was lost under James I, when Bacon deplored the 'brigues and canvasses' to which Salisbury resorted in trying to form a court party in the House of Commons.[1] The social foundations of unity rested on class divisions which, though not rigid, were yet deep; so deep, indeed, and tacitly recognized that they admitted of a greater freedom of actual social intercourse than in the much less formally hierarchal society of the eighteenth century. The period between Henry VIII and Charles II was the great age of the country grammar school, where the sons of burgesses and of the neighbouring gentry were educated together. School registers and numerous autobiographies and memoirs show how common this custom was under the Stuarts, when it produced political leaders of the importance of Hampden and Cromwell. The earlier evidence is slighter and there is no aspect of Elizabethan history about which we would wish to know more. But we do know that Sir Philip Sidney and Sir Fulke Greville were educated at Shrewsbury, Burghley at Stamford, Coke at Norwich and Sir Walter Raleigh at one of two or three grammar schools in Devonshire. The number of ordinary members of Parliament educated in this way must, we may suppose, have been considerable and of justices of peace larger still. The only pupil at Stratford grammar school for whom there is any documentary evidence at this time was, as it happens, of gentle birth: Henry Dineley, of the ancient landed family of the Dineleys of Charlton, near Evesham.[2] The influence of this educational background, common to gentle and simple, is, of course, impossible to estimate precisely. The sons of squires and the sons of tradesmen who learned their Latin together would have had many opportunities of contact in after life, for the official and business connections between the boroughs and the local magnates were too numerous and close to be discussed here. But it must have had an effect, which is often overlooked, on the tone of society which was lost when the grammar schools declined and the great public schools began to emerge as the accepted training grounds for the sons of the aristocracy.

If we may try to reconstruct the outlook of the average Elizabethan on the state and on public affairs, we find it so closely bound within a theological and juridical framework as to leave little room for what we understand by politics. In a sermon at Whitehall on 15 November 1601, when the Commons were debating the Queen's demand for an unprecedentedly large grant of supply, Lancelot Andrewes took occasion to comment on the text in Romans xiii, 'for this cause pay ye tribute also': 'For this', he says, 'that while we intend our private pleasures and profits in particular, we have them that study how we may safely and quietly do it, that counsel and contrive our peace, while we intend every man his own affairs; that wake while we sleep securely, and cark and care while we are merry and never think of it.'[1] Many of his hearers would soon have to confront their country neighbours and constituents with the unpalatable news of further heavy taxation and persuade them to pay it without demur. We may regard his remarks, therefore, as soothing court doctrine, to encourage them in their task. None the less, he can be taken as expressing the attitude which most ordinary men were contented to adopt. Parliament, or 'the Parliament', to use the Elizabethan phrase—the definite article is itself significant—was as yet no part of the regular machinery of government and outside Parliament there was no lawful means at all for the organized expression of political opinion. Anything like the movements and agitations which have characterized English political life during the past two centuries were not only officially regarded as seditious and treasonable, but were apt to become so, however law-abiding the intentions of their leaders. This is abundantly clear from the history of most sixteenth-century rebellions. Characteristically, the nearest approach to modern political organization was made by the Puritans, for religion had more power than any secular issue to stir masses of men. Nor could this be otherwise so long as politics were centred on the Court. To those outside this charmed circle, and unconnected with it, they might be a matter of interest and wonder, a theme perhaps for moral reflection on the doings of

> packs and sects of great ones
> That ebb and flow by the moon.   (*Lear*, v, iii, 18)

But they could be no part of their daily lives. If we judge the Elizabethan monarchy from the modern political standpoint, with its conceptions of discussion and public opinion, it may well appear as a despotism. But the ideal of the Commonwealth, as Shakespeare and his contemporaries understood it, was not, in our sense, a political ideal. It was an ideal of justice, of duty, of unity rather than freedom to differ, of the manifestation of the will of God. The field of activity was thus narrowed down, was, as we might say, more than half withdrawn from this world and from the influence of any one generation. In any analysis of Elizabethan political thought these limitations have to be borne in mind. It is a measure of the greatness of the age that they were still consistent with a vigorous communal life and that they released rather than confined such a tremendous outburst of creative energy.

9

DISSENT AND SATIRE

'The malice of this age'

I

Half a century ago, in the opening chapter of *Shakespeare's England*, Sir Walter Raleigh boldly declared that

Our most intimate knowledge of Elizabethan England is given us by writers who found in the life and changes of the time matter for complaint and protest. Town or country makes no difference, all were agreed that the world was hastening to decay.

Such statements, clearly contentious, will receive no more approval than any other generalizations about the familiar subjects of Elizabethan and Jacobean pessimism, cynicism and discontent. Yet the changes in the life of the age were so momentous, religious, social and literary, and the divisions so extreme, that for Englishmen of roughly Shakespeare's generation the sheer contrariety of experience presented an exceptional intensity, at once the condition of their everyday lives, a pattern for thought, and a stimulus to art. For many the condition was intolerable, the pattern fragmented, and the stimulus a goad, provoking controversy and ridicule. Such were the religious martyrs, social malcontents and literary satirists, opponents of the establishment in the English Church, of the Court factions, or of the social and literary hierarchy of established values and reputations.

Their voices tell us directly of an England about which Shakespeare speaks only obliquely, but they are necessary for the fullest understanding of his time. For it is a paradox worthy of a literature that so constantly asserted contradiction that its greatest writer came to maturity as an age declined and its ideals came under severe scrutiny. It seems probable indeed that most historians, while subscribing to Tawney's famous dictum that during Elizabeth's reign England attained 'a balanced society', would share Sir John Neale's qualified view that

The balance did not last long; and one may doubt whether it could have done so. It was not there in November 1558 when Elizabeth came to the throne, and it was in jeopardy in March 1603 when she died. Like other societies, the Elizabethan age contained the seeds of its own decay.[1]

The seeds of religious dissent, political discontent and social complaint were sown early in the reign and were flowering profusely at its close; they are arguably of so similar stock that there is sufficient justification for treating them in close relationship.

II

Throughout Elizabeth's reign religious dissent offered, on the one hand, the prospect of international aggression to re-establish the old religion, and, on the other, domestic discord fostered by demands for further reformation in the Church established. The Bills of Uniformity and Supremacy of 1559 made clear the reaffirmation of the breach with Rome and of complicated relationships with the reformed churches of the continent. Bishop Jewel's 'Challenge Sermon' of that year, preached twice at Paul's Cross and once at Court, challenged Catholics to prove— from Scripture, Church doctors, Councils, or the general example of the primitive Church— twenty-seven articles of belief or practice, from the doctrine of the real presence in the sacrament to communion under one kind, or the use of Latin. His *Apologia Ecclesiae Anglicanae* (1562), in Latin and English, maintained that the English Church preserved the whole substance of the Catholic faith, a position unacceptable to papists and an emphasis disliked by puritans.

The challenge was directly taken up by Catholic scholars forced by the Act of 1563 into exile, 'the more learned sort', according to Persons, concentrating within the University of Louvain.[1] Their quality was indeed high: Nicholas Sander, Regius Professor of Canon Law at Oxford, headed a body of Wykhamists there, and there, too, went William Allen, former Principal of St Mary's Hall, Oxford, future Cardinal, eventual founder of the English College at Douai in 1568, and ultimately leader of the exiled Catholics. His *Apologie and true declaration of the institution and endeauours of the two English Colleges* (1581), describes their aims as, first, 'to draw diuers youths, who then for their conscience liued in the low Countries, from sole, seueral, and voluntarie studie, to a more exact methode and course of common conference'; second, since 'age, emprisonment, or other miserie' must eventually reduce the older men, it was 'a necessarie duety for the posteritie, to prouide for a perpetual feede and supply of Catholikes, namely of the Clergie'; and third, for the 'better furnishing of meete men' and 'for disaduantaging the adversarie part therin' it was hoped to attract 'the best wittes out of England, that were either Catholikly bent, or desirous of more exact education then is these daies in either of the Vniuersities'.

The success of this last intention became evident, particularly at Oxford, and was a cause of contention for many years after; it was small consolation that the superiority of their English training was recognized in the remodelling of European seminaries under the belated influence of the Council of Trent, and its insistence upon spiritual renewal, scholarly and cultural improvement. These were precisely the main concern of the early exiles, 'nothing mistrusting' said Allen, 'but the time and opportunities would come (were they neere, were they far of) when they might take advantage for restitution of religion, no Sect euer being liked long, nor permanent without enterchange'.

The permanence of the Elizabethan compromise in religion, then, was not foreseen by papists or accepted by puritans. 'Enterchange' was a notion natural to a generation which had seen the successive alteration in religious practices under Henry VIII, Edward VI, Mary Tudor and now Elizabeth. The 'Great Controversy' was to continue for more than twenty years, occasioning above sixty works, and drawing from Gabriel Harvey special praise for those 'two thundring and lightning Oratours in diuinity', Jewel and Harding. By 1576, when Robert Bellarmine became Professor of Controversial Theology at the Roman College, the thunderous tirade and the learned lightning were long confirmed as the climatic condition of Europe.

But the bull of 1570, *Regnans in Excelsis*, excommunicating Elizabeth as 'a heretic and an abettor of heretics' and absolving her subjects from allegiance, had brought a latent issue from the sphere of polemics to that of action, and though it clarified matters for the English government, it raised a dilemma for the English Catholics which more than any other single cause divided them and ensured their self-defeat. Government response was swift. Recusancy, in the broad sense of non-attendance at the English service, was made punishable by fine. Acts of 1571 provided penalties of praemunire for the introduction of devotional objects into England; and to deny Elizabeth's lawful title, to attempt the subversion of her subjects by proselytizing, or to possess papal bulls, became treason. In 1573 Edmund Campion made representations at Rome about the issue of loyalty, and after Pius' death Gregory XIII ruled in 1580 that obedience might be given to Elizabeth as *de facto* ruler until the provisions of the bull could be put into effect.

The Jesuit missionaries from that year onwards made repeated use of this ruling in allaying the fears of English laymen. But to Elizabeth and her ministers it constituted a sword of Damocles. However much the missioners' rule of conduct forbade involvement in matters of state, the borderlines were difficult to distinguish, and controversy had already crossed them. Most notably, John Leslie's *A Treatise of Treasons* (Louvain, 1572), accused Lord Keeper Bacon and Lord Treasurer Cecil of political treachery. A proclamation of 1573, one of many, banned all Catholic books.

The attempted separation of pastoral duties from the larger international issues became impossible to maintain. While the memory of the Northern Rising of 1569 was fresh, while Mary Stuart lived, plotting was inevitable; as the Ridolfi affair and its successors proved, rebellion was possible, the Spanish danger insistent, and the religious wars of France and the Netherlands ominous portents. It was perhaps as much tacit recognition of the insoluble dilemma that prompted Campion to place himself under the leadership of his junior Persons on the first mission of 1579|80: the submission of the martyr to the politician reflects to some extent the changing pattern of Catholic dissent. For, though friends, they typified extremes of simplicity and subtlety. With a wholly Elizabethan confidence in his accomplished oratory Campion wrote his 'Letter to the Lords of the Council' of 1580, printed as *The great bragge and challenge*, and demanding 'iii sortes of indifferent and quiet audience', of the Council, of University representatives, and of spiritual and temporal lawyers, proposing to resolve the tremendous issues by 'combat with all and every one of them'. The outcome was complex: Elizabeth and Leicester offered patronage, in return for conformity, to the man whom Cecil had called 'one of the diamonds of England'; he was tortured to reveal the names of Catholic adherents and the whereabouts of mass-centres; and Bishop Aylmer arranged four Disputes in the Tower with scholarly opponents before his execution. The issues were never to be so simply presented as in Campion's famous *Decem Rationes*, or so neatly displayed as in their surreptitious printing and circulation in St Mary's Oxford on the eve of Commencement. Persons, by contrast, began his extensive epistolary work with a brief discourse offered to Elizabeth of the *Reasons Why Catholiques Refuse* (1580) to attend service, and maintaining the cause of conscience rather than obstinacy. Alban Langdale's contention that attendance should be permitted to avoid the increasing penalties and persecution shows the extent of disagreement among English Catholics over authority, aggravated by the reluctance of Rome to nominate bishops to the English sees. The brief flurry of support for Langdale shows topical sensitivity and the arising of a new kind of controversy.

Tempers had changed significantly. The earliest exiles had dedicated works to Elizabeth, and the incidental sarcasm of their writings was often likely to appeal to her own known prejudices, such as the mockery of married clergy ('But is it grauitie for a Bushop with a graye bearde in his extreme age to waxe wantone, and to wade in loue with a light mayde?' asked Lewis Evans),[1] or the ridicule of language and conduct used by the extreme reformers. But as the debate increasingly centred on national survival, so both the polemical tone, and the penalties, worsened. A proclamation of 1581 recalled those 'subjects which under pretence of studies do live beyond the seas both contrary to the laws of God and of the realm'; and the relatives of seminarists were required to recover them or lose civil rights. The Council gave renewed prominence to existing laws, under which to say or attend mass was punishable by fine, priests were outlaws and to harbour them was treason and sedition. The murder of William of Orange in 1584, the formation of the Protestant Association in that year under Leicester's leadership, the publication of *Leicester's Commonwealth*, all showed new tensions in international and home affairs, and the scurrility of the attack on Leicester touched a new vein of impotent violence more seriously reflected in the fanaticism of the Babington conspiracy. From then on, as a broadside put it,

> A seminary Priest, like Comets Blaze,
> Doth always Blood-shed and Rebellion Raise.

The seminaries also raised mutinous voices among their own flock, and while some answered Campion's cry of 'alarm spiritual', others made renewed efforts, encouraged by the Council under Cecil's prominent lead, and activated by renewed quarrels between secular clergy and Jesuits over problems of discipline, to reach some measure of accommodation with the state. The pre-Armada decade was crucial for the Catholics in all aspects. Politically, the execution of Mary Stuart in 1587 brought new complexities of competiton among the Franco–Scottish and Spanish factions of the exiles, and divisions between them and Catholics at home widened with the years. Socially, the punitive precaution of 1587, declaring lands and all goods of a convicted recusant forfeit to the Crown, brought lawlessness in support of the law, widespread insecurity and much local treachery. For the system of pursuivants ranged from legally controlled Servants of the Privy Council and Queen's Messengers, and officials of the Bishops, to marauding individuals, among whom apostate priests were the most dangerous, and organized bands of profit-sharing protectionists and extortioners.

In the face of a divided spiritual leadership and a heavily penalized lay leadership, coupled with a growing detestation of foreign influence, it is scarcely surprising that Cardinal Allen's eventual call for rebellion, in his *Admonition* on the eve of the Armada, went unanswered. For the accumulated experience of a bitter decade can be seen clearly in Robert Southwell's *An Humble Supplication to her Majestie* of 1591, which contrasts so strikingly with Campion's challenge to the Council, or the tone of Persons' own *Admonition to the People of England* of 1588, declaring Elizabeth 'the offspring of adultery and incest, a heretic and maintainer of heretics, a lascivious tyrant and unholy perjurer, a woman odious alike to God and man'. Southwell affirms loyalty to the Queen, and believes that the loyalty of Catholics had been sufficiently demonstrated during the Armada scare, though in the absence of a landing the point was unproven. More importantly, he acknowledges that proper conduct in a future crisis must be pacifism. The value of Southwell's appeal, however, does not lie in its handling of international policy, its rejection of fanatical plots, or its attempt to defend the conduct of Allen and Persons against their derogatory description in a proclamation of 1591 as 'vnnatural subjects of our

Kingdom (but yet very base of birth)' who have gathered together 'a multitude of dissolute young men...Fugitives, Rebelles, and Traitors'. More important for the understanding of these difficult years is its frank picture of the social chaos occasioned by persecution. He writes[1] of 'the continual hel we suffer by the merciles searching and storming of pursevants and such needy officers', who 'build their houses with the ruines of ours', who 'make our willes before we be sicke', and 'by displanting our ofspring adopt themselves to be heirs of our lands, beging and broking for them, as if we were either condemned for fooles, or in perpetual minority'. The summing up is passionate and precise: 'We are accounted men, whom it is a credit to pursue, a disgrace to protect, a commodity to spoil, a gaine to torture, and a glory to kill.'

Southwell was no politician: he did not realize that loyalty to Elizabeth as her reign neared its end was irrelevant and embarrassing. His book was left unprinted in his lifetime. Had it been so printed, it is doubtful if its plea for toleration would have been acknowledged, for as the international threat of direct Spanish domination receded, Government anxiety was freshly alerted and transferred to the subject of renewed Puritan vitality.

III

The sudden emergence of this threat is vividly conveyed by Bishop Thomas Cooper's *An Admonition to the Church and People of England* (1589):

Oh my good Brethren and louing Country men, what a lamentable thing is this, that euen nowe, when the view of the mightie Nauie of the Spaniards is scant passed out of our sight; when the terrible sound of their shot ringeth, as it were, yet in our eares...when our Christian duetie requireth for ioy and thankesgiuing, that we should bee seene yet still lifting vp our hands and hearts to heauen...and saying, 'The Lorde hath triumphed gloriously, the horse and the Rider, the Ships and the Saylers, the souldiers and their Captaines hee hath ouerthrown in the Sea: the Lorde is our strength, the Lorde is become our saluation, &c' That euen nowe (I say) at this present time, wee should see in mens handes and bosomes, commonly slaunderous Pamphlets fresh from the Presse, against the best of the Church of Englande.[2]

By the best, of course, were meant the bishops, and by the pamphlets those of the Marprelate controversy. It was by no means an unprepared onslaught, but its dangers were of a new kind. The stages of Puritan dissent had shown an increasing intransigence. At the beginning of the reign their objections had most directly been made against vestments and liturgy laid down in the Ornaments Rubric of 1559. There was a diversity of practice which caused Elizabeth to seek uniformity and prompted the vestiarian controversy, but long though this continued it was less momentous than the succeeding troubles over all matters of discipline. For rule and ceremony could not be divorced from accepted authority, and just as Catholic dissent had brought conflict inevitably with the State itself, so Puritan dissent was always to find its natural opponents in the bishops and its ultimate quarrel with an authority beyond theirs. Where Catholics directed their arguments to individual controversialists, or more generally to Queen, Council or people, it is significant that Puritans more frequently addressed themselves to Parliament. Here lay not only power, but a considerable measure of support. Many parliamentarians were Puritans in sympathy, more so as the universities began to supply members. The challenge to discipline came most strongly after the dismissal of Thomas Cartwright from his Chair of Divinity at Cambridge in 1570, when Cecil was Chancellor and Whitgift Vice-Chancellor.

It was a two-fold attack by direct appeal and by subsequent organization of reformist congregations. The *Admonition to Parliament* of 1572 sets out the 'true platform of a church reformed, to the end that it beyng layd before your eyes, to beholde the great unlikeness betwixt it and this our english church'. To purify the Church three things were declared necessary—'preachynge of ye worde purely', 'ministering of the sacramentes sincerely', and 'ecclesiastical discipline'.

Despite their champions, such as the Wentworths, in Parliament, and their sympathizers, such as Leicester, among ministers, the Puritans found more immediate progress with the building of a 'true platform' in the gatherings known as the prophesyings. These joined clergy and laity in the study and exposition of Scripture, in imitation of the *classis* of the reformed churches. John Field, co-author with Wilcox of the *Admonition*, lived like John Foxe in Grub Street and had collected material for the *Acts and Monuments*. Suspended from preaching because of refusal over vestments, Field became the leader of the extremist faction, condemned by older Puritans in much the same way as the later Marprelate controversialists were to be disowned. Cartwright's teaching at Cambridge had trained a new generation of young men, and in their different activities Field and Cartwright sought to contain this new element and prevent it from the continuing danger of a separatist movement. Archbishop Grindal supported the prophesyings, as a necessary educative influence better retained and controlled than suppressed, and was himself suspended by Elizabeth when the meetings were suppressed in 1577. By then Cartwright was abroad in the Palatinate and the Low Countries, and Field was lying low, under protection. The contacts with continental reformers maintained by such appointments as Walter Travers to the congregation of the Merchant Adventurers at Antwerp, where he was succeeded by Cartwright, was a further means of intellectual cross-fertilization, and it has been well demonstrated that 'English puritanism, far from being the insular phenomenon which it is sometimes represented, was part of an internationally revolutionary movement'.[1]

The total nature of the demands concerning discipline was becoming evident. The vestiarian controversy was declining in importance: Gabriel Harvey reported 'No more adoe about Cappes and Surplesses'[2] in Cambridge in 1580. But the crucial issue of ecclesiastical authority carried clearly irreconcilable views of the interpretation of scriptural teaching on church government.

The discussion of matters arising from the desired transformation from an Episcopal to a Presbyterian Church revived more openly in the 1580's, which saw government concentration upon Catholic activities. In 1583 Whitgift's appointment as Archbishop of Canterbury was followed by the drawing up of fresh articles demanding uniformity. The use of Catholic surreptitious printing presses, at Tower Hill, in Greenstreet, and at Smithfield, together with the traffic in continental printed books both Catholic and Puritan, caused fresh stringency in printing regulations.

More than any other cause, the tensions generated by restraint, both in direct censorship and indirect (such as the restriction imposed upon Cartwright's refutation of the Rheims *New Testament*), together with an atmosphere made favourable by hostility to Catholic activities, occasioned the temper of the Martin Marprelate tracts. The ponderous tone of the official contributions to this controversy contrasted markedly with the spirited mockery of 'Martin's' writings and induced an audience tired of 'admonitions' to follow the lively cut and thrust of a new propaganda, conducted with a vigour reminiscent of Tudor interludes.

The lesson was clear to the authorities, who took direct and indirect action. While the Ecclesiastical Commissioners sought for the authors of the tracts, discovering and destroying the presses but failing to identify the writers, Bancroft found more effective ways of answering their damaging popularity, by finding work for the idle hands of impecunious University Wits, Greene, Nashe, Lyly and Richard Harvey. Furthermore, 'Martin' was brought on the stage 'attired like an Ape', or in ludicrous make-up, or in 'a cocks combe, an apes face, a wolfs belie'; he was whipped, and wormed; it was feigned that he attempted the rape of Divinity, and poisoned her with a vomit. Some of this dramatic farce failed to pass the official censors. The City protested against the mob appeal of the plays, and a new cynicism was being bred as a consequence of helpless authority. But though 'Martin' was never caught, by 1593, when Udall died in prison under suspicion, and Penry was executed for complicity, the immediate threat was much diminished.

IV

In fact, by about 1593, when Shakespeare was established as a playwright, both major parties of religious dissent were in confusion and dismayed. The varieties of experience among their members, extreme and moderate, testify to the fragmentation of late Elizabethan society in certain aspects, and Stratford, during Shakespeare's formative years, was perhaps as divided as any town. Francis Smith, for instance, Lord of the Manor of Shottery, was Catholic in 1564 and had conformed by 1586. The younger William Clopton, the only esquire in Stratford in 1580, and his wife Anne, were recusants. Fervour and fanaticism were both evident; Thomas Cottam, younger brother of schoolmaster John Cottam (who was teaching from 1579 to 1581), was executed with Edmund Campion; and John Somerville of Edstone in 1583 set off on his strange journey to London with the intention of murdering Elizabeth. John Shakespeare appears twice in the recusancy rolls, and William bought New Place from the recusant William Underhill in 1597.[1] The old religion was in retreat in Stratford, and Puritan dominance in local affairs was becoming evident, most markedly shown by the ban upon players visiting the town in 1602. That the town was divided is plain enough from the manner in which old grievances burst into public disorder a few years after Shakespeare's death.

Of such dissentious matters Shakespeare's plays give us little enough reference. 'Old Poysam the papist and young Charbon the puritan' are not brought upon his stage; pursuivants make images ('These grey locks, the pursuivants of death', *1 Henry VI*, II, v) not characters; his stage church is medieval, not that of the counter-reformation or the reformed religion; and Malvolio is no puritan. Yet the experience is there, sometimes explicitly revealed in such topical references as those to 'equivocation' in *Hamlet*, *Macbeth* and *Othello*, transmuted more deeply in the discussion of grace in *Hamlet*, *Macbeth* or *Measure for Measure*. And in part such transmutation was possible because of the clarification of extreme issues for men of Shakespeare's generation, the equal poise achieved by Hooker and later by Bacon, could be won afresh in the arts, most significantly at a period when its tensions were still vital, and imbalance always an alternative.

126

V

The point of balance in national affairs had indeed been passed during the last decade of the century, if realization of the fact was slow to come. For though that universal upheaval and destruction of empires prophesied by Regiomontanus, and given wide European currency for many years, had been decisively disproved, 1588 was to remain, in the terms of John Harvey's refutation, the 'Great-wonderful and Fatel Yeare of our Age'. The wonder lay in the victorious climax to thirty years of patiently sought national unity; the fatality simply in that the unity depended so directly upon the Queen. While the 'great deliverance', as S. T. Bindoff observes, 'served to grapple Queen and nation together with the steel hoops of tried comradeship' it also 'loosened the bands forged between them by the fears of the past. Those fears had proved to be liars, and their explosion cracked and weakened the crust of ideas and habits which had accreted round them'.[1] Moreover, those whom he calls 'The Old Guard of Elizabethan England' were passing from parade. Leicester barely survived the Armada, Chancellor Mildmay and Secretary Walsingham were dead by 1590, followed by Shrewsbury, Hunsdon, Knollys; Drake, last of the sea captains for an era, died in 1596, Burghley in 1598. And Sir John Neale notes that the 'new generation coming into power in the 1590's was out of touch with the old Queen and her ways'.[2] Donne's 'Utopian youth, grown old Italian' were being replaced by men of new policies.

The struggles for reversion to office among the factions at court, notably Robert Cecil, the Earl of Essex, and the cryptic Bacon, were a reflection of the larger problem of the Succession. The situation, long precarious, both paralysed and demanded action.

> Actions crowne vertues, and like pulses proue
> Whither the soul of's greatnes sweetlie moue
> With natures harmoney: which standing still
> Or faintlie beatinge shew them dead or ill.[3]

Raleigh was to say cruelly of Elizabeth that she was 'a lady whom Time had surprised', and the remark has been applied to Burghley also.[4] For though the cult of personality was intensified, in popular ballad, acrostical sonnet, court compliment, and devotional prayer, that chastity which had been the shield of England and the bait of dynastic courtship was ultimately to be acknowledged as a barrenness breeding problems graver than the strange progenies of Elizabethan broadsides.

As Elizabeth approached the grand climacteric of 63 years in 1596 both the specific discussion and the general pessimism can be seen displayed in two tracts of the times. 'Hispaniolated' Persons turned his interests from the papal deposing power to legitimatist claims to the English Crown, and presided over the composite work known briefly as the *Book of Succession*, issued at Antwerp in 1594, and dedicated to Essex.[5] Aquaviva, seeing that the topic 'touches and can cause offence to great persons and princes' tried to suppress it. Robert Beale, Clerk of the Council, thought the dedication would bring Essex 'into jealousy and disgrace here'. Rowland Whyte reported to Sir Robert Sydney that the Earl 'was observed to look wan and pale, being exceedingly troubled at this great piece of villainy done unto him'. The malice was probably unintentional, the dedication most likely by Sir Francis Englefield. A week later Essex had 'put off the melancholy he fell into by a printed book'. But the argument was more pernicious.

Its central thesis was that a sovereign could be deposed for failing to honour the compact with the people, from whom power was derived. Central to the compact was true religion, a more important factor in succession than nearness of blood. Thus, as a heretic, James VI had less claim than other foreign claimants, among whom Persons preferred the Infanta of Spain. The book came out against a background of fear generated by report of a Jesuit and Portuguese conspiracy which was to cost Dr Lopez, the Portuguese Jew, his life. A more direct result was Cecil's investigation, necessarily secret, of the Infanta's claim and the nature of her support, which brought unjustified suspicion upon him. The book was used both against Persons by his enemies among the exiles, and against Essex at his trial, but when the latter rode through the London streets crying 'The Crown is sold to the Spaniard' he was the victim of rumours rather than the revealer of secrets.[1]

By contrast William Covell offered to Essex, perhaps in recompense, *Polimanteia, or the meanes lawfull and vnlawfull to iudge of the fall of a commonwealth, against the frivolous and foolish conjectures of this age* (1595). His preface declares that 'We are fallen into the barren age of the world', and he is concerned to dispel pessimism by common sense. He gathers up philosophy, history, divinity, and astrology. The latter teaches us 'prestigious and false surmises'; of Bodin's historical fears about September Covell remarks 'In every month great states have died'; of commonplaces about the harmony of the spheres he reminds his readers of the equal importance and protection in the 'harmony of good laws'. Dismissing arguments against impending disaster, he allows weight to the evidence of sheer time, since 'the most parte of the greatest kingdomes, haue not endured *five hundred yeares*', or seven hundred years, which happens to be the time since Charles the Great 'established the westerne Empyre'. However, though this 'seemeth to threaten some great ruine' Covell concludes that there is 'nothing so of necessitie, but as it pleaseth God to dispose all things for the best'.[2] Ultimately, Scripture tells us of three sins especially ruinous to a commonwealth, impiety in the church, injustice in the commonwealth, lechery destroying the family.

Such moralizing is familiar enough at all times, and it is understandable that this period of particular difficulty should produce propositions long current among philosophers, poets and divines concerning mutability and ruin, touched with fresh intensity. That there was a 'sensible decay and age in the whole frame of the world' as Donne would phrase it, was not, of course, a discovery of the new learning, but traditional teaching, Stoical and Christian, classical and medieval. Similarly, the fiction of the Golden world was transmitted not only by poets of moral allegory, but by moralists of prosaic literalness. Philip Stubbes approved the opinion of Theodorus that 'we are fallen into...*Ferrea* or *Plumbea aetas*, the yron or leaden age, in as much as now men are fallen from all godlinesse whatsoeuer, and are as it were wedded to iniquitie'.[3]

Few Elizabethan writers avoided sententiousness or remained unmoved by moral commonplaces. Most cultivated habits of mind which saw interrelation and interpenetration between divine, cosmic and human affairs found earthly corruption mirrored in the heavens, believed pestilence a punishment for sin, and conceived that 'her Maiestie and Counsell is as it were *primum mobile*, whatsoeuer moueth must begin from thence, and by direction from thence, must all the rest moue as vpon the axetree, which carieth about al the gouernment of this commonwealth'.[4] For minds so habituated Nature too evidently conspired with Time in the closing years of the sixteenth century: the last seven harvests failed, famine joined with plague in 1592 and recurred in 1602 and 1603, reducing the population and aggravating the economic setback in almost every area of trade (that of East India excepted), to such an extent that in 1597 'the purchasing power of wages fell lower than perhaps at any time between the thirteenth century and the present day'.[1]

Ultimately, it is against such real and sombre evils as the political stagnation caused by an aging administration, 'a government running out of ideas', natural disasters, expediency in political behaviour, an inability to cope with long-established corruptions such as monopolies, rack-rents, enclosures and usury, that we must set both the phenomena of real and affected melancholy, and the bold movement of 'satire, keen and critical' in the decades before and after 1600.

VI

That the changing tone and increased popularity of satire in the 1590's is predominantly the work of younger men is clear enough. The men coming to literary power then were the heirs of a social revolution in literature as in society. The bitter experience of the University Wits was apparent; they had turned from the professions of their fathers to attempt careers in literature with conspicuous social insecurity. The dangers of the expansion of educational opportunities without any serious corresponding provision of employment had long been foreseen, as Mulcaster wrote in 1581:

To have so many gaping for preferment, as no gulf hath store to suffice, and to let them roam helpless whom nothing else can help, how can it be but that such shifters must needs shake the very strongest pillar in that state where they live, and loiter without living?[2]

Those who, like Daniel, found patronage among the great, were sensitive to the thought that

> this busy world cannot attend
> Th'untimely music of neglected lays.
> Other delights than these, other desires,
> This wiser profit-seeking age requires.

It was not easy, however, to leave

> the left and outworn course
> Of unregarded ways, and labour how
> To fit these times with what is most in force;
> Be new with men's affections that are new.

For many of the University Wits had tried precisely to effect such an adjustment, cynically observed in Daniel's lines, from the world of their education to the wider world of their future living. They had appealed to all, had sought independence as artists, and met discouragement from patron and public alike. Their rewards were to be summed up with succinctness in Lyly's famous letter to Elizabeth in 1598; 'But three legacies I bequeath, Patience to my creditors, Melancholy without measure to my friends, and Beggary without shame to my family'.

Nashe stands at the cross-roads in this matter of patronage, and hesitates in several directions. In *Pierce Penniless* (1592) he offers to repay 'any Mecoenas' for 'rough liberalitie' with as much honour as 'any Poet of my beardless yeeres in England'; or alternatively, to 'raile on him soundly' if 'sent away with a Flea in mine eare'.[1]

The Wits, by working at full stretch, could make a precarious living, yerking up their pamphlets at short notice, patching, reworking and repeatedly self-plagiarizing, alike in roguery and romance. They could also appeal to a public and express something of their own insecurity by turning back to the traditions of medieval homily and didactic moralizing. Much of *Pierce Penniless*, for instance, presents the Seven Deadly Sins, satirically portrayed in contemporary dress and behaviour, but still labelled conventionally Avarice, Pride or Drunkenness.[2] Lodge's *Wits Miserie and the Worlds Madness* (1596), indebted heavily to this most popular of Nashe's works, augments these sins with a new brood, such as Derision, Hypocrisy or Boasting (who sits daily in the stationer's shop 'Iibing and fleering ouer euery pamphlet with Ironical iests'). Lodge makes a notable effort to bring in view both old and new devilry, like Vainglory, son of Pride, stalking in Paul's in the guise of a gallant, or sycophantic Adulation 'ietting in Noblemens cast apparrell', or Sedition flying overseas for 'colours of religion'. But the Apocalyptic tone and the burden of moralizing demanded by popular taste, and indulged in by Nashe and Lodge, is shed when prose gives way to epigrammatic ease, in verse satire and quick prose character. Nor is the contrast merely formal, for the work of young men such as Donne, Sir John Davies, Guilpin and Marston at the Inns of Court, or of Joseph Hall at Emmanuel College, is markedly different in temper from that of the University Wits. That these men began a new satirical movement is attested by Francis Meres in 1598. They shared similar subject-matter, though their attitudes towards it are often distinct.

This is perhaps plainest in their treatment of religion, especially if the work of younger men is contrasted with an old reprobate like Sir John Harington, whose superior social position and cast of mind make him unique among Elizabethan epigrammatists. He jibes at many matters, but fundamentally, and particularly in religious affairs, he displays a tolerance, not much removed from indifference, amply shown in his epigram 'Of two religions', where the major spiritual crisis of his lifetime is resolved, as it probably was for many people, in a quibble. A father asks his son whether he finds the reformed church or the unreformed church 'safest for his soule':

> 'Sure' quoth the sonn, 'a man had neede be crafty
> To keepe his soule and body both in safty.
> But both to save, this best way to houlde;
> Live in the new, dy yf you can in th'olde'.[3]

For Donne such hypocrisy is a target of satire not its substance. His 'Satyre III' offers the famous debate, a mimicry of the momentous choice of Paris, between the loves of Rome, Geneva and Canterbury, wherin the suitably named Mirreus, Grantz and Graius court respectively true religion, at Rome

> because hee doth know
> That shee was there a thousand yeares agoe,

at Geneva, where she is called

> Religion, plaine, simple, sullen, yong,
> Contemptuous, yet unhansome,

or 'at home here' because

> Some Preachers, vile ambitious bauds, and lawes
> Still new like fashions, bid him thinke that shee
> Which dwels with us, is onely perfect.

Three other young men, however, find further possibilities: 'Carelesse Phrygius' scorns all, 'Graccus loves all as one', and the unnamed, because untypical, seeks truth and moves beyond satirical observation;

> Hee's not of none, nor worst, that seekes the best.
> To adore, or scorne an image, or protest,
> May all be bad; doubt wisely; in strange way
> To stand inquiring right, is not to stray.

Donne's satires are excoriating of postures which seem inviting, cherishing persons and attitudes offering protective sanity. His recusant origins are exposed like sores to the competing corruptions of a hostile society, but throughout his long progress from private fears to public faith he refrains from arrogating to himself the role of didactic moralist. He had been in

> A Purgatorie, such as fear'd hell is
> A recreation to, and scarse map of this.

And his judgement on the whole tumultuous variety of vanities and malicious practices which he itemized in his scrutiny of the court world preserves a distinction:

> Preachers which are
> Seas of Wit and Arts, you can, then dare,
> Drowne the sinnes of this place, for, for mee
> Which am but a scarse brooke, it enough shall bee
> To wash the staines away.

This serious concern with the purpose of satire is found most appropriately among the future preachers, Donne, Hall, Marston or Thomas Bastard. It is least evident in light-witted humorists, like Sir John Davies or Guilpin, for whom all matters and all manners can be compounded in felicitous salacity. Primed with classical precept, light-fingeredly indebted to past authority or present accomplice, such wits set out to make short spokes of the long stakes of men. Easy victims are the gallants, fops and gulls of court, city or Bankside: Cornelius, sitting 'o're the stage', tobacco-pipe in mouth, seems 'new printed to this fangled age',

> He weares a Ierkin cudgeld with gold lace,
> A profound slop, a hat scarce pipkin high,
> For boots, a paire of dagge cases: his face
> Furr'd with Cads beard: his poynard on his thigh...
> Yet this Sir Beuis, or the fayery Knight,
> Put vp the lie because he durst not fight.   (*Skialetheia*, no. 53)

The significance of the great vogue of facile criticism, its defacing of the whole gallery of gorgeous gallants, lies in its cultivation of social self-awareness, through broad typifications, 'close libell or open satyre', personal allusion, and the continuous ridicule of achievement and fame-seeking in so many areas of life, from peasant hopes to princely pride:

> Gaeta from wool and weaving first began,
> Swelling and swelling to a gentleman.
> When he was a gentleman, and bravely dight,
> He left not swelling till he was a knight.
> At last (forgetting what he was at first),
> He swole to be a lord: and then he burst.　　　　*(Chrestoleros, Bk 5, Ep. 4)*

> When Priscus, raised from low to high estate,
> Rode through the street in pompous jollity,
> Caius, his poor familiar friend of late,
> Bespake him thus: 'Sir, now you know not me'.
>   'Tis likely, friend (quoth Priscus) to be so;
>   For at this time my self I do not know.　　　　*(Davies, Epigrammes, 31)*

Such naïve exemplary tales are the ground bass to more individualized notes, like Guilpin's 'great Foelix passing through the street', which glances at Essex and Bacon:

> Who would not thinke him perfect curtesie?
> Or the Honny-suckle of humilitie?
> The deuill he is as soone: he is the deuill,
> Brightly accoustred to bemist his euill:
> Like a Swartrutters hose his puffe thoughts swell,
> With yeastie ambition: Signior Machiauell
> Taught him this mumming trick, with curtesie
> T'entrench himselfe in popularitie,
> And for a writhen face, and bodies moue,
> Be Barricadode in the peoples loue.　　　　*(Satyre I)*

Such pointed allusion, rarely to political figures, and more frequently to his own associates in the world of law and literature, Guilpin boasts:

> I care not what the world doth think, or say,
> There lies a morral vnder my leane play;

and the sub-title of *Skialetheia*, 'A shadowe of Truth', was intended to attract a public quick to catch references now stumbled after by commentators. Joseph Hall's *Virgidemiae* (1597) offered 'His Defiance to Enuie', rejected all poetry save satire, all poets save Spenser, and castigated the malpractices of some professions, learning, law, medicine or the Church, setting the vanity of the age against the 'time of Gold'. When these 'Toothlesse Satyrs' were joined in 1598 by three books of 'Byting Satyres', the urbanity gave way to calculated, allusive and riddling abuse. The portrait of England painted by Hall is of a devastated countryside and a misspent inheritance:

> Old driueling Lollio drudges all he can,
> To make his eldest soone a Gentleman.

While another may

>   shine in tissues and pure gold
>   That hath his lands and patrimony sold
>   Lolios side-cote is rough Pampilian
>   Guilded with drops that downe the bosome ran,
>   White Carsy hose, patched on eyther knee,
>   The very Embleme of good husbandrie,
>   And a knit night-cap made of coursest twine,
>   With two long labels button's to his chin;
>   So rides he mounted on the market-day
>   Vpon a straw-stuft pannel, all the way.

The discrepancy is insisted at every point:

>   When Lolio feasteth in his reueling fit,
>   Some starued Pullen scoures the rust spitt.
>   For else how should his sonne maintained bee,
>   At Ins of Court or of the Chancerie:
>   There to learne Law, and courtly carriage,
>   To make amendes for his meane parentage,
>   Where he vnknowne and ruffling as he can,
>   Goes currant each-where for a Gentleman?   (*Virgidemiarum*, IV, ii)

This Quixotic figure and his unprodigal son are minutely observed, but Hall's anger is charged with a seriousness distinct from the flippancy of Lolio's sons' companions:

>   How I fore-see in many ages past,
>   When Lolioes caytiue name is quite defas't,
>   Thine heire, thine heyres, & his heyre againe
>   From out the loynes of carefull Lolian,
>   Shall climbe vp to the Chancell pewes on hie,
>   And rule and reigne in their rich Tenancie;
>   When pearch't aloft to perfect their estate
>   They racke their rents vnto a treble rate;
>   And hedge in all the neighbour common-lands,
>   And clodge their slauish tenant with commaunds.

Similarly, the accumulating sneers at 'vaunted pedigree', or the mottoes of the new gentry (Nashe's 'Not without Mustard'), are strengthened by Hall's contempt for affected and true descent either way:

>   What boots it Pontice, tho thou could'st discourse
>   Of a long golden line of Ancesters?...
>   Or call some old Church-windowes to record
>   The age of thy fayre Armes,
>   Or find some figure halfe obliterate
>   In rain-beat Marble neare to the Church-gate,

Vpon a Crosse-leg'd Toombe, what boots it thee
To shew the rusted Buckle that did tie
The Garter of thy greatest Grand-sires knee?
What to reserue their reliques many yeares,
Their siluer-spurs, or spils of broken speares. (IV, iii)

Impatient of the appeal to antiquity, sceptical of heroic postures, such as 'Martius in boystrous Buffes' who goes 'brabling Make-fray at ech Fayre and Sise', hostile to manifest religious power and authority (Juvenal's ghost 'would stampe and stare | That Caesars throne is turn'ed to Peters chayre'), Hall, the future bishop and author of *The Mischief of Faction*, has a thoroughgoing disillusionment at the age of twenty-three.

The precision of his sarcasm, and the subjects which arouse it, are in some contrast to the sweeping range of Marston, whose *Pigmalion's Image and Certain Satires*, and *The Scourge of Villainy*, appeared in 1598. The latter is a tripartite sacrifice, dedicated 'To his most esteemed, and best beloued Selfe', presented next to 'Enuies abhorred child Detraction', and consigned in the conclusion 'To euerlasting Obliuion' that 'mighty gulfe, insatiat cormorant'.

Marston's is the largest claim among Elizabethan satirists to

> beare the scourge of iust Rhamnusia,
> Lashing the lewdnes of Britania.

Imploring the assistance of 'Ingenuous Melancholy', crowned with 'Blacke Cypresse', Marston sets out to plough

> The hidden entrailes of ranke villanie,
> Tearing the vaile from damn'd Impietie.

With endlessly repeated rhetorical questions ('Who'le coole my rage? who'le stay my itching fist | But I will plague and torture whom I list?), and by constant conversation with accompanying confidants, Marston probes his own mind, tests his reactions, and rails full stretch against the 'fustie world'. For all the parade of figures, the constantly changing scene and vantage points of observation, Marston's is in some ways a more restricted, claustrophobic world of satire than that of less ambitious censurers. The figures of folly jump at his lash, but they turn their faces from us; Marston 'greeued sees, with red vext eyes', and the mists of lust which envelop all his creations settle thickly again before the chastisement is finished. But the agitation sometimes pauses sufficiently for us to contemplate the horror:

> O stay, thou impious slaue,
> Teare not the lead from off thy Fathers graue,
> To stop base brokerage, sell not thy fathers sheete,
> His leaden sheete, that strangers eyes may greet
> Both putrefaction of thy greedy Sire,
> And thy abhorred viperous desire.
> But wilt thou needs, shall thy Dads lacky brat
> Weare thy Sire halfe-rot finger in his hat? (*Scourge*, Satire III)

The overwhelming impression conveyed by Marston's satires of his contemporary society is anticipatory of the later created worlds of Jacobean tragedy, of man brutalized, a prey to appetite, a broker of the mind and body of himself and others, perverted in his appearance, corrupted in his essence:

> He hath no soule, the which the Stagerite
> Term'd rationall, for beastly appetite,
> Base dunghill thoughts, and sensual action,
> Hath made him loose that faire creation.
> And now no man, since Circes magick charme
> Hath turn'd him to a maggot, that doth swarme
> In tainted flesh, whose foule corruption
> Is his faire foode, whose generation
> Anothers ruine.

Simple men are charmed to simple beasts, 'an Oxe, that with base drudgery | Eates vp the Land', or a 'muckhill ouer-spred with snow': the 'sencelesse, sensuall Epicure' is 'sprightlesse, sence or soule hath none, | Since last Medusa turn'd him to a stone': Nestor who 'Eates Nectar, drinks Ambrosia, saunce controule', is 'but a sponge, and shortly needs must leese | His wrong got iuce, when greatnes fist shal squeese | His liquor out'. Men are metamorphosed into their animal, mineral or vegetable properties, atomized away into 'apparitions, | Ignes fatui, glowworms, fictions, | Meteors, rats of Nile, fantasies, | Colosses, pictures, shades, resemblances!' (*Scourge*, Satire VII). Their outward show begins to usurp their proper nature, the ridicule of fashionable extravagance yields more sombre metaphysical scrutinies of men and women:

> Her maske, her vizard, her loose-hanging gowne
> For her loose lying body, her bright spangled crown,
> Her long slit sleeues, stiffe buske, puffe verdingall,
> Is all that makes her thus angelicall.
> Alas, her soule struts round about her neck,
> Her seate of scence is her rebato set,
> Her intellectuall is a fained nicenes,
> Nothing but clothes, & simpering precisenes.   (*Scourge*, Satire VII)

For the satirists, of course, all women are Ophelia seen through Hamlet's eyes, and the technique of hyperbole familiar in the praises of love poets is adapted to the new overstatement of annihilating scorn. In all matters those little sparks of dissension among young men become fanned until they burst into Donne's 'satyrique fires which urg'd me to have writt in skorne of all'.

The mood was general. 'England's wits', as Guilpin wrote, were 'now mounted the full height', and 'puft up by conquest'. Nor was this only a literary phenomenon. During the last decade of the century Star Chamber was being appealed to increasingly for redress against libellous attacks.[1] There were ample provocations, therefore, in 1599, for the Bishops' Ban on controversial literature, the writing of histories, and on scurrilous publications, by which the satires of Hall, Marston, Guilpin, Rankins and Middleton, the epigrams of Davies and Marlowe's scandalous elegies of Ovid, were ordered to be burned. That the ban on the future printing of 'Satyres or Epigrams' was not wholly effective may be shown easily from the subsequent appearance of numerous later collections. But, in fact, in the very year of the edict, the spirit of more severe satire was already passing by Pythagorean transmigration into the drama. There had been discovered 'the need of a Democritus to laugh at Democritus, one jester to flout another: a great Stentorian Democritus, as big as that Rhodian Colossus'.[1] Such a role Ben Jonson was destined to fill, more ephemerally in the 'Poetomachia', with his summons to Envy in *Poetaster*, his purging of poets reminiscent of the treatment meted out to 'Martin', and more permanently in *Every Man Out of His Humour*. Here the most prominent figures critical of Elizabethan society are themselves arraigned, and the ideal, ingenious and free spirit of Asper, bearing marked resemblance to Jonson's own image, alone wins approval.

To some extent this is Jonson's England, and though Shakespeare's representation of it is less direct than Jonson's he is in some measure indebted to the changes effected by the satirists. It is perhaps notable that the only society which Shakespeare treats with consistently humorous satire is that early, privileged world of *Love's Labour's Lost*, where pedantry is punctured with its own quill, and the gallants are indulgently rebuked. Shakespeare was notoriously envied by the unhappy Greene, and it seems clear that however much Shakespeare's sonnets imply some distaste for his theatrical occupation, its independence as a sphere of artistic endeavour brought him compensations greater than those of either University men or patronized poets. The anger of Shakespeare's characters is directed less specifically at his particular society. When the figure of a contemporary satirist such as Jaques intrudes into Arden his critical opinions earn respect, but ultimately it is the regard due to an alien, whose way of life is solitary and unreconciled, as the Duke admonishes him:

> For thou thyself hast been a libertine,
> As sensual as the brutish sting itself,
> And all th'imbossed sores, and headed evils,
> That thou with licence of free foot hast caught,
> Wouldst thou disgorge into the general world.   (*As You Like It*, II, vii)

The conviction of young men that dire reproof may suffice to 'Cleanse the foul body of th'infected world', is not shared by Shakespeare's major characters, and in *2 Henry IV*, composed in the crucial phase of late Elizabethan society and Shakespeare's most extended satirically tragic contemplation of a 'general world' conspicuously resembling his own, the moral earnestness of angry young men falls from Falstaff's lips:

Virtue is of so little regard in these costermongers' times that true valour is turned bear-herd, pregnancy is made a tapster, and his quick wit wasted in giving reckonings: all the other gifts appertinent to man, as the malice of this age shapes them, are not worth a gooseberry. You that are old consider not the capacities of us that are young, you measure the heat of our livers with the bitterness of your galls, and we that are young, I must confess, are wags too.

These gross lies receive the rebuke of the Lord Chief Justice: 'Is not your voice broken, your wind short, your chin double, and every part about you blasted with antiquity, and will you yet call yourself young?' Many times Falstaff pretends to be young, in the unsettling manner of a deceitful vice, but the stage tableau of Vice rebuking Justice in the accents of Juventus implicitly ridicules those wags in the vaward of their youth so strenuously critical of their society.

The cynicism and malice of which Falstaff complains are written on his own features and substantially embodied in his person. With him bills are unpaid; lies are the commonest conduct of an argument; honour is catechized and fails examination; military office is used for self-interest, and simple, indeed simpleton humanity is recruited as 'food for powder'; the defeated body of dead chivalry, in this post-Armada world, is mutilated for fame and profit; the cushion of luxury is worn in emblematic parody of crowned royalty. These are fit matters for castigation, yet the indulgence we accord such violations of human and social codes is freely given in the theatre, and their restraint, inevitable, necessary and accepted, involves a rejection of more than a stage vice; for Falstaff is compounded of the grossest humours of our clay.

In Shakespeare's works, the satirical representation of society, whether of the heroic past in *Troilus and Cressida*, or the historically immediate in *2 Henry IV*, together with the most severely pessimistic presentation of social man in the legendary and permanent worlds of *King Lear* and *Timon of Athens*, remain inseparable from the criticism of individual man. The malice of the age is a part only of that greater malice of time, age and nature. The 'infected world' is set against that long sickness of life itself which begins to mend at Timon's death. And Timon, Shakespeare's fiercest satirist and critic of man in society, wrote his own injured epitaph only to have its nobleness capped by a sententious senator with more crushing objectivity:

> His discontents are unremovably
> Coupled to nature.

10

SCIENTIFIC THOUGHT

'Nature's mystery'

> To solemnize this day the glorious Sun
> Stays in his course and plays the alchemist,
> Turning with splendour of his precious eye
> The meagre cloddy earth to glittering gold.[1]

A cursory glance at Shakespeare's imagery immediately demonstrates that, like all men of the Elizabethan age, the science he knew best was astronomy. Typical of the times also is his interest in the mystical (or as he would have said practical) application of astronomy to astrological prediction. And to Shakespeare, as to the Danish astronomer Tycho Brahe (1546–1601), alchemy was a natural corollary to astrology, a terrestrial form, borrowing its terminology from its older and better established relation. (We still retain a trace of this association when we call the most elusive metal, mercury, after the most elusive planet, which was itself named for the most slippery of the gods.)

The basis for the widespread acceptance of astrology in Shakespeare's day lay in a universally accepted cosmology which combined to render the world at once compact and full of wonder: the forces presumed to govern nature were mysterious, unknown and perhaps unknowable, though the universe had been made for man, whose abode was at its centre. In its essentials this cosmology was Aristotelian, Christianized and modernized by generations of medieval teachers and commentators. Though technical astronomy had made many advances in the fifteenth and sixteenth centuries, the basic system of the world recognized by scholar and layman alike remained virtually unaltered until the end of Shakespeare's life. That the system proved highly resistant to change was the result of certain conspicuous virtues: it appealed to common sense as reasonable, and it enjoyed the advantage of apparent empirical confirmation together with the ability to explain a wide range of observed facts. It postulated a unique, unified universe where every part knew its proper place, behaved in expected fashion and was neatly related to the whole. No wonder, in Shakespeare's day, there could be no higher praise for a well-run State than to compare it to the cosmos.

The Elizabethan universe was, physically, a vast enclosed sphere, within whose surface were contained the heavens and the earth. At the centre was 'the huge firm earth',[2] a fixed, inert, immovable globe, which could never be other than at the centre:

> As true as steel, as plantage to the moon,
> As sun to day, as turtle to her mate,
> As iron to adamant, as earth to the centre,[3]

quoted Troilus; and indeed there was no reason to suppose otherwise. Between the terrestrial spheres (which ended just below the moon) and the outer sphere of the universe nested a series of crystalline spheres 'of one entire and perfect chrysolite';[1] these served to support and, where necessary, move the stars and planets. (Stars and planets were not clearly distinguished in nature until after 1610, the date of the publication of Galileo's telescopic observations; earlier planets were thought to be merely wandering stars.) The outermost sphere was that of the fixed stars; within this lay the planetary spheres in order. Each planet was located on the circumference of its own sphere and thereby located at a fixed and definite position in the universe. The 'nobler' the planet the farther its sphere from the base earth and the nearer to the divine heavens—for the outermost sphere, the *primum mobile* for Aristotle, came to be regarded as the Christian heaven or firmament. Hence Helena's plaintive lament in *All's Well*

> 'Twere all one
> That I should love a bright particular star
> And think to wed it, he is so above me:
> In his bright radiance and collateral light
> Must I be comforted, not in his sphere.[2]

With all this, the sun yet retained a special place, as giver of light and heat.

The spheres of stars and planets moved in regular fashion, carrying their heavenly bodies round and round the earth. Because, as every natural philosopher since Plato's time had agreed, circular motion, which is perfect, belongs to the perfect crystalline matter out of which the spheres are made, there is no need to ask why the stars, sun, moon and planets rise and set daily: it is the nature of crystalline spheres to move endlessly and smoothly in a circle; that is, to rotate. And in this way, though there is motion there is no change, and the heavenly regions are perfect, unchanging and eternal: death, corruption and generation being restricted to the imperfect and 'cloddy' terrestrial regions.

It was these crystalline spheres which by their motion were thought to produce the 'music of the spheres'. This concept, which can be traced to the Pythagoreans, was mathematical in origin, and described certain 'harmonic' ratios and proportions of the sizes and distances of the planetary spheres. This was what the term meant to Shakespeare's younger contemporary Johann Kepler, who was to publish, three years after Shakespeare's death, a mathematical treatise entitled *Harmonices Mundi* which enshrined both the astronomically important 'Third Law' of Kepler (that the squares of the periodic times of revolution of planets in their orbits are to one another as the cube of their radii) and also an elaborate restatement of the existence and precise nature of the music of the spheres. This is the same music as that which Lorenzo so poetically described to Jessica:

> Look how the floor of heaven
> Is thick inlaid with patines of bright gold:
> There's not the smallest orb which thou behold'st
> But in his motion like an angel sings,
> Still quiring to the young-eyed cherubins;
> Such harmony is in immortal souls;
> But whilst this muddy vesture of decay
> Doth grossly close it in, we cannot hear it.[3]

And it is also that music which Olivia was prepared to rate less agreeable to the ear than the prospect of a declaration of love from the disguised Viola.[1]

The technical astronomy of the Renaissance was highly mathematical, and increasingly specialized.[2] Gone were the days when a knowledge of the existence of spheres, zodiac and ecliptic constituted a university course. This much knowledge allowed one to consult an almanac (as Shakespeare's characters so frequently did)[3] but little more. Fifteenth-century astronomers had insisted on the necessity of a thorough mastery of Ptolemy's *Almagest*, more revered than read in the previous three centuries; consequently, sixteenth-century astronomers were ready to take issue with Ptolemy and strike out on their own. This meant that they were competent to handle the complex mathematical methods devised by the Hellenistic mathematicians to represent the somewhat irregular observed motions of the planets in their orbits, and to trust their own observations and calculations when these differed from those of the Greek masters.

The aim of sixteenth-century astronomers was still that suggested by Plato: to represent the apparent motions of the planets by a combination of circular motions. (The chief difficulty lay not in the fact that planetary orbits are elliptical rather than circular—for the eccentricity is in all cases small—but in the fact that the planets in fact 'go round' the sun rather than the earth. Since the inner planets, Mercury and Venus, go faster than the earth and the outer planets, Mars, Jupiter and Saturn, go more slowly than the earth, obvious complexities will appear; the most important and famous case is the 'retrograde' motion exhibited by the outer planets, when they appear to go backward for a space, apparently tracing out a small loop in the midst of an otherwise circular path.) Three chief devices were used: eccentric, epicycle and equant. The eccentric, originally devised to represent the varying brightness of most planets, caused by their varying distance from the earth, was a circle whose centre was near but distinct from the earth; by the sixteenth century it was usually the inner surface of a crystalline sphere. The epicycle was a small circle carrying the planet on its circumference; its centre was on the circumference of a larger circle, the deferent, which might be concentric or eccentric to the earth; both epicycle and deferent rotated, and their combined motions explained many observed peculiarities of planetary motion, like retrogradation. The equant was a point, different from the earth, with respect to which the planet's motion was uniform; it accounted for the phenomena described in Kepler's Second Law. None of these circles was other than a mathematical device, though by the mid-sixteenth century most had been given concrete existence by treating them as parts of crystalline spheres. The motions of sun and moon were handled by the same mathematical methods. It was the job of technical astronomers to devise combinations of these mathematical figures to represent observed motions of the planets, and at the same time to use their computations to predict future positions of the planets for inclusion in Ephemerides (for the learned) and almanacs (for the layman).

Clearly Shakespeare, who used zodiac as a synonym for ecliptic and as a metaphor for year,[4] was no amateur of mathematical astronomy; still less was he aware of the revolutionary ideas being tentatively developed by his contemporaries. Since the early sixteenth century astronomers had been growing increasingly dissatisfied with both the predictive inaccuracy of the established astronomical system and with its complexity. (They were not, initially, in any way dissatisfied with the prevailing cosmology.) Various suggestions, mainly based on the work of pre-Ptolemaic Greek astronomers, were offered by humanist-astronomers; the only one of lasting importance was that of Copernicus (1473–1543) enshrined in his monumental *De Revolutionibus orbium coelestium* (*On the Revolution of the Celestial Spheres*, 1543). *De Revolutionibus* was the first attempt to combine a cosmological system with detailed mathematical development since Ptolemy's *Almagest* (*c.* A.D. 150). Copernicus retained the crystalline spheres, epicycles and eccentrics of conventional astronomy (though he dispensed with the equant); but he turned the universe inside out by insisting that it was the earth which moved, not the sun, and that all the planets revolved around the sun, not around the earth. This failed to account for many peculiarities of the earth (the only planet to have a moon, for example) and was manifestly contrary to common sense; but it did explain retrograde motion, and it could be said to make the paths of the planets more nearly circular. Copernicus was no revolutionary: in good humanist fashion he claimed to have found the inspiration for his work in Greek texts, and he retained the essential features of conventional astronomy as well as of Aristotelian physics; but his system, if taken literally, meant an end to the comfortable and familiar world where things were truly as they appeared to be.

Copernicus had no proof of his system, and no observational confirmation. (On the contrary, to explain the lack of observational support he was forced to postulate what then seemed an outrageously large radius for the sphere of fixed stars.) Little wonder then that he and his work received more praise than acceptance; nor that many computational astronomers used his calculations and tables without accepting his cosmology. Yet the main tenets of his system—the rotation and revolution of the earth—were astonishingly well known in the later sixteenth century. The layman often jeered—as did Guillaume du Bartas whose didactic poem *La Sepmaine, ou Création du Monde* (1578) was much read in English translation in the early seventeenth century, Jean Bodin, and Montaigne to name but three Frenchmen—but this very scorn displayed awareness, if not knowledge. Astronomers, whether friendly or hostile, were invariably respectful of what all recognized to be a truly monumental achievement.

English astronomers were more than respectful: they were favourably inclined from a very early period. In 1556 there appeared the first Copernican ephemeris in English (by an obscure mathematician named John Feild) and also the first detailed reference in English to the new astronomy. This was in an elementary textbook, *The Castle of Knowledge* by Robert Recorde; it was too elementary, as Recorde realized, for a proper exposition, but he could not resist a passing reference to 'Copernicus, a man of greate learninge, of muche experience, and of wonderfull diligence in observation' who 'affirmeth that the earthe not only moveth circularlye about his owne centre, but also may be, yea and is, continually out of the precise centre of the world 38 hundreth thousand miles'.[1] Recorde's treatise, cast in the form of a dialogue between Master and Student in the manner so common to Renaissance school texts, is the kind of book which Shakespeare might well have studied had he been interested in pure astronomy (as he evidently was not). Twenty years after Recorde's work, an English translation of the Book I of Copernicus' *De Revolutionibus* (the non-technical description of his cosmology) was made available in a form which even Shakespeare might have looked at. For Thomas Digges (*c.* 1543–95), a highly competent observational and mathematical astronomer, published in 1576 a new edition of his father's *Prognostication Everlasting*, a popular perpetual almanac, with an appendix entitled *A Perfect Description of the Caelestiall Orbes according to the most auncient doctrine of the Pythagoreans, lately revised by Copernicus and by Geometricall Demonstrations Approved.* Digges' own contribution was to suggest that there was no sphere of the fixed stars; rather the stars were scattered through space from the region beyond the sphere of Saturn to the abode of God and the angels, the stars serving, as Digges said, to 'garnish' the 'pallace of foelicitye'. This is the first step towards the infinite universe, although in itself it is more mystical than practical. *A Prognostication Everlasting* was even more popular with its Copernican appendix than it had been before, and seven editions appeared between 1576 and 1605. No wonder that there were more English than continental Copernicans—especially since Digges' own master, John Dee, was a powerful influence on English mathematics and astronomy. Copernicanism continued to reach the layman, and there were many Copernican almanacs besides that of Digges.

Further advances in astronomy belong to the later years of Shakespeare's life. The great observational astronomer, Tycho Brahe, published his most important books in 1573 and 1588, but these were read by relatively few; his ideas and discoveries became much better known after 1602, when a collected edition of his works was published posthumously. All Tycho's theoretical developments stem from the excellent observations in which he had a well-warranted faith: from his observations of the new star (nova) in Cassiopeia (1572; also observed by Digges) he concluded that the heavens are subject to change, since this new star manifestly belonged to the celestial regions beyond the moon; from his observations of the great comet of 1577 he concluded that it too lay in the celestial regions, and that its path crossed the spheres of several planets; from this he concluded that there were no solid crystalline spheres. This in turn led him to devise the so-called Tychonic system, in which all the planets revolve around the sun which in turn revolves around the earth, beyond the sphere of the moon. Tycho rejected the Copernican system, on the grounds that a moving earth was contrary to common sense, to the Bible, and to the observational evidence; these were such excellent reasons that many more astronomers espoused the Tychonic than the Copernican system, and it was not long before no competent astronomer dared to defend the Ptolemaic universe.

Although Tycho rejected the novelties of the Copernican system his own system was, in many ways, more radical. For in totally rejecting crystalline spheres he turned the cosmos from a nest of Russian eggs, wherein each planet was held in its place by a solid structure, into a vast, open universe, in which the planets moved and remained in place for no known reason, and in which heavens and earth were one, with no distinction in physical attributes. Hence Francis Bacon, who praised Tycho above all other astronomers, doubted whether there was any 'system of the world' and conjectured that there might only be planets and stars scattered through immensities of space—though Tycho himself had, somewhat illogically, retained the bounding sphere of a finite universe.

Most astronomers preferred to retain their belief in the order of nature, and to do so felt compelled to explain what kept the planets in their orbits, a problem Tycho had never contemplated. (He also ignored the need to work out a detailed mathematics for his system.) Ultimately, of course, this was to be solved by a clear understanding of gravity, arrived at in the first instance through a study of terrestrial bodies. Preceding this was the attempt to make use of magnetic attraction. This was first done by the English physician William Gilbert (1540–1603), whose *De magnete* (1601) climaxed a detailed experimental investigation of magnetism with the suggestion that it was because the earth was a magnet (his own discovery) that it rotated daily on its axis. Gilbert was not a Copernican, for he did not accept the annual revolution of the earth around the sun. But he did believe (with Digges) that the fixed stars were scattered at varying distances; and he did postulate that magnetism which clearly, as he thought, extended to the moon was the force that kept the moon circling the earth in a fixed orbit. This idea was adopted and extended by Johann Kepler (1571–1630), especially in *Astronomia nova* (1609), which also contains his first two eponymous laws: that the planets move in ellipses with the sun at one focus; and that the radius vector drawn from the sun to the planet sweeps out equal areas in equal times. But Kepler's work, based firmly on the marvellous observations of Tycho Brahe, was too mathematical for the laymen, and indeed for most astronomers as well.

Just outside Shakespeare's working lifetime lie the astounding telescopic discoveries of Galileo, announced in *Sidereus Nuncius* (1610) and eagerly discussed in England by those who read Latin. Here Galileo announced the terrestrial nature of the moon; established clearly the difference between planets and stars; discovered that stars need not be so huge as naked-eye observation had previously suggested in order that the Copernican universe be possible; announced the discovery of Jupiter's satellites, and the existence of many previously unsuspected stars. Though nothing of this was proof, the Copernican system now seemed much more probable: the terrestrial appearance of the moon suggested that the earth *could* move; and the existence of the moons of Jupiter showed that the earth was not unique in having a satellite. It was in reaction to Galileo's achievement, so widely publicized, that John Donne cried out in despair. Now, after nearly seventy years, the Copernican system was seen as a scientific force with which all thinking men had to reckon.

To be able to gain accurate knowledge of the future position of the various celestial bodies was the end to which all astronomers looked; in many ways it was thought to be more important than the devising of cosmological systems, since it was more immediately useful. Applied astronomy took many forms in the sixteenth century. One of obvious importance in Elizabethan England was the application of navigation. For though Drake, Hawkins and the rest depended in part on luck and a flair for navigation, they were by no means without navigational aids, and as the century wore on transatlantic sailors expected such assistance from the learned as sailors in European waters were already beginning to take for granted. Coastwise sailors depended principally on 'rutters' (*routiers*), pilot books describing banks, currents, landfalls and tides; with this, lead, line and compass they were pretty sure of finding their way, possibly assisted further by map and chart. Deep-sea sailors needed something more: map and chart for the coast, but also methods for determining position during the long weeks out of sight of land.

By Shakespeare's time sailors had been taught by astronomers how to take the altitude of the Pole Star with navigational quadrant, cross-staff (both introduced in the fifteenth century), or back staff (new in Shakespeare's day); and with tables prepared by the scholar and craftsman the navigator could then determine his latitude. Since there was no practical method of determining longitude at sea, in spite of ingenious suggestions by astronomers, sixteenth-century navigators usually made their way to the desired latitude and then 'ran down it' to their destination. Basic to all navigation was dead-reckoning. Here the compass was essential for determining direction; distance was determined by estimation of the ship's speed, assisted by such new English inventions as the log (first described in print by William Bourne in *A Regiment for the Sea*, 1573). Further aids to dead-reckoning were better tables and calculating aids (like Gunter's sector, first described in 1607), all prepared by mathematically trained landsmen. The sixteenth century also saw improvements in the method of mounting compasses, and more knowledge about deviations of the compass from true North, from which it was hoped some day to determine longitude after gathering data for drawing a magnetic grid of the terrestrial globe. (This was a fruitless hope, as it turned out, for both magnetic variation and declination vary in any given place with the passage of time.)

Cartography also experienced a most flourishing period in the later sixteenth century. Scientific cartography, utilizing a knowledge of the mathematical art of projecting a spherical surface on to a plane sheet of paper, was revived early in the fifteenth century by the rediscovery of Ptolemy's geographical writings. New discoveries and the art of printing created a thriving trade, centred in Germany and the Low Countries. It was a Portuguese mathematician (Pedro Nuñez) who first pointed out the difficulties of representing high northern or southern latitudes on a sea chart, since the meridians on a globe converge; a Dutch mathematical instrument-maker, map-designer and publisher who arbitrarily spaced out the meridians on his world map of 1569, and thereby had his name immortalized in 'Mercator's projection'; but an English mathematician, Edward Wright (1558–1615), who first solved the mathematical problems of the projection and taught map-makers how to use it.[1] The great advantage to sailors was that a line of constant compass heading was a straight line on the new projection, which greatly facilitated the plotting of a course.

So widely was it recognized that the trained mathematician was essential to progress in navigation that the crisis of 1588 prompted a group of London citizens to establish a lectureship in the mathematical sciences; the first and only incumbent, Thomas Hood, gave his inaugural 'speech' on 4 November, and continued to lecture for about four years thereafter. Similarly, among the professorships established by Sir Thomas Gresham and begun in 1598 were those in geometry and astronomy; the first professor of geometry (until 1619) was Henry Briggs, decidedly interested in computational problems; the second (1619) and third (1626) professors of astronomy, Edmund Gunter and Henry Gellibrand, made important contributions to navigation. Though the public to whom these lectures were delivered was smaller than their founders had intended, there was in London a genuine interest in navigational problems. And maps, whether for decoration or information, were enormously popular.[2] Even Shakespeare, remote from the sea affairs of England as he evidently was, knew something of this; he shared the passionate interest which most men bestowed on the progress of discovery, knew a little of the cartographic results, and could make Maria compare Malvolio's face to 'the new map with the augmentation of the Indies' for its many lines.[3] Clearly, strange as it seems in retrospect, it was possible to live in sixteenth-century London without associating with men of sea-faring interests, especially if one stayed away from the Court. Even so, no one could escape knowing that the Pole Star was the sailor's guide and friend,[4] or that shipwreck was a constant peril.

Shakespeare knew far more of other applications of astronomy to the needs of everyday life. An almanac, prepared initially by an astronomer, was available to every literate man, even to the mechanics of *A Midsummer Night's Dream*. And, like his audience, Shakespeare was remarkably well informed about astrology, the application of astronomical prediction to the future of man's affairs. The belief in astrology was shared by most men, whether learned or not: only humanists, moved by Plato's warning, had ever seriously attacked its validity; the best astronomers of the day practised astrology and, on the whole, accepted it. The theoretical justification lay in the ancient doctrine of the microcosm. Surely the events of the great universe, the macrocosm, must influence the earth at its centre and man, the cosmos in little; it must be true that

> It is the stars
> The stars above us, govern our conditions.[1]

By the late sixteenth century there was a variety of attitudes towards astrology. There were strong partisans, practitioners of 'judicial astrology' who cast horoscopes for individuals and insisted that the whole of man's life was determined by his birth. Even in the early sixteenth century this was an extreme position among learned men; the Italian physician and mathematician Cardan was severely dealt with by the authorities of the city of Milan for computing horoscopes of his patients, of his distinguished contemporaries and even, it was said, of Jesus Christ. (Indeed, the Medical Faculty of Paris sternly repressed the practice among its students.) The more usual belief was that signs and portents in the heavens had a general influence upon human affairs; it was the duty of the astrologer to point these out, so that everyone could govern his life accordingly. Some 'portents' were clearly celestial, and indeed of regular occurrence. 'Saturn and Venus this year in conjunction. What says the almanac to that?'[2] (A planet was 'in conjunction' when the earth, the sun and the planet all lay in a straight line, with the sun between the earth and the planet.) 'These late eclipses in the sun and moon portend no good to us.'[3] It was the job of the almanac-maker to note such predictable occurrences and indicate their meaning for the world: it was taken for granted that this would be dire, and any astrologer could be sure of success if he predicted war, famine and civil unrest. It was a measure of the utter novelty of the new star (nova) in Cassiopeia in 1572 (there had been only one previously reported in the history of astronomy, that of the second century B.C.) that Tycho Brahe could regard it as a cheerful sign: he noted that it was reinforced by the conjunction of Saturn and Jupiter nine years before, and by a comet five years later, and concluded that it portended the arrival of a new age of peace and plenty which should begin in fifty years. Even Tycho admitted, however, that 'These Prognostic matters are grounded only upon conjectural probabilitie'.[4] Tycho, like his contemporaries, was sure that God, who was directly responsible for these prodigies, would not mock the world by producing them without significance. In the late sixteenth and early seventeenth centuries, there was an amazing abundance of bright, naked-eye comets, of the sort which have been singularly scarce in this century. There had been a famous series in the 1530's; after the great comet of 1577 Tycho was able to observe six more again in the early years of the seventeenth century, including an appearance of Halley's comet in 1607. No wonder that comets are so frequently referred to in the plays, always 'importing change of times and states'.[5] Shakespeare subscribed to the belief that such great heavenly portents applied to affairs of state rather than to individuals; as evidence we have not only Calpurnia's famous warning

> When beggars die, there are no comets seen;
> The heavens themselves blaze forth the death of princes;[6]

but Othello's exaggerated grief-stricken declaration

> Methinks it should be now a huge eclipse
> Of sun and moon, and that the affrighted globe
> Should yawn at alteration.[7]

Eclipses and conjunctions certainly lay in the celestial regions: the case was not so clear for new stars and comets. Part of the revolutionary nature of Tycho's astronomy lay in his declaration that these belonged in the heavens; for he thereby proclaimed that the heavens, like the terrestrial regions, were subject to change. (He even, more daring still, suggested that at least some comets might be recurrent phenomena.) This statement of the possibility of change in the celestial regions was to be reinforced ten years after Tycho's death by the telescopic observation of sun-spots by Galileo and others. But the position was not clear in Shakespeare's time, even to astronomers, and most people continued to believe with Aristotle that all such phenomena, together with shooting stars, haloes, mock suns and the 'ignis fatuus or...ball of wildfire'[1] were atmospheric phenomena (and hence named meteors), the result of strange exhalations, miasmata, fumes and smokes from the earth, such as were common in mining districts and marshes filled with rotting vegetation. If this were the case, it was even easier to see why such phenomena must influence those who lived immediately beneath them; at the same time it was impossible to suppose that God could not have intended these things as signs. Only the cynical, like Edmund, or those lead astray by pride, like Cassius, could argue against the direct influence of the stars.[2] Most reasonable men agreed with the metaphor employed in Henry IV's rebuke to the rebel lord:

> This is not well, my lord, this is not well.
> What say you to it? will you again unknit
> This churlish knot of all-abhorred war?
> And move in that obedient orb again
> Where you did give a fair and natural light,
> And be no more an exhaled meteor,
> A prodigy of fear and a portent
> Of broached mischief to the unborn times?[3]

Like astrology, alchemy moved on two levels, the practical and the theoretical. Theoretical alchemy was mystic in the extreme, with its language drawn from astrology, magic and theology. Practical alchemy varied from the search for a method to turn base metals into gold to the smelting of ores to produce the common metals such as iron, tin, lead, antimony or even silver. Since ores were thought to 'grow' in the earth (because it was profitable to work old slag heaps) and there was evidence of iron being turned into copper after infusion in mineral springs (actually these springs were strongly impregnated with soluble copper sulphate) and lead turning into silver (because silver occurs in small quantities in conjunction with lead ore), it seemed obvious that alchemy was a natural process, a craft practised by nature deep in the earth.

> Plutus himself,
> That knows the tinct and multiplying medicine,
> Hath not in nature's mystery more science...[4]

Clearly not all the wonders and prodigies of the world lay in the higher spheres when so many were to be found on or below the earth's surface.

It was, of course, not only the stars that belonged in appropriate spheres: each of the elements had its proper place in the terrestrial regions. Below the moon lay the sphere of fire; below that, the sphere of air, the atmosphere; below that again, the sphere of water, and lowest of all, at the very centre of the universe, the sphere of earth. An element displaced from its sphere was quite literally out of place, and if not constrained would seek to regain its proper region. So a stone in water or air falls to earth; water bubbles out of the earth in springs, but falls out of the air as rain, flames rise, and so on. In Aristotelian terminology 'light' and 'heavy' only meant tendency to rise or fall; so earth was always heavy, and fire light, but water and air might be either, depending upon where they are. Hence Lear's objuration

> Hysterica passio, down, thou climbing sorrow,
> Thy element's below![1]

These elements were not those of modern chemistry—the last product of chemical analysis—but of a more 'elemental' kind, being the stuff out of which all matter was thought to be composed; when any lump of terrestrial matter was mentally analysed it would be found to be composed of earth, air, fire and water in varying proportions. This is why Iago could say of Desdemona

> She's framed as fruitful
> As the free elements.[2]

The elements themselves were composed of the universal matter filling the universe on which had been impressed various 'forms': of cold and dry for earth, hot and moist for air, hot and dry for fire, cold and moist for water; as the distinction between the elements rested only on form, they could be changed into one another by change of form.

'Does not our life consist of the four elements?' asked Sir Toby Belch,[3] emphasizing the corporeal aspect of mortal man. Greek physiology had associated the elements and their forms with the four humours or temperaments; sanguine, phlegmatic, choleric and melancholic, which indicated, in turn, the possession of an excess of blood, phlegm, yellow bile and black bile. These were a commonplace of speech, and by Shakespeare's day were on the way to become mere temperaments, rather psychological than physiological. As yet, however, they had real meaning for medical practice: illness was the result of an imbalance in the humours, clearly to be re-dressed by depletion to restore the balance.

> Wrath-kindled gentlemen, be ruled by me;
> Let's purge this choler without letting blood:
> This we prescribe, though no physician;
> Deep malice makes too deep incision;
> Forget, forgive; conclude and be agreed;
> Our doctors say this is no month to bleed.[4]

Phlebotomy was an almost invariable remedy, practised for all complaints, though not yet in the deliberately heroic manner of a century later. But sudorifics, purgatives and diuretics were also used in profusion, the manner of administration and the drug chosen depending upon the prescribing physician; all were aimed at purging one or other of the four humours.

Technically, only a doctor of medicine was licensed to practise; and his preparation was long. The medical faculty of a university admitted only M.A.'s; the curriculum consisted of the study of selected texts, primarily Galen's therapeutic works supplemented by the *Canon of Medicine* of

Avicenna and various commentaries. By the beginning of the sixteenth century there were always lectures in anatomy, held in the winter and making use of the right gained by all medical schools of having the bodies of one or two executed criminals for instructional purposes. The professor read or paraphrased a text, illustrating his remarks with reference to the cadaver; by the mid-sixteenth century most professors either were anatomists or wished to be thought so, and so had dispensed with the demonstrator shown in earlier illustrations. At the same time the medieval textbook was replaced by the newly discovered (and far superior) text of Galen, so that Galen's name became doubly authoritative.

At the same time, a new and independent school, centred mainly in Padua, developed by following the precepts rather than the text of Galen; these men, though leaning on Galen, endeavoured to undertake original anatomical research. The most famous was Andreas Vesalius (1514–64) whose great book *De Humani Corporis Fabrica* (1543) is the largest, most impressive and most beautifully illustrated work of its kind. Vesalius typified the anatomical efforts of his day: he made new discoveries, corrected Galen, revised Galenic physiology, and yet repeated much of what Galen had already done, both good and bad. (The illustrations and much of the material appeared in England in the *Anatomy* of Thomas Geminus, 1545.) Vesalius' contemporaries and successors also produced much that was new and important. The major discoveries were those connected with the blood supply: the discovery of the lesser or pulmonary circulation (first enunciated in print by Servetus in 1553 in a work of theological polemic, and first effectively announced by Realdus Columbus in 1559, though he had discussed it for some years in his lectures at Padua); and the discovery of the valves in the veins (noted by various anatomists, most fully by William Harvey's teacher Fabricius of Aquapendente in a work published in 1603). These discoveries were only fully understood by Harvey (1578–1657) who tentatively announced his own discovery of the circulation of the blood in 1618 to the College of Physicians, publishing his final account in 1628. The later sixteenth century also saw important work in embryology (notably by Fabricius) and in comparative anatomy.

Besides anatomy, the physician learned the arts of diagnosis (including uroscopy), therapeutics, prognosis and general medical philosophy. He also learned medical ethics, together with pride in his profession and scorn for lesser practitioners. These were many, mostly unlicensed, but in demand because of the shortage of trained physicians; because, in the then state of medical knowledge, even the physician could do little to cure a disease; and because there was widespread the not altogether unfounded belief that physicians killed as often as they cured. Though the physician was legally the only person licensed to prescribe drugs, then as now pharmacists and apothecaries were frequently called upon by the sick to suggest appropriate drugs from their stock.

The commonest drugs were of plant origin, their origin and properties described in the herbals and materia medica which traced their origin back to that of Dioscorides, a Greek army doctor of the first century A.D. Herbals were half botanical, half medical: they combined descriptions of plants and identifying pictures (which make them handsome examples of Renaissance printing) with careful summaries of the medical application of various parts of each plant. The physical characteristics of some part of the plant commonly dictated its function: the blue flowers of eyebright were thought, in infusion, to aid the eyes; liver-wort cured diseases of the liver, and so on. The theory that God had purposely made parts of plants in the shape of the organ they affected was known as the doctrine of signatures; its widespread acceptance reveals the strong magical element still present in medical practice, however remote it might be from up-to-date medical theory.

Herbal remedies might be simple infusions, decoctions or sugary syrups; by the sixteenth century they might also be alcoholic 'essences' prepared by distillation. Cordials (so called because they were thought to strengthen the heart) were prepared by distillation from a vast variety of substances of vegetable origin, and were particularly recommended in time of plague. Even newer were the drugs of 'mineral' origin (mostly metals and their salts), whose use was advocated by the followers of Paracelsus, and whose preparation, at first secret, was fully described in textbooks of chemistry for the use of apothecaries after about 1610. During Shakespeare's lifetime there was relentless and much publicized war between those physicians who favoured herbal 'Galenicals' and those who favoured the 'chymical' drugs of the Paracelsans. This struggle, expressed in wordy polemic and legal regulation, was known to the lay public, who, however, often confused chemical drugs with the secret remedies of wonder-working empirics. (Juliet's 'potion' is a case in point.) Gradually the 'chymists' won: popular opinion opted for the newer and more violent purges and emetics of the chemists (mainly mercurial and antimonial compounds) over the more familiar herbal preparations. Though Paracelsus (1493–1541) had been a thorough mystic, his name after his death connoted his 'school' of medical chemistry, which laboured hard to increase the number of chemical drugs on the shelves of the apothecaries' shops.[1]

Given the contemporary controversies and the almost total inability of the physician to cure serious diseases it is no wonder that the gravely ill so often resorted to unlicensed 'empirics'. Empirics were those who, rebelling against orthodox practice as derived from Galen (the one name known to all),[2] professed to derive their knowledge from experience alone. Generally they relied upon some secret remedy deemed infallible, usually indiscriminately applied to all ills. The father of Helena was such a one, of a manifestly successful reputation; yet the King of France was properly wary:

> We thank you, maiden;
> But may not be so credulous of cure,
> When our most learned doctors leave us, and
> The congregated college have concluded
> That labouring art can never ransom nature
> From her inaidible estate; I say we must not
> So stain our judgement, or corrupt our hope,
> To prostitute our past-cure malady
> To empirics, or to dissever so
> Our great self and our credit, to esteem
> A senseless help when help past sense we deem.[3]

Characteristically, Helena protested that her secret remedy could hurt no one (though it could cure an otherwise incurable disease), and that it would work within the space of a mere two days. As so often must have been true, even the hope of a cure was irresistible; and in keeping with the reputation of the dead empiric, the treatment was wholly successful. It can seldom have been so in actual fact; nor could any but the great expect the services of so well-bred a healer. The empiric whom lesser folk knew was the quack of the fair and market place, an alternative to the wise women or herb gatherers of the villages.

One other form of medical practitioner was employed in all walks of life—the surgeon. Technically there were two types of surgeon, the barber-surgeon who cut hair as readily as he did veins being the lowlier. But a reform antedating Shakespeare's birth had, in England, amalgamated the two branches and tended to raise the status of the lowlier; it is evident that surgeon and barber were usually separate individuals. The English surgeon was supposed to have had a grammar school education and therefore to know some Latin, though unlike the physician he wrote in English. Surgeons trained in London were expected to attend anatomy demonstrations provided by the Surgeons' Company; the lecturers were commonly university-trained physicians. The main training came in practice, as such a work as the delightfully autobiographical case-book of William Clowes (1544–1604) painfully demonstrated.

The surgeon dealt with a specialized range of ills. All wounds and fractures lay within his province, not that of the physician, and most of the famous sixteenth-century surgeons began their careers as army or navy surgeons, technically attached to a general or admiral, but in fact serving regiment or ship. (Othello's surgeon is a case in point.) Because ulcers, fistulas and running sores were common, and all injuries slow to heal (in large part the result of the chronic dietary deficiencies which made scurvy so widespread in the winter and early spring), the surgeon's skill was needed in civil life as well. Even more necessary was the surgeon's skill with the lancet: though the physician prescribed phlebotomy, it was the surgeon who actually let blood. Very often indeed the patient acted as his own physician; in that case the surgeon, not quite legally, usually prescribed any drugs required. The surgeon also handled the epidemic or semi-epidemic diseases newly associated with armies in the field at the end of the fifteenth century; of these syphilis (the 'new disease of the armed forces', the 'French', 'Spanish' or 'English' disease, or to Shakespeare's England simply 'the pox') was at once the most common and the most important. The use of mercury to purge the peccant humours by salivation (mercurial ointment was an old standby in skin diseases) was a powerful stimulus to the introduction of mercurial preparations into general usage.

Perhaps because medicine was in so curiously unprofessional a state, most men knew more about medical practice and the administration of drugs than they did about the rest of animate nature. The love of nature expressed by fifteenth-century humanists was more often a learned man's sentiment, described in Latin treatises, than a sentiment of the non-academic. In Elizabethan England external nature seems to have appealed mainly either through the love of gardens or the delights of hunting. Herbals were Latin works of specialization until the very end of the century; John Gerard (whose immensely popular English *Herball* was first published in 1597) was, typically, a gardener. Town and country dweller alike knew the names of herbs and flowers used in cookery, household remedies and gardens. Interest in animals, except those connected with the chase, was also limited. John Caius, the physician, wrote on dogs, but even this work was in Latin, and first published as part of the Latin *History of Animals* of the Swiss humanist Conrad Gesner, an encyclopedia published in the 1550's. Zoology for the English-reading public was poor until the early seventeenth century brought translations: first of the *Natural History* of the Roman Pliny in 1601, then of parts of Gesner by Edward Topsell (1607–8), both widely read.

PLATE I

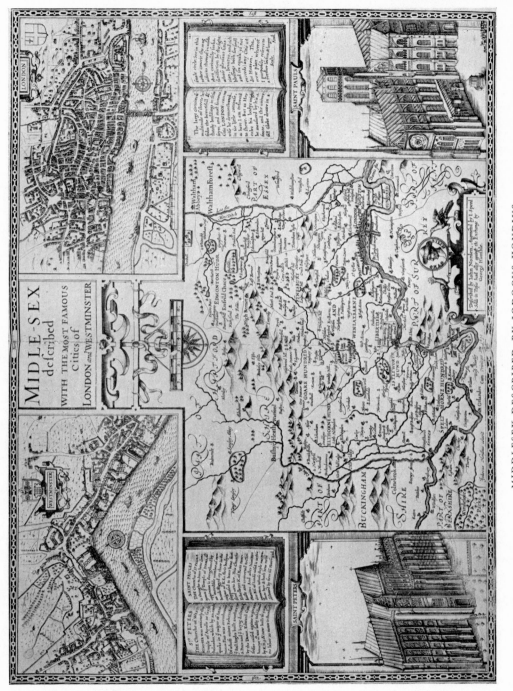

MIDDLESEX DESCRIBED, BY JODOCUS HONDIUS

In John Speed, *The Theatre of the Empire of Great Britaine*, 1611–12

PLATE II

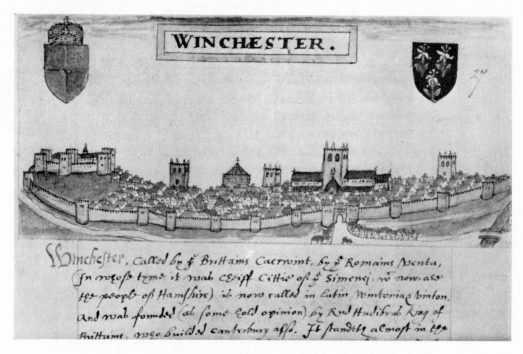

A. BIRD'S-EYE VIEW OF WINCHESTER, BY T. SMITH

B. PLAN OF NORWICH, BY WILLIAM CUNNINGHAM
In *The Cosmographical Glass*, 1559

PLATE III

ELIZABETHAN SAILOR IN SIXTEENTH-CENTURY COSTUME

PLATE IV

A. *The Revenge* (500 tons)

B. *The Tiger* (200 tons)

C. *The Swiftsure* (400 tons)

SHIPS OF 1580

PLATE V

A. *The Aid* (250 tons)

B. *The Victualler* (50–60 tons)

C. *The Jack* (10–15 tons)

SHIPS OF 1580

PLATE VI

PROBABLY DRAKE'S FLAGSHIP, 'ELIZABETH BONAVENTURE' (600 tons)

PLATE VII

MAPPA MUNDI, *c.* 1500

PLATE VIII

A. CHICHESTER MISSAL

B. DOUCE MS

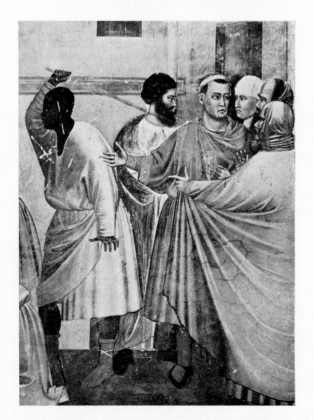

C. 'MOCKING OF CHRIST', BY GIOTTO

D. FROM LUDWIG LAVATER,
'DE SPECTRIS', 1683

PLATE IX

TITLE-PAGE OF 'PURCHAS HIS PILGRIMES', 1625

PLATE X

A. WESTMINSTER HALL IN THE EARLY SEVENTEENTH CENTURY

The Court of Chancery is on the right, the King's Bench on the left

B. CONSISTORY COURT OF CHESTER

PLATE XI

COURT OF WARDS AND LIVERIES

PLATE XII

A. SIR EDWARD COKE, ATTORNEY-GENERAL, 1593

B. AN ATTORNEY IN THE REIGN OF CHARLES I
From George Ruggle, *Ignoramus*, 1603

PLATE XIII

PRESSING TO DEATH

From *The Life and Death of Griffen Flood Informer*, 1623

PLATE XIV

A. The Counter Scuffle

B. The Counter-Ratt

TITLE-PAGES OF 'THE COVNTER SCVFFLE, WHEREUNTO IS ADDED
THE COVNTER-RATT', 1628

PLATE XV

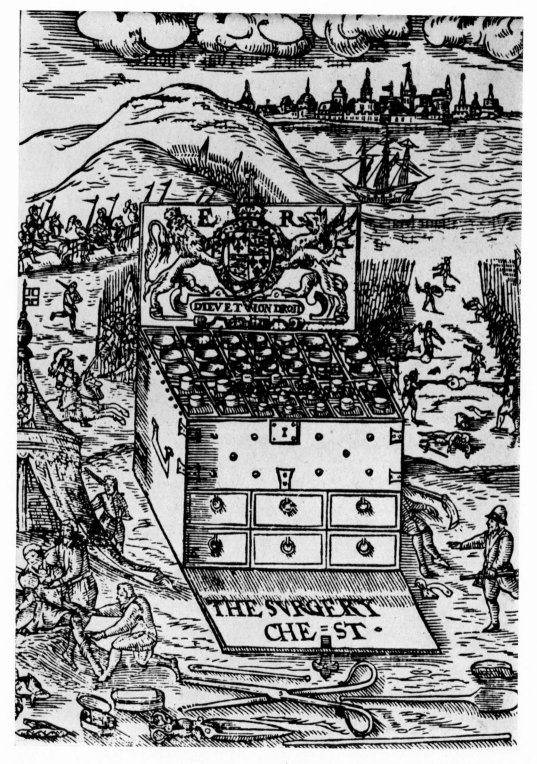

THE SURGEON'S CHEST

From William Clowes, *A profitable and necessarie booke of observations*, 1596

PLATE XVI

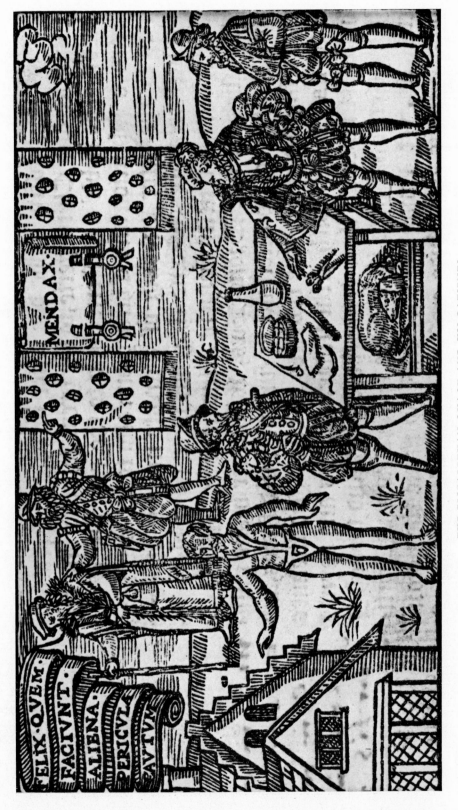

THE ELIZABETHAN QUACK AND HIS PATIENTS

From William Clowes, *A briefe and necessarie treatise*, 1585

PLATE XVII

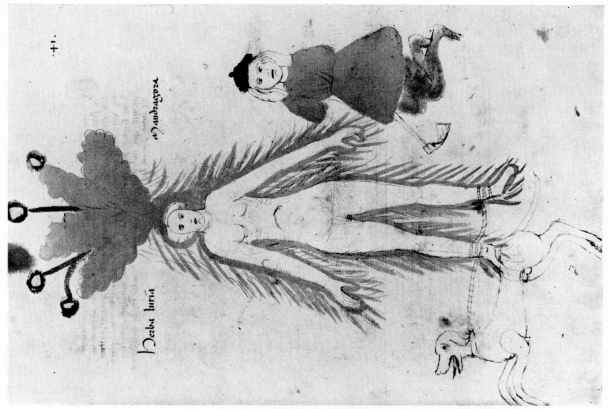

B. HERBAL, WITH NAMES OF MEDICINAL PLANTS, C. 1475

A. TITLE-PAGE OF JOHN GERARD'S 'THE HERBALL', 1597

PLATE XVIII

A. THE DEVICE CALLED LONDINIUM, BY WILLIAM KIP

From Stephen Harrison, *Archs of Triumph*, 1604

B. PART OF A CIVIC PROCESSION

Anonymous, after John Norden, 1600

PLATE XIX

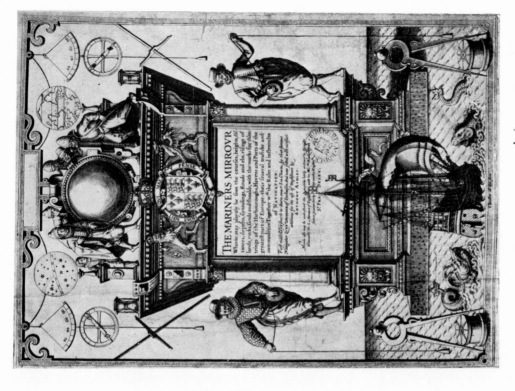

B. TITLE-PAGE OF WAGENAER'S 'MARINERS MIRROUR', BY THEODORE DE BRY

A. TITLE-PAGE OF HENRY PEACHAM'S 'MINERVA BRITANNA'

PLATE XX

B.   The Salamander
'I nourish and I extinguish'

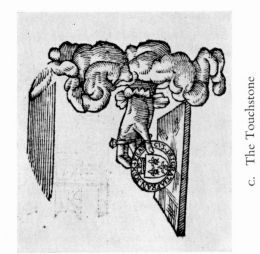

C.   The Touchstone
'So is faith to be tried'

'THE HEROICALL DEVISES OF M. CLAUDIUS
PARADIN', 1591

A.   ELIZABETH BETWEEN TWO COLUMNS

PLATE XXI

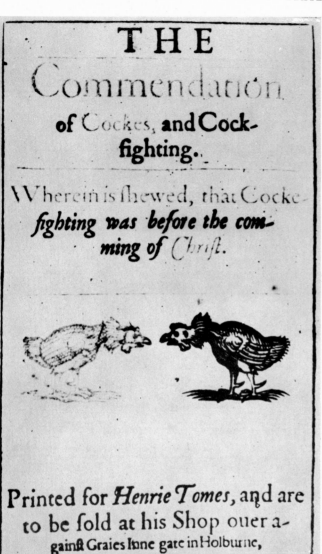

From George Wilson, *The Commendation of Cockes and Cock-Fighting*, 1607

The cock-fighting season lasted from the end of August till the end of May. Wilson's book, written to defend the sport against Puritan attack, tells of a cock of his called Tipsy who fought so valiantly at Bury St Edmunds that he was carried round the town followed by a procession of gentlemen, the City waits, the trainbands and the cock masters

B. A GAMESTER PLAYING DICE

'Noethrift', from *A Pake of Knaves*

PLATE XXII

A. The world a whipping top

His vertitur orbis.

O Lord thou knowest my foolishness & my Sins are not hid from thee Ps: 09: 5.

B. The hobby horse

'CHILDISH BAUBLES'

From Francis Quarles, *Emblems Divine and Moral*

PLATE XXIII

Utriusq⁹ crepundia Merces.

A. GALLANT PLAYING BOWLS

From Francis Quarles, *Emblems Divine and Moral*

The gallant, Mammon, plays against Cupid; the bowls are sinful thoughts, the prize a crown for fools: Satan is the 'juditious Fiend' who 'gives the ground', and Gill Fortune stands by the jack, which represents the world.

B. CUPID PLAYING BILLIARDS
WITH AN ANGEL

From Francis Quarles, *Emblems Divine and Moral*

The billiard player's aim was to get through the arch and touch the ivory king (here represented by a crown of thorns) without knocking it over: also to put an opponent's ball into the hazards, or pockets. Here, Cupid's path is short and free from rubs, the way to hell: the right way is through the thorny and narrow gate. (Elizabethan tables were covered with green cloth; but they were not very true.)

Erras hâc itur ad illam

104

PLATE XXIV

A. QUEEN ELIZABETH AT A HUNT-PICNIC

From George Turberville, *A Book of Faulconrie*, 1575

B. A PICNIC, BY SIMON VAN DE PASSE

PLATE XXV

A. PORTRAIT OF HENRY VIII

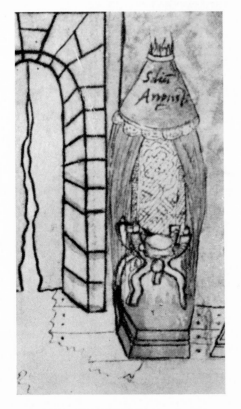

B. CANOPIED THRONE

C. TITLE-PAGE WOODCUT FROM 'THE SPANISH
TRAGEDY', 1615

PLATE XXVI

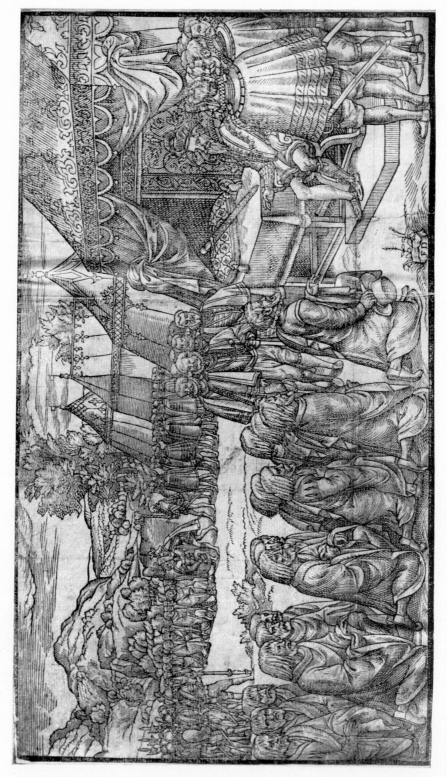

JOHN DERRICKE'S 'THE IMAGE OF IRELAND', 1581

PLATE XXVII

A. DU BARTAS' 'DIVINE WEEKES
AND WORKES', 1621

B. RICHARD BRAITHWAIT'S 'THE
ENGLISH GENTLEWOMAN', 1631

C. TITLE-PAGE OF 'TRUTH BROUGHT TO
LIGHT AND DISCOVERED BY TIME', 1651

PLATE XXVIII

MODEL OF WOODEN PRINTING PRESS AT UNIVERSITY COLLEGE LONDON

Both these works combined much interesting zoological information. Pliny suffered from the fact that he described the Mediterranean world, but though Topsell had a wider range and more exact information Pliny's style had the greater charm. Both offered much to appeal to the Renaissance love of the marvellous, fed on a long tradition, derived ultimately from Pliny but Christianized and allegorized in medieval bestiaries. But though Shakespeare knew of mermaids, he apparently was not well read in the lore of the bestiary, since he was confused about the unicorn, properly subdued only by a virgin.[1] He did know one of the most famous of all Christian zoological allegories, no doubt repeated in a hundred sermons in sixteenth-century pulpits—that of the pelican. The origin of the fable can be traced to the early Christian Greek treatise *Physiologus*, known later in many Latin versions: the pelican's young rebel as they grow, and in her anger she strikes and kills them. Then, in remorse, she feeds them with blood from her own breast, and they revive.[2] The pelican was said to represent God, her young the human race. In the same way the bear who licked her unformed cubs into shape, or the ostrich hiding her head in the sand, though originally mistaken accounts of animal behaviour, took on religious significance with time. When all was strange it was not difficult to believe in strange monsters elsewhere; the Middle Ages cherished the fable of the barnacle goose, born in the far north from barnacle-covered logs;[3] the Renaissance, with a wider range of strange lands and stranger tales from discoverers, had even stranger zoological monsters to tell of. When even the elephant was known only from Pliny's description, what was one to make of the even more curious marvels described by sailors and travellers? The descriptions grew in wonder as they were repeated. Well might the Bermudas be described as 'the Ile of Divels'[4] and be thought to contain the wonders of *The Tempest*. Shakespeare's age was still the age of credulity and wonder, and the investigations of the new science as yet touched man's life and thought but little.

II

MEDICINE AND PUBLIC HEALTH

'Nature and sickness'

In no other subject discussed in this volume, except possibly the natural and physical sciences, has there been so fundamental a break between past and present as there has been in the development of medicine and public health. Unless we can leap back across that gap and regard what we find on the other side without the superiority of 'hindsight' we shall never be able to appreciate fully the significance of the numerous medical allusions in Shakespeare. The emotional colouring which always surrounds sickness and death, the horror which is naturally aroused by the very thought of great epidemics of plague or smallpox, the aesthetic revulsion which is now the normal reaction to dirt, unwashed bodies and bad smells, the mixed feelings provoked by the spectacle of grave physicians consulting the stars before treating a patient, these are only a few of the obstacles which stand in the way of a fair appraisal.

I

The unprecedented developments in medical science and practice during the past century have brought us far from the doctors and diseases familiar in Shakespeare's world. They have also, by their complexity and by the highly technical language which has grown around them, removed the whole subject from the body of general knowledge accessible to the ordinary well-educated man or woman. In Shakespeare's day medical knowledge was as commonplace and necessary as a knowledge of other domestic skills. Medical books were just as likely to be found in any gentleman's library as literary or historical works.[1] Families in the higher ranks of society often had their own manuscript volume of prescriptions and remedies, collected either from reading or from friends and neighbours, which was passed down from generation to generation and which even the local doctor would not disdain to consult.[2] The ladies of the household often attained great skill and experience in the art of healing and were noted for their 'good neighbourhood',[3] so that there is nothing out of the way in Helena (*All's Well*, II, i, 107–17) being entrusted with the 'secrets' of her father, a professional physician. Although the College of Physicians attempted to stop the practice, many professional physicians and surgeons saw nothing unethical in preserving their own secret remedies which were regarded as valuable properties.[4]

Many striking and memorable phrases from the classics of medical literature had become a part of popular wisdom and it is not at all surprising that Mistress Quickly (*Henry V*, II, iii, 9–28) should, when describing the death of Falstaff, come so close to the classic description by Hippocrates of the physical changes which precede death and which is still widely known among physicians as the 'Hippocratic facies'. Nor is it surprising to find in the plays direct translations of phrases from one of the most enduring of all medical writings, the *Aphorisms* of Hippocrates, such as

...Diseases desperate grown
By desperate appliance are relieved,
Or not at all,   (*Hamlet*, IV, iii, 9–11)

and

For to strange sores strangely they strain the cure,
                                    (*Much Ado About Nothing*, IV, i, 254)

both of which have their origin in the sixth aphorism.

It is probable that at least some of this aphoristic lore had become well known through the celebrated Regimen of Salerno, a code of simple rules for the preservation of health written in easily learned verses. It was the product of the School of Salerno which was founded in the eleventh century, being the first medical school in Europe. One of the most popular medical texts during the Middle Ages, it was widely circulated in manuscript, both in the original Latin and in several vernacular translations, and was later often printed. The first English translation appeared in 1528 and went through a dozen editions, but in 1607 there was published a fresh translation by Sir John Harington, entitled *The Englishmans Doctor. Or, The Schoole of Salerne*, which was reprinted four times within twenty years.

Best known among amateur physicians is the Marquis of Dorchester (1606–80) who became so well known for his skill that he was elected a Fellow of the College of Physicians in 1658 and left his valuable library to the College at his death. Among his predecessors was the Earl of Derby (Edward Stanley, 1508–72) who 'was famous for chirurgerie, bone-setting and hospitalitie'. Men such as he and Lord Lumley, who founded the Surgery Lecture at the College of Physicians in 1582, could well have provided the model for Shakespeare's Lord Cerimon (*Pericles*, III, ii, 26–48), but many anonymous humble folk did just as well. There could have been few living at that time who had not seen advanced disease and injury at close quarters from their earliest years. The sick were not rushed off to hospital but treated within the family circle. Such hospitals as there were—St Bartholomew's, St Thomas's, and Bethlem (Bethlehem) for the insane—were no places for respectable folk but were reserved entirely for the sick poor.

Midwifery was entirely in the hands of women, a few of whom may have gone to the trouble of acquiring an episcopal licence to practise, but it was customary for any woman to be called upon in this capacity and it was usual for five or six 'gossips' to be present at a birth. Among them would be found many like the Nurse in *Romeo and Juliet*. The birth-rate was very high and many women died young from excessive child-bearing, the figure of ten or more children before the age of thirty often appearing in the records. This factor may account for the paradox that despite the medical conditions of the time and the widespread epidemics there were some years during the reign of Elizabeth when the birth-rate was as much as 25 per cent higher than the death rate, a figure rarely attained in any modern societies. Infant mortality however was also very high and almost certainly exceeded the appalling rate of 50 per cent still common in London in the mid-eighteenth century.

All this amateur practice was legally permitted by the third of the Medical Acts of Henry VIII, unjustly known among the medical profession as 'the Quacks' Charter', passed in 1542.[1] Because, it seemed, the surgeons were 'minding only their own lucres', freedom to practise was granted to 'divers honest persons, as well men as women, whom God hath endued with the knowledge of the nature, kind and operation of certain herbs, roots and waters, and the using and ministering of them to such as be pained with customable diseases'. The results achieved by such people often compared favourably with those of the learned physicians restricted within the close bounds of ancient medical theories.

Fiercer and more unscrupulous competition came from the many quacks and mountebanks whose sole aim was money and whose activities often resulted in death for the trusting patients. Latin was for long the language of medicine and, apart from the eccentric Dr Andrew Boorde and his *Breviary of Helthe* (1547, etc.), it was left to the surgeons of the time, Thomas Gale, William Clowes, John Banister, John Hall and others, to write books in English for their fellows. They apologize for using their native tongue, mainly because their 'secrets' were revealed to those outside the fold, but they justify it by reminding their readers that Hippocrates and Galen wrote in theirs. Most of the books contain bitter attacks on the rogues and cheats who battened on the credulous. According to Clowes they were made up of

Tinkers, Tooth-drawers, Pedlers, Ostlers, Carters, Porters, Horse-gelders, & horse-leeches, Ideots, Apple-squires, Broomemen, bawds, witches, cuniurers, South-saiers, & sow gelders, Roages, Rat-catchers, Runagates, & Procters of Spitlehouses, with such other lyke rotten & stincking weeds, which do in town & Countrie, without order, honestie, or skil, daily abuse both Phisick & Chirurgerie, hauing no more perseuerance, reason, or knowledge in this art, then hath a goose: but a certain blind practise, without wisdome or iudgement, & most commonly useth one remedie for all diseases, and one waye of curing to all persons, both olde and young, men, women and children, which is as possible to be parformed, or to be true, as for a Shoomaker with one last to make a shew fit for euery mans foote, and this is one principall cause, that so many perish.[1]

Shakespeare has less to say about the members of this gallimaufry than other contemporary dramatists, but his Pinch in the *Comedy of Errors* (v, i, 236–48) is clearly one of them. The more prosperous and respectable of these quacks would be accorded the title 'Doctor', for the border-line between qualified and unqualified practice was never very clear and their pretensions were accepted without much question.

II

Early in the reign of Henry VIII, in 1512, an attempt had been made to regulate the practice of medicine by Act of Parliament and to suppress rampant superstition and quackery. The only system of administration covering the whole country at that time was the Church, and this Act introduced a scheme by which honest and respectable practitioners obtained a licence to practise from the Bishop after they had been approved by qualified medical assessors. Many men and some women with no formal training or degree were eventually licensed in this way. The establishment of the College of Physicians in 1518 was a further step in the effort to control a widespread evil, but was not remarkably successful in achieving its aim. Membership of the College was open only to those who already had the degree of M.D. from Oxford or Cambridge and throughout the sixteenth century admissions were at the rate of less than one a year, the total being so small that it could do little more than supply the needs of the Court and the great households. By its original Charter the College was entrusted with the control of medical practice in London and within seven miles thereof, but the extension of this right in 1522 to cover the whole kingdom was unrealistic, for the College had no officers outside London to enforce the regulations. Recent research[1] has shown that in fact it represented little more than 5 per cent of all the medical graduates in the kingdom, most of whom had received their degrees from foreign universities.

Their medical training had consisted almost entirely of textual study, anything from six to eleven years being spent on the writings of Galen and Hippocrates and their medieval commentators. The medical education offered at the universities of Oxford and Cambridge was in fact of a very low standard and many of the leading physicians of the time had preferred to study abroad, especially at the celebrated university of Padua, where Thomas Linacre, the founder of the College of Physicians, John Caius, a President of the College and founder of Gonville and Caius College at Cambridge, as well as the great William Harvey, discoverer of the circulation of the blood, all carried out their medical studies. Even there all teaching was based on the ancient classics and the Galenic system with its elaboration of the old Greek ideas of the four elements (air, earth, fire, and water) and the four humours (blood—hot and moist; phlegm—cold and moist; yellow bile—hot and dry; and black bile—cold and dry) with their accompanying complexions (sanguine, phlegmatic, choleric, melancholy).

Perfect health depended upon the balance of the humours, and disease was caused when this balance was temporarily lost, as when Chatillon, using the term metaphorically, speaks of the 'unsettled humours of the land' (*King John*, II, i, 66). In order to restore it the peccant humours were corrected by blood-letting or purgation. The theoretical nature of this pathology fitted perfectly into an age which knew little of the real causes of disease but which delighted in logical, theological and philosophical systems, and so familiar was it as a way of thought that nobody ever dreamed of questioning its validity.

One other important factor in judging the course of a disease and its treatment was the influence of the stars. Chaucer's physician was 'grounded in astronomy' and so were his successors, for astrology was for long an important branch of orthodox medical science. Galen himself had written a treatise on 'critical days' and there is a similar one in the Hippocratic writings. Even in seventeenth-century England, in the time of Harvey, Boyle, and Newton, it is commonplace to find highly qualified physicians following Galen closely in these matters. So generally accepted were these ideas that even classes, professions and trades were arranged in a hierarchy within the scheme. Thus, the doctor was properly under the influence of the planet Mars, his dominant humour was yellow bile (hot and dry) and his temperament choleric. This may have some bearing on the fact that he so often figures in comedy, for the short bursts of anger so characteristic of the choleric temperament are always good for a laugh from the onlooker.

But there is no satire in accounts of a doctor casting the horoscope of his patients and judging from the position of the planets whether the disease was in the ascendant or the decline, and whether it was, astrologically speaking, a proper time for bleeding, purging, or taking physic. When Richard II appealed to his nobles:

> Let's purge this choler without letting blood

and added

> Our doctors say this is no month to bleed   (I, i, 153, 157)

he was repeating phrases familiar to most of the audience of the time.

According to the humoral system every disease went through three phases: (1) preliminary; (2) the stage of coction or digestion in which the humours acted upon each other; (3) the crisis, during which the excrementitious humours evolved by coction were expelled, their presence being detected by the various 'colours' of the urine. In the older medical works there are often elaborate charts where all the colours of the urine are arranged in a circle or table according to the offending humour or combination of humours which have brought about the disease—a kind of diagnostic ready-reckoner. The inspection of urine for diagnosis by this method was known as *urinoscopy*, and the physician was said to 'cast the patients' water'. The analogy with casting a horoscope is obvious. The phrase is used by Shakespeare: Macbeth says:

> If thou couldst, doctor, cast
> The water of my land, find her disease,
> And purge it to a sound and pristine health,
> I would applaud thee to the very echo. (*Macbeth*, v, iii, 50–3)

The 'urinal' or urine flask, which was shaped like the human bladder, was regarded everywhere almost as the physician's badge of office. When he is teasing his master Valentine, Speed declares that

these follies are within you and shine through you like the water in an urinal, that not an eye that sees you but is a physician to comment on your malady. (*Two Gentlemen of Verona*, II, i, 42–6)

The presence of the patient was not thought to be necessary and a doctor's waiting room in those days would have presented a picture of husbands, wives, fathers, mothers, serving men and women, waiting patiently for Master Doctor to look at the flasks which they clutched tightly in their hands or held carefully in a specially made small wicker carrier. Falstaff sent a page with his and greeted him on his return:

> Sirrah, you giant, what says the doctor to my water?

to which the page replies:

He said, sir, the water itself was a good healthy water; but, for the party that owed it, he might have more diseases than he knew for. (*2 Henry IV*, I, ii, 1–6)

This practice lasted well into the seventeenth century, despite the condemnation of the College of Physicians, who preferred to recommend the indications from the pulse, although the Galenic pulse lore was full of error. Apart from judging the extent of fever by feeling the forehead with the back of his hand, the doctor had no other means of diagnosis than sight, smell or taste, for the stethoscope was an early nineteenth-century innovation and the clinical thermometer came later still. It was therefore considered normal that the doctor should diagnose at a distance, basing his judgement on what he was told by the patient's family or the apothecary. Any active treatment was beneath his dignity and such menial tasks as letting blood were left to the barber-surgeon.

In the normal course of his duties the physician at court was in a position to learn many secrets and to use his knowledge of drugs and poisons in dynastic intrigues, a situation which provided sensational material for some dramatists but which was not greatly exploited by Shakespeare. He does however allude to the doctor's wealth and influence:

> The doctor is well money'd, and his friends
> Potent at court... *(Merry Wives of Windsor*, IV, iv, 88)

It is the physician's ignorance and the danger of his remedies rather than his malice which provides the target of Timon's bitter gibe:

> trust not the physician:
> His antidotes are poison, and he slays
> More than you rob... *(Timon of Athens*, IV, iii, 434–6)

or when Richard II prays:

> Now put it, God, into the physician's mind
> To help him to his grave immediately. *(Richard II*, I, iv, 59–60)

Cornelius, in *Cymbeline*, far from carrying out the Queen's evil designs, risks his life to counteract them. The doctor who is called in to see Lady Macbeth is honest and cautious, if not unmindful of his fees. He cannot 'minister to a mind diseased', but the doctor in *King Lear* (IV, iv, 1–15; vii, 14–25, 78–82) can and does, most successfully, and in a humane manner then far removed from the orthodox treatment such as that meted out to Malvolio (*Twelfth Night*, III, iv, 93–154) and referred to by Rosalind when she says that

Love is merely a madness, and, I tell you, deserves as well a dark house and a whip as madmen do.
(As You Like It, III, ii, 420–2)

Mental illness was from earliest times thought to be caused by demoniac possession and only to be overcome by harsh physical means.

Two of the physicians who appear as characters in the plays bear the names of well-known doctors; they are Dr Butts in *Henry VIII* and Dr Caius in *The Merry Wives of Windsor*. Sir William Butts was physician to the king and his role in the play is that of a sober and experienced counsellor rather than a medical attendant, but Shakespeare's Dr Caius has no resemblance to the serious and scholarly John Caius who was President of the College of Physicians. However, considering the limitations of the physician's practical abilities, his prized latinity and his pompous bearing, it is perhaps not unnatural that he should be made the butt of comedy.[1]

III

Much more down to earth and one of the ordinary folk was the surgeon, whose Company of Barber-Surgeons, established by royal charter in 1540 under the leadership of Thomas Vicary, supervised his training and regulated his practice. As a rule he was educated in a grammar school and was apprenticed at the age of fourteen for seven years. It was at the bidding of Henry VIII that a version of the great anatomical work of Vesalius,[2] with plates engraved by Thomas Geminus, was printed in London in 1545. In the following year John Caius, who had shared lodgings with Vesalius at Padua, began a course of anatomical lectures at Barber-Surgeons' Hall which was to continue for 21 years. The Company was allowed the bodies of four executed criminals each year for the purposes of dissection and instruction and there is little doubt that the surgeon of 1595 was much more knowledgeable in practical anatomy than the best of surgeons fifty years earlier. Facilities for anatomical study were not limited to these few permitted dissections, for post-mortem investigations to discover the cause of death were not unusual, especially among the higher ranks of society (perhaps to ensure that poison had not been used), a practice referred to by Lear (III, vi, 80–1).

Although technically they were supposed to operate only under the direction of a physician, the surgeons did of course carry on an independent practice, but they were not allowed to encroach upon the preserve of the physician and were restricted to the treatment of wounds, fractures, injuries and 'outward diseases'. In the frequent wars of the time many untrained surgeons were called into service so that the reputation of the whole craft suffered. Amputations on the battlefield, without anaesthetics or antiseptics, were frequent, and a responsible surgeon like William Clowes followed the practice then recently introduced by the famous French surgeon Ambroise Paré. By skilful ligation of the arteries and conservative after-care he saved many a patient to walk the streets of London on a wooden 'peg-leg'. The opening of the abdomen or thorax was never attempted deliberately, but a penetrating sword-wound of the chest was successfully treated by Clowes, as also was a depressed fracture of the skull in one of the victims of the accident at the Bear Garden in Southwark on 15 January 1583, when the gallery collapsed beneath the weight of the spectators. Deep wounds were cleaned out (or 'searched') with a roll of lint called a 'tent' before being dressed with a variety of unguents and plasters, this same treatment being given to the wounds left after the removal of ulcers and tumours.[1] Blood-letting was of course the commonest of the surgeon's tasks and he was also employed to drain excess fluid from dropsical patients. Stone of the bladder was far more frequently found than it is today, but its removal by surgery was dangerous and often fatal so that few regular surgeons cared to attempt it, preferring to leave it to the itinerant lithotomists (mostly German or Italian) whose methods seemed to meet with better success. To them too was usually left the treatment of hernia (see the truss in Pl. XVI) and cataract ('the pin and web' or 'web of the eye') which called for great experience and skill. Being concerned with 'outward diseases', the surgeon found a great part of his practice in treating syphilis and skin diseases, both of which were extremely common. It is interesting to find that a woman surgeon who had remarkable success with skin diseases was officially appointed in 1620 to care for such cases in St Bartholomew's Hospital.

None of Shakespeare's plays has any specific role for a surgeon and only four times are surgeons referred to. On one of these occasions (*Twelfth Night*, v, i, 202) he is said to be too drunk to appear on the scene. Such behaviour was probably not unusual among many who called themselves surgeons, but no such misdemeanour is known of any of the band of energetic and responsible men who controlled the affairs of their profession from Barber-Surgeons' Hall, although two of them were once reprimanded for fighting outside the Hall.

When the physician 'feared for his patient' and saw the approach of death he 'gave over', received his fee and departed, but the surgeon, especially if he operated, undertook a 'cure' and was often sued in the courts if he failed. Even William Clowes, Surgeon to the Queen, was involved in such a suit and had to return his fee. The fear of actions by dissatisfied patients made the more respectable surgeons very cautious in accepting cases and they would sometimes refuse one which seemed particularly difficult or dangerous. The risks of post-operative infection were great and rich patients would ensure the surgeon's presence by paying large sums for him to remain in their homes until the wound was healed.

IV

Both physicians and surgeons used large quantities of drugs, for although the basis of most of them was 'simples', the oils, tinctures, electuaries, pills, unguents and plasters of the time usually combined many of them in a single prescription, for which the patient paid dearly according to their number. The drug trade was in the hands of the apothecaries, at first a part of the Grocers' Company but from 1617 an independent Society with a royal charter. Familiarity with the prescriptions of the physicians for the common diseases gave the apothecaries some grounds for commencing independent medical practice and even in the sixteenth century a number of them were acting in the capacity of general practitioners. They were generally prosperous and the poverty of Friar Lawrence in *Romeo and Juliet* would, apart from his membership of a religious order, at once mark him out as a 'stranger' for contemporary Londoners.

As there was little or no knowledge of physiology so there was no scientific pharmacology and nobody knew how or why precisely the plants, minerals and parts of animals used in medicine had their effects, although the results of their administration were at times only too apparent. Patients were as avid then as now for medicines which had a powerful effect and the old pharmacopoeia contained enough purgatives and vomitories to satisfy the most determined hypochondriac. Knowledge of medicinal plants was traditional and empirical, the most authoritative text of the time being that of Dioscorides, a Greek surgeon in the army of Nero. It was the subject of numerous commentaries in the sixteenth century and out of these, and the work of Turner, Fuchs, Matthiolus, Dodoens, and Lobel, gradually developed the modern science of botany. The old 'herbal' was essentially a medical book containing a comprehensive account of all the plants used in orthodox medicine, which is now the unorthodox medicine of the 'herbalist'. Because most of them were recommended in the books of Galen they came to be called 'galenicals', a term still found at the head of the pharmacists' list of vegetable drugs. The part of the plant—leaf, stem, root, or fruit—which was effective was known, but chemistry was still in the primitive stage of alchemy and nobody had extracted or isolated the active principle of any one of them. There were several famous remedies which were looked upon as panaceas for all ills and were consequently of great price. Among these was the horn of the mythical unicorn (usually the tusk of narwhal), bezoar stone, an organic concretion sometimes found in the stomachs of goats and other animals, mithridatum, a mixture of more than a hundred ingredients named after King Mithridates of Pontus and supposed to be an antidote for all poisons, and Venice treacle or theriac, so called because it was an official preparation made in Venice and carrying the republic's official seal. Most commonly used of all drugs were such simple purgatives as rhubarb and senna (*Macbeth*, v, iii, 55–6), but narcotics such as opium and mandrake (*Othello*, iii, iii, 330–3), were also available. Many popular beliefs and superstitions had grown around the 'magic' properties of certain drugs and poisons and it is believed that it is there rather than to any drug actually known at the time that we must look for an explanation of Juliet's coma. Mandrake (Atropa mandragora, Linn.) was also highly prized for its supposed aphrodisiac properties and had long been regarded as a 'magic' plant. The resemblance of its forked root to the human form had caused it to be endowed with more than vegetable qualities which made its collection very difficult:

> And shrieks like mandrakes' torn out of the earth,
> That living mortals, hearing them, run mad.   (*Romeo and Juliet*, IV, iii, 47–8)

How the problem was ingeniously solved in practice is illustrated in Plate XVII B.

The few mineral remedies in the ancient *materia medica* had been extended by the Arabs in the ninth and tenth centuries and their use had been greatly encouraged by the work of that great rebel against Galen's authority, the Swiss physician Paracelsus, sometimes called the 'Luther of Medicine'. Medicine was split into two camps with Galen as the acknowledged champion of one and Paracelsus of the other, a situation which is satirized in *All's Well That Ends Well* (II, iii, 1–30). Mercury, sulphur, antimony and arsenic were the best known of minerals used in medicine, and quacks made great play with those products of the alchemist's laboratory, the philosopher's stone, the elixir of youth, and 'aurum potabile' (potable gold) which is referred to by Shakespeare (*2 Henry IV*, IV, v, 161–3) and was the subject of a treatise by Francis Anthony in 1616.

Exciting possibilities opened up for the apothecary with the introduction of medicinal plants from the New World. An excellent account of them by Nicholas Monardes was translated from the Spanish by John Frampton and published as *Joyfull Newes out of the New Founde Worlde* in 1577. The most rapidly and widely adopted of these new 'herbs' was tobacco, which was thought to be beneficial for colds and catarrh. The value of the potato as a food was not immediately appreciated, but the apothecary seized upon it as an aphrodisiac comparable with eryngo (*Merry Wives of Windsor*, V, v, 20; *Troilus and Cressida*, V, ii, 56). The most precious of all the new American drugs, cinchona or Peruvian bark, from which quinine was later isolated as a specific against malaria, was not introduced until the middle of the seventeenth century. Protesting in vain against the expensive foreign importations, Dr Timothy Bright wrote a little book on 'the sufficiencie of English Medicines' (1580),[1] a theme taken up during the Commonwealth period by Nicholas Culpeper.

Very few indeed of the most useful plants were in fact indigenous to Britain and little progress had been made in distinguishing the species of English plants from those found in the Mediterranean area and recommended by Galen. There were no institutional physic gardens, for the Oxford Physic Garden and later the Apothecaries' Garden at Chelsea were established in the following century. The small herb garden was however considered a necessary part of any private garden and some apothecaries had their own commercial gardens. John Gerard, an apothecary-surgeon who published a catalogue of his plants in 1596, had an excellent garden near Chancery Lane in Holborn. In 1597 he published his famous *Herball* which was largely based on traditional sources, coming at the end of a long line rather than at the head of a new one. The work which was to supersede all the old-style herbals and to survive to our own time was the official pharmacopoeia, specimens of which had already appeared in Italy and Germany by the middle of the sixteenth century. The first English pharmacopoeia was that of the College of Physicians, *Pharmacopoeia Londinensis*, first published in May 1618, then hastily withdrawn because of the number of errors and republished in a corrected version in December of the same year. This was designed to be the official guide for the apothecaries in selecting and making up their medicines. The Society of Apothecaries had the duty of inspecting the drug stocks of their members and ensuring that they were genuine and in good condition, but the College also had this right of inspection and often exercised it. Their *Pharmacopoeia* was often republished in successive editions until the middle of the nineteenth century, when it was superseded by the *British Pharmacopoeia* (1864, etc.) drawn up by the Pharmacopoeia Commission working under the direction of the General Medical Council. The first and even some later editions of the *Pharmacopoeia Londinensis* remained distinctly medieval in character, retaining many features of the old herbal. We are particularly shocked today by the number of offensive and nauseating remedies to be found in it, many of which would qualify for inclusion in the witches' brew in *Macbeth*. Not only were they officially recommended but were also, it seems, frequently used in treatment, even by physicians to the Court. How long they persisted may be seen in the vivid account of the last illness and death of Charles II written by the late Sir Raymond Crawfurd.[1]

V

Compared with the public health regulations in many continental towns and cities, where officially appointed Town Physicians supervised the sanitary conditions, those gradually introduced into England were often too little and too late. During outbreaks of epidemic disease hasty measures were taken which were allowed to lapse as soon as the immediate threat had passed. The principles of preventive medicine, based on common sense as they are, were not so obvious at a time when 'common sense' consisted of acceptance of the prevailing humoral doctrine, and of the belief that disease and suffering were God's punishment for sin operating through the influences exerted on all living things by the planets. Evil conjunctions of the planets produced a 'poisoned' and 'corrupt' air which infected all who breathed it. The Hippocratic texts on *Epidemics* and on *Airs, Waters and Places* had already in the fourth century B.C. associated epidemics of certain diseases with climates, atmospheric conditions, and certain geographical features, but in a manner far more natural and reasonable than anything to be found in the elaborate astrological lore of the sixteenth century, for malaria was one of the great killing diseases of ancient Greece and was always to be met with in marshy districts. The 'miasmatic' origin of disease was therefore already established in classical times and to the Elizabethans the planetary origin of 'miasmas' seemed a logical scientific development.

The signs of corrupt air were unpleasant odours, but where the Victorian sanitary reformers (who also believed in 'miasmatic contagion') sought to remove these dangerous odours at their source, the Elizabethans were content to mask them by a variety of perfumes, fumigating rooms and houses, and sometimes the very streets, with the smoke of burning herbs (rosemary, rue, wormwood) or by the more pungent odours of boiling vinegar or burning pitch. Individuals carried about with them small posies of sweet smelling herbs or pomanders made from dried oranges stuck with cloves. The odours they tried to overcome came from cesspools, middens, and the 'laystalls' or dunghills which were to be seen in the overcrowded suburbs just outside the city walls, sites in such places as Shoreditch, Aldgate, and Whitechapel, which were still used for the same purpose until the 1850's. The 'channels' in the centre of the narrow streets were often as offensive as a sewer for, despite regulations, they were the repository of household filth and of offal from slaughter houses and butchers' shops. In London, the main ditches, Fleet Ditch and Moor Ditch, which carried all this unsavoury waste into the Thames, were periodically so obstructed that their stench became intolerable and idlers and vagrants were set to work to clear them out. Shakespeare refers to 'the melancholy of Moor-ditch' and has Falstaff call it 'a most unsavoury simile' (*1 Henry IV*, I, ii, 88).

Although London was the home of the Court and special efforts were made from time to time to ward off the threat of disease implicit in these conditions it remained, especially in its suburbs, one of the unhealthiest spots in the country. A magnet for all those who were left without a livelihood by the inclosures and the conversion of arable land to pasture, as well as for the many rogues and vagrants who sought an easy living in the capital, its population continued to grow steadily in spite of the heavy inroads made by frequent epidemics. Strict limits were set to the city's outward growth and every available plot within the walls was seized upon for building, with a consequent loss of light and air to the surrounding houses. Many older houses were grossly overcrowded so that a statute of 1593 (35 Eliz. c. 6) declared that 'great mischiefs daily grow and increase by reason of pestering the houses with divers families, harbouring of inmates, and converting great houses into several tenements, and the erecting of new buildings in London and Westminster'. This and other attempts to remedy the evil met with little success.

Inside the houses of all but the rich rushes were still the most usual floor covering and were generally changed too infrequently for health or comfort, fresh rushes being strewn to cover those already filthy. The smoke of 'sea-coal', burned on hearths beneath the new but badly designed chimneys, gave rise to many public and private protests, providing Londoners both inside and outside their homes with their first taste of the air pollution which Evelyn was to write against a century later.

Sewage disposal was of a primitive kind and the one sewer which ran beneath London to the Thames was quite inadequate even if it had not been periodically choked. The water closet which Sir John Harington invented[1] was taken no more seriously than its author took himself and remained a mere novelty. The water supply was conveyed through the city in wooden pipes from the Thames and stand pipes were placed at street junctions from which the channels could be sluiced down each morning. When the supply was insufficient all householders who had wells of their own were required to contribute a certain number of buckets of water for this purpose. In 1580 a Dutch engineer named Peter Maurice began to instal beneath the last two arches at the north end of London Bridge the water pumps which were to ensure a much more adequate supply of water under pressure. Considering what went into the Thames it is surprising that Londoners were ready to drink its water, and it is little wonder that outbreaks of typhoid (not then recognized as a distinct disease) were a common occurrence. It was from this disease that Prince Henry died in 1612, just as Prince Albert died in 1861, when it was found that the cesspits in Windsor Castle had overflowed and contaminated the water supply.

The system of disposal of the dead, which would have been quite suitable for a rural parish, proved inadequate for a populous city. In 1583 twenty-three London parishes, which had let their own churchyards for building small tenements, began to use St Paul's for their burials. By 1584 it became necessary to impose restrictions 'by reason of former burials so shallow, that scarcely any graves be made without corpses being laid open'. Here again, precisely similar conditions prevailed in the nineteenth century and were the subject of one of Edwin Chadwick's classic reports. It was strictly forbidden to bury plague victims in any of the churchyards, and when evasion was practised by burial during the hours of darkness new regulations were made fixing certain hours during which burials were permitted. Special plague pits, or communal graves, were dug and set aside for those who died of plague.

If all the regulations with regard to street cleaning had been observed to the letter London would have been much pleasanter for its inhabitants. In each parish there were two scavengers—minor magistrates who were unpaid and held office for a year—whose duty it was to supervise the work of the rakers and to collect dues from householders for their pay. Every householder was supposed to keep clean the street along his own frontage and to repair any broken paving. Many added to the filth in the street instead of removing what was there and paid the scavenger's dues either grudgingly or not at all.

More strictly kept than any of these regulations were those by which the Lord Mayor and Aldermen, directed by the Lords of the Council, supervised the supplies of food and fuel for the city and the conditions of sale of the chief necessities of life, corn, beer, meat, fish, butter, candles, and even the meals offered in ordinaries and hostelries. The city had its own granaries and could requisition or divert supplies of corn from export if it was needed to keep them filled. In 1614 the Lord Mayor complained that there was great waste of corn in brewing strong beer and supported his claim by reporting that 40,000 barrels of beer were counted at one time in London. Acts of Edward VI and Elizabeth had ordered abstinence from meat in Lent as well as on certain 'fish-days', observed chiefly for the benefit of maintaining fishermen as reserves for the navy. As a strengthening diet was an important part of the medical treatment for some diseases, exemptions were granted for the sick, at first for poultry only, but later for mutton and veal, a privilege alluded to in *Measure for Measure* (III, ii, 192). There was no regular inspection of meat or other foods and unless it was obviously rotten it could be sold. Considering the other sanitary conditions of the time food poisoning (caused by *salmonella*) must have accounted for a good deal of illness which was given other names. It was bad food and bad water which accounted for much of the disease in the military expeditions of the time, by which more died than ever fell by the hand of the enemy. Overcrowding in camps and small ships led to outbreaks of the deadly typhus ('camp fever' or 'gaol fever') and spotted fever. At sea on long voyages the lack of fresh vegetables produced scurvy (caused by lack of vitamin C) from which many of the pioneering seamen died.

In many of the descriptions of disease of the sixteenth century we can find precise means of identifying them, but the whole group of 'fevers', which were not finally separated into the different diseases with which they are associated until the nineteenth century, are usually ambiguous. The fevers or 'agues' so frequently mentioned by Shakespeare as the 'tertians' and 'quotidians' certainly refer to malaria, for it was endemic in London and in the marshy districts to the south and east along the Thames estuary. Then, as now in England, coughs and colds were perennial and it is amusing to find Harrison attributing them to the new-fangled chimneys and the houses of brick which had made people soft.[1] Shakespeare refers to them on several occasions, as he does to pulmonary tuberculosis, or 'consumption' (*Much Ado About Nothing*, v, iv, 97). Tuberculosis of the lymph nodes of the neck, or scrofula, was known everywhere as the 'King's Evil', so called because it was supposed to be cured by the touch of the sovereign, a tradition which went back to Edward the Confessor and was practised by successive monarchs until Queen Anne, who so touched Samuel Johnson when a boy. It is believed that the detailed account of the healing ceremony which occurs in *Macbeth* (IV, iii, 140–59) was introduced as a tribute to James I, before whom the play was acted. Shakespeare also has an interesting reference to goitre, the thyroid disease caused by lack of iodine which leads to cretinism and which was once common in the Swiss Alps. In the Peak district of Derbyshire it was so common that it used to be known in England as 'Derbyshire neck'. Gonzalo says:

> When we were boys,
> Who would believe that there were mountaineers
> Dew-lapp'd like bulls, whose throats had hanging at 'em
> Wallets of flesh? (*Tempest*, III, iii, 43–6)

Leprosy, which had been brought into western Europe by the Crusaders and was at one time so common that England had a number of 'lazar houses' or leper hospitals, had died out and the site of the lazar house at St James's was used for a new park and palace. Some skin diseases, however, especially the 'tetter' or ringworm, although its resemblance was closer to the 'French crown' or *corona Veneris* of syphilis, often reminded people of the dread disease as in *Hamlet* (I, v, 71). The vivid and persisting recollections of it, sharpened by the penal laws associated with it, are also reflected in the frequency with which the terms 'leper' and 'leprous' occur in the plays and other popular literature of the time in connection with moral taint.

Smallpox was not recognized as a serious disease in England until the second half of the century when there were frequent outbreaks among the poor. Elizabeth herself contracted it in 1572 and had medals struck to celebrate her recovery. The 'pox' which was used so frequently as an oath referred to *la grosse vérole*, the great pox, or syphilis, so named after the shepherd hero (Syphilus) in the celebrated poem of the Italian Fracastoro (1530),[1] which has a classic description of the disease. It is thought that it was brought to Europe by the sailors of Columbus and the first severe outbreak occurred in 1495 among the troops of Charles VIII in Italy, hence the names *morbus gallicus*, 'the French disease', or the 'Neapolitan disease'. Because of the symptomatic joint pains it was also referred to euphemistically as 'the bone-ache' (*Troilus and Cressida*, II, iii, 21). It spread through Europe with frightful rapidity, especially among the rich, and in a form far more acute and deadly than was to be known later. Clowes tells us that 'It is wonderfull to consider the huge multitudes of such as be infected with it, and that dayly increase'. He adds that during a period of nine or ten years one-half of all patients admitted to St Bartholomew's suffered with this disease, to say nothing of 'Saint Thomas hospitall, and other houses about the Citie, wherein an infinite multitude are dayly in cure'.[2]

In London it was spread from the brothels on Bankside where their vicinity to the theatres must have made it well known to both actors and audience. The ravages of the tertiary stage must have been only too obvious in many among those who thronged the narrow streets of London. They are depicted with the greatest accuracy in *Timon of Athens* (IV, iii). Its treatment was by mercurial inunction to the point of salivation (a desperate remedy for a desperate disease) or by mercurial fumigation in the sweating tub, the patients often being confined for this purpose in the 'spital', the equivalent of the modern lock-hospital. Pistol tells us that Doll Tearsheet was to be found in 'the powd'ring tub of infamy' (*Henry V*, II, i, 79) and that

>   my Nell is dead i'th'spital
>   Of malady of France.   *(Henry V,* v, i, 86)

However, syphilis did not kill so suddenly or so dramatically as plague, which was the most deadly and most feared of all the diseases in England between 1350 and 1665. Outbreaks which were exceeded in their severity only by the Black Death itself and the 'great plague' of 1665 occurred during many years between 1550 and 1650 and in 1603 and 1625 it has been estimated that one-sixth of London's population died in each of the two outbreaks. The facts concerning these epidemics and the measures taken against them are all to be found in the scholarly and comprehensive work written by F. P. Wilson nearly forty years ago,[1] but this account of health conditions in Shakespeare's world would be incomplete without some reference to them.

The theories of its causation have already been mentioned and we find Shakespeare writing of

>   a planetary plague, when Jove
>   Will o'er some high-viced City hang his poison
>   In the sick air.   *(Timon of Athens,* IV, iii, 108)

Writing to Burleigh in 1580, the Lord Mayor requested the aid of the Council

for the redress of such things as were found dangerous in spreading the infection and otherwise drawing God's wrath and plague upon the City, such as the erecting and frequenting of infamous houses out of the liberties and jurisdiction of the City,—the drawing of the people from the service of God and honest exercises, to unchaste plays,—and the increase of the number of the people.[2]

The frequent closure of the theatres and other places of entertainment, often for many months, was one of the steps taken to prevent the spread of the plague. Nothing was done to destroy the black rats, then commonly found in older houses, whose fleas carried the plague through the overcrowded slums. Dogs, which might have killed the rats, were incriminated and hunted ruthlessly during epidemics. In 1546 Fracastoro[3] had published his new theories which held that pestilent fevers were spread by the 'seeds of contagion' which were carried on the air and persisted in the form of 'fomites' in the bedding, clothing, and other personal belongings of those who had been infected. In Venice even letters were not allowed to be delivered from a plague centre unless they had gone through a process of 'quarantine', when they were handled only with tongs, pierced and fumigated.[4] This practice may be referred to in *Romeo and Juliet* (V, ii, 14) when Friar John can find no messenger to take the letter from him. This theory gave a scientific basis for the London order that all such articles should be burnt, an order which was often evaded in practice, for there would always be some needy wretch prepared to risk using them.

The haemorrhagic spots (*petechiae*), known as the 'tokens' (*Love's Labour's Lost,* V, ii, 423; *Antony and Cleopatra,* III, x, 9) were the first unmistakable symptoms to appear on those who were 'visited' or infected. It was these which the official 'Searchers' (*Romeo and Juliet,* V, ii, 7) looked for as they went to suspected houses with their wands of office, affixing the 'Lord have mercy on us' bill to the doors of those where cases were confirmed. This measure of isolation or house arrest was for long the most carefully observed of all the rudimentary quarantine regulations but in the worst plague years even that broke down completely.

At a certain stage, as the climax mounts in these severe epidemics, the bubonic form changes to the much more infectious and fatal pneumonic plague which can kill within hours. It is then that

> good men's lives
> Expire before the flowers in their caps,
> Dying or ere they sicken. (*Macbeth*, IV, iii, 171)

All the 'approved remedies', chiefly a variety of 'drinks' and some plasters for applying to the plague bubo, were pitifully useless, even when they were officially recommended, as in one tract issued by the College of Physicians 'for the poorer sort'. The richer sort clearly believed the only remedy to be flight from the stricken city, where grass grew in the main streets, and consequently few of them ever died of plague.

In 1583 the Queen expressed

surprise that no house or hospital had been built without the City, in some remote place, to which the infected people might be removed, although other cities of less antiquity, fame, wealth, and reputation had provided themselves with such places, whereby the lives of the inhabitants had been in all times of infection chiefly preserved.[1]

Because of the expense, nothing was done for a decade, and then, on 10 May 1593 (another plague year) the City, having had a windfall of £6000 from the sale of the treasure in the captured *Madre de Dios*, set aside one-third of that sum for erecting the first London pesthouse beside an alley to the north of St Bartholomew's. This was named Pesthouse Row (now Bath Street, E.C. 1) and there it remained until 1736.

Viewed in isolation, the medical aspects of Shakespeare's world certainly provide the darker tones in the scene, and seem difficult to reconcile with the traditional picture of a robust, healthy, and even 'glorious' age of English history. It may explain the fact that 'melancholy' was the most fashionable distemper of the time, but the true answer to the paradox lies in that 'piece of work' which Hamlet marvelled at, which suffers but endures and survives even the wrath of God and the focused evil of the planets.

12

THE FOLDS OF FOLKLORE

'Fables and antique toys'

I

When we are considering the treatment of folklore and of supernatural traditions in Shakespeare's plays we are almost forced to attempt some exploration of the atmosphere in which his childhood was passed.

Indeed, if we could discover all the stories, rhymes, songs and games known to the poets in their nurseries, we should know much more of their art and minds than we do now. Few of us can recall so translucent a childhood as Traherne's, but for most of us some scenes and stories have a special power, and kindle a glow in the mind which nothing but memories of childhood can light. It may be that childhood is not the happiest time in a man's life; if joys are keen, grief is often at that time most helpless and insupportable. Children are specially liable to fear, and are defenceless against grown-up exploitation, and the uncomprehended assault of grown-up emotions; but in spite of that, the senses are so brilliantly perceptive in childhood, and sense and emotion move together so harmoniously, that childhood is commonly remembered as a golden age, even in times when children suffered more hardships than they do at present. The poet's mind is more open to his childhood than that of the average man; and many recurrent symbols of this poet or that might be traced back, if we had but the key, to some nursery rhyme or fairy tale of his early youth.

It is seldom that we can find an example of this so neat as that unconsciously provided for us by Richard Willis in his *Mount Tabor*. Willis was a Gloucester man, born the same year as Shakespeare, into the same burgess class, and not far removed from him in locality. A part of the following passage was quoted by E. K. Chambers to illustrate the way in which the travelling companies arranged their performances.[1] It has an even greater interest in the picture it gives of the impression made upon a childish mind:

In the City of *Gloucester* the manner is (as I think it is in other like corporations) that when players of Enterludes come to towne, they first attend the Mayor to enforme him what noble-mans servants they are, and so to get licence for their publike playing; and if the Mayor like the Actors, or would shew respect to their Lord and Master, he appoints them to play their first play before himselfe and the Aldermen and common Counsell of the City; and that is called the Mayors play, where every one that will comes in without money, the Mayor giving the players a reward as hee thinks fit to shew respect unto them. At such a play, my father tooke me with him, and made me stand betweene his leggs, as he sate upon one of the benches where wee saw and heard very well. The play was called (the Cradle of Security,) wherein was personated a King or some great Prince with his Courtiers of severall kinds, amongst which three Ladies were in speciall grace with him; and they keeping him in delights and pleasures, drew him from his graver Counsellors, hearing of Sermons, and listning to good counsell, and admonitions, that in the end they got him to lye downe in a cradle upon the stage, where these three Ladies joyning in a sweet song rocked him asleepe, that he snorted againe, and in the meane time closely conveyed under the cloaths where withall he was covered, a vizard like a swines snout upon his face, with three wire chains fastnd thereunto, the other end whereof being holden severally by those three Ladies, who fall to singing againe, and then discovered his face, that the spectators might see how they had transformed him, going on with their singing, whilst all this was acting, there came forth of another doore at the farthest end of the stage, two old men, the one in blew with a Serjeant at Armes, his mace on his shoulder, the other in red with a drawn sword in his hand, and leaning with the other hand upon the others shoulder, and so they two went along in a soft pace round about by the skirt of the Stage, till at last they came to the Cradle, when all the Court was in greatest jollity, and then the foremost old man with his Mace stroke a fearfull blow upon the Cradle; whereat all the Courtiers with the three Ladies and the vizard all vanished; and the desolate Prince starting up bare faced, and finding himselfe thus sent for to judgement, made a lamentable complaint of his miserable case, and so was carried away by wicked spirits. This Prince did personate in the morall, the wicked of the world; the three Ladies, Pride, Covetousnesse, and Luxury, the two old men, the end of the world, and the last judgement. This sight tooke such impression in me, that when I came towards mans estate, it was as fresh in my memory, as if I had seen it newly acted.[1]

We cannot doubt that Shakespeare was equally impressionable. In the year 1569 the Earl of Worcester's Players played at both Stratford and Gloucester.[2] If William Shakespeare stood between his father's legs and watched, it was no wonder that Death was ever after a sergeant to him. 'This sergeant death is strict in his arrest' would come so naturally to his lips as hardly to be a simile. Other children must have been equally impressed; for the play seems to have passed into a children's game. In an anti-prelatical tract published in 1644 we find:

So have I seene at Children's festivalls the gaudie King and Queene followed by an awfull blacke Coat neither crowned nor Robed, yet well maced who cold at pleasure, though a pawne, give Checkemate to both *Rex et Regina imbeati*.[3]

This same Willis gives us an insight into the factual nature of the fairy belief in the time of Shakespeare's childhood and among the same class of Midland people:

When we come to years, we are commonly told of what befel us in our infancie, if the same were more than ordinary. Such an accident (by relation of others) befell me within a few dayes after my birth, whilst my mother lay in of me being her second child, when I was taken out of the bed from her side, and by my suddain and fierce crying recovered again, being found sticking between the beds-head and the wall; and if I had not cryed in that manner as I did, our gossips had a conceit that I had been quite carried away by the Fairies they know not whither, and some elfe or changeling (as they call it) laid in my room.[4]

It was a mental background of such beliefs that writers of yeoman stock carried up with them to London in Elizabeth's day. They met there a more fully intellectualized life, and were assailed by all the scepticisms of the learned, of travellers and of materialists, so that they came for the most part to regard the country beliefs as no more than pretty fancies; yet these were winged by the glamour of childhood memories, and it was the glow behind them that brought the fairy poetry into fashion. Until this time the fairies of literature had been of human or more than human dimension, but the country fairies were of very varying sizes, from the giant-like spriggans of Cornwall and the fairy ladies who married human husbands down to the tiny fairies who stole the Hampshire farmers' wheat and 'the smallest elf, no bigger than an ant' of the Danish ballad. The most usual size was perhaps about three foot, but it is clear that in Warwickshire, as in other parts of England, the tiny fairies who lurked among the flowers were taken as a matter of course. Shakespeare accepted them so readily that he made the fairies of *A Midsummer Night's Dream* small enough to creep into an acorn cup or to find a bumble bee a formidable adversary, when, for the purpose of the stage, child-sized faries would have been more convenient. Lyly and the anonymous authors of *The Mayde's Metamorphosis* and *The Wisdom of Dr Dodypol* took the same line, as did Drayton, another Warwickshire man, and Herrick. On the whole their treatment of the fairies betrays no fear of them; indeed, Shakespeare gives us the only example before the nineteenth century of the changeling regarded from the fairies' point of view. Titania no doubt left a lingering substituted image in the Indian King's nursery, but she adopted his child out of her love for its mother, and she treated it with only too much fondness. Imogen's prayer against 'fairies and the tempters of the night'[1] reminds one of the Incubus and Love Talker who had a fiendish office, but as a rule the fairies' tricks are pure mischief, pricking and pinching and misleading and playing puck-like pranks. The worst and most commonly mentioned trait is that of stealing human babies and leaving changelings in their place. As we have seen from Willis, this was a real fear among country people. The poetic mentions of the fairies are in the general tradition of English fairy lore. Darker things are expected from the fairy people of Ireland and the Scottish Highlands, but most of the English fairies may say with Fairy Patch:

> But to the good I ne'ere was foe:
> The bad I hate and will doe ever,
> Till they from ill themselves doe sever.
> To helpe the good Ile run and goe.
> The bad no good from me shall know.[2]

The pixies in the still-living traditions of Somerset are of the same kind as Shakespeare's fairies. Such a story as *Farmer Mole and the Pixies*, collected on Exmoor by Miss Ruth Tongue in the early years of this century, comes from a world with which young Shakespeare must have been familiar. It is perhaps worth transcribing for its childlike ruthlessness towards the bad husband.

They'll tell 'ee three things about an Exmoor pony. 'Can climb a cleeve, carry a drunk an' zee a pixy.' And that's what old Varmer Mole's pony do. Old Varmer Mole were a drunken old toad as lived over to Hangley Cleeve, and he gived his pore wife and liddle children a shocking life of it. He never come back vrom market till he was vull of zider. He'd get on pony hind zide avore, and zinging and swearing till er rolled into ditch and spent night there. But if his poor missus didn't zit up all night vor'n he'd baste her and the children wicked. Now the pixies they did mind 'n, and they went to mend er ways. 'Twadn't no manner of use to try and frighten pony. He were that foot-sure and way-wise he'd brought Varmer safe whoam drunk or asleep in years, wheresoever the vule tried to ride 'n to. But one foggy night the old veller were wicked drunk, and a-waving his gad and reckoning how he'd drub his missus when he gets to whoam, and her zee a light in the mist. "Whoa, thou vule," says he. "Us be to whoam." But pony he wouldn't stop. He could a-zee the pixy holdn' the light, and 'twere over the blackest, deepest bog they zide of the Chains,—zuck a pony down in a minute 'twould, rider and all. But the old man keeps on shouting, "Whoa, vule. Us be whoam!" and rode straight vor bog. But pony digged in his liddle veet, and er stood. Varmer gets off, and catches 'n a crack on the head and walks on to light. He hadn't gone two steps when bog took and swallowed 'n. Zo old pony trots whoam. And when they seed 'n come alone with peat mud on his legs they knowed what had come to Varmer, and they did light every candle in house and *dance*. Arter that missus left a pail of clear water out at night vor pixy babies to wash in, pretty dears! and swept hearth vor pixies to dancey on, and varm prospered wonderful, and old pony grew zo fat as a pig.[1]

This is rural tale, and it may be objected that the Shakespeares were burghers of a small town and not countrymen. John Shakespeare, however, came of country stock, and his children had a country, not a bourgeois, background in their mother's family. Even now to visit the Ardens' house after seeing Shakespeare's birthplace is to feel oneself stepping back for another hundred years. The Ardens were gentlepeople, not citizens, but in their manor a much more primitive life was lived than that of Stratford. There we find ourselves in a virtually medieval atmosphere. There was the great hall in which the menservants slept, and at either end of it was a kind of elevated Black Hole of Calcutta, a cock-loft without a window and approached only by a ladder. In that, at the kitchen end, the mistress, her daughters and the female servants slept, at the other end the lord, his sons and the best of the menservants. In the earlier days of the marriage the lord and lady would occupy one loft and the children and maidservants the other; but as the children grew up the sexes would be divided. In the Arden family there was no problem of accommodating the first-born sons, for all the children were girls. The family was unusual, and indeed famous, because all the eight daughters grew up to maturity. The forest came near to the house, or even surrounded it, and Mary Arden would bring tales of goblins and ghosts and outlaws into Stratford town to entertain her son. Snitterfield Farm, where Shakespeare's grandfather and uncle lived, was on the Arden estate, and William himself was heir to Asbies, his mother's inheritance, until it had to be sold to meet his father's necessities. He may fairly then be regarded as a country boy, who had a full share in all the fairy, witch and ghost beliefs that were current in the countryside. There were forest customs too. One of them, the horn-dance of the successful hunters, is reproduced for us in *As You Like It*.[2]

The belief in fairies had long been regarded by the literate as dead or dying, but it has lingered on obstinately until the present day, so that, even now, fairy beliefs emerge from wherever a Celtic strain is to be found. The taboo against the mention of fairies has buried the belief out of sight, and has in many places tended to kill it. With ghosts and witches it is a different matter. In Elizabethan times the belief in witches was so generally held, so fully conscious and so firmly based on scriptural and literary sanctions that one could hardly regard it as folklore at all if a strong strain of oral and very ancient tradition had not been mixed with the more intellectualized concepts. Folk countercharms against witches were commonly used in the country, and folk methods of testing for witchcraft were brought forward in the witch trials and are evidence of a traditional belief, but the white witch was part of the ordinary pattern of rural life, and not till the witch fever had become really hysterical was she lumped with the black witch in a general condemnation. When Fabian says, 'Carry his water to the wise-woman',[1] he is merely following the usual practice. True, the wise woman would probably diagnose witchcraft and work a counter-spell, and if the practical jokers had cared to carry on the joke there might have been a tragic conclusion for someone; but, in all probability, it would only have been a matter of knocking a nail into the suspected witch's footprint or boiling up a bottle of Malvolio's water in a closed room, and no legal remedy would have been sought. The evidence brought by country people at the witch trials shows that there was a real fear of black witchcraft, and that many wretched old women with no other means of subsistence levied supernatural blackmail on their neighbours. But this fear seems only at times to have become intolerable; as a rule countrymen trusted in their own simple counter-spells, and, if we can judge from the pamphlets, there was even a kind of pride in the notable wise women like Mother Shipton. In the earlier plays witches are often half humorously treated, Lyly's Mother Bombie is a sympathetic character, Dipsas in *Endimion*, wicked though she is, is pardoned in the end, and such magicians as Peter Fabell and Friar Bacon are sympathetic characters. Shakespeare's earlier references to witchcraft—except in the doubtful Pucelle passages of Henry VI—are nearly always comic. In *A Comedy of Errors* we have:

> Some devils ask but parings of one's nail,
> A rush, a hair, a drop of blood, a pin,
> A nut, a cherry stone;
> But she, more covetous, would have a chain.
> Master, be wise: an if you give it her,
> The devil will shake her chain and fright us with it—.[2]

and Sir Hugh Evans mistakes the disguised Falstaff for a witch: 'I like not when a 'oman has a great peard.' In *Macbeth*, for the first time, the witches are horrific creatures, with some of their activities copied from *Newes from Scotlande*, so that they must be treated as to that extent factual; but here, as in Ben Jonson's *Masque of Queens*, there is a zest and poetic heightening that suggests an imaginative and poetic belief rather than a factual one; it is not till we get to *The Witch of Edmonton* and *The Lancashire Witches* that we find the down-to-earth treatment of real witch trials. Probably both Shakespeare and Jonson had listened in delighted horror to country witch stories, and some of that glamour hung over the subject still.

It is probable that only a few of the stories that were known to Shakespeare and his contemporaries survive now. The collector set to work late in this country, and many masterpieces, both of ballads and stories, must have perished. *Childe Roland*[3] is one of the finest which survived. Shakespeare must have known it much as we do, for the Elf King's ogreish cry is given in *King Lear*. Mr Fox,[4] the English Blue-Beard story, was certainly known to both Shakespeare and Spenser, for Benedick quotes, 'It is not so, nor 'twas not so',[5] and the cumulative inscription, 'Be bold, be bold', is used in the *Faerie Queene*.[6] Probably Shakespeare, at any rate, knew some Welsh fairy stories. Robert Graves in *The White Goddess* suggests rather fancifully that the characters in *The Tempest* are founded on the Welsh fairy story of Creirwy and Afagdda.[7] Perhaps it is equally fanciful to suggest that the plot is a retelling of the *Nix Nought Nothing*[8] or *The Battle of the Birds* story with the Magician as the hero. I have already remarked that in *A Midsummer Night's Dream* we have the only version before the nineteenth century of the changeling from the fairy's point of view. Imagine the story of *Nix Nought Nothing* told from the Wizard's point of view, and so turned as to give it a happy ending. If it is to end in a triumph for the Wizard he must have planned his daughter's marriage with the prince, manœuvred him there, simulated anger and imposed dangerous tasks in order to interest his daughter in her predestined husband.

As he grew older Shakespeare seems to have returned to the stories and the imaginative background of his childhood. In *King Lear* he treated what was virtually a fairy story, a variant of *Cap o' Rushes*,[1] but he refused the fairy story conclusion which the earlier play, *The Chronicle History of King Leir*,[2] had used. He knew that historically Cordelia was hanged in prison; and though according to history she was immediately successful, and restored her father, he would not falsify the general historical impression, and turn the truth to prettiness. Still, perhaps the association with the old fairy story stirred him, for the play is full of snatches of song and nursery rhymes and references to old tales. In the Reconciliation Plays he returned to fairyland. *The Winter's Tale* was treated as a solar myth in Constance Armfield's production, and certainly it could be interpreted in that way, though it is highly improbable that such an interpretation would have occurred to Shakespeare. The play has the fairy story readiness to pass great swathes of time, seven long years and seven long years, and the fairy story casualness about killing off innocent people and forgetting them. *Pericles Prince of Tyre* is even more a medley of fairy stories, drawn from that old repository of fairy tales, the *Gesta Romanorum*.[3] Gower, who had retold the tale in the *Confessio Amantis*, is used as the narrator to mark the sense that it is an antique tale and that too much credibility is not to be expected of it. In the course of the play one seems to move down the ages. The first scene is the most archaic, dating from that time when modern science had just discovered paternity and modern morality had set up a new taboo, which was not yet valid everywhere, and from that civilization in which the king was forced to set riddles at his own peril, and to the still greater peril of the man who wished to succeed him. In the next we come to a gentler time, to the stranger cast on the land and the contest for the hand of the princess; to a matrilineal succession, in fact. Next we have the old story of the seemingly dead Princess, washed ashore in a chest and brought to life by a wise physician. Then we have a story which seems most at home in a medieval setting, that of the jealous woman who commands a servant to kill a young girl, generally a step-daughter, though here it is an adopted daughter. In the brothel scenes we arrive at the seventeenth century, but at the end we return to the fairy story world in the grieving father, who like the grandfather in *Tattercoats*[4] had refused to cut his hair or to do anything but weep.

Fairy story plots are common in the drama of the time, and from them we can gather something of the stories known to the children in those days. *The Old Wives Tale* will occur to everyone, for it is not only a fairy story but a portrait of an old woman telling one. There must have been some version of *The King's Daughter of Colchester*[5] extant then, for the three gold heads come from it, and also of *The Faithful Servant*,[6] the ghost of the dead man whose body has been saved from insult, which has almost disappeared from this country except in Celtic folklore. The enchanted bear suggests that there was some version of *Snow-White and Rose-Red* known to Peele which is lost to us now.

Beaumont and Fletcher often used fairy story plots for their plays but after a sophisticated and literary manner. In *The Knight of the Burning Pestle*, however, which is a burlesque rather than a fairy tale, there is a real folk character in the Citizen's Wife. She refers to a fairy story which is nearly lost to us, that of Lob-Lie-by-the-Fire, the giant who had a witch for his mother,[1] surely a less friendly character than the Lob who has survived. A variant of this tale has lately been found by Hamish Henderson among the Scottish tinkers.[2] A Brownie, who haunted Fincastle Mill by night, was scalded to death by a lass who had gone there to grind corn against her wedding day. His witch mother, Maggie Moloch, could do nothing to avenge him because the girl had told him that she was called 'Me Myself'. Later, however, the invisible witch-wife heard the girl describing her victory, and killed her with a three-legged stool. Though Maggie Moloch was described as a witch she was actually a Brownie, like her son, and did a Brownie's work. The Citizen's Wife, too, uses the old Scandinavian name for giants, which still occurs in Scottish fairy tales, 'the Giants and Ettins of Portugal'.[3]

Reginald Scot seems to have heard more of fiends and goblins, and he mentions his grandmother's maids as the chief story-tellers.[4] Shakespeare's Mamillius, on the other hand, preferred to tell his stories himself, and chose a grim one to relieve the tension of nerves strung up over emotional problems he did not understand:

> *Mamillius.*   A sad tale's best for winter.
> I have one of sprites and goblins.
> *Hermione.*   Let's have that, good sir.
> Come on, sit down: come on, and do your best
> To fright me with your sprites; you're powerful at it.
> *Mamillius.*   There was a man—
> *Hermione.*   Nay, come, sit down; then on.
> *Mamillius.* Dwelt by a churchyard.[5]

What the story was we never hear. It might be a version of the *Man whose Wife had a Golden Arm*;[6] the child was in that state of repressed misery which is glad to vent itself in a shout. But possibly neither Shakespeare nor Mamillius had decided.

II

Children have always been great conservers and repositories of tradition; and if one wants to study the folk mind it is wise to turn to the children of a place, as well as to the old people. There we shall find a rich mixture of new and old which will enable us to understand why the descendants of the ancient gods of Ireland smoke tobacco,[7] and how Napoleon has taken his place in the prehistoric mummers' play. It is for these reasons that it seems relevant to our subject to make some attempt to recreate the atmosphere of an Elizabethan childhood.

Childhood in those days was passed in a world at once harsher and richer than the present. There were great brutalities at that time, some of which must have pressed hard upon children; but, on the whole, the emotional temper was congenial to them. Pity is a plant that requires some tending, and it is to be feared that not many children were of a nature compassionate enough to suffer with the shrovetide cock and the baited bull and the mumbled sparrow. In a rough-and-tumble world the children took their chance. Not much effort was expended on understanding them, though quite a lot on training them. Our modern cult of childhood does not emerge until the beginning of the seventeenth century; and, except in the household of the

Sire de Montaigne, there was no attempt to produce that special, rarefied atmosphere which so many educationalists recommend now.

On the other hand, the children, Folk themselves by temperament, were surrounded by Folk, and the rich pageant of the folk year passed before their eyes. The wealthy and noble might be forced by their masters into an intellectual mould unsuited to their age, but outside lesson hours the men and maids had a store of legends suited to childhood, even if some of it was strong meat, and seasoned with horrors. The games which grown-up people played were congenial to children, the land rang with music, and the recurrent festivities held the right balance between excitement and stability. Life was rooted in custom; and so gave the children what they most needed, a sense of security.

Games and sports at that time were half-way on the long descent from religious ceremonies to an amusement for children. Some retained a memory of ritual significance; it was felt to be lucky and good to perform them. A few were even recognized as heathen rites. Some were still played more by grown-up people than children, and some the children had taken over completely. Brand quotes from MS. Harleian 2057 a rhymed list of sports called *Auntient Customs in Games used by Boyes and Girles, merrily set out in verse*, which is a slightly altered quotation from Rowlands' *Letting of Humor's Blood in the Head Vaine*,[1] where it is not specially meant to apply to children. It is a fairly comprehensive list:

> Any they dare challenge for to throw the sledge,
> To jumpe or leape over ditch or hedge;
> To wrestle, play at stoole ball, or to runne,
> To pich the barre, or to shoot of a gunne;
> To play at loggets, nine holes, or ten pinnes,
> To try it out at foote-ball by the shinnes;
> At tick-tacke, seize nody, maw, and ruffe,
> At hot-cockles, leape-frogge, or blind-man's buffe,
> To drink the halper pottes,[2] or deale at the whole cann,
> To play at chesse, or pue, and ink horne,
> To daunce the morris, play at barley brake,
> At all exploits a man can think or speak:
> At shove groate, venter poynte, or cross and pile,
> At beshrew him that's last at any stile;
> At leaping over a Christmas bonfire,
> Or at the drawing Dunne out of the myer;
> At shoote cocke, Gregory, stoole ball, and what not;
> Picke poynt, toppe and scourge to make him hott.[3]

Some of these are not games at all; and some, like tossing the hammer, or the half pote, could never be children's games. Some literary mentions of most of them can be found; but of them all, with the exception of morris dancing, barley break seems to have been felt the most significant.

This game in its earlier form is extinct now, though the name survives in Scotland for a form of hide and seek played in a stack yard. Lady Gomme's description of it is vague,[4] and the strictly limited number who played would make it dull, unless the interest was sustained by some ritual excitement. It was a game played before spectators, and it was considered by the poets suitable for fairies, nymphs and pastoral characters. It is generally, though not always, spoken of as an amorous game. The sports engaged in by the fairies are of special interest, for they are often ritualistic. The three fullest descriptions of the game are Sidney's,[1] Suckling's,[2] and Herrick's.[3] Between them we can make out something of how it was played, though there are discrepancies in their accounts. Other references to the game are to be found in Braithwaite, Browne, Drayton, Fletcher, Holiday, Massinger, Middleton, Randolph and Wither.

Stoolball is another game often mentioned because it was appropriate to pastoral characters. There is a reference to it in Sidney's pastoral poems:

> A tyme there is for all, my Mother often sayes,
> When she with skirts tuckt very hy, with girles at stoolball playes.[4]

It was the milkmaid's game, and is still played in some places. It is supposed to have been the ancestor of cricket, but is more like baseball or rounders.

To discuss morris is to enter on too large a subject, and it is certain that it would be rather a spectacle for children than a game played by them, though presumably they would have to learn it. *Kemp's Nine Daies Wonder* makes it clear that in his time girls danced the morris as well as boys.[5] If we can judge by *The Two Noble Kinsmen*[6] and *The Witch of Edmonton*[7] the morris characters, Robin Hood and the Hobby Horse and the rest, who were afterwards subsidiary, took part in the dance at this time. The often-quoted fragment, 'For O, for O, the hobby horse is forgot', may have come from a lost play after the style of the Sword Dance Play.

Football, which had not gone far from its ritual origin, was played at definite times by all the men of a village against a rival neighbour, but would be played by boys at any time in the winter. It was a rough game, with a good deal of tripping and kicking at the shins, as Kent's speech in *King Lear* shows, and as Stubbes in his *Anatomie of Abuses* states with his usual emphasis.

Pulling the Dunne out of the Mire is mentioned in several places; in *The Dutches of Suffolk*, Beaumont's *Woman Hater, Romeo and Juliet*, and as early as Chaucer. Lewis Spence believes it to have been the mimic slaying of an afanc or similar monster. A log of wood represented the dunne, and one after another of the players joined the string of people that was heaving at it. The game seems to have been to drop the log upon another player's toes and to avoid getting it on one's own, but there was no doubt a good deal of drama in the presentation of it. Some of the games played at the Highland Ceillidhs up to the end of the last century were something of this kind.

Primero, maw and noddy were card games, and specially popular at Christmas time, and hotcockles, leap-frog and blind man's buff were Christmas sports for grown people too, but were played by children all through the year.

Whipping tops has long been a boy's game only, though a seasonal one; but at one time every parish had a large top, which was whipped in cold weather to keep the men warm when the frost was too hard to allow them to work in the fields. Sir Toby speaks of his brains turning on their toe like the Parish Top.[8] It does not seem that one top could go very far towards restoring the circulation of a whole village. Originally the top may have represented the lazy sun, and the whipping was a piece of imitative magic. This is the more probable as it is said that the scourge was made of eel or snake skin, a symbol of immortality. Shirley has:

> Thou art the town top;
> A boy will set thee up, and make thee spin
> Home with an eel-skin.[1]

One of Quarles's emblems is of the World as a Whipping Top.[2] During the seventeenth century the sport seems to have passed from men to boys. Bunyan treats it as a boy's sport:

> Tis with the Whip the Boy sets up the Top,
> The Whip makes it run round upon it's Toe;
> The Whip makes it hither and thither hop:
> Tis with the Whip, the Top is made to go.[3]

The Christmas bonfires must have had the same origin as the need fires of Beltane, through which the cattle were driven and the young people leaped. By the seventeenth century, it seems to have become a boy's sport in England. In *The Two Noble Kinsmen* we have:

> Whose youth like wanton boys through Bonfires
> Have skipt thy flame.[4]

Shoeing the Wild Mare was an accomplishment of Ralph the Prentice.[5] The only survival of it today is in the baby's rhyme, 'Shoe the colt, shoe! Shoe the wild mare.'[6] 'Beshrew him that's last at any stile' is the same as the Scots game, 'The black Sow tak' the hindmost'. Cherry pit is a game several times mentioned in literature. It is a form of marbles, played with cherry stones and small holes in the ground. Some sinister implication was attached to the game, to judge from Herrick's short poem on it, and from Sir Toby's ''Tis not for gravity to play at cherry-pit with Satan: hang him, foul collier'.[7]

Shakespeare mentions several games too childish for Rowland's catalogue, as for instance, handy-dandy. 'Hark in thine ear; change places; and, handy-dandy, which is the justice, which is the thief?'[8] This was familiar to most of us in childhood as 'Handy-pandy, which hand will you have?' Hamlet's 'Hide Fox and all after'[9] probably refers to a form of hide-and-seek very like *Black Beast*, as played in Scotland today, in which the catcher hides. This is possibly the older form; though the more generally known hide-and-seek, in which one seeks and the rest hide, was probably that under cover of which James II escaped from the Parliament's custody as a boy.[10] There is an allusion to this form in *Satiromastix*:

> Our unhandsome-fac'd Poet does
> play at bo-peepes with your Grace,
> and cryes all-hidde, as boyes do.[11]

A fine catalogue of country sports is to be found in Herrick's poem to Endimion Porter:

> For Sports, for Pagentrie, and Playes,
> Thou hast thy Eves, and Holydayes:
> On which the young men and maids meet,
> To exercise their dancing feet:

Tripping the comely country round,
With Daffadils and Daisies crown'd.
Thy Wakes, thy Quintels, here thou hast,
Thy May-poles too with Garlands grac't:
Thy Morris-dance; thy Whitsun-ale;
Thy Sheering-feast, which never faile.
Thy Harvest home; thy Wassaile bowle,
That's tost up after Fox i' th' Hole.
Thy Mummeries, thy Twelfe-tide Kings
And Queenes; thy Christmas revellings.[1]

Of the old brutal sports which probably had a sacrificial origin, bear-baiting and bull-baiting were grown-up occupations, and pursued with an almost religious ardour, but the Shrovetide cock-throwing was the special prerogative of schoolboys, who each brought a penny to their schoolmaster to buy a cock for Shrove Tuesday. The sport is sufficiently described in Llewellyn's poem:

Cocke a doodle doe, tis the bravest game,
Take a Cocke from his Dame,
And bind him to a stake,
How he *struts*, how he *throwes*,
How he *swaggers*, how he *crowes*,
As if the Day newly brake.
How his *Mistris* cackles,
Thus to find him in *shackles*.
And tyed to a *Packe-thread Garter*?
Oh the *Beares* and the *Bulls*
Are but *Corpulent Gulls*
To the valiant *Shrove-Tide Martyr*.[2]

Jack a Lent, a kind of spring guy dressed in greenery, which was drenched with water, also provided sport for schoolboys on Shrove Tuesday. St Stephen's Day wren hunting was another sacrificial sport peculiar to boys, but it has left little impress on literature. The rhymes on it that survive are real folk rhymes.

Schoolboys' holidays, if brief, were frequent in those days, for the year was spangled with festivals. Most of them have been celebrated by the poets. In the country there were Wakes and Whitsun Ales, Plough Monday and Haysel and Hocktide, in London there was Pancake Day and the Lord Mayor's Day, with its giant figures of Gogmagog and Corineus; but everywhere the two great festivals were those of Christmas and May Day, the Mid-winter and Summer festivals of the Celtic year. These were so written of that it is hard to know where to choose our examples. Jonson's *Christmas his Masque*[3] gives a good idea of some of the sports of the time. The verse is a rough jog-trot, in imitation of the old Christmas mumming plays, and Father Christmas introduces his sons in very much the style of one. They are *Mis-rule, Caroll, Minc'd-Pie, Gamboll, Post and Paire, New-Yeares-Gift, Mumming, Wassall, Offering,* and *Babie-Cake.* The torch-bearer of each one carries his appropriate emblem. Gamboll's is a cole staff and a blinding cloth for blind-man's buff, Post and Paire's a box, cards and counters, and the Babie Cake's a great cake with a pea and a bean in it, by which the King and Queen of Twelfth Night were chosen.[1]

The title of Shakespeare's *Twelfth Night* tempts one to look for some allusion to Twelfth Night customs in the shape and plot of the play, but there is not much to bear this out. There is perhaps some faint shadow of the choosing of Kings and Queens in the marriages of Viola and Sebastian, and the disguise motif belongs to the Twelfth Night customs, but the same kind of suggestions could be drawn from any of the comedies. Certainly, Helena's pursuit of Bertram in *All's Well that Ends Well* shapes better as a hock-tide play, where the girls pursue and kiss the men, than *Twelfth Night* does as a Twelfth Night one. Sir Toby's persistent revelry echoes the spirit of the time, and the jest played upon Malvolio by Maria might be part of the Christmas Saturnalia, but the comparison cannot with any common sense be pushed very far.

May games have an even larger part in English literature than Christmas revels. They were sacred to youth rather than to childhood, but when they were neglected by the rest of the world children continued to celebrate them. It is not many years since children were showing May garlands on Magdalen bridge; and Flora Thompson's description of May Day in *Larkrise* tells how large a place it took in country children's minds even till the beginning of this century. The Puritans, who did so much to destroy the May Day celebrations, have helped to preserve the memory of them by the zest of their denunciations. Stubbes is one of the liveliest:

Against May, *Whitsonday*, or other time, all the yung men and maides, olde men and wives, run gadding ouer night to the woods, groues, hils, & mountains, where they spend all the night in plesant pastimes; and in the morning they return, bringing with them birch and branches of trees, to deck their assemblies withall. and no meruaile, for there is a great Lord present amongst them, as superintendent and Lord over their pastimes and sportes, namely, Sathan, prince of hel. But the cheifest iewel they bring from thence is their May-pole, which they bring home with great veneration, as thus. They have twentie or fortie yoke of Oxen, every Oxe hauing a sweete nose-gay of flouers placed on the tip of his hornes; and these Oxen drawe home this May-pole (this stinking ydol, rather) which is couered all over with flouers and hearbs, bound round about with strings from the top to the bottome, and sometime painted with variable colours, with two or three hundred men, women and children, following it with great deuotion. And thus beeing reared vp with handkercheefs and flags houering on the top, they straw the ground rounde about, binde green boughes about it, set vp sommer haules, bowers, and arbors hard by it; And then fall they to daunce about it, like as the heathen people did at the dedication of the Idols, whereof this is a perfect pattern, or rather the thing it self.[2]

The Puritans were not mistaken in tracing the May games from heathen times, and certainly the Church had never christianized May Day, as she had done Christmas, perhaps because the summer rites were dispersed between May Day and Midsummer Day. According to Stubbes the Lords of Misrule were even more characteristic of the summer than the winter festivities. He blames the winter celebrations for gambling and gluttony, but his Lords of Misrule belong to the summer. After describing how the Lord of Misrule is chosen and picks twenty to a hundred men for his followers, dressed in green, yellow, or some other light wanton colour, and tricked out with bells and with handkerchiefs in their hands, he goes on:

Thus al things set in order, then haue they their Hobby-horses, dragons and other Antiques, togither with their baudie Pipers and thundering Drummers to strike up the devils daunce withall. (then, marche these heathen company towards the Church and Church-yard, their pipers pipeing, their drummers thundring, their stumps dauncing, their bels iyngling, their handkerchefs swinging about their heds like madmen, their hobbie horses and other monsters skirmishing amongst the route: and in this sorte they go to the Church (I say) and into the Church, (though the Minister be at praier or preaching), dancing and swinging their handkercheifs over their heds in the Church, like devils incarnate,) with such a confuse noise, *that* no man can hear his own voice. Then, the foolish people they looke, they stare, they laugh, they fleer, and mount vpon fourmes and pewes, to see these goodly pageants, solemnized in this sort. Then, after this, about the Church they goe againe and again, and so foorth into the church-yard, where they haue commonly their Sommer-haules, their bowers, arbors, and banqueting houses set up, wherein they feast, banquet, and daunce al that day, and (peraduenture) all the night too. And thus these terrestriall furies spend the Sabaoth day.[1]

Many writers defended or lamented the May Day celebrations, but few conveyed such a sense of energy as this denunciation, though some of the praises are pretty enough. The boys who ran behind this pageant of life and colour had something to feed their fancies.

13

SYMBOLS AND SIGNIFICANCES

'All such emblems'

I

The potent force exerted by symbols, translated into diverse emblematical forms, upon sixteenth- and seventeenth-century life, thought, painting and literature can hardly be overstressed. Unless we fully realize the current faith in these symbols and learn to recognize the many ways in which they were made to play their effective role, we shall fail to appreciate what may be termed the inner spirit of that age. Monarchs used emblematic devices to glorify their states, to emphasize their policies and to sway their subjects; subjects, in turn, utilized similar methods in order to demonstrate their loyalty or, on occasion, tactfully to make royalty aware of their grievances, their hopes and their fears. Queen Elizabeth thus had her portrait painted holding a sieve, which symbolized not only chastity (derived from the legend of the Vestal Virgin Tuccia who carried water in a sieve to prove her chastity), but also her ability to distinguish good from bad—a *double voir* typical of such devices. She was also engraved flanked by the pillars of Hercules, a device appropriated from Emperor Charles V, to express her expanding empire; besides ships in the offing the engraving also includes the pelican in piety and the phoenix, both 'personal devices of the Queen', placed strategically on top of the pillars.[1] By the use of such emblems, she clearly disseminated an image of herself which has largely survived to this day. Similarly, her subjects, by the choice of device in costly and sumptuous pageants and *tableaux*, indicated to her what they wished from the monarchy. The first pageant presented to her by the citizens of London on her pre-coronation procession was on the theme of 'The vniting of the two houses of Lancastre and Yorke'. It consisted of a 'stage' (presumably a triumphal arch) extending across the street with a representation of the Tudor dynasty (Henry VII and Elizabeth of York, Henry VIII and Ann Boleyn—notably excluding Edward VI and Mary, as well as Henry VIII's other wives), wreathed with a profusion of red and white roses, 'and all emptie places thereof were furnished with sentences concerning vnitie'. A contemporary reported that 'it was deuised that like as Elizabeth [of York] was the first occasion of concorde, so she another Elizabeth might maintaine the same among her subiectes, so that vnitie was the ende wherat the whole deuise shotte'. We cannot but be impressed by the young Queen's earnestness, in spite of the difficulties caused by the noise and press of people, to see, hear and understand the 'devise' of the pageant:

her grace caused her chariot to be remoued back, & yet hardly coulde she see, because the children were set somewhat with the farthest in. But after that her grace had vnderstode the meaning therof, she thanked the citie, praised the fairenes of the worke, and promised, that she wuold doe her whole endeuour for the continuall preseruation of concorde, as the pageant did emporte.[2]

These pageants, or devices as they were often called, which greeted the queen on state occasions and on her progresses through the country, united the visual and aural arts, the 'loude noyses of musicke' to the elaborately costumed *tableaux vivantes* and the set verses in both English and Latin; but they also inextricably wedded art to morality in a way which may seem naïve and foreign to us. The endeavours of their art were to make morality vivacious and interesting, and the mentality which now turns to the comparative triviality of the crossword puzzle, then pondered on the sophistical riddles of the emblems and *imprese*. 'These devices,' Bishop Hurd later pronounced, 'composed out of the poetical history, were not only vehicles of compliment to the great on solemn occasions, but of the soundest moral lessons, artfully thrown in and recommended by the charm of poetry and numbers.'[1]

II

Throughout the whole of Renaissance painting, embracing in its folds artists as various as Pinturicchio, Leonardo da Vinci, Mantegna, Bellini and Raphael, the symbol and the emblem formed the soul of many a work of art. And in literature not only did these images illuminate and enrich poetic concepts, they also produced an important genre of their own, those emblem books in which literary and pictorial artists collaborated in presenting series of symbolic devices designed to appeal both to the mind, through the words (or 'mottoes'), and, through the designs, to the imagination.

For the development of this emblematic literature an explanation may be found in the coalescing of numerous intellectual currents. From the medieval period there came the idea that poetry should have a didactic function—and what more adroit way could be found to introduce such didactic elements than the employment of emblematic images? To the men of the Renaissance this made particular appeal, since there is everywhere evident during that period a desire, sometimes even a passionate desire, to find cryptic expression of thought, to proceed in the imaginative realm curiously rather than straightforwardly. This trend, so clearly marked both in poetry and painting, found added support from that typically humanistic endeavour—the attempt to delve into the mystery of Egyptian hieroglyphics and to evolve for them a Renaissance equivalent.[2]

It is true that, while other European countries produced during this period a vast and flourishing 'emblem-book' literature, England brought forward comparatively little in that kind; yet this fact by no means should be interpreted as meaning that in the Elizabethan and Jacobean world the power of these symbols was less than it was on the continent. Many of the continental collections were well known to Englishmen, and towards the close of the sixteenth century the emblematic vogue was as strong in London as it was in Paris or Rome. Even before that vogue was fully established, the celebrated *Emblemata* of Andrea Alciati was beginning to circulate, and with it was associated the no less well-known work of another Italian author, the *Hypnerotomachia Poliphili* of the humanist, Francesco Colonna—both preparing the way for what was to come.[3]

To Alciati goes the credit of having first inaugurated the 'emblem-book' literature. Although he had to wait for ten years before his manuscript, completed in 1521, came from the press, his volume soon became one of the most widely read and deeply admired books of the period. The first edition of 1531 was soon followed by a second at Paris three years later, and thereafter printing succeeded printing. Almost immediately imitators sought to copy and expand upon his style. Such, for example, was the celebrated *Symbolicarum Quaestionum…Libri V* of Achille Bocchi, issued at Bologna in 1555, and embellished with excellent copper-plates by Giulio Bonasone, which were to have, for the second edition of 1574, a very able retouching by Agostino Carracci. From Italy the mode passed quickly into France, where works such as *Le Théâtre des bons engins* (1539) by Guillaume de la Perrière and the *Hécatomgraphie* (1540) by Gilles Corrozet demonstrate very clearly—even if the authors do not admit it—their great indebtedness to the work of Alciati. Those works include collections of historical apologues, of proverbs, of shrewd maxims concerning love, of wonderful adventures, or even of fables, always in accordance with the line of development indicated by their forerunner.

The credit for having inaugurated the genre in England goes to Geoffrey Whitney, who was to entitle his book, published in 1586, *A Choice of Emblemes, and other Devises*. Little originality was exhibited here—so little, indeed, that the author was constrained to give warning that he intended merely to present a selection of emblems 'for the moste parte gathered out of sundrie writers'. To simplify things for his reader Whitney divides his emblems into three categories, with further subdivisions into historical, natural and moral:

Historicall, as representing the actes of some noble persons, being matter of historie. *Naturall*, as in expressing the natures of creatures, for example, the love of the yonge Storkes, to the oulde, or of such like. *Morall*, pertaining to vertue and instruction of life, which is the chiefe of the three, and the other two maye bee in some sorte drawen into this head. For, all doe tende unto discipline, and morall preceptes of living.

Whitney himself was to furnish part of the material required for the next book of emblems that appeared in England: this was a work entitled *The Heroicall Devises of M. Claudius Paradin*, published in 1591, edited by an anonymous P.S. and illustrated with many woodcuts, accompanied by descriptions in prose which comment in a fairly adequate manner on the plates. Although much of this book is devoted to explanations of coats of arms and crests belonging or supposed to belong to French cavaliers, to emperors of ancient Rome and even to famous personages of classic antiquity, many pages are given over to the explanation of maxims and sayings. The manner in which emblem collections of this kind penetrated beyond the pages of books is well demonstrated by the fact that there is still to be seen, at Hawstead Hall in Suffolk, a small wainscoted closet adorned with no less than forty-one devices taken from Paradin's volume. The emblems thus were not restricted to the library shelves: a man's physical surroundings reflected his moral preoccupations. Wall paintings and tapestries—such as those at Hatfield House based on Whitney's work—were placed on display for constant contemplation.[1]

The fashion of turning to France for ideas was to continue meanwhile with another emblem book, Thomas Combe's *The Theater of Fine Devices*, of which we now possess only an edition of 1614, although it had been entered as early as 1593 in the Stationers' Register and was mentioned soon after that by Meres. In effect, this work is a translation from the French of Guillaume de la Perrière's *Le Théâtre des bons engins*, a book crammed with erudition and intended to demonstrate, in a very full discussion, the remote origin of emblems.

So far, therefore, the English essays in this style had been translations or rehashings. The first truly English emblem book is Andrew Willett's *Sacrorum Emblematum Centuria Una*, which was published, without illustrations, about 1591 or 1592. This, however, was a very modest performance, which demonstrates little more than an earnest yearning after the marvellous, edited with particular care. That it is without illustrations does not constitute a novelty or exception, as numerous books were similarly printed on the continent.

By far the most important of all the English works of this kind came from the pen of Henry Peacham, and this author of *The Compleat Gentleman* well shows how deeply the emblematic fashion in the early seventeenth century had established itself in at least courtly circles. His *Minerva Britanna or a garden of Heroical Devises* appeared in 1612, and it is significant that, although obviously there is a considerable debt to the *Iconologia* of Cesare Ripa, the illustrations are almost all original and that the verses used to illuminate the moral problems are in English. Rich in themes borrowed from the classical world, in fables and in analogues, *Minerva Britanna* is indeed a sumptuous volume.

It is important, too, to bear in mind the fact that, before the preparation of this book, Peacham had prepared, for presentation to the king, a magnificent manuscript entitled *Basilicon Doron*, illuminated with charming illustrations apt to charm a prince who was ever diligent in deciphering the emblematic devices displayed by participants in tournaments. Indeed, the quatrains used to explain or enrich the illustrations were all specifically based on royal 'instructions'.

In spite of all this interest, however, England lacked a true 'emblem-book' tradition. The number of such volumes issued by London publishers was meagre indeed compared with the mass of kindred writings put forth by Parisian and Italian presses; and, above all, there was little in that country which may be set alongside the quite considerable volume of continental theoretical discussion on the subject. Henri Estienne's *L'Art de faire les devises* finds no English parallel, nor does Giovanni Ferro's *Teatro d'Imprese*; among other important studies of a similar kind—Scipione Bargagli's *Dell'imprese*, Luca Contile's *Ragionamento sopra la proprietà delle Imprese*, Emmanuele Tesauro's *Il Cannocchiale Aristotelico, O sia Idea delle Argutezze Heroiche Vulgarmente chiamate Imprese*—only one, Paolo Giovio's *Dialogo dell'Imprese* was given an English dress, Samuel Daniel translating it in 1585.

III

If, however, there was in England no firmly set 'emblem-book' tradition, based on scholarly theory and poetic practice, it is clearly evident that the aims of the continental writers were strongly reflected in Elizabethan and Jacobean literature, even if sometimes they assumed variant forms, and that the spirit which animated the French and Italian authors was equally dominant in the Elizabethan and Jacobean world. During recent years the prevalence of the emblematic style in English literature has been widely exemplified by several scholars, and, despite the excellence of their work, still more remains to be done on this theme. We need turn, for example, only to Spenser in order to realize how the allegory in many passages can be clarified and deepened by observing his use of methods and procedures closely related to the technique established by the authors of emblem books.

Among the playwrights who were Shakespeare's contemporaries especially deserving of attention from this point of view are John Marston, George Chapman and Ben Jonson. In Marston's dramas, many significant emblematic devices are introduced, even while satirical reference is made to the vogue itself. One such device mentioned in *Antonio and Mellida* is derived from Girolamo Ruscelli's *Le Imprese illustri* (Venezia, 1584, pp. 126 ff.) and Achille Bocchi's *Symbolicarum Quaestionum* (Bologna, 1555, symb. LV). In *The Malcontent* the device of the bear alluded to by one of the characters is to be found in the *Hieroglyphica* of Horapollo.[1]

In much the same way George Chapman frequently presents moral lessons put forward almost exactly in accordance with the typical *forma mentis* of an author of emblems; as a consequence, many images in his plays may be regarded as true emblems cast precisely in the form they might have taken in formal emblem-books. In *Byron's Conspiracy*, for example, Savoy describes Byron on his horse as an emblem of the state:

> Your Majesty hath miss'd a royal sight:
> The Duke Byron on his brave beast Pastrana,
> Who sits him like a full-sailed Argosy
> Danced with a lofty billow, and as snug
> Plies to his bearer, both their motions mix'd;
> And being consider'd in their site together,
> They do the best present the state of man
> In his first royalty ruling, and of beasts
> In their first loyalty serving (one commanding,
> And no way being mov'd; the other serving,
> And no way being compell'd) of all the sights
> That ever my eyes witness'd; and they make
> A doctrinal and witty hieroglyphic
> Of a blest kingdom: to express and teach
> Kings to command as they could serve, and subjects
> To serve as if they had power to command.   (II, ii, 66)

Ben Jonson, too, deserves particular attention in this connection; learned author as he was, he made abundant use of devices and emblems not only in his masques but in his plays as well. His delight in this kind of theme is well testified by the enthusiasm he displayed when telling Drummond of Hawthornden of a device consisting of a 'Compass with one foot in Center, the other Broken, the word. *Deest qūod duceret orbem.*' It is, of course, in the masques that these emblematic forms assume greatest significance. Jonson himself called his masques 'Court Hieroglyphics', and here the figures taken from emblem books and from iconology were to be transplanted into appropriate surroundings. Nor was Jonson alone in building these courtly displays upon emblematic foundations: all such works, including the great *Coelum Britanicum* of Carew and Shirley's *Triumph of Peace*, are packed, in their characters and in their stage settings, with references to mythographical and emblematic works of the time.[2]

In noting this direct indebtedness of the English poets to the continental emblem-books, it is particularly important to observe that the former did not see in the emblematic figures merely a visual quality—the quality which we today are inclined to think their chief attraction: for them other qualities were equally important. We shall, for example, do well to remember that in contemporary books dealing with problems of eloquence the emblem was considered as a distinctive element in rhetoric. The emblem book was thus transformed into a kind of precious jewel-box for writers of the time. Bearing this in mind, we can now appreciate the significance of what otherwise might be considered merely the work of idle brains and the useless pastime of a particular moment in the story of civilization.

IV

When we turn to Shakespeare's works in this connection we must, of course, go cautiously, since it is all too easy to try to prove too much. Nevertheless, we can say with absolute assurance, not only that Shakespeare shared the general dependence of his age upon the power of symbols, but that he also was well acquainted with the emblem-book literature. The fact that he devised an *impresa* for Lord Rutland, to be painted by Burbage, by itself demonstrates how much he shared the taste of his time.

No doubt the attempt to relate all the various sayings or mottoes in Spanish, Italian, Latin, or French which appear in some of the plays to particular devices presented by this emblem writer or that yield little that can be regarded as certain. In any case, even if we could demonstrate with assurance that Shakespeare had borrowed or quoted from particular volumes, we should not have before us anything more than evidence of his reading. What is much more significant is the undeniable fact that in various passages he shows himself akin in spirit to the emblem writers, thinking as it were in their terms. Take, for instance, the casket scene in *The Merchant of Venice*: the Prince of Morocco is speaking:

> The first, of gold, who this inscription bears,
> 'Who chooseth me shall gain what many men desire';
> The second, silver which this promise carries,
> 'Who chooseth me shall get as much as he deserves';
> This third, dull lead, with warning all as blunt,
> 'Who chooseth me must give and hazard all he hath'. (II, vii, 4)

These words could have been composed to adorn, at the bottom of a page, some rich engraving in wood or copper. We must fully recognize that here, and elsewhere, Shakespeare reveals without doubt the mentality of the emblem author.

The dramatist's use of emblematic material is here obvious, but in reading his works we must seek also for things not so obvious, and therefore even more significant. We turn, for instance, to a scene in *Hamlet*. 'Besides,' cries the Prince, 'to be demanded of a sponge!'

What replication should be made by the son of a king?

Rosencrantz. Take you me for a sponge, my lord?

Hamlet. Ay, sir, that soaks up the king's countenance, his rewards, his authorities. But such officers do the king best service in the end: he keeps them, like an ape, in the corner of his jaw; first mouthed, to be last swallowed: when he needs what you have gleaned, it is but squeezing you, and, sponge, you shall be dry again.

Rosencrantz. I understand you not, my lord.

Hamlet. I am glad of it: a knavish speech sleeps in a foolish ear. (IV, ii, 12)

Nothing, it might be said, of emblem material here. Yet, if Rosencrantz has not read his Whitney[1] or his Alciati, Hamlet has, and as he speaks he recalls the picture of a king squeezing out a sponge: in the background is a gallows with several bodies hanging from it, and these, as the accompanying verse makes clear, are the greedy courtiers who suck their sustenance from the monarch and, when full, are squeezed dry again. The malicious Claudius and the opportunist Rosencrantz and Guildenstern are set down with as great clarity as the 'image' of his uncle which Hamlet had already put into his 'tables', with the motto, or 'word', to remind him of that uncle's villainy.

Among the plays one in particular merits close attention from this point of view. In *Pericles* Shakespeare not only brings in emblem-like material, but also demonstrates clearly his indebtedness to various authors of emblem-books. The scene of special importance is that in which the princess's suitors display their shields to her and her father:

Thaisa. A knight of Sparta, my renowned father;
And the device he bears upon his shield
Is a black Ethiope reaching at the sun:
The word, '*Lux tua vita mihi*'.
    Simonides. He loves you well that holds his life of you.
Who is the second that presents himself?   [*The second Knight passes over.*
    Thaisa. A prince of Macedon, my royal father;
And the device he bears upon his shield
Is an arm'd knight that's conquer'd by a lady;
The motto thus, in Spanish, '*Piu por dulzura que por fuerza*'.
                                [*The third Knight passes over.*

    Simonides. And what's the third?
    Thaisa.   The third of Antioch;
And his device, a wreath of chivalry;
The word, '*Me pompae provexit apex*'.   [*The fourth Knight passes over.*
    Simonides. What is the fourth?
    Thaisa. A burning torch that's turned upside down;
The word, '*Quod me alit me extinguit*'.
    Simonides. Which shows that beauty hath his power and will,
Which can as well inflame as it can kill.   [*The fifth Knight passes over.*
    Thaisa. The fifth, an hand environed with clouds,
Holding out gold that's by the touchstone tried;
The motto thus, '*Sic spectanda fides*'.   [*The sixth Knight passes over.*
    Simonides. And what's
The sixth and last, the which the knight himself
With such a graceful courtesy deliver'd?
    Thaisa. He seems to be a stranger; but his present is
A wither'd branch, that's only green at top;
The motto, '*In hac spe vivo*'.
    Simonides.   A pretty moral;
From the dejected state wherein he is,
He hopes by you his fortunes yet may flourish.   (II, ii. 18)

As is easily seen, we are dealing here with mottoes and devices calculated to appeal directly to the emblematic culture of the spectators: this being so, obviously Shakespeare could not effectively introduce emblems easy to identify, since the audience's pleasure would lie, partly at least, in interpreting them for themselves; on the other hand, they could not be too difficult to understand, since, if they were, the effect of the scene would be lost. We must not forget that, in a very short space of time, the public is being presented with six different mottoes for which no preparation has been made.

A close examination of the dialogue seems to indicate that here the playwright has combined several things: on occasion he has invented a device of his own, on occasion he has used a device taken from a particular source, and on occasion he has modified an already existing motto and design. The motto and emblem of the First Knight seem to be original: at any rate, no emblem-book published before 1609 yields '*Lux tua vita mihi*' or the image of a black Ethiope reaching at the sun. When, however, we turn to the second shield, with its '*Piu por dulzura che por fuerza*', we recognize that this is a modification of the '*Plus par doulceur que par force*' which appears in emblem 29 of Gilles Corrozet's *Hécatomgraphie* (Paris, 1540). The design and motto of the third Knight—'a wreath of chivalry' and '*Me pompae provexit apex*'—are to be found in the 1562 edition of Claude Paradin's *Devises heroïques* and reproduced in the English edition of 1591. Paradin also gives us the fourth cavalier's 'burning torch that's turned upside down' and the motto '*Quod me alit me extinguit*', but this might also have been known to some of the audience from its appearance in Gabriello Symeoni's *Imprese heroiche* (1559) and in the 1586 edition of Whitney's volume. Almost certainly Whitney gave to Shakespeare the fifth emblem, the hand environed with clouds and the motto '*Sic spectanda fides*'. Finally, with the sixth emblem we come back apparently to the playwright's own invention: nowhere else can be found the withered branch and the motto '*In hac spe vivo*'. The whole effect of the scene, therefore, would seem to be based on an adroit admixture of the familiar and the completely unknown, together with an equally adroit counterpoise between the comments made on the stage by Simonides and the interpretations which the spectators might themselves put upon the various devices.

This scene, then, may be taken in itself as an emblem of the spirit of the age. It would make its appeal to audiences of the time precisely because it accorded so well with a trend, a taste and a style which was part of their intellectual and spiritual being; and it appears to demonstrate how Shakespeare, like so many of his contemporaries, not only found delight and satisfaction in contemplating the emblematic devices originated by others, but also had in himself the inclination and power to invent similar devices of his own. The appeal of the symbol is indeed one of the chief features of this age's intellectual temper.

ART AND ENTERTAINMENT

14

ACTORS AND THEATRES

'Players that offer service'

I

Acting is an ephemeral art. A great actor can enrich his patrons with an unforgettable experience but it is a matter of luck if they include a Hazlitt or a Lewes or a Beerbohm capable of resurrecting the experience through the power of the written word and carrying it living into the minds and hearts of later generations. No writers of this kind emerged during the age of Shakespeare; how Burbage played Hamlet is almost as conjectural as what song the sirens sang. But though we lack detailed word-pictures of the great performances of the period, the scholarly excavations of the last fifty years have brought to light numerous fragments of evidence about the various troupes of actors and it is now possible to piece some of them into mosaics which provide an outline of some of their histrionic styles and methods of casting. Some parts of these mosaics have rough edges and contrasting colours, but they coalesce sufficiently to permit some generalizations and to show that Shakespeare's references to acting exhibit a fuller awareness of the various histrionic traditions at work during his lifetime than those of any of his contemporaries.

During Shakespeare's lifetime, medieval miracle plays were still being performed in certain parts of England, notably at Chester, Norwich, Coventry, York and Perranzabulo. Most Elizabethan allusions to the acting of these plays are disparaging, and Shakespeare's most important reference to the subject is no exception and may have been prompted by first-hand knowledge. To Hamlet the ranting of the periwig-pated actor who tears a passion to tatters 'out-herods Herod'. This comparison may derive from Shakespeare's having seen the role of Herod acted at Coventry in the pageant of the Shearmen and Tailors during his boyhood or his 'teens. The Coventry miracles, as E. K. Chambers has noted, 'were played regularly, except in 1575, until 1580', and were 'probably the most famous in England'.[1] Roscoe E. Parker's comparison of the Herods of the Coventry, York, Towneley, Chester, and Ludus Coventriae plays has revealed that the Coventry one far surpasses the others in rodomontade and furious action.[2] How he registered rage when his plan to trap the Three Kings was frustrated is shown by the following quotation and stage direction:

> I stampe! I stare! I loke all abowtt!
> Myght I them take, I schuld them bren at a glede!
> I rent! I rawe! *and* now run I wode!
> A! thatt these velen trayturs hath mard *this* my mode!
> The schalbe hangid yf I ma cum them to!
> *Here Erode ragis in the pagond and in the strete also.*[3]

That Shakespeare may have seen the most famous of our medieval stage directions translated into action is a nice speculation. Herod's appearance evidently matched his action; the Coventry

191

accounts of the sixteenth century include payments for an iron crest, a gilt falchion, a painted wig, and a painted face for this character.[1]

One of the special merits of D. M. Bevington's book *From Mankind to Marlowe*[2] is that it gives preciser details of the personnel and casting methods of the early Tudor professional troupes than any earlier study. It shows, for instance, that in the earliest troupes the leading actor usually took the role of the Vice, that he had less doubling to do than any of his colleagues, and that his was the dominant role in their productions.[3] The popularity of this performer with his long fool's coat and coxcomb or dagger of lath is picturesquely explained by John Gee: 'It was wont', he recalls, 'when an Enterlude was to be acted in a Country-Towne, the first question that an Hob-naile Spectator made, before he would pay his penny to get in, was, Whether there bee a Divell and a foole in the play? And if the Foole get upon the Divels backe, and beate him with his Cox-combe til he rore, the play is complete.'[4] Ben Jonson caustically dismissed such practices as 'antique reliques of barbarisme',[5] but Shakespeare's Feste whimsically recalls them to tease Malvolio when he promises to come back quickly like the ubiquitous 'old Vice',

> Who, with dagger of lath,
> In his rage and his wrath,
> Cries, ah, ha! to the devil.[6]

Shakespeare glosses in more detail the next phase of histrionic development revealed by the casting lists of the professional troupes. As Bevington has shown, certain leading actors abandoned the Vice and began to impersonate human heroes and villains.[7] This transition is particularly well illustrated by the scheme for casting in the first edition of Thomas Preston's *Cambises*, published about 1570. It shows that the actor who played Ambidexter, the Vice, also had to take the minor role of Trial. The pre-eminence of the actor who played Cambises is attested not only by the exceptional length of this part but also by the fact that the only other lines assigned to him are those of the epilogue, which ensured him a central place on the stage at the end of the play. Passion, not the mischief-making of the Vice, is the *forte* of Cambises; stumbling through fourteen-syllabled lines, he runs the gamut of anger, jealousy, and lust. The fustian expedients and inflated histrionics of performers of this role are recalled in *1 Henry IV* when Falstaff prefaces his parody of kingship with the command, 'Give me a cup of sack to make my eyes look red, that it may be thought I have wept; for I must speak in passion, and I will do it in King Camby-ses' vein', and when Mistress Quickly delightedly proclaims that 'he doth it as like one of these harlotry players as ever I see!'[8]

Shakespeare had the same phase in the evolution of Tudor acting in mind when he wrote *A Midsummer Night's Dream*. Bottom's emphatic preference for 'Ercles' vein, a tyrant's vein'[9] links the endeavours of the rude mechanicals to the period when the Vice was being superseded as a leading role by flamboyant character parts drawn from classical myth and legend, and the scenes in which they rehearse and perform *Pyramus and Thisbe* mirror many of the characteristics of the small professional troupes of the mid-sixteenth century which Bevington has documented.[10] The burlesque element in these scenes is much closer to fact than has sometimes been assumed. That Quince's troupe has professional aspirations is implicit in Flute's estimate of Bottom's quality: 'an the duke had not given him sixpence a day for playing Pyramus, I'll be hanged'.[11] The size and the personnel of his troupe—six men only—was common in the mid-sixteenth century, when women's roles were frequently taken by men, not boys. The scheme for the casting of *Cambises* reveals that the actor who played Smirdis and Ruf also took the part of Venus, so the casting of Flute as Thisbe is not so fantastic as it might seem. It was also a common practice for one man to double three or four parts; sometimes he had to switch roles in the course of a single scene, so lightning transformations were often imperative, and beards and masks to enable the player to effect them were indispensable items in his equipment. Hence Quince tells Flute that he can play the part of Thisbe 'in a mask', and when Bottom considers which beard will be best for Pyramus—'either your straw-colour beard, your orange-tawny beard, your purple-in-grain beard, or your French-crown-colour beard, your perfect yellow'— he is surely itemizing the stock in trade of the professionals.[1] The stage directions of mid-century professional pieces often require actors to improvise parts of their roles, so Quince is asking for nothing out of the ordinary when he tells Snug that he can play the lion 'extempore, for it is nothing but roaring'.[2] Similarly, when Quince alters his play to suit the supposed tastes of his aristocratic patrons, he is following known precedents; John Rastell, for instance, prepared two versions of his *Play of the Four Elements*, a longer one for educated audiences, and a shorter one for less intellectual spectators which could be performed by five actors.

Songs and dances were an accepted part of the professional repertoire, and Bottom provides another pointer to the professional pretensions of his company when he proudly offers Theseus the alternative entertainments of an epilogue or a Bergomask dance. The same pretensions are also implicit in the jargon of professional actors with which these aspiring artisans interlard their discussions and rehearsals, as they talk glibly of their 'interlude', of their 'bill of properties', of the 'scroll' on which a part is written, of 'studying' and 'conning' their lines, of doing the piece 'in action' with everyone rehearsing 'according to his cue', of Bottom's 'condoling' vein in one role and his 'tearing a cat' and 'making all split' in another.[3] A full appreciation of the travesty, in short, demands an awareness of its multiple connections with what professionals actually did and said in their rehearsals and productions, and Theseus' genial comment, 'The best in this kind are but shadows; and the worst are no worse, if imagination amend them',[4] shows a nice assessment on Shakespeare's part of the relativity of the best professional playing and of blundering attempts to emulate it.

Shakespeare was less tolerant of the new histrionic fashion which surged to the fore in the 1580's. Inflated though it was, the tyrannical vein of Cambises and Hercules offered some scope for rudimentary character acting, but in the 1580's it was superseded in popularity by the comic clowning, extemporal wit, and lively jigs of Richard Tarlton and Robert Wilson. The contrast between the two vogues is vividly suggested by Joseph Hall's censorious lines:

> Now, least such frightfull showes of Fortunes fall,
> And bloudy Tyrants rage, should chance appall
> The dead stroke audience, mids the silent rout,
> Comes leaping in a selfe-misformed lout,
> And laughs and grins, and frames his Mimik face,
> And justles straight into the princes place.
> Then doth the Theatre Eccho all a loud,
> With gladsome noise of that applauding croud.[5]

These 'vile russettings' of the clown seemed indecorous to Hall. Shakespeare, for his part, deplored the extemporized speeches and loud laughter of the clown as an unpardonable intrusion when 'some necessary question of the play'[1] was about to be discussed. This item in Hamlet's advice to the players is often interpreted as a criticism of the clowning of Will Kempe, a former member of Shakespeare's company, but the aptest contemporary illustration of what Hamlet had in mind occurs in *Tarltons Jests*, where we are told of a performance of *The Famous Victories of Henry the Fifth* in which Tarlton unexpectedly took the part of the Lord Chief Justice, received the customary box on the ear from Prince Hal, then reappeared in his usual role of the clown and, on being told of the prince's action, improvised the mirth-provoking lines, 'the report so terrifies me, that me thinkes the blow remaines still on my cheeke, that it burnes again'.[2] Tarlton's squint, flat nose, and low stature were unmistakable whatever part he played, and his well-known gifts as an extemporiser of witty retorts in rime were liable to cause any play or jig in which he appeared to be interrupted by 'themes' shouted from the auditory expressly to provoke an exhibition of these powers.

In his most characteristic moments, Tarlton was a primitivist of genius who revived what Richard Southern has described as the first age of the theatre, in which the performer works his magic on his audience with no aids other than his spontaneous words, his body, and his costume. No other Elizabethan player received so many written tributes from his contemporary admirers. It is clear, however, that some Elizabethan playwrights saw the dangers of Tarlton's atavism and succeeded in curbing some of his disciples. So much emerges from the passage in Richard Brome's *The Antipodes*, where Letoy censures By-play for improvising additions to his roles and for addressing the audience instead of his 'coactors in the scene'. When By-play protests that such practices have been permitted 'On elder stages, to move mirth and laughter', Letoy sternly rejoins,

Yes, in the dayes of Tarlton and Kempe,
Before the stage was purg'd from barbarisme
And brought to the perfection it now shines with.
Then fooles and jesters spent their wits, because
The poets were wise enough to save their owne
For profitable uses.[3]

The latter remark implies that a reform eventually came when poets began to take more interest in the stage. The earliest manifesto of this histrionic reformation is the prologue to *Tamburlaine*, where Marlowe's diatribe against the '*iygging vaines of riming mother wits, And such conceits as clownage keepes in pay*', coupled with his commendation of the *high astounding tearms* of his conquering hero,[4] heralds the supersession of the jigs, gags and doggerel of Tarlton and his rout by the dignified action and sonorous elocution of Edward Alleyn, creator of the role of Tamburlaine. Marlowe's crusade was not immediately successful, however. Ironically, the printer of the first edition of *Tamburlaine* (1590) found it necessary to omit '*some fond and friuolous Iestures, digressing (and in my poore opinion) far vnmeet for the matter*' which had found their way into the acted version of the play.[5]

By 1590 Tarlton was dead; during the next ten years Will Kempe was his acknowledged successor, famed for his grimaces, jigs and extemporal wit. But some playwrights, including Shakespeare, took measures to prevent him from dominating the stage as Tarlton had done. In the title-page of *A Knack to Know a Knave* (1594), the reference to 'ED. ALLEN and his companie' takes precedence over 'KEMPS applauded Merrimentes | of the men of Goteham'. As Kempe appeared only in these 'Merrimentes', and as they have no bearing on the plot and run to barely a page and a half of the text, the anonymous dramatist obviously did his best to isolate and restrict the clowning in his play. Similar conclusions can be drawn from the two Shakespearian roles that Kempe is known to have played: Peter in *Romeo and Juliet* and Dogberry in *Much Ado About Nothing*. The very limited scope of the former role and the peculiar humour of the latter suggest that Shakespeare was taking effective measures to prevent the comedian who played them from disrupting the plots and 'necessary questions' of the plays concerned. Peter has nothing to do with the main action; he has only one short speech in II, iv, a brief and silent appearance in II, v, and only in IV, v is he conceded a modest interlude of puns, songs and riddles with the musicians. As for Dogberry, it is the very nature of his self-regarding vanity to make him veer away from the 'necessary question' which he could help to solve; the bumbling discursiveness of the characterization seems designed to accommodate and motivate such digressions, by-play and improvisations as Kempe may have brought to the role. That Shakespeare's clowns were shaped to fit the actors who played them seems beyond question, for when Robert Armin took Kempe's place in the Lord Chamberlain's Company, Shakespeare created for him the parts of Touchstone and Feste, which were exquisitely attuned to the more delicate, introspective, and sophisticated style of fooling in which Armin had already begun to specialize. It is also significant that in a pamphlet on clowning published not long after he had joined Shakespeare's company, Armin endorses a discipline in stage-fooling more in keeping with Hamlet's advice than with the Tarlton tradition:

> True it is, he playes the Foole indeed;
> But in the Play he playes it as he must.[1]

II

There is a marked increase in the frequency of critical references to the art of acting in plays written after permanent theatres had been established in London, probably because the dramatists were then able to participate more regularly in the business of staging their pieces. In an interesting note, 'Did Shakespeare Produce his Own Plays?' David Klein has given an affirmative answer to his title-question and has claimed that 'the system of author-direction prevailed throughout the period'.[2] It is important to realize, however, that 'produce' as a theatrical term was unknown to Elizabethans and implies more comprehensive powers of direction than were accorded to the playwright in some, if not all, Elizabethan productions. 'Instruct', 'instructor', and 'instruction' are the terms most frequently employed by Elizabethan writers to describe a playwright's participation in rehearsals. Thus John Aubrey speaks of Ben Jonson as 'an excellent instructor',[3] and Domitia tells Caesar in Massinger's *The Roman Actor* that she has been 'instructing the players how to act' in a tragedy that she has arranged.[4] The earliest English writers known to have given 'instruction' of this kind were the masters of the boys of the various royal chapels, notably William Cornish, Nicholas Udall, Richard Edwards, William Hunnis, Richard Farrant and Sebastian Westcote, who not only organized and managed juvenile companies, but wrote plays for them and directed their rehearsals. The term 'instruction' has academic over-tones and the Elizabethan application of it to the direction of actors may be due to the pedagogic status of its earliest exponents.

That the juvenile troupes competed successfully with adult professional companies until the latter two decades of the sixteenth century may have been partly due to the superior artistic discipline imposed on them by their masters. That the adults gained the upper hand may have been partly due to the 'instruction' given them by their playwrights once they acquired per-manent headquarters in London. This theory of a creative collaboration between dramatists and actors is certainly upheld by Richard Flecknoe's remark à propos of Shakespeare, Jonson, and Beau-mont and Fletcher: 'It was the happiness of the Actors of those Times to have such Poets as these to instruct them, and write for them; and no less of those Poets to have such docile and excellent Actors to Act their Playes, as a *Field* and *Burbidge*.'[1] This seems to me a more accurate account of the relationship between the instructors and the instructed than that given by Johannes Rhenanus, a German who visited England in 1611 and afterwards wrote, 'So far as the actors are concerned, they, as I have noticed in England, are daily instructed, as it were in a school, so that even the most eminent actors have to allow themselves to be taught their places by the dramatists...'.[2] The King's Men were obviously not as deferential as this when they undertook *The New Inn* for the formidable Ben Jonson, whose title-page (1631) describes the play 'A COMOEDY. | As it was neuer acted, but most negligently play'd, by some | the Kings Seruants'. At the end of *The Antipodes*, Brome glumly informs his readers that parts of it were 'left out of the presentation for superfluous length, as some of the players pretended'.[3] The Elizabethan dramatists obviously did not possess the absolute powers of playwright-producers like W. S. Gilbert and A. W. Pinero.

Having made this reservation, we may usefully survey some of the fragmentary indications of the way in which Jonson, Fletcher and Shakespeare instructed their players. Jonson reacted as violently against the heroic style of acting made popular by *Tamburlaine* as Marlowe had reacted against the stock in trade of Tarlton; so much emerges from his scornful reference to the '*scenicall* strutting, and furious vociferation' of 'the *Tamerlanes*, and *Tamer-Chams* of the late Age'.[4] After Jonson's death, according to Robert Herrick,

> The Cirque prophan'd was; and all postures rackt:
> For men did strut, and stride, and stare, not act.
> Then temper flew from words; and men did squeake,
> Looke red, and blow, and bluster, but not speake.[5]

These references concur with Jonson's own critique of players who '*ouer-act prodigiously in beaten satten, and, hauing got the tricke on't, will be* monstrous *still, in despight of* Counsell'.[6] The special virtue of the 'Counsell' given by John Fletcher appears to have been the creation of a high degree of stage illusion. 'How didst thou sway the Theatre!' wrote one of his admirers

> make us feele,
> The Players wounds were true, and their swords, steele!
> Nay, stranger yet, how often did I know
> When the Spectators ran to save the blow?

Frozen with griefe we could not stir away
Vntill the Epilogue told us 'twas a Play.[1]

As an instructor, Shakespeare apparently made it his business to establish in detail the lines along which his leading roles were to be interpreted. John Downes, who attended the rehearsals of Sir William Davenant's company after the Restoration, records that the part of Henry VIII was 'right and justly done by Mr *Betterton*, he being Instructed in it by Sir *William*, who had it from Old Mr *Lowen*, that had his Instructions from Mr Shakespear himself', and that when Betterton played Hamlet, 'Sir *William* (having seen Mr *Taylor* of the *Black-Fryars* Company Act it, who being Instructed by the Author *Mr Shaksepear*) taught Mr *Betterton* in every Particle of it'.[2]

Limited though they are, these details of playwrights' instructions run counter to the theory that Elizabethan acting was a fixed and formalized art based upon the techniques of gesture and diction laid down in contemporary treatises on rhetoric and practised in grammar schools and universities. The acting of *Tamburlaine* and Jonson's histrionic principles were too much at variance to have come from a common source. Some performances of Fletcher's plays, far from being formalized, were highly naturalistic. If a settled system of acting was in use, it would hardly have been necessary for actors of a later generation to hark back to the particular advice given by Shakespeare to Lowen and Taylor. We can be certain that to a dramatist-instructor the play was the thing. In Elizabethan school and university productions, however, it is clear that the play was subordinate to the opportunities which it gave for practising the arts of forensic gesture and elocution outlined by books on rhetoric. At Westminster School, for instance, the annual Latin play was performed so that the pupils, in accordance with the school statutes of 1560, might 'the better become accustomed to proper action and pronunciation'. In the universities, as Thomas Heywood tells us, the purpose of plays was 'the emboldening of their *Iunior* schollars...*against they come to be imployed in any publicke exercise*, as in the reading of Dialectike, Rhetoricke, Ethicke, Mathematicke, the Physicke, or Metaphysicke Lectures'.[3] There are good reasons for believing that the consciously rhetorical style of acting used by academic amateurs differed considerably from the technique employed by professional Elizabethan players. A number of plays contain pointed criticisms of academic histrionics. In *The Return from Parnassus* (Part II), Will Kempe finds it ridiculous that the amateur actors at Cambridge 'neuer speake in their walke, but at the end of the stage, just as though in walking with a fellow we should neuer speake but at a stile, a gate, or a ditch, where a man can go no further'.[4] In *The Antipodes*, Letoy criticizes other artificialities of the academic player when he tells Quailpipe, a curate turned actor, that he 'dreamt too long upon his sillables' in the speaking of a prologue, and orders him not to perform

> In your Scholasticke way you brought to town wi' yee,
> With see saw sacke a downe, like a Sawyer;
> Nor in a Comicke Scene play *Hercules furens*,
> Tearing your throat to split the Audients eares.[5]

These criticisms suggest that professionals thought the 'scholasticke' technique slow, mannered, over-deliberate, and inflexible.

The Elizabethan professional actor was, of course, capable of rhetorical graces when his part required them. After the titular hero of *The Roman Actor* has addressed the Senate in defence of his profession, the admiring comment of one of his fellow-players,

> Well pleaded, on my life! I never saw him
> Act the Orator's part before,[1]

proves that the Elizabethan professional could act the orator. It does not follow, however, that stage oratory was the same as academic oratory, or that all the skills of the professional player were of a formalized kind. Various references reveal that not only were there different styles of acting at different theatres, but that the leading company had more than one style, that the more naturalistic of these styles was preferred by judicious observers, and that Burbage's methods as an actor were those which we associate with impersonation of a naturalistic kind rather than the exhibition of a formalized technique. In 1630, for instance, Thomas Carew condemned the Red Bull and the Cockpit as theatres '*where not a tong Of th'untun'd Kennel, can a line repeat Of serious sense*', and singled out the Blackfriars company for special praise as '*the true brood of Actors, that alone Keepe naturall vnstray'nd Action in her throne*'.[2] At the Globe, the King's Men evidently used a louder and more emphatic style than they did at Blackfriars, for in his prologue to *The Doubtful Heir*, James Shirley candidly informs the audience that the play was written for the smaller Blackfriars Theatre and that '*we have no Heart to break our Lungs* at the Globe'.[3] It is reasonable to assume that the Queen's Men, who performed *The Antipodes* at Salisbury Court, had some naturalistic virtues in common with the Blackfriars company, for this play contains passages condemning players who talk into the audience instead of addressing their 'coactors in the Scene' and who turn round at the end of every speech, 'not minding the reply',[4] and Brome would not expect his actors to censure faults of which they themselves were guilty. The ideals of consistency, naturalness, and completeness of impersonation underlying this passage were surely realized by Burbage as Flecknoe describes him: 'a delightful *Proteus*, so wholly transforming himself into his Part, and putting off himself with his Cloathes, as he never (not so much as in the Tyring-house) assum'd himself again until the Play was done...never falling in his Part when he had done speaking; but with his looks and gesture, maintaining it still to the heighth...'.[5]

III

Some critics have doubted whether a naturalistic style would be possible on the Elizabethan stage because some spectators sat so close to the actors. But the criteria of naturalism and the conditions of stage illusion change from age to age, and the spectators of the sixteenth and early seventeenth centuries had a capacity for make-believe which enabled them to accept stage conventions even more various than those of medieval drama. This claim is borne out by the unprecedented number of different types of stage setting used by Tudor and Stuart playwrights. In addition to the simultaneous setting which they had inherited from the Middle Ages, they used the fixed setting, painted canvas settings inside a proscenium arch, and the scenic system which E. K. Chambers has described as 'successive staging'. The fixed setting was directly or indirectly inspired by Serlio's invention of a single scene for satyric drama and by neo-classical theories about the unity of place. Its use is illustrated by John Lyly's employment of a single woodland setting of trees and shrubs for the entire action of *Love's Metamorphosis*. In *Love's Labour's*

Lost, Shakespeare followed suit, but most Elizabethan playwrights found the dramaturgy of the fixed setting too restrictive, too much at odds with the flowing variety of action demanded by their audiences. Settings of this kind were rarely used.

Simultaneous settings, on the other hand, were used throughout the period. Shakespeare's *The Comedy of Errors*, for instance, requires at the back of the stage three structures representing the Priory, the house of Antipholus, and the Courtesan's house. The same scenic system is found in a play staged at Blackfriars as late as 1640 or 1641, James Shirley's *The Imposture*, in which the fifth act demands a simultaneous representation of a wood, St Felice's chapel, and Father Cyprian's cell. When this system was employed, spectators were usually expected to concentrate their attention on the particular setting in use and to assume that the other settings were temporarily non-existent. In *Histrio-Mastix*, however, John Marston characteristically abandons this convention for a more sophisticated and experimental one of his own when the simultaneous settings representing Fourchier's study and Velure's shop are simultaneously used, with passages of dialogue alternating between the two places and a stage direction instructing Fourchier and Lyon-rash to '*sit and whisper whilst the other two speake*'.[1]

The use of painted settings also led to a significant experiment in stagecraft. Scenes of this kind, consisting of painted wings and back flats arranged on a stage framed by a proscenium arch, appear to have been used in special productions of Sir John Suckling's *Aglaura*, William Habington's *The Queen of Arragon*, and Thomas Nabbes's *Hannibal and Scipio*, staged at the Cockpit or Salisbury Court or Blackfriars between 1635 and 1640.[2] In his prologue to *Hannibal and Scipio*, Nabbes declares that

> The Places sometimes chang'd too for the Scene,
> Which is translated as the musick playes
> Betwixt the acts,[3]

which indicates that each of the five acts had a special painted setting. This production seems to have encouraged Nabbes to try to employ in ordinary productions a principle often observed on the modern stage—that of restricting each act to a single scene. His stage directions in *The Unfortunate Mother* show that the five acts were respectively intended to take place in 'The Presence', 'the Dutchesse Chamber', 'the presence', 'the gallery', and '*the Grove*'. In his dedicatory epistle to the first edition, Nabbes boasts that his method was 'without president', but, significantly, its austerity did not commend it to the actors. The prefatory verses which follow the epistle reveal that the play was never performed because the actors rejected it.[4]

The rejection of *The Unfortunate Mother* may well have been due to the players' instinctive preference for the freedom of the system of successive staging, which permitted the platform and the tiring-house façade to represent successively an unlimited number of specified or unspecified localities by the use of significant actions, words, or properties, or even by the mere entry of particular characters. This convention enabled Shakespeare to unfold the imperial theme of *Antony and Cleopatra* without act or scene divisions in a rhythmical sequence of episodes set in Africa, Europe, Asia, and on the Tyrrhene Sea. The same convention permitted the imaginative elaboration of a particular locality as well as the deployment of an unlimited number of different places. In Act V, scene iii of *The Duchess of Malfi*, for instance, Delio's opening words to Antonio required the audiences of the Globe and Blackfriars to metamorphose the platform and the façade behind it into a scene consisting of three places with a river separating one of them from the other two:

> Yond's the Cardinall's window: This fortification
> Grew from the ruines of an auncient Abbey:
> And to yond side o' th' river, lies a wall
> (Peece of a Cloyster) which in my opinion
> Gives the best Echo, that you ever heard.[1]

One can identify the window with a casement on one side of the tiring-house, the fortification with the outer part of the forestage on the same side, the wall with part of the tiring-house on the other side, and the river with the bare boards between Delio and this 'wall', but the power of the passage derives essentially from the reverberant associations rather than the specific localization given to these structures. The 'Cardinall's window' is a reminder of the sinister forces still at work in the background, the dividing 'river' of the other-worldly condition into which the Duchess has crossed, and the 'fortification' of the new-found resolution with which Antonio is imbued. In some plays, the dramatists even enfranchise themselves from the liberal conventions of successive staging by using a character with supernatural powers to juxtapose places and persons many miles apart. In the sixth scene of *Friar Bacon and Friar Bungay*, for example, when Prince Edward gazes into the magic glass in Friar Bacon's study at Oxford, he sees events at Fressingfield in Suffolk which are actually performed by the characters concerned on another part of the stage. Simultaneous actions are represented here in a manner best compared to the use of montage in a film.

A 'study' with curtains in front of it figures prominently in the stage directions of *Friar Bacon and Friar Bungay*, and as there has been much controversy among reconstructors of Elizabethan playhouses since John Cranford Adams took over the word as a generic term to describe an alleged curtained recess or inner stage at the Globe, it is appropriate to consider the evidence relating to the use of curtained properties or structures by professional companies during the sixteenth and seventeenth centuries. An early instance of such a usage occurs in a play probably acted in the 1520's, John Heywood's *The Play of the Wether*, in which Jupiter's throne appears to have been equipped with a canopy from which practicable curtains were suspended. The direction following line 178—'*the god hath a song pleyed in trone*'—indicates the presence of a throne. Immediately afterwards Jupiter says, 'A whyle we will wythdrawe our godly presence',[2] and as there are no directions for an exit and re-entry by him, it can be inferred that he temporarily concealed himself by drawing together curtains attached to his throne. A commodious throne of the kind required for this play is depicted in the portrait of Henry VIII in the patent for Cardinal College, Oxford, of 25 May 1529 (see Pl. XXVA). A similar throne, complete with dais, canopy, and curtains, appears on the stage shown in the picture of the setting for *Laurentius*, performed at Cologne in 1581 (see Pl. XXVB). The same method of concealment and discovery seems to have been used in a play acted in the 1580's, *The Famous Victories of Henry the Fifth*, in the episode which begins when Henry IV gives the following command to his lords, 'Draw the curtaines, and depart my chamber a while', and afterwards falls asleep. Immediately afterwards, Prince Henry takes away his father's crown. That the king went to sleep wearing his crown and sitting on a chair is clearly indicated when he wakes up and gives the order, 'take off my crown.

Remoue my chair a little backe, and set me right'. After the prince has returned the crown, we again have the formula, 'draw the curtaines, depart my chamber'.[1] As these are the only references to curtains in the play, the use of a canopied throne seems highly probable. It may have stood on the stage throughout the performance and have been used by the Lord Chief Justice and Henry V as well as by Henry IV. Even when not in use, it would have an emblematic value in this play.

Another curtained structure in use before the first public theatre was built was the tent. The interlude called *Jacob and Esau* (published in 1568) contains the direction, 'Esau entring into Iacobs te[n]t shaketh Ragan off'.[2] Between 1576 and 1613, tents were used with some frequency in plays by Peele, Greene, Marlowe, Shakespeare, Barnabe Barnes, and Thomas Heywood. The most interesting instance occurs in Peele's *Edward the First*, which was acted at the Rose, where a big tent was used to represent a room in a palace. Edward's remark,

> We will goe see my beautuous louely Queene,
> That hath inricht me with a goodly boie,

is followed by the direction '*King Edward, Edmund, and Gloster goes* (sic) *into the Queenes chamber, the Queenes Tent opens, shee is discovered in her bed, attended by Mary Dutches of Lancaster, Ione of Acon her daughter, & the Queene dandles his young sonne*'.[3] This episode ends with a direction '*They close the Tent*'; soon afterwards another refers to it as '*The Queenes Tent*', whereas a still later one specifies it as '*the Chamber*'.[4] Two significant facts emerge from these quotations: (*a*) a tent was used to make a discovery representing '*the Queenes Chamber*', (*b*) it was a structure large enough to accommodate six persons and a bed. After the christening of the young prince there is another interesting episode when Gloucester says 'let us now goe visite the King and Queen', and we have the direction '*Then all passe in their order to the kings pauilion, the king sits in his Tent, with his pages about him*'. After the child has been presented to the king, we have the directions '*Sound Trumpets, they all march to the Chamber. Bishop speakes to her in her bed.*'[5] These directions show that another fairly large tent was erected on the stage to represent the '*kings pauilion*' and that in conjunction with the queen's tent it provided two simultaneous settings. If, as seems likely, the queen's tent was placed at the rear of the Rose stage, it may have resembled the big pavilion shown in the twelfth woodcut in John Derricke's *The Image of Ireland* (London, 1581), which has front hangings drawn well to the sides to reveal Sir Herbert Sidney in his chair, a table, and attendants (see Pl. XXVI). But when tents like King Edward's had to be placed well forward on a platform with spectators at its sides as well as at its front, they cannot have been the same as the tents used in everyday life because their interiors had to be open to view on every side. A pavilion canopy mounted on posts with hangings which could be opened on every side may have provided the necessary transpicuous structure. Such a structure may have evolved from a type of booth used by early professional companies. 'Booth' and 'tent' were synonymous terms in sixteenth-century parlance, as the quotations under 'booth' reveal in the *Oxford English Dictionary*, which include a sentence published by Coverdale in 1535: 'We came to the tentes of the Sirians, and beholde, there is no man there...but...the bothes as they stonde.'

A third type of curtained structure was the arbour or bower. The outstanding example of its use occurs in Peele's *The Love of King David and Fair Bethsabe*, where the speaker of the prologue, according to a direction, '*drawes a Curtaine, and discouers Bethsabe with her maid bathing ouer a spring: she sings, and Dauid sits aboue vewing* (sic) *her*'. That Bethsabe and her maid were inside a bower with foliage attached to it is shown when Bethsabe tells Zephyr that 'this shade (sun proofe) is yet no proofe for thee' and urges him 'To play the wantons (*sic*) with vs through the leaves', and when David says,

> Let all the grass that beautifies her bower,
> Beare Manna every morne in stead of dew.[1]

This episode resembles one performed on the Rederyker stage at Antwerp in 1561, when allegorical characters led Man to 'an arbour, made all open that what happens within may be seen from all sides'.[2] The bower used in Peele's play was probably a trellised arch like the one depicted in the title-page woodcut of the 1615 edition of *The Spanish Tragedy* (see Pl. XXV c).

'Bower' was evidently a fluid term for the word 'cabin' and is used interchangeably with it to describe a curtained structure in Fletcher's *The Faithful Shepherdess*;[3] George R. Kernodle has recorded how a 'bower' used in a court entertainment in 1606 had 'cloth of crimson taffeta and a canopy on top'.[4] 'Canopy' appears to have had three distinct meanings in Elizabethan theatrical terminology. As we have seen, it could mean the cloth of state suspended over a throne. It could also mean a portable canopy mounted on poles and carried over a person of high rank, like the canopy borne by '*four of the* Cinque-ports' over the queen in 'The Order of the Coronation' in Shakespeare's *Henry VIII*.[5] In other directions, 'canopy' apparently refers to a tent-like structure used for the staging of interior scenes in the Blackfriars, Cockpit and Paul's private theatres. In Marston's *Sophonisba*, which was acted at Blackfriars, a direction states that '*Syphax hasteneth within the Canopy as to Sophonisba's bed*',[6] and the ensuing dialogue and action make it clear that a bedroom setting was arranged '*within the Canopy*'. A canopy was also used in the staging of a play probably written for the Cockpit, William Hemings' *The Fatal Contract*, in which a direction tells us that the Eunuch '*solemnly draws the Canopie, where the Queen sits at one end bound, with Landrey at the other, both as asleep*'.[7] In Chapman's *Bussy d'Ambois*, first staged at Paul's, the ghost of the friar interviews Tamyra '*in a canapie*' which represents her private room. 'Canopy' recurs in the directions of another play prepared for presentation at Paul's, William Percy's *The Faery Pastoral*, where the fairy chapel with seats on degrees mentioned in Act v, scene v was intended to occupy the 'Canopie'.[8]

Directions like the latter ones led E. K. Chambers to assume that at the back of the Paul's stage there was 'a curtained recess, corresponding to the alcove of the public theatres, and known at Paul's as the "canopy"'.[9] But one must reckon with the possibility that the canopy used at Paul's, Blackfriars, and the Cockpit was a curtained, roof-like projection from the rear wall of the stage. In support of this suggestion, it is worth remarking that when Charles V was formally welcomed to London in 1520, 'the *tableaux vivants* had projecting canopies in front of both castle walls and single towers',[10] and that the vignette on the title-page of N. Richards' *Messallina* (1640) depicts a wide ledge hung with curtains and projecting from the rear wall of a stage. In his definition of *scena* as '*properly the fore-part of a Theater where Plaiers make them ready, being trimmed with hangings, from out which they enter vpon the stage*',[11] John Florio may have been referring to a projecting canopy (*fore-part*) equipped with curtains (*hangings*) and enclosing an area to which the players had access via a door or opening in the tiring-house façade. In his inventory of the properties of the Admiral's Men, Henslowe lists 'j wooden canepie'.[12] Hung with curtains and attached to the rear wall of a stage and supported with posts, this solid canopy may have been used for discoveries and interior scenes at the Rose and other public theatres. The general appearance of a projecting canopy equipped with curtains and being used for a discovery scene is suggested by parts of the title-page engravings in Joshua Sylvester's translation of Du Bartas' *Diuine Weekes* (London, 1621) and Richard Braithwait's *The English Gentlewoman* (London, 1631). The former work depicts a canopy with partly drawn hangings; Judith has just slain Holofernes and is carrying his head away: within the canopy is a bed with part of the decapitated corpse showing (see Pl. XXVII A). The latter shows a canopy with curtains drawn up and knotted at either side of the allegorical figure of Apparel, who is described on the page opposite as 'being by a Curtaine first discouered, where she appears sitting in a wardrobe richly furnished' (see Pl. XXVII B).

It has been one of the purposes of the foregoing discussion to show that there is a considerable body of evidence indicating that a variety of curtained structures—thrones, tents, arbours, and canopies—were placed on the platform and used for discoveries and interior scenes. For a number of reasons, however, I do not think that the existence and dramatic use of a recess in the tiring-house can be ruled out of court. Admittedly, no such recess appears in De Witt's drawing of the Swan Theatre, but when such an area was not required in a performance or rehearsal in an open-air theatre of that kind it would surely have been closed with a screen, partition, or wooden 'traverse' to protect the interior of the tiring-house. That recesses in the tiring-houses of certain theatres were put to dramatic use is proved by directions calling for discoveries to be made by the opening of stage doors. *Eastward Ho!* (acted at Blackfriars) contains the direction '*At the middle dore, Enter Golding discouering a Gold-smiths shoppe*'.[1] In *The Renegado* (acted at the Cockpit) Asambeg, according to the directions, '*plucks out a guilt key*', opens a door, and '*Paulina discouered comes forth*'.[2] Another Blackfriars' play, *Alphonsus, Emperor of Germany*, requires a scene to be acted in a large doorway recess because Alphonsus asks his page for the master-key of all the doors and afterwards '*opens the door and finds* Lorenzo *asleep aloft*'.[3] A later remark reveals that Lorenzo was 'sleeping in his chair' on this occasion. The ensuing episode takes place near the chair in the recess.

Lexicographers of the period give us good reason for believing that by 'stage' Elizabethan stage directions mean specifically the platform or scaffold in front of the tiring-house. Cotgrave defines 'Eschafaut' as '*A Scaffold, or high Stage*';[4] Florio defines 'palco' as '*a stage, or scaffold*', and 'palco basso' as '*a low stage, or scaffold*'.[5] These definitions are especially relevant to certain episodes in a Globe play by Barnabe Barnes, *The Divils Charter*. In Act IV, scene i we have the direction, '*Alexander in his studie beholding a Magicall glasse*', followed by the highly significant addition, '*Alexander commeth vpon the Stage out of his study*'.[6] Taking *Stage* to mean the platform, one cannot but infer that the *studie* was a recess in the tiring-house behind it. The definitions of the lexicographers also encourage one to believe that the well-known direction in Greene's *Alphonsus King of Arragon*—'*Let there be a brazen Head set in the middle of the place behind the Stage*'[7]—means that a recess beyond the rear edge of the platform was used here. Barnes' study had curtains in front of it; in the last scene of his play '*Alexander draweth the Curtaine of his studie where he discouereth the divill sitting in his pontificals.*'[8] This discovery can be related to the engraving at the top of the title-page of the anonymous *Trvth Brought to light and discouered by Time* (1651); it shows Truth and Time drawing aside curtains which are suspended from a rail, not a canopy, to reveal a figure seated on a throne with a table by him in a small area bounded at the rear by an arras (see Pl. XXVII C). In Jonson's *The Poetaster*, Tucca warns Histrio against representing him in a play: 'an you stage me, stinkard, your mansions shall sweat for't, your tabernacles, varlet'.[1] As 'tabernacle' can mean a canopied niche or recess in a wall, this passage opens up the possibility that in some Elizabethan theatres the recess had a curtained canopy projecting from the wall above it. An arrangement of this kind would combine the advantages of the alleged 'inner stage' with those of the tents and canopies known to have been used in some Elizabethan playhouses.

Speculation of the latter kind is admissible in discussions of the Elizabethan stage for its usages abound in variety and elasticity of method. Soon after *Antony and Cleopatra* had spanned continents at the Globe, Jonson was treating its patrons to a unique concentration of locality in *The Alchemist*, with a setting representing nothing more than the inside and the outside of a wall with three doors and a window in it. Such contrasts are typical. Simultaneous settings and successive staging often occur in the same play. While some actors and playwrights are developing the arts of naturalism and stage illusion at the Blackfriars and Salisbury Court, such comedians as John Singer and Andrew Cane are cheerfully maintaining the music hall techniques of Tarlton and Kempe at the Red Bull and the Fortune. It is wise to think of such an age in terms of various traditions and syntheses rather than as settled systems of acting and stagecraft.

15

THE PRINTING OF BOOKS

'Whole volumes in folio'

'Whole volumes in folio' has a fine expansive ring about it, but we do well to remember that in the first place few, if any, Elizabethan and Jacobean dramatists could expect to have their works presented to the reading public in so sumptuous a form, and that in the second place few of them seem to have harboured any such ambition. There is not, it is true, a great deal of evidence from the dramatists themselves about their attitude to this question. Yet it seems probable that many of those who thought about it at all would have subscribed quite cheerfully to the view expressed by Thomas Heywood in his Epistle to the Reader prefixed to his play *The English Traveller* (1633): 'True it is, that my playes are not exposed vnto the world in Volumes, to beare the title of *Workes* (as others), one reason is, that many of them by shifting and change of Companies, haue beene negligently lost, Others of them are still retained in the hands of some Actors, who thinke it against their peculiar profit to haue them come in print, and a third, that it neuer was any great ambition in me, to bee in this kind Voluminously read.' This statement should be taken in conjunction with an earlier one by Heywood, prefixed to his play *The Rape of Lucrece* (1608): 'It hath beene no custome in mee of all other men (curteous Readers) to commit my plaies to the presse...for though some haue vsed a double sale of their labours, first to the Stage, and after to the presse, for my owne part I heere proclaime my selfe euer faithfull in the first, and neuer guiltie of the last.' It would be improper to assume that these opinions were necessarily shared *in toto* by all Heywood's fellow-dramatists. Nevertheless, we find neatly summarized in these two passages the hard facts which must have occurred to many of them as they contemplated the circumstances of dramatic production at this time: that a play was intended to be acted, and had to be sold to an acting company if the dramatist was to earn his living; that the fate of a play was quite intimately bound up with the fortunes of the company which had bought it, and that its future, both on the stage and in print, depended to a considerable extent upon the attitude of the actors; and that for many dramatists there was nothing further to be gained by chasing after the dubious immortality of print. If we bear in mind also the date of the passage in *The English Traveller*, it seems possible to detect something of a sneer at such men as Ben Jonson and William Shakespeare whose works had been 'exposed vnto the world in Volumes', and in Folio volumes, the former having gone so far as to correct and revise his material, and to take some pains to ensure that the printer made a respectable job of the result!

It seems desirable at this point to consider briefly a few more statements either by authors or by printers which seem to support the notion that in general the attitude towards the printing of plays was one of indifference; these statements will also help to illustrate the most common reasons adduced for publication when a play actually reached that point.[1] As early as 1570 John Day, the printer of *Ferrex and Porrex*, explained to the readers that the authors never intended the play to be published; but 'one W. G. getting a copie therof at some yongmans hand that lacked a litle money and much discretion', a badly corrupted version was put out while the authors were absent from London, and it now seemed proper to try to put things right. Eight years later the printer of George Whetsone's *Promos and Cassandra* told his readers that the author was about to leave the country, and had no time to revise or to correct his text; he, the printer, had done his best with the material, and craved pardon for any faults that may have escaped him. In 1590 the printer of *Tamburlaine* felt himself free to omit certain 'fond and friuolous Iestures' which, although they may have been admired on the stage by 'vain conceited fondlings', were out of place in the serious history which he proposed to print. Heywood's reference to 'shifting and change of Companies' has an echo in John Charlewood's preface to his edition of *Endymion* in 1591: ' 'Since the Plaies in Paules were dissolued, there are certaine Commedies come to my handes by chaunce...'; he has printed this one as an experiment, and he will print the rest if its reception proves satisfactory. John Marston, addressing readers of *The Malcontent* in 1604, was unhappy 'to thinke that Scenes invented, meerely to be spoken, should be inforcively published to be read' (recalling Heywood's distinction between the stage and the press); but this particular play has been so much misunderstood that 'I have my selfe therefore set forth this Comedy'. Even so, his absence made it necessary for him to rely to a great extent on the printer's discretion, and he apologized for any errors that might occur. Heywood's attitude has already been fully quoted, but we may note briefly that in the 1639 edition of *If You Know not Me, You Know Nobody* he complained of an earlier text printed without his consent and based on a copy produced by 'stenography'; and that in prefaces to *The Rape of Lucrece* (1608), *The Golden Age* (1611), and *The Four Prentises* (1615) he remarks on the fact that these plays had come to the press without his knowledge but that he is happy to claim them as his own. Thomas Middleton made a similar complaint in the preface to *The Family of Love* (1608): 'Too soone and too late, is this work published: Too soone, in that it was in the Presse, before I had notice of it, by which meanes some faults may escape in the Printing. Too late, for that it was not published when the general voice of the people had seald it for good, and the newnesses of it made it much more desired, then at this time....' Writing a preface to *Greene's Tu quoque or The City Gallant* in 1614, Heywood could say without a tremor, 'Nor can I tell whether this worke was diuulged with his [i.e. Cooke's] consent or no'. Finally Bernard Alsop, the printer of *The Two Merry Milkmaids* (1620), sums up a number of the points already raised when he says: 'It was made more for the Eye, then the Eare; lesse for the Hande, then eyther: and had not false Copies trauail'd abroad (euen to surbating) this had kept in; so farre the Author was from seeking fame in the publishing that he could haue wisht it bound about with the Ring.'

These statements speak for themselves, and seem to indicate clearly enough indifference on the part of the author, except when he felt moved to complain about the way in which his text had been handled, a considerable element of chance in the passage of a text from actors to printer, and a general assumption that the printer had the right to proceed with his activities, and even to take liberties with his material, without consulting the author. Certainly there was no generally accepted idea of author's copyright as we understand it today. Sir Walter Greg put the position very clearly when he said: 'The notion of copyright in the modern sense of an author's right to the fruits of his own labour was for all practical purposes unknown at the time with which we are concerned. When we use the term in connexion with an Elizabethan work what we mean is the exclusive right of publication accruing under the ordinances of the Stationers' Company to one of its members who had issued an edition of a work after duly registering it as his copy in the Hall Book.'[1] The troublesome and still widely disputed question of the establishment of a printer's or publisher's copyright will have to be dealt with later; for the moment our concern is with establishing the background of relations between author and printer. Greg quotes elsewhere[2] the charges brought against the typical member of the Stationers' Company by George Wither in his *Scholars' Purgatory* (c. 1624), and while he agrees that Wither was not altogether an impartial witness (since he was smarting under defeat by the Company) and that some of his remarks are highly coloured, there is nothing in his statement 'that can be shown to be contrary to usage, and for much of it confirmation is forthcoming'. According to Wither, the typical stationer, 'If he get any written copy into his power likely to be vendible, he will publish it: and it shall be contrived and named according to his own pleasure, which is the reason so many good books come forth imperfect and with foolish titles', and he goes on to say that 'by the laws and orders of their corporation they can and do settle upon the particular members thereof a perpetual interest in such books as are registered by them at their Hall in their several names; and are secured in taking full benefit of those books, better than any author can be by the King's grant, notwithstanding their first copies were purloined from the true owner or imprinted without his leave'. Allowing for all possible exaggeration this leaves us with a picture just about as different as it can be from the one to which modern author-publisher relations have accustomed us; yet it is one that we must be fully aware of if we are to understand many of the important aspects of the transmission of the texts of Shakespeare and his fellow-dramatists from their own day to ours.

A dramatist wrote his play primarily for an acting company, and he was paid by this company for his work; there is ample evidence for this part of a play's history in Philip Henslowe's *Diary*, the entries in which record his transactions as owner of the Rose Theatre and banker and money-lender to the Lord Admiral's Men with such leading dramatists as Dekker, Chapman, Webster, Jonson, Chettle and Heywood. It is a great pity that we do not have a corresponding record of the activities of the Lord Chamberlain's Men, Shakespeare's company, but the most recent editors of the Diary have argued with some plausibility that there is perhaps no real reason to believe that the organizations of these two companies were essentially different from each other.[3] Not quite so easy to define are the ways in which the plays passed from the acting companies to the printers, and there is still considerable difference of opinion about the relations between companies and printers from time to time. One clear fact does emerge from E. K. Chambers' examination of the printing of plays at this time which deserves mention here. He counts up the number of plays which have survived, mainly in print but a few in manuscript, from the period 1586–1616. 'The resultant total of three hundred and seven is', he says, 'considerable, but there is reason to suppose that it only represents a comparatively small fraction of the complete crop of these thirty pullulating dramatic years. Of over two hundred and eighty plays recorded by Henslowe as produced or commissioned by the companies for whom he acted as banker between 1592 and 1603, we have only some forty and perhaps revised versions of a few others.'[4] These figures seem at least to confirm in part what was suggested earlier in this essay, that the majority of dramatists were not over-interested in the publication of their plays; presentation on the stage was their major concern—and probably their major source of income.

Most of the plays which found their way into print did so, we may assume, as the result of a straightforward sale by the actors to the printer concerned. But we may also assume that from the actors' point of view there would be no advantage in such a sale as long as the play was enjoying success in the theatre; as Chambers remarks, 'the danger was not so much that readers would not become spectators, as that other companies might buy the plays and act them'.[1] Heywood certainly seems to have had such considerations in mind when he referred, as we saw above, to the reluctance of actors to part with plays in their possession. Chambers also gives two examples of this reluctance being put into practice, the Admiral's Men borrowing forty shillings in 1600 to pay to the printer to stop the printing of *Patient Grissel*, and the King's Revels syndicate entering into formal agreement in 1608 to debar any of its members from putting into print any of the play-books jointly owned by them.[2] Other circumstances might, of course, intervene and make it desirable for a company to depart from its normal jealous care of its play texts. We saw above that in 1591 *Endymion* and other plays came into the hands of the printer as the result of the dissolution of the children's company at St Paul's, and a later closing of St Paul's in 1607 coincides with another rise in the number of printed plays; the comparatively large number of plays coming into print in 1594 may no doubt be linked up with the fact that at this time 'the companies were reforming themselves after a long and disastrous spell of plague; and in particular the Queen's, Pembroke's, and Sussex's men were all ruined, and their books were thrown in bulk upon the market'; while in 1599–1600, when many of the plays published belonged to the Chamberlain's and Admiral's companies, a 'reason might be found in the call for ready money involved by the building of the Globe in 1599 and the Fortune in 1600'.[3] We also saw above, in John Day's reference to a 'yongmans hand that lacked a litle money and much discretion', that plays might reach a printer by more surreptitious methods which would not meet with the actors' approval. There are examples, too, of the authors themselves selling their plays to a printer apparently independently of the company for which they were working (thus falling under Heywood's condemnation of those who 'vsed a double sale of their labours, first to the Stage, and after to the presse'); Fredson Bowers suggests that this may have been the case with Dekker's *Westward Ho!* in 1605, and that the delay of two years between the play's entrance in the Stationers' Register and its eventual publication may have resulted from the acting company's refusal to allow the play to be printed.[4] Similarly, J. R. Brown argues that Webster's *The White Devil* probably reached the printer from the author rather than from the players' company, and quotes Webster's preface as showing 'an independent attitude, critical of the theatre in which this company was habitually acting'.[5]

We must next consider what kind of copy was handed over to the printer. There is still a good deal of work to be done in this field, and for many individual plays the answer is still far from certain. Bowers has put the matter briefly but succinctly when he remarks that 'the copy, on the evidence, seems to have been of every conceivable variety', and he goes on to discuss no fewer than thirteen possible categories.[6] In what follows I shall rely largely on his classifications and shall indicate for each category some of Shakespeare's plays which, in Greg's opinion,[7] seem to fall into that category. It should be emphasized, however, that there is still much speculation involved; this is a very important matter for anyone who has to do with the editing of plays from this period, since it is clear that the kind of copy used by the first printers of the plays will have considerable influence on the form in which the text has been transmitted to us, and it is a healthy sign that so much detailed research is being directed to the answering of the many questions that arise. By the nature of things a manuscript used as copy in a printing shop was unlikely to survive for long once its purpose had been served, and much of what we know, or hope to know, can only be ascertained from a study of the end product—the printed quarto or folio.

In the first place the printer may have received the author's 'foul papers', defined by Bowers as 'the author's last complete draft in a shape satisfactory to him to be transferred to a fair copy'.[1] In these we might expect to find certain loose ends and inconsistencies, in the designation of characters in speech-headings and stage-directions for example, which would be cleared up when the play was being rehearsed for production. This kind of copy seems to be extant in the manuscript of Heywood's *The Captives*,[2] and Greg sees it behind *Romeo and Juliet* Q2 (although certain deficiencies in the manuscript appear to have been made good by the printer's consulting Q1), the quarto of *Love's Labour's Lost*, *Richard II* Q1, and a number of other Shakespearian quartos. Secondly, a printer might receive an authorial or scribal fair copy not intended for direct theatrical use, and Greg seems to find this kind of copy behind the First Folio texts of *Measure for Measure* and *All's Well that Ends Well*, and the quarto text of *Othello*. Thirdly, the printer's copy may have been the author's foul papers, or a fair copy of these, partially annotated by the prompter with notes for properties, effects, and the like, before being transcribed into the prompt book itself. Such phenomena appear in the manuscript of *The Captives* already referred to, and such a copy may lie behind the Fisher quarto of *A Midsummer Night's Dream*. Fourthly we have to bear in mind that copies were sometimes made by scribes for private individuals, based on the author's foul papers or on a fair copy of these, but not intended to be used in the theatre. This kind of copy is extant in the manuscript of the Beaumont and Fletcher tragedy, *Bonduca*,[3] perhaps made by one Knight, the book-keeper of the King's Men, and the manuscript of Fletcher's *Demetrius and Enanthe*, made by the well-known scribe Ralph Crane, and presented to Sir Kenelm Digby in 1624.[4] There seems to be no evidence of such 'private copies' behind any of the printed versions of Shakespeare's plays; on the other hand it is likely that Crane was employed to some extent in the preparation of texts for the First Folio, and that he transcribed for this purpose the texts of *The Two Gentlemen of Verona*, *The Merry Wives of Windsor*, *The Tempest*, and *Measure for Measure*. Fifthly, the printer might receive the company's manuscript prompt-book itself, the copy which had been annotated and used in the theatre for the actual production of the play. There has, perhaps, from time to time been too great a readiness to see prompt-book origin behind a number of Shakespeare's printed texts, and Greg is commendably cautious in this field. It is possible that such a copy was used for the Folio text of *As You Like It*, the Folio text of *Macbeth*, and the Folio text of *Cymbeline*, but we should always bear in mind that a company of actors could not normally be expected to part easily with their prompt-books, and that those features of a printed text which seem to point to such an origin may just as easily have survived through scribal transcripts of a prompt-book. Such transcripts are treated by Bowers as his sixth class, and are seen by Greg as likely to be behind the Folio texts of *The Two Gentlemen of Verona*, *Julius Caesar*, *Twelfth Night*, and *The Merry Wives of Windsor*.

Bower's remaining categories of printer's copy have to do very largely with reprinting from an earlier printed form of the text. The printer might use an unrevised earlier printed edition; or one that had been revised in some way, the revisions having no authority from the author;

or one which had been marked by the author so that it contained his own revisions; or an earlier printed edition which had been annotated by comparison with some manuscript, either the author's own manuscript or a prompt-copy, preserved in the theatre's archives (the kind of copy which may lie behind the Folio texts of *Richard II*, *A Midsummer Night's Dream*, *The Merchant of Venice*, *Much Ado about Nothing*, *Troilus and Cressida*, *Othello*, and *King Lear*); or an earlier printed edition which had itself been used in the theatre as a prompt-book; or, finally, the foul papers, fair copy, prompt-book, or transcript of a prompt-book of a memorial reconstruction of the text without direct transcriptional link with any manuscript derived from the author's autograph, in other words, the copy for a so-called 'bad quarto' (the kind of copy which may lie behind the quartos of *2* and *3 Henry VI*, *Romeo and Juliet* Q1, *Henry V* Q1, *Hamlet* Q1, and possibly the quarto of *King Lear*).

It should be clear from what has been said that right at the start of the printing process we are faced with a great variety of circumstances which will have their influence on the finished text. We must make an effort to rid ourselves of our modern conceptions of printer's copy, an author's typescript (not normally manuscript) which has been carefully prepared in accordance with a number of widely accepted conventions, as free as possible from errors and from any other features which will interfere with the business of transferring the work into printed form as cheaply, as quickly, and as accurately as possible. But when we have accepted this preliminary hurdle of many kinds of copy we are faced with another enormous one, the nature of the printing process itself in Elizabethan times. Once again a great deal of research has been, and still is being, directed towards lifting the veil from the Elizabethan printing shop,[1] but there is still much to be learned, and the process of learning is not made easier by the general reticence of the printers themselves about their work. Certain things we do know, or may reasonably assume. There must have been, for example, some process of 'casting-off' copy, so that the printer would know the size of the book that he was about to print, and so that the work could be divided among the compositors efficiently and equitably. Yet it is only comparatively recently that scholars have come to see that this casting-off could have been done, and indeed was done, in two quite different ways: the result could be that the pages of type were composed in seriatim order (as was generally assumed to be the case), or were composed for immediate setting by formes.[2] The implications of this discovery are still being worked out, but two studies, one of *A Midsummer Night's Dream* and the other of *The Duchess of Malfi*, will indicate some of the editorial considerations that arise as a result.[3] We know that the type was set, one letter at a time, by a single compositor or by more than one sharing the work, and we know that compositors varied in their spelling habits. It has indeed been possible to identify a number of the compositors engaged in setting the First Folio by close attention to these habits as they appear throughout the volume. Yet there is still a wide area of uncertainty when we come to consider such questions as how far we may expect an individual compositor to be faithful to his copy in matters of spelling and punctuation, how far he may be expected to impose his own habits on his copy, how far either of these possibilities may be complicated by the necessity for varying spelling to justify a line of type or by the occasional shortage of certain letters in his composing cases.[4] These are not matters which can readily be decided by the application of strict blibliographical techniques, though such techniques can and do help to limit considerably the possibility of error and misunderstanding; but the unexpected, accidental, human element is there all the time, and has been well summed up by one scholar who says, 'The curious reader should always remember that, when there is a book, Men have been At Work'.[1]

Other aspects of the printing process give rise to difficulties which are rather easier to handle. A knowledge of Elizabethan handwriting, for example, will enable an editor to make intelligent emendations of those errors in his text which arise from the compositor's misreading of his copy; it should be remembered that the setting of type by hand, letter by letter, does not help a compositor to grasp the sense of a long passage, perhaps not even of a single line, and he may easily be misled by some of the letter-forms in his manuscript. Combinations of the various minim letters, *i*, *u*, *n*, and *m*, for example, may give him trouble, while the misprints of *u* for *n*, *g* for *h*, *f* for long *s* are too common to need more than a passing mention. A hand such as that of Thomas Heywood must have been a continual thorn in the side of his printers, and it is interesting in this context to read his own apology for it in the preface to *The Exemplary Lives and Memorable Acts of Nine the Most Worthy Women of the World* (1640), and to study the errata list which follows; almost every conceivable misreading of an Elizabethan letter occurs, and many examples may be paralleled in the printed quartos of Heywood's plays. We know little enough about Shakespeare's hand—if, indeed, it is his hand which appears in a section of *Sir Thomas More*—but certain errors which appear in his printed quartos may certainly be accounted for by an assumption that some of his letter-forms too were capable of misleading a compositor. More mechanical errors are likely to occur as a result of the operation of the printing press. A glance at Pl. XXVIII, which shows the reconstructed press at University College London, based largely on the details given by Joseph Moxon in his *Mechanick Exercises* (1683) and on a study of a great many pictures of the press appearing in printers' devices, ornamental capitals, and so on, will show that it is a fairly simple structure, effective enough in use but not by any means a refined piece of engineering. It is possible, while the press is in operation, for a forme of type to shift slightly, gradually, but inevitably, until odd words or parts of a line are cut off by the frisket, the protecting sheet which comes between the inked type and the sheet to be printed and allows only the type face to come into contact with the paper; the resulting 'frisket bite' can often pass unnoticed by the printer, especially if he is working hurriedly, until it has reached considerable proportions. The inking of the type with ink balls after each sheet has been printed may easily result in the pulling out of loose letters; Elizabethan type seems to have been fairly roughly cast, so that it was not often possible to ensure that a line would be set without a certain looseness. The piece so displaced may or may not be seen at once, but in any case the line from which it was pulled will quickly begin to shift and the gap into which the letter is replaced may not be the original one.

Further difficulties arise when we consider the question of proof-reading. Again we must rid ourselves of twentieth-century conceptions; there was not normally any process corresponding to that by which a printer runs off a set of proofs, sends them to the author for correction, holds up the printing until these are returned, and if necessary sends out further proofs and makes the required corrections before printing is allowed to continue. The evidence seems to show that proof-reading, if it took place at all, was largely a matter for the printer himself, and was carried out in a somewhat haphazard and desultory way. Normally one side of a printed sheet (containing, in a quarto volume, four pages) would be read and corrected, but the actual passage of sheets through the press would not be stopped while this was being done. And even after the press had been stopped for corrections to be made in the type, there was no question of throwing away the uncorrected sheets already printed; paper was much too expensive for that, and they would eventually form part of a finished copy. The result is that individual copies of a play printed as part of one and the same edition will often vary considerably in the readings they contain. Often enough the variants are simply the result of the corrections of obvious misprints, turned letters, and so on, matters which would be well within the competence of an intelligent printer. Sometimes they are rather more serious, and the modern editor has to decide whether they are still the result of more or less intelligent guess-work on the part of the printer, or whether they arise from the presence of the author himself in the printing house, or whether the printer has taken the trouble to consult another source in order to get over the difficulties of his copy. Jonson, we know, did interest himself in this part of the work on his own plays, and it is probable that on occasion Dekker and Webster did too; but there are many more examples, some of which were mentioned earlier in this article, of authors who were prepared, for one reason or another, to leave this business to the printer.[1] In view of what was said earlier about the value of paper and the retention of uncorrected sheets to form part of finished copies, it may also be mentioned that proof-sheets themselves, that is, sheets with the corrections marked by the printer or his reader, sometimes turn up in these copies. They too often tend to show that the process of proof-reading was not altogether a careful or a consistent one; what seem to be obvious errors are sometimes overlooked, while comparison with a corrected version of the same sheet in another copy will often show that some of the corrections were disregarded, or that new errors were introduced in the process of putting the old ones right.[2] 'Printers are madde whoorsons', said Thomas Nashe, and while we need not agree with him wholeheartedly we may perhaps be allowed to regard them as great levellers. For there is no reason to think that their approach to the printing of Shakespeare's quartos differed markedly from their approach to the work of other dramatists; indeed it is probable that for a long time they saw no particular profit in the printing of plays. It has sometimes been suggested that the appearance of the initials W. S. on a play's title-page (those, for example, of *Thomas Lord Cromwell* in 1602, *The Puritan* in 1607, and *Locrine* in 1595) was a deliberate attempt on the part of the printers involved to take advantage of the selling power of the name of a popular and successful dramatist. But Baldwin Maxwell, who examined the problem carefully, came to the conclusion that no case of deliberate attempt at fraud could be made against them.[3] It is 1622 when we find Thomas Walkley telling the reader of the *Othello* quarto that 'the Authors name is sufficient to vent his worke', and the considerations which apply to the publication of the First Folio in 1623 are rather different.

It is clear, therefore, that although enormous advances have been made in our knowledge and understanding of the circumstances in which Elizabethan plays were printed, we are still very much in the dark on some vital matters. The authors and the printers themselves are annoyingly silent about their normal relations; often enough the only time we hear anything at all about these happens when one side or the other feels itself aggrieved—and anger is not a good friend to truth! For Shakespeare himself we know practically nothing about this side of his life, and perhaps we can only conclude that it was very similar to that of his fellow-dramatists, a mixture of indifference, occasional mistrust when the interests of his company were at stake, and occasional outright hostility. We need to know much more about the day-to-day workings of the Stationers' Company, particularly as these affected questions of copyright; if we are to trust the reviewer of the third and fourth volumes of Greg's *Bibliography* in *The Times Literary Supplement*—and I think we may—this scholar's 'last thought on the problem why so many works, often reputable works, were not entered for copyright in the Stationers' Register is that we do not know'.[1] We need to know much more about the activities of individual printing houses, what instructions, if any, were given to their compositors, what their stocks of type and ornaments were like,[2] and many other matters which affected their handling of copy. And we still need more careful analyses of the printed quartos to clear up a number of doubts about the kind of copy from which many of the plays were set. Above all we must not lose sight of the fact that Shakespeare was very much part of this world; we see him now in a very different light, but to the printers of his day there was probably nothing particularly unusual about him. For this reason the answers to many of the problems concerning the text of his plays may well be found in the general and normal run of printed books from his time.

16

MUSIC AND BALLADS

'Marvellous sweet music'

We know that the role of music in Elizabethan life was far from negligible, yet to assess its significance in that golden age is difficult since the conditions governing twentieth-century attitudes and requirements are so distinct from the earlier epoch. Our historical knowledge permits us to avoid some of the pitfalls of exaggerating or minimizing the importance of music in the life of the average Elizabethan, and a famous quotation from Thomas Morley's *Plain and Easy Introduction to Music*[1] may serve for orientation:

But supper being ended and music books (according to custom) being brought to the table, the mistress of the house presented me with a part earnestly requesting me to sing; but when, after many excuses, I protested unfeignedly that I could not, every one began to wonder; yea, some whispered to others demanding how I was brought up....

This passage is frequently quoted to prove that the art of singing was cultivated with equal zeal in every grade of social rank, though recent scholarship is inclined to hold that Morley had good reason[2] to exaggerate the social advantages of musical capability. He was, after all, not only the author of a textbook on music, but also a prolific composer. Moreover, about this time he was petitioning Queen Elizabeth for a patent granting him the monopoly to print music, a suit in which he was successful in 1598. To assume, then, that the average Elizabethan could read at sight the part of a madrigal or other music set in parts would give an unrealistic picture of the age. Before we bewail the imperfections of the twentieth century we are bound to admit that there is little evidence to show that the number of musically literate laymen of our own time is substantially below that present in the reign of Queen Elizabeth. Morley was undoubtedly exaggerating. Guests at an average Elizabethan supper party were probably entertained by musical professionals or by members of the household versed in the art. It is useful to remember, also, that the only music they were ever likely to hear was live music, not the product of a loud speaker. To be sure, mechanical instruments were known as curiosities: Queen Elizabeth presented Sultan Murat III with a mechanical organ, and the 'ingenious instrument' mentioned in *Cymbeline* seems to refer to some contraption 'that goeth with a wheel'.[3] These exceptions merely stress the rule that, for all practical purposes, Elizabethan voices and instruments made live music, and since the occasions demanding music were many, extending from church to banqueting hall, from theatre to tavern, the number of performers in demand was likely to be greater than it is today and thus affected the position of music in Elizabethan life.

Another important aspect, in which our civilization, heir to the industrial and scientific revolutions, differs from that of the Elizabethans, is the ease and readiness with which the average person, whilst engaged in discourse, might refer to the philosophy of music. The connection between the macrocosm of the music of the spheres and the microcosm of human affairs, let alone man-made music, was a commonplace of Elizabethan rhetoric, readily referred to by preacher or playwright. The division of music by medieval theorists into *musica mundana*, the music of the spheres, *musica humana*, the well-ordered and harmonious commonwealth, and *musica instrumentalis*, the vocal and instrumental music performed by men, was still alive in Shakespeare's age, as anyone who ponders Ulysses' speech in *Troilus and Cressida* will realize:

> Take but degree away, untune that string,
> And hark what discord follows!

The frequency with which such ideas were referred to declined steadily after 1600 and, by the time Milton died, what was still a major tenet in treatises of the sixteenth century had become a pretty and somewhat anaemic figure of *licentia poetica*. But in the days of Queen Elizabeth the political writings of Jean Bodin[1] and the plays of Marlowe, Rowley and Shakespeare, still referred to the music of the spheres with serious intent. Pericles does not listen to a figure of speech when he exclaims

> The music of the spheres! List my Marina.

He listens to actual music which may, or may not, represent his conscience or intuition, and spectators of the early seventeenth century accepted the playwright's introduction of supernatural music as part of the Elizabethan world picture, not as a quaint device of a private or esoteric imagination.

Such interventions of miraculous music, harbingers of good and evil to come, were to be read in the history books of Shakespeare's contemporaries, such as Plutarch's *Lives*, englished by North. There the followers of Mark Antony, before their leader's downfall, suddenly

…heard a marvellous sweet harmony of sundry sorts of instruments…as they use in Bacchus feasts….Now such as in reason sought the depth of the interpretation of this wonder, thought that it was the god unto whom Antonius bare singular devotion…that did forsake them.

This 'marvellous', that is, divine, or at least supernatural, music was considered no more out of the ordinary than the prophecy of a seer or of one possessed and, indeed, Shakespeare was quick to utilize both the musical and the dramatic ingredients of this passage when, in his *Antony and Cleopatra*, IV, iii, the soldiers hear a strange music, emanating from an invisible source—actually produced by oboes from under the stage.

> *1st Soldier.* What should this mean?
> *2nd Soldier.* 'Tis the god Hercules, whom Antony lov'd,
> Now leaves him.

Indeed, against the background of these beliefs the interventions of Ariel in the *Tempest* are not fantastic, since Ariel, as the servant of the demi-god Prospero, moves to the accompaniment of strains traditionally associated with his nature. The famous passage (III, iii, 19) in which Alonso and Gonzalo react to the 'solemn and strange music' which accompanies the dance of shapes—

> *Alonso.* What harmony is this? my good friends, hark!
> *Gonzalo.* Marvellous sweet music!—

is, quite likely, a verbal echo from the passage in North's Plutarch. Beyond this it demonstrates the ubiquity of beliefs and superstitions shared alike by courtiers and common folk, on the stage as well as in the audience.

We meet another belief with equal frequency in political and philosophical treatises and in lyrical and dramatic poetry, namely, the view that music was a means to influence the disposition of men. The Pythagorean notion of ἦθος was, of course, in many ways related to the theory of the music of the spheres. If the eternal deities and verities had their expression in *musica mundana*, reflected to greater or lesser degrees in *musica humana*, then an obvious means to elevate the minds and souls of human beings would be through music of a dignified and pious character. Such beliefs were held by doctor and quack, by recusant, Anglican and Puritan; by the Master of the Revels and the humblest entertainer. In the course of the eighteenth and nineteenth centuries these views were apt to be ridiculed by a good many rationalistic commentators, but in the wake of the Second World War the use of music in hospitals and factories has provided a curious pragmatic footnote to a once scorned philosophical tenet. However this may be, our main concern here is with the continuity of the tradition which transmitted Pythagorean, Platonic and neo-Platonic thought to the sixteenth century. Understandably, Latin sources took precedence over Greek, notably Cicero's *Somnium Scipionis*, which plays so prominent a part in English literature, from Chaucer's *Parliament of Fowles* to Drummond's *Cypress Grove*. There was, besides, the neo-platonic tradition extending from Plotinus to Ficino, continuing to Agrippa, Pomponazzi and Pico. While Catharine de' Medici was Queen Mother these views exercised their power at the French Court and, in turn, the practices of her sons Charles IX, Henry III and the Duc d'Alençon could not fail to add prestige to the beliefs and traditions already well established across the channel.[1] When Othello apostrophizes 'the shrill trump, the spirit-stirring drum, the ear-piercing fife' he is referring to the customary music of war which aims to put neighing steeds, knights and commoners on their mettle. It would be an anachronistic error to view the military bands of cavalry and infantry merely as conveying signals, a musical cipher, so to speak. Whether the aristocratic trumpet or the common drum were employed, all intruments were 'spirit-stirring' to Elizabethan ears. Indeed, a well-executed military exercise was considered a 'symphony of war' because the organized and systematic employment of courage which the actual 'symphony' of battle music induced resembled the martial strains in its well-ordered proportions, much as microcosm and macrocosm were related in the philosophic view of the world.

As he that daunceth procedeth with the time of the music...even so an army obeying and moving itself to the same sound doeth not disorder

was a maxim of Machiavelli, faithfully reflected in the dramas of Heywood, Jonson and Shakespeare. In Thomas Wright's treatise on *The Passions of the Mind* (1604) music as an influence on a man's humour is compared with more mundane stimulants:

...just as certain foods delight the palate, so in music diverse consorts stir up in the heart diverse sorts of joys, sadness, or pain...Let a soldier hear a trumpet or a drum, and his blood will boil and bend to battle....

Nor were the Elizabethans unmindful of the other side of the coin of the theory of the Ethos of music. If religious music could turn the mind to God, martial music bend the soldier to battle, surely, lascivious music would degrade those easily tempted. Many of the injunctions against public playhouses, taverns, and brothels, voiced by preachers, parents, and solid citizens, mention lewd music as one of the means which could corrupt the youth of the country. These stern monitors do not deny that David sang a song unto the Lord and consoled Saul with his harp, but most of the space in their tracts is taken up by the opposite view, as it is in William Prynne's *Histriomastix*—

That music of itself is lawful, useful, and commendable, no man, no Christian dares deny....But that lascivious, amorous, effeminate, voluptuous music (which I only here encounter) [i.e. in the theatre] should be either expedient or lawful unto Christians, there is none so audacious as to justify it, since both Scripture, Fathers, modern Christian writers, yea and heathen nations, states and authors, have passed a doom upon it.

This intemperate attack on the theatre and 'light' music—the two are usually linked together—had both its sympathizers and its opponents, as Prynne's career was to show: initially he was deprived of his Oxford degree and condemned to lose both his ears in the pillory, but the outbreak of the civil war changed his fortune; the accused turned accuser and had his triumph in the closing of the theatres (as well as the executions of Archbishop Laud and King Charles).

The kinship between loose morals and lewd music is brought out frequently in the plays of the period. In Jonson's *Volpone* the jealous husband upbraids his wife

> Get you a cittern, lady vanity,
> And be a dealer with the virtuous man.

It should be noted, in passing, that Corvino's vulgar suggestion refers to the popular cittern with wire strings, not to the soft-spoken aristocratic lute, with its gut strings. In Jonson's *Silent Woman* the unhappy Morose who finds himself saddled with a sharp-tongued wife, exclaims

> I have married a cittern that is common to all men.

And in the *Alchemist* the dubious Dol Common plays on the cittern while Dapper is robbed. But perhaps no other play emphasizes music's divergent powers, to debase or to elevate, more truly than *Pericles* (disregarding the question whether or not it be wholly by Shakespeare). In the first Act Pericles apostrophizes the daughter of Antiochus in a manner which distinguishes sharply between heavenly music (here symbolized by the soft and dignified viol) and the dance of hell—

> You are a fair viol and your sense the strings,
> Who, fingered to make man his lawful music,
> Would draw heaven down and all the gods to hearken,
> But being played upon before your time,
> Hell only danceth at so harsh a chime.

In the second Act Pericles' mastery of chivalrous music is praised by Thaisa's father as 'sweet', as full of 'delightful pleasing harmony'. The wooer is declared 'music's master'. But it is in the third Act, when Thaisa is brought back to life, that Cerimon, that ancestor of Prospero, performs his white magic with the aid of divinely inspired music:

> The still and woeful music that we have,
> Cause it to sound, beseech you.
> The viol once more; how thou stirr'st thou block!
> The music there! I pray you give her air.
> Gentlemen,
> This queen will live———

(Again, the instrument chosen[1] is drawn from the family of the soft-spoken, aristocratic string group.) Now the play proceeds to chronicle the musical accomplishments of Pericles' and Thaisa's daughter Marina who, we are informed in the Prologue to Act IV, was 'trained in music' and 'made the night-bird [nightingale] mute' when 'to the lute she sung'. Upon her abduction and sale to a brothel, Marina's accomplishments might have proved a valuable asset to the trade of Dol Common. But nature and nurture prevent her from accommodating herself to this environment. Instead, Marina insists that the keepers of the brothel advertise her accomplishments so that she may earn them money by teaching young gentlewomen:

> Proclaim that I can sing, weave, sew, and dance.

By the fifth Act her fame is established, 'she sings like an immortal', we are told, and the governor ventures to employ her art to restore the distraught Pericles to sanity:

> We have a maid in Mytilene———
> She questionless, with her sweet harmony
> And other chosen attractions, would allure
> And make a battery through his deafened ports.

The scene which follows, in which Marina's music and pleading make successful 'battery', is one of the most moving in Shakespeare's plays. It presages the intervention of the music of the spheres later in the Act. This curious 'miracle play' of the seventeenth century utilizes music prominently and extensively to mark the intervention of powers greater than man. In this respect it functions as a preliminary study to the *Tempest*. As a matter of fact, in their reliance on musical means to symbolize the redemption of human imperfections, both plays have a kinship with such works of the eighteenth century as Mozart's *Magic Flute*. *Pericles* also reminds us that an Elizabethan or Jacobean audience was ever aware of music's divine as well as profane functions. Whether the playwright used a figure of speech, a verbal description, or actual music on the stage, the entire gamut from marvellous sweet music to hell's harsh chime was readily conjured up for his listeners.

So far this essay has dealt only with supernatural music. Yet, he would distort the picture of Shakespeare's world who would omit its complement: the matter-of-fact, work-a-day world of simple song, the treasure of Elizabethan balladry, admired from Sidney's *Apology for Poetry* to Addison's *Spectator* and so enthusiastically revived in the last century or two.

One is inclined to illustrate the ubiquity of balladry in Shakespeare's England by reference to

Autolycus and the glorious sheep-shearing in the *Winter's Tale*, or perhaps to the ballad singer Nightingale in Jonson's *Bartholomew Fair*. But these examples restrict the performance of ballads to professional vendors and singers, whereas ballads were part and parcel of Elizabethan life quite apart from commercial considerations. True, the combination of printing, hawking and public performance brought the ballads to a much wider public. But that public, once introduced to easily remembered tunes, rhymes and phrases, continued to enjoy and remember them on all kinds of occasions. Nor was this fondness for popular ditties restricted to the lower classes. Ophelia in her mad-scene and Desdemona in the privacy of her bedroom demonstrate to us that young gentlewomen knew their ballads too; whether their familiarity with popular lyrics was acquired from the counterpart of an Autolycus or a Nightingale or, more likely, from a nurse or attendant, is of no importance to this study. Indeed, so readily might a quotation from a ballad slip into the everyday parlance of the Elizabethans that the reference, often in the form of a joke that was easily recognized by Shakespeare's contemporaries, tends to be obscured for the modern reader. When Armado exclaims in *Love's Labour's Lost* (I, ii, 179) 'Love is a familiar; love is a devil. . . . Yet was Samson so tempted, and he had an excellent strength: yet was Solomon so seduced, and he had a very good wit', we may surmise that the fantastical Armado, wearing his learning none too lightly, refers to the obvious biblical *exempla*. But an acquaintance with the work of that most popular of Elizabethan ballad-makers, William Elderton, shows that Armado's reference combines tags from two widely distributed ballads. One tells of strong Samson meeting a beautiful lady in Timnath:

> When Samson was a tall young man
> His pow'r and strength increased then...[1]

The other speaks of how wise Solomon was ravished by feminine beauty:

> And was not good king Solomon
> Ravished in sundry wise,
> With every lively paragon
> That glistered before his eyes?
> If this be true, as true it was,
> Lady, lady,
> Why should not I serve you alas,
> My dear lady?[2]

The second stanza, here quoted in full, contains the celebrated refrain 'lady, lady' which occurs in so many love-sick ballads and is quoted in many stage-plays:

> Farewell, ancient lady, Farewell,
> [*Sings*] lady, lady, lady   (*Romeo and Juliet*, II, iv, 151)

> Am not I in blessed case
> Treasure and pleasure to possess?
> I would not wish no better place.
> If I may still have wealthiness,

And to enjoy in perfect peace,
 My lady, lady,
My pleasant pleasure shall increase,
 My dear Lady   (*Trial of Treasure*)[1]

And was it not a worthy sight
Of Venus' child, King Priam's son,
To steal from Greece a lady bright
For whom the wars of Troy begun?
Nought fearing danger that might fall
 Lady, lady,
From Greece to Troy he went with all,
 My dear lady   (*Horestes*)[1]

Of course, if one merely reads the words of these ballads, it is sometimes difficult to understand why they were so popular. The rhymes and the measure are often of a humdrum kind, and one is loath to think that playwrights would include a line here or an allusion there for the sake of poetic excellency. But ballads were not meant to be read, they were intended to be sung. It is usually the rubric in the printed broadside or in the registers of the Stationers' Company which informs us of the melody to which the words were to be fitted. For instance, the 'most excellent and famous ditty of Samson Judge of Israel' was to be sung 'To the tune of the Spanish Pavin'. It was no doubt this attractive tune, preserved in many printed and manuscript sources, that made the words, if not memorable, at least familiar. In fact, the enormous ballad literature of the late sixteenth and early seventeenth centuries is based on the popularity of a comparatively small repertoire of well-known melodies which wandered from text to text. The task of the printer thus became simpler and more economical; instead of reproducing the music he could frequently restrict himself to a brief remark, 'to the tune of...'.

But in suggesting that well-known melodies acted as the carriers of amorous, topical, and other ballads, we must beware of regarding the musical undercurrent as a mere mechanical conveyance. Usually the tune of an older ballad carried to its successor also a variety of verbal elements apart from the metrical scheme. A phrase here, a rhyme there are quickly identified and a family of texts, held together by the same tune, offers a fascinating body of material for a study of sixteenth- or seventeenth-century verse written for music. Within the same sing-song similarities and dissimilarities, the expected and the unexpected stand out sharply, and were no doubt recognized by Elizabethans both in life and in the theatre.

As an example of the criss-cross of relationships existing between various texts sung to the same tune, we may quote the opening stanzas of the following eight ballads, all sung at one time or another to the tune of 'Flying Fame'.[2]

(1) *The Death of King Lear*

King Lear once rulèd in this land
With princely power and peace,
And had all things with heart's content,
That might his joys increase.

(2) *Noble Acts of Arthur*

When Arthur first in court began,
And was approvèd King,
By force of arms great victories won,
And conquest home did bring.

(3) *Chevy Chase*

God prosper long our noble king,
Our lives and safeties all;
A woeful hunting once there did
In Chevy Chase befall.

(4) *Death of Fair Rosamond*

When as King Henry ruled this land,
The second of that name
Besides the queen he dearly loved
A fair and comely dame.

(5) *Marriage of Sir Gawain*

Sir Launcelot and Sir Steven bold,
They rode with them that day,
And the foremost of the company,
There rode the steward Kay.

(6) *Coverdale's Certain most godly...letters*

Some men for sudden joy did weep,
And some in sorrow sing:
When they that lie in danger deep,
To put away mourning.

(7) *Heywood, 'Rape of Lucrece'*

When Tarquin first in court began
And was approvèd King:
Some men for sudden joy did weep,
But I for sorrow sing.

(8) *Shakespeare, 'King Lear'*

Then they for sudden joy did weep,
And I for sorrow sung,
That such a king should play bo-peep,
And go the fools among.

A detailed analysis of the verbal echoes in some of the longer, narrative ballads, such as (3) and (5), would go beyond the scope of this essay. But when the King is named in the opening line, as in (1), (2) and (4), the similarities and the likely mutual influences are obvious at a cursory glance. Another subdivision of this large family of ballads derives from (6), first printed by Coverdale in 1564, and referred to among others by Thomas Nashe. With the wealth of associations carried by the one tune, conflations and distortions were easily contrived, and dramatists were quick to seize so easy a vehicle for evoking overtones and undertones. The two instances here quoted, (7) and (8), occur in plays printed in 1608. In Heywood's tragedy, the serious business of state is repeatedly interrupted by the merry songs of Valerius who acts, dramatically, as a chorus but also adds musical variety to an otherwise fairly steady diet of speech. (The theatre-going Elizabethans wanted their music not only between the acts, but as part of the play as well.) The ballad which Valerius improvises on the tyranny of Tarquin clearly derives from the ballad of King Arthur and points to the contrast between legendary goodness and the evil of unconstitutional rule. The intermingling of lofty tragedy and popular balladry in *King Lear* is, naturally, of a more complex and refined order. Yet, it would be a mistake to overlook the fact that the function of the fool in *Lear* is dramatically akin to that of Heywood's merry Valerius: Lear's witty fool does not merely act as a chorus, he also provides the audience with music, and with familiar ballads to boot. It is precisely because he is 'so full of songs', that is to say, because he is by his profession expected to be a storehouse of well-known lyrics, that he may dare to adapt a ballad and so audaciously tell his king that to have given irrevocable power to Goneril and Regan was an egregious mistake:

> *Lear.* When were you wont to be so full of songs, sirrah?
>
> *Fool.* I have used it, nuncle, e'er since thou mad'st thy daughters thy mothers—for when thou gav'st them the rod and putt'st down thine own breeches,
>
> [*Sings*] Then they for sudden joy did weep,
> And I for sorrow sung,
> That such a king should play bo-peep,
> And go the fools among.

17

THE FOUNDATIONS OF
ELIZABETHAN LANGUAGE

'This goodly speech'

I

'We speak the tongue that Shakespeare spake' is a figure of speech rather than a statement of fact, and it has an ironic flavour in these days of the retranslation of the Authorized Version. It can imply that kinship which Shakespeare's Queen phrased memorably, in the common idiom of her day, when she declared herself to be 'mere English'; but no one is likely to be 'so bold or daring hardy' as to claim parity of esteem for the impoverished and diminishing vocabulary of our familiar speech, if they agree with H. C. Wyld that '"the tongue that Shakespeare spake" was the tongue which he wrote'.[1] We know what it sounded like on the stage of the Globe, and that in spite of differences in pronunciation Shakespeare's English, unlike Chaucer's, is 'modern'. Nevertheless, its vocabulary and rhythms apparently seemed remote enough to that sensitive artist, the late Rose Macaulay, to make her say she could never write a novel set in a period earlier than the seventeenth century, 'because the language they talked was just too different from ours to make easy dialogue which wouldn't sound affected'. She was discussing More's *Dialogue of Comfort against Tribulation* and, passing over Elizabeth's reign and omitting Shakespeare from her argument, referred specifically to the early 1500's when she said, 'there is much less available of colloquial talk and one doesn't quite hear them talking':

By the seventeenth century this isn't so. And there is such a mass of letters, diaries, memoirs, plays, essays, of this period that one can soak oneself in the language and easily reproduce it.[2]

Curious as it may seem, it is this omission from the argument of the richest linguistic artist of all sixteenth-century writers which arouses our instinctive protest and helps to make us aware of a residuum of simple truth in that now almost banal poetic tag. We know that Shakespeare was an extender of the power and range of our language; a creator, a coiner, a borrower, a critic of words and of men's treatment of them; an inventor of harmonies, a connoisseur of sound and sense in words, an artist who could stretch their capacities to unimagined limits, combine five of them to sparkle like a jewel 'on the stretch'd forefinger of time' for ever, or take a very jelly-fish of a word and set it to shine star-like in the heavens. And yet, lord of language as he is, we regard his words as familiar and 'household' words, and this not because we quote him, consciously and unconsciously, in ordinary talk, more freely than any other writer, nor yet because our drafts upon the common fund of English gnomic wisdom are paid in his coin more often than we know—how many people who affirm that 'one touch of nature makes the whole world kin' or that 'the end crowns all' realize they are quoting *Troilus and Cressida*?—but because we sense an affinity, if doubtful how to express it. We recognize rhythms and phrasing which are still natural to our ordinary speech. Scholarship warns us not to assume, when the first recorded use of such a phrase as 'what the dickens' is found in Shakespeare, that it is therefore his invention. All dramatists are pickers-up of unconsidered fresh and lively trifles from the racy talk of the man-in-the-street. Ear and instinct tell us that 'I know a trick worth two of that', 'a poor, lone woman', 'I'll be hanged', 'I have not slept one wink' are even more likely to be borrowings from the common stock; and we are equally convinced that in countless original lines which characterize an individual in perhaps ten words, we 'hear' the everyday speech of his time, as in the First Citizen's rebuke to Coriolanus—'the price of the consulship is to ask it kindly'.

The scholars are with us. Like Wyld, J. W. H. Atkins, discussing English as a literary medium, affirms that in the Elizabethan period 'men wrote very much as they spoke; the literary language has probably never stood nearer to the colloquial'.[1] F. P. Wilson attributes to Shakespeare 'an instinct for what was permanent in the colloquial language of his day, stronger than that of any contemporary dramatist', and believes that the conditions of the art of drama

did not permit him to stray far from popular idiom, but even if they had his mind was of a cast that would still have found the material upon which it worked mainly in the diction of common life.[2]

Helge Kökeritz points out, when discussing his pronunciation, that his radical reduction of unstressed syllables and his 'nonchalant treatment of consonants' makes his verse, as spoken, 'more colloquial' than we might think proper today.[3] And both G. D. Willcock and Madeleine Doran[4] insist that his use of rhetorical art in the language of the plays is of a kind common to all who reached an average educational level. As the former says, 'the "alms-basket of words" was freely scattered among the humble'. These are merely a token indication of the clouds of witness that have gathered over the subject during the first half of this century. The whole weight of competent opinion comes down in Falstaffian bulk on the side of instinct. Why, then, should Rose Macaulay have left him out of her reckoning and have felt that 'one doesn't quite hear them talking' until the seventeenth century?

I do not know why she omitted Shakespeare, but I can guess why she could not quite hear the sixteenth century talking. Instinct makes us all think we know when we are listening in Shakespeare to the talk of ordinary men; but I never feel confident that in contemporary Elizabethan non-dramatic prose I am hearing the natural accents of colloquial speech so that I can 'soak' in it. The rhythms are wrong. Naturally there are exceptions: no one could miss the ring of truth in Deloney's conversational and gossipy passages, for example.[5] But the mass of prose writing is either too formal, over-elaborate and self-consciously 'literary', or else too forced in its verbal liveliness to be credible as speech, though enjoyable for its ingenuity and exuberance, like W. S. Gilbert's patter songs. The explanatory simplicity of much narrative writing has that tone of patient nursery heartiness still sometimes employed in speaking to and writing for children, and the good, direct narrative writing which offsets extravagances and lumbering, heavy-footed rhythms still does not equate with talk.

'Drab and transitional prose' is C. S. Lewis's apt title for his chapter on the early work, 'adorned' and 'plain'; and as he so rightly insists, with reference to the flatter utilitarian style, 'not all plain prose is good'. The effect of a 'plain Drab' specimen is 'as of a man speaking with his mouth full of gravel', referring, for comparison, the written to the spoken language—the known to the unknown; and of Edward Hall, the historian, he says, 'Hall is deliberately trying to write better than he talked'.[1] By implication Lewis has, like Rose Macaulay, an idea of the spoken language of the time; but no one has yet assembled any real body of evidence to enable us to proceed from this negative inference that speech is not like the written 'literary' language to a positive concept of natural writing by which to check our instinctive belief that in Shakespeare we really do hear the sixteenth century 'talking'. That we can, as Dr Johnson suggests, take 'the diction of common life' from Shakespeare is a proposition which needs to be proved, instead of being treated as a basic assumption, and I think Rose Macaulay felt that the documents in the case were missing. She had not found in the sixteenth century the kind of material that had enabled her to get on terms of intimacy with the seventeenth—the written material that lies outside the domain of 'literature', such as the 'letters, diaries, memoirs' she mentions.

II

My own obstinate questioning of Elizabethan prose found no answer; but going back to the first half of the century I realized that not the least of its attractions was that it yielded more and better information than the later years, to help towards the establishment of a general idea of Tudor speech. For the foundations of the current spoken language of the century we must catch the vernacular before it becomes critically and aesthetically self-conscious, when, on the evidence of those who loved it, from Wilson and Elyot to Ascham and Mulcaster, it was, as Florio says, 'so written as it is spoken and such upon the paper as it is in the mouth'. Most people write colloquially and with no thought of effect, so runs their general conclusion; but it is a fine language and full of possibilities, so men must cultivate greater elegance and eloquence and acquire a greatly expanded vocabulary or more 'copie'. If, therefore, we go back to those early decades which are almost barren of literary achievement, back to the pre-Prayer Book period, when writing is primarily a functional activity, an extension and recording of speech instead of an endeavour of art, we can see what kinds of prose rhythms and what range of vocabulary and mastery of composition, sentence structure and the devices of style characterized the writing of ordinary people of all classes before professional writers began to write better than they talked. We shall catch the vernacular before it was taken up, patronized, enthused over, criticized, lectured on and cultivated for its own good—before scholarship and national feeling combined to encourage its development and make it truly conscious of its responsibility and high destiny as a proper medium for literature.

The material is available, and in more than sufficient bulk. What is needed is that most personal form of expression, the letter—especially the familiar letter—as written by ordinary men and women, of all ages, in the two generations immediately preceding Shakespeare's. Here, and in such special documents as signed depositions containing reported speech, we shall find the manuscript material that the Oxford Dictionary and literary studies in general have perforce left practically unexplored. If we tried, theoretically, to pin-point the most propitious moment for studying the language in this pre-literary, pre-1549-Prayer Book period we should inevitably choose the 1530's, historically the reign's most significant decade. It is, therefore, a crowning piece of good fortune that the finest collection of personal letters in the whole Tudor century happens to belong to this central decade.

This collection, known as the Lisle Letters, provides some 3000 items, covers the years 1533–40 and represents the major portion of the personal and official correspondence which accumulated in the household of Arthur Plantagenet, Viscount Lisle, the illegitimate son of King Edward IV, during his term of office as Lord Deputy of Calais.[1] It includes some 500 letters all written by one man, John Husee, gentleman, of London, Lisle's confidential man of business. Holograph and dictated letters are nicely balanced: there are rough drafts, with copies, showing spoken first thoughts adjusted to a final, more judiciously phrased written style: there are hastily scribbled notes, carefully calculated compositions, official as well as personal letters written by the same individuals, and letters to and from Lisle's second wife, born Honor Grenville, their family, members of their household and all their friends, acquaintances and dependants. Practically everyone of importance in society and representatives of all classes are included. But primarily this is the right material for an investigation of 'this goodly speech' because, in the mass, these are the normal letters in which men and women pursue the businesses and pleasures, and face the troubles, the problems, the disasters, the frustrations and hopes deferred of everyday life, celebrate their small personal triumphs, record their fears, beg for help, advise, rebuke, persuade, and even occasionally speak the language of intimacy and affection. They handle the stuff from which dramatic art is made, and it is this that gives them the advantage, as an index to speech habits, over the great Elizabethan collections of letters, which are mainly concerned with politics, diplomatic negotiations and the business of governing the kingdom—subject-matter which does not lend itself in the same way to the rhythms and vocabulary of common speech. These later collections do not include such a wide variety of correspondents of all classes and occupations: too often the writers are infected by the general desire to write more stylishly and fashionably than they speak; and, in learning 'to write', forget or reject the simpler, tunable, speakable rhythms of the earlier generation.

In the Lisle Letters the self-conscious stylists are few, the 'naturals' many. The former are impressive, the latter more relevant in this particular context, partly for their evidence of ease and fluency, but above all because such a high proportion yield passage after passage as eminently speakable as any dramatic dialogue written seventy to a hundred years later. This is only what we should expect, in the given circumstances. Though dramatic dialogue in prose was non-existent until Gascoigne's *Supposes* (1566), what his grounding in rhetoric taught the schoolboy was to express himself in speech. Expression *was* speech. Instruction in rhetoric meant the teaching of style for oratory, 'well-saying'. As Hardin Craig says, 'the faculty of speech was dignified in Renaissance thinking as the chief accomplishment which God had chosen to bestow upon man, to distinguish him from the brute beast'.[2] The writing of themes in English was no part of the educational method which reared these letter-writers, who cover an age-span of eighty to eighteen, from the middle of the fifteenth century to the grandfathers and fathers of Shakespeare's generation; but they had learned to love and enjoy words and they applied their education in rhetoric and Latin to the practical purpose of expressing themselves effectively in the vernacular, so that to write a letter, having mastered the protocol of address and subscription, was simply to write down what one wanted to say. In the majority of cases, mercifully for us, they might never have heard of the *ars dictaminis*. They look in their hearts, listen with their ears, and write. Whether we call it the art or the business of letter-writing, it seems to come easily enough to the average correspondent in this collection.

To some it was obviously a pleasure and opportunity to 'open' their minds freely to their betters and say their say. As John Hutton, quoted below, remarks, 'He that talketh alone may say what he will'. A few are hampered by lack of skill and their own bad handwriting, like James Hawkesworth, who excuses himself because 'I am so ill a writer causes me oft times that [I] do not write.' But he is the exception, who may be found in any class—the tongue-tied writer of every century for whom Sir Henry Sidney 'speaks' when he asks Queen Elizabeth's pardon for so seldom reporting on Irish affairs, 'so bad a delivery of my mind I have by pen, and so illegible it is when I do it myself'. And even here, surely, in each case, is the manner of the man's speech.

Except when they compose official letters, stuffed with official jargon and bowings and scrapings of compliment, they write vigorously and simply. Some achieve genuine distinction. Only very rarely is one conscious of the striving to write better than they speak, and some of them make the connection between speech and writing explicit. John Hutton, Governor of the Merchant Adventurers at Antwerp, has 'none other matter unto your ladyship but to devise what I may write to cause your ladyship to be merry', so takes up his pen 'thinking myself that I should be present with you talking' (2 March 1537). It is in this same spirit that, nearly a hundred years later, Lady Katharine Paston concludes a letter to her son William at Cambridge: 'I am so straited of time as I cannot tarry longer to talk with thee now.'[1] The tradition of the familiar letter was and is the tradition of familiar talk.

The editing of the Lisle Letters over a period of many years has naturally involved much wider exploration of manuscript material, and examples quoted are not all taken from them. But I believe that within the compass of this collection we can study every degree of sophistication—and the lack of it—belonging to this talking-writing—from Hutton, the conscious conversationalist who writes pleasantly about nothing at all, to the real gossips on paper, not confined to any one social class, who flow on, with no attempt at order or composition, writing as they think and speak, without premeditation, with much repetition, many digressions and abrupt transitions, a great deal of vehemence, a complete lack of punctuation and a speed and urgency betokening strong feeling. They look forward, by way of Launce and Lancelot Gobbo, to such agreeable rattles as Miss Bates and Flora Finching, and link up over the centuries with our own spontaneous talkers who lack formal educational advantages and inhibitions and pour out their hearts and grievances on paper as they do in conversation, invoking us by name in every other sentence. To quote them briefly is to ruin their effects, but they offer good evidence, such as we still meet at first hand, of the direct connection in the unsophisticated, un-literary mind between speech and letter-writing.

The temptation, of course, as with Shakespeare, is to put in one's thumb and pull out a plum and say, Look how colloquial this is! Instinct again tells us we hear the very accent of speech when Husee writes, 'The King enquired how the man was slain, and I answered that one of them, or both, was drunk', or when Lisle dictates, 'Now, good Master Page, stick to me in this matter'—'stick to', in this sense, being common in the 1530's and still one of our colloquialisms, but not Shakespeare's. We shake hands across four centuries with Sir Brian Tuke when he describes his daughters' governess as a 'treasure',[2] or with John Husee when he refers to the grocer who refuses any more credit as 'a limb of the devil'. We have lost Husee's favourite 'off or on' for 'one way or the other', but 'too good to be true' and 'now or never' are still current, and we still say 'wouldn't hurt' or the variant 'would do no harm', like Husee urging his master that 'a gentle letter would not hurt'. Not one of these phrases occurs in the plays.

III

But the haphazard sampling of colloquialisms does not 'prove' that this is speech 'so written as it is spoken', and a more methodical approach 'would not hurt'. The touchstone for speech is speakability. Does the ear say *Yes* as we read? Do we—would Rose Macaulay—'hear them talking'? And can we establish a fundamental relationship between these familiar letters and Shakespeare's dramatic writing, verse and prose? We can certainly establish the necessary links of vocabulary and phrasing, but we also discover a lavish use of synonyms, amplification by similitudes and proverbs, and other characteristics which we tend to regard as symptoms of the self-conscious 'literary' style of elaborate Elizabethan writing. The real case should rest primarily, I believe, upon the evidence supplied by rhythm and by direct speech and *oratio obliqua*.

The ordinary reader, if he 'soaks' himself in these letters, will be struck by the familiarity and the speakable quality of their prose rhythms. The natural 'tunes' or phrase-lengths of our speech, which by their recurrence give balance as well as variety and make patterns of sound within the complex sentence, are the usual five-, four- and three-beat units or time-periods which we recognize in characteristic combinations in Shakespeare's prose passages or in Sir Thomas Browne's writing, to take two extremes. The predominance of the five-beat phrase, or the blank verse line, in its infinite variety of syllabic cadence, reflects a natural tendency in our speech. It is such a normal speech- and breath-length that we have to take thought to avoid it, as all writers and speakers know, even in conversational and colloquial remarks. We shall find this unit of five time-periods used in these letters with any number of syllables from nine to fifteen, as freely as in blank verse. The following examples were not chosen, but are simply odd phrases that happen to remain in memory. Shakespearian examples of syllabic equivalence are given for rhythmic comparison only.

Mistress Anne is sworn the Queen's woman	(9)
(Stay! The King hath thrown his warder down)	
I live by hope and comfortable words	(10)
(Observe degree, priority and place)	
There to abíde the cóming of your lórdship	(11)
(Ángels and mínisters of gráce defénd us)	4-beat
Money was never so scant since this King reigned	(11)
(Injurious time, now with a robber's haste)	5-beat
Divers religious men are in the *Tower*	(10/11)
(Shall blow the horrid deed in *every* eye)	
Here is nothing but *everyone* for himself	
(The *heavens* themselves, the planets and this centre)	(11/12)

Seeing I have begun I would fain make an end }
(The enterprise is sick. How could communities) } 4-beat

Be content, Husee: thou shalt speedily be rid (12) }
(As you have ever been my father's honour'd friend) } 5-beat
They that promised me horses to ride deceived me }

Privy dissimuled friends and familiar enemies (13)
(Remorseless, treacherous, lecherous, kindless villain)

Before I hear of it again I cannot be merry 5-beat
The augmentation and amendment of my poor living (14) } 4-beat
(What honey is expected? Degree being vizarded) }

Fifteen and sixteen are the longest syllabic runs: 'But yet I assure you I would be glad to do him pleasure'; 'Your ladyship may be glad that ever ye bare Mr Basset'. I cannot recall Shakespeare parallels, nor yet an eight-syllable run from the Letters for John of Gaunt's 'Think not the King did banish thee'. (To say that this 'is a foot short' may be metrical rule-of-thumb but is *speech* nonsense. The five stresses, with strong pauses, are clearly indicated by the first half of the next line, 'But thou the King'.) There is, however, a seven-syllable line, 'Here cometh my Lord Lisle's man'; unless, as is sometimes said, we ought to pronounce the name as Lisley or Lesley, in which case we have our eight-syllable equivalent. 'His Grace spake few words that day|to those that came' is another seven-syllable example, with a concluding two-stress phrase to balance the Shakespearian parallel completely.

There is no monotonous sequence of this five-beat phrasing: four- and three-beat units are equally characteristic: 'The saying is, the abbeys shall down'; 'Now is the time to speak or never'; 'When we are gone, all is gone'; 'I spake with his Grace an hour together'; 'It is a solemn gentleman!' ('It is an ancient mariner'): 'Grant me a lodging at Umberleigh'; 'My lord, the debt is great'; 'many and importunate suitors'; 'sore diseased with the cough'; 'He shall have my heart while I live'. All are eminently speakable: they have pace, and come 'trippingly off the tongue'. Their simplicity refers this kind of basic phrase-rhythm to speech, just as surely as elaborate structure and the skilful handling of long periodic sentences, in the King's diplomatic correspondence, place certain letters in the class of written compositions.[1]

Analysing continuous passages that at once strike the ear as good, we find that the pleasant, speakable rhythm of the whole derives from varying combinations of these simple units which wing and mark sense with sound, and by their recurrence balance thought against thought, phrase against phrase. These three-four-five patterns frequently have a central supporting core, existing solidly as a single thought-and-speech unit, or a prose stabilizer, which has no regular recognizable pattern or tune as a whole and cannot be profitably analysed in terms of sound, balance, accent, recurrence, etc. In longer passages there is sometimes more than one of these larger sense-units and they occur similarly in Shakespearian prose.

The following extract, from one of Husee's letters, though providing no exact parallel in thought or expression, has never been known to fail to draw from hearers surprise at its likeness to Mrs Quickly's account of Falstaff's death.

Christopher Vyllers is departed...I spake with Crowder, his man, who shewed me that your lordship is not overseer, but he bequeathed your lordship v marks in money, and a salt of five marks. And he sayeth that iij hours ere he died he commoned nothing but of your lordship, and after he had made his executors he could never abide the sight of them. If your lordship had been here he thinketh verily that you should have had a great part of his substance, for he had more mind of your lordship than of all the world at the hour of his death (21 August 1537).

There is one verbal link: 'abide' reminds us that 'a' could never abide carnation: 'twas a colour he never liked'; but a certain tonal and rhythmic similarity probably has more to do with the recognition that they are of the same quality, and the 'patterns' of both, as the reader can hear for himself, are the result of the three-four-five-beat combinations of sound units with one 'sense-unit' in each. Both have the absolute ring of truth to common speech. A shared idiom of valediction is established. They authenticate each other.

These three-four-five tunes compose the most usual recurrence patterns, sometimes almost as obviously as in verse, at other times muted, less noticeable, but to be found when looked-for within the pleasantly harmonious general impression. In their modest way these people know how to write. Already the unit—whether sentence or paragraph—that is determined by sense, the statement made as straightforwardly and clearly as possible, which yet runs smoothly to its individual music, is just as much in evidence as these native recurrent rhythms. Take for example the following announcement of the death of one of her step-daughters, sent to Lady Lisle in 1536 by her 'old servant' John Davy, in which a simple Devon gentleman illustrates the rhythmic ease and simplicity of the ordinary letter.

It may please your good ladyship to perceive that Mistress Thomasine Basset is deceased, whose soul I pray Jesu take to mercy; and she deceased the Friday before Palm Sunday, full well and virtuously, with all the sacraments of the Church. She died at Bery's house, and lieth at Dowland. She was sick at Marrais and desired to go to Bery's, and this was about the Purification of our Lady that she came there (11 April 1536).

One is not really conscious of any formal stress-pattern till the three-beat phrase at the end of his first sentence. Then we get two sentences with three five-beat units in a sequence, ending with a 'dying fall' reminiscent of 'to weep there'. His postscript begins with five and two: 'I do intend to see Mistress Thomasine's month's mind | honestly to be kept.' 'Madam ye know very well she is your friend (or, 'she is your friend') and no fool', is another good example of this same characteristic movement. On the other hand, Dan Nicholas Clement, a monk of Christ Church, Canterbury, will combine the melodic and the intellectual so that no accustomed pattern asserts itself. The music is his own:

I am very sorry at heart that I have no good thing able to present unto you at this time; but nevertheless I have sent unto you by this child a beast, the creature of God, sometime wild, but now tame, to comfort your heart at such time as you be weary of praying (30 April 1536).

Lisle's own writing illustrates both tendencies. He has three styles—the familiar, the business and the high official. In the last everything is laid on thick—long involved sentences, inkhorns, nouns, verbs and adjectives in triplicate, and every possible form of amplification. One hopes and believes it had no resemblance whatever to speech. In ordinary business letters he is fluent and direct and the phrasing runs easily, as when he describes a 'wanted' person as 'a man of honest conversation and of few words, being of a good age and a draper of wool, dwelling in Mechlin', with the smooth five-five-two rhythm. In the personal letter he is brisk, spontaneous and more colloquial, with a rather impetuously run-on, simple-continuous movement; but in all three styles we find the same admixture of the free and the predictable balancing rhythms. There seems little, if any, difference between the dictated letters and those he writes himself. Making up a quarrel with his old friend, Sir William Kingston, he speaks his thoughts to a secretary:

Right worshipful, In my most hearty wise I recommend me unto you, and am right sorry that any inconvenience should cause writing to be spared of so long time between us that have been of so long familiar acquaintance; ensuring you no cause on my behalf, whatsoever have been informed you: for if it had, I should neither have eaten nor yet slept quietly until I had written unto you. Nevertheless, it is forgotten on my behalf, praying you it may so be on yours: And that we may hear the one from the other after our old accustomed wont. And ye shall have me after the old fashion (August 1534).

He 'speaks' in his own hand in a note to his cousin, Antony Wayte, in a similar conversational manner:

Cousin Wayte, I commend me unto you, and have received the letter you sent to my wife,[1] and well perceive the contents of everything therein, thanking you of your news concerning priests, which I would a' been gladder of xxti year gone, that I might a' made one priest cuckold (23 November 1535).

In the first he seems to be using an entirely 'free' continuous prose rhythm: in the second he falls into the accustomed four-five pattern, with a concluding nine-syllable five-beat phrase.

Whatever the number of syllables it contains, | the insistence of the phrase that carries five stresses | —as these do when spoken—| remains the dominant rhythmic impression, | with the four-stress clause, just used, | as the next most noticeable unit, | and three or two, for a coda, | equally common. They were and are natural to the language, and just as it is impossible to miss these same combinations in the sense structure of blank verse paragraphing, so, in a passage like the following, one can hear how easily this five-stress base lent itself to fluent 'prose' runs: 'My Lord Privy Seal called me to him on Thursday | and said that it was time for your lordship now to wax grave | and not to give credit to every light flying tale.' There is, literally, no end to the examples of this five-stress bias throughout the Letters, and it dominates their commonplaces even as it does ours. 'Concerning news, here be none worth the writing'; (Remember me to Janet if you're writing.) It is the way we speak, the way we have always spoken.

Recognizing, then, in early sixteenth-century writing the dominance of this normal English speech-and-breath length of five time-periods, with four or five stresses, and finding in it also the same customary syllabic extensions and variations that give such infinite flexibility to our dramatic blank verse line, it seems reasonable to believe that they both reflect the speech habits of the century, and it is hard to see how the English drama could possibly have avoided blank verse as its natural medium. When the enduring rhythmic bias of our speech asserts itself thus vigorously in the familiar writing of the thirties we cannot choose but accept the contemporary verdict that it was indeed 'such upon the paper as it is in the mouth'. More than half a century lies between the Elizabethan dramatists and these writers, and naturally, among thousands, we find many clumsy, confused, repetitive letters, much awkward syntax and occasional illiteracy. But the ready speaker, with a natural ear for native rhythms, expresses himself in sufficient numbers, without clumsiness and without reliance upon ornament or formal tricks, to show that already, before the 'Drab Age' of printed prose, Englishmen could write in the vernacular with ease and clarity, often with an individual voice and a touch of distinction, and a mastery of structure and sense-rhythm which controls and varies the basic under-hum without losing it and creates sustained complex sentence and paragraphing effects comparable to those found in dramatic writing.

IV

Rhythm is, of course, only one aspect of speech, but it is the most fundamental when trying to discover how men talked in past ages. Vocabulary and phrasing are a study in themselves, fascinating and important, and vital to anyone who wants to soak in the language of the period, but even less susceptible than rhythm to brief handling. One can only sample, more or less at random, to register changes or persistence of idiom. Reverberations of turns of phrase met in the Letters still echo in Shakespearian lines: 'If they come not now it shall come with the next' (If it be not to come, it will be now); 'Yet did I repent me after I had delivered them' (Yet did I repent me of my fury); 'surest and secretst means' (secretst man of blood); 'I shall tomorrow in hand...' (I will tomorrow—And betimes I will—); 'Unto his speech can I not come' (Out of this wood do not desire to go). The omission of a verb of motion, very usual in the Letters— 'they will to Boulogne', they 'will over' (to Calais, understood)—is paralleled in the plays: 'I'll to England. To Ireland, I'; 'I'll not to Rome', etc. Among common phrases which we have lost but which continually recur in the Letters and are used by Shakespeare we may note 'to be bold upon' or 'make bold with', to 'well perceive by', to 'cull (out)', to 'open' a matter or one's mind to someone, to have 'much (little, what) ado', 'bolt (out)', i.e. to sift, 'there is no remedy' or simply 'no remedy'.

There are also interesting changes in word usage, of which 'occupy' is an outstanding example, upon which Shakespeare himself comments (2 *Henry IV*, II, iv, 161). It is used throughout the Letters with the meaning of to be busy or occupied in, to work, to do business, to use something, but has dropped out of polite conversation—and the plays—by the end of the century, and has given occasion for a useful note in the *Oxford English Dictionary* mentioning that it occurs only twice in Shakespeare, equivocally, and means 'to deal or have to do with sexually'— hence his comment that 'the word occupy, which was an excellent good word before it was ill-sorted', is now 'odious'.

The losses—or are they Shakespeare's rejections of colloquialisms and words and phrases which occur throughout the letters?—are equally interesting. 'God pardon his soul' or 'whose soul God pardon', which always qualifies the names of the dead, has disappeared—a striking if accountable loss. The only parallels are the Nurse's 'God rest all Christian souls!' and 'God be with his soul!' No one describes herself as 'your bedewoman', though .there are some references to 'beads' and Valentine swears he will be Proteus' 'bedesman' and the unhappy Richard II's 'very bedesmen learn to bend their bows' against his state. Shakespeare's characters neither write nor receive 'gentle' or 'thankful' letters, nor yet 'sharp ones': they do not 'conceive any displeasure' with their friends or servants, though they agree in 'taking' it (*Tempest, As You Like It, Pericles*), in 'finding' it (*Lear*) and in 'running into' it (*All's Well*); they do not 'apply' their learning, their books, their devotions or their business; they are never 'at the finding' of their employers; they do not get 'in a fume' or make others 'participant' or 'parttaker', in their news or their good fortune, though they 'partake' and are 'partakers'. They do not 'remove', though Birnam Wood does, like Henry VIII in these letters and Queen Elizabeth in the letters of John Chamberlain[1] (though Ralph Winwood insists on saying 'the Queen goes back again to Richmond on Monday').[2] They do not 'set store by' things or people, or 'shew' their mind, though they 'open' it. They do not say 'I ensure you' for 'I assure' or 'I promise you'; and there are only two instances of that favourite early Tudor word 'incontinent' to signify haste and immediate action. 'Clean cast away' (i.e. utterly undone), which appears in every kind of begging letter, has vanished from the language of supplication and despair in Shakespeare. But he uses 'clean' in ten instances as an intensive, as we do in such phrases as clean forgotten, and as the letters do in 'clean contrary to the Act', etc. He is fastidious in his use of colloquialisms when a word has both a serious and a slangy meaning, but like the letter-writers he accepts both senses of 'abide' and relishes the popular one. Master Ford 'cannot abide the old woman', Mistress Quickly 'cannot abide swaggerers' and Jane Nightwork 'could not abide Master Shallow', like Christopher Vyllers who could never abide the sight of his executors after he had made his will.

Nothing short of systematic investigation would enable one to say with any certainty how far their Latinisms and foreign borrowings reflect current spoken usage. But if anyone imagines these are characteristic of late Elizabethan writing only, these Letters will quickly undeceive him. From any random selection an impressive list can be compiled, and it seems unlikely, therefore, that such words were not freely used in speech in an age when the schoolboy talked Latin and some of Lisle's bailiffs still kept the manorial accounts in it. They occur even in letters obviously composed, if not written, by women 'uneducated' in the formal sense. If Maria can speak of 'the new map with the augmentation of the Indies', I see no reason to doubt that when in 1535 Jane Basset wrote to her stepmother for help 'towards the augmentation and amendment of my poor living' her writer put down the words she actually said.

Inkhorn or bookish and learned terms are another matter. They may have attained some currency in speech for a time, but their use in these letters is of interest to the historian of language mainly because they are not, in this decade, the calculated extravagance of literary experiment but part of the already copious vocabulary used by ordinary writers, who were neither avowed scholars nor pedants but had an adventurous taste in words and a real love for them. Thomas Broke, of the Calais retinue, defending himself to Cromwell against a charge of sedition, produces two fine specimens:

I had rather that Almighty God should by his hasty messangier Death send for me, rather than by like messangier this realm should be orbated or denudated of one so prudent and sage a counsellor as your good lordship, by your very proper deeds and industries, have from time to time approved yourself to have been (4 August 1539).

'Orbated' and 'denudated', otherwise practically unknown to lexicography, might well be inkhorns of the nineties, of the kind Shakespeare parodies.

How much of this bookish borrowing was used in ordinary pre-Elizabethan writing could only be estimated from a general check of manuscript sources; and the process of adoption, trial and rejection tempts us to ask—does their non-appearance in the plays warrant the belief that, although the words occur in letters and literature, they had never taken root in current speech? What is it that condemns all the following, with 'orbated' and 'denudated', after a brief trial? Their appearance in the Letters argues currency at some time for 'aggradation', 'charitative', 'obtemper', 'suppeditation', 'vilipende', 'inspeculation', 'scrupulosity', 'propice', 'occurrents', 'reconciliate', 'pre-mentioned', 'dilations', but the only one of that odd dozen that Shakespeare took up was 'occurrents', for use, once, in *Hamlet* (v, ii, 68), though it was common enough in the seventeenth as well as the sixteenth century. 'Aggradation'—a word favoured by Lisle and Husee for the subscription of a letter—can hardly have been peculiar to them, though I do not recollect any other specimens. Its only recorded use is in the form 'agrade', employed by Florio in 1611 to translate 'gradire', to be pleased with (cf. *Ital.* aggradare). For 'inspeculation', which Husee attributes to Honor Lisle in 1537—'Your ladyship saith I have good inspeculation'—only a solitary mid-seventeenth example has been noted. 'Propice' and 'obtemper' are medieval: all of them have interesting histories; but only 'vilipende' survived to the last century. All we can say is that learned borrowings were never merely a literary affectation of Elizabethan style but are a noticeable feature in ordinary letter-writing fifty years earlier.

Speech, directly quoted or recapitulated, is an important source of evidence for the spoken language. In certain cases it provides interesting clues to the rhythms and mannerisms of individuals, such as Henry VIII's use of 'Well,' at the beginning of a sentence. Tricks of speech were repeated literally, especially the King's or Cromwell's, to both of whom, apparently, we must credit that habit of repetition for emphasis that we notice in Hamlet. In the following we hear Cromwell, as reported by Thomas Broke, winding his way into a pleading before the King's Council with an adroit bit of softening-up:

...he said himself 'thus, Perchance, my lords, you do think that I speak thus for affection that I bear my Lord Lisle, by reason of some great rewards or gifts. But I assure you, on my faith, it is not so; nor I never received of his lordship anything, unless it were a piece or ij of wine, or a dish of fish or wild fowl. But yet I assure you I would be glad to do him pleasure; and moreover I do know so perfectly well this matter, that I must needs speak in it.'

Opposing counsel asked to have the case referred to the trial of the Common Law:

With that answered Mr Secretary in this manner, 'The King's Grace being his good lord, say you? Yes, marry, I warrant you! He is and will be his good lord. His good lord, quod a! Marry, ye may be sure he is and will be his good lord. Doubt ye not of that.' And thus he repeated it, iij or iiij times, that the King's Highness was and would be good lord unto your lordship (17 October 1534).

In the next two we listen to Henry VIII dealing first with a complaint, then with a request:

(*a*) His Grace said a'was sure, once, twice or thrice, it was not so. I shewed his Grace it was of truth. His Grace asked me, 'Who?' I shewed his Grace one Leonard Snowden, your servant. Then his Grace answered incontinent, 'What? So soon? So soon? Well,' said his Grace, 'resort unto us again' (9 June 1536).

(*b*) His Grace answered me by these words...'Well', said his Grace, 'think you that it is meet that I shall put both the baillyship and the searchership in one man's hands? No, nor I will not!' (8 January 535).

In the following we hear three brief specimens from Husee's remarkable anthology of the sayings of Thomas Cromwell, though alas without any of his detailed descriptions of their interviews:

He made me answer by these words, 'If I should not remember my gentle Lord Lisle I would I were buried! Be content, Husee, thou shalt speedily be rid.'

There are innumerable examples of indirect reporting such as 'My Lord Privy Seal shewed me this day that he remembereth your lordship oftener than he hath fingers or toes'; or, 'And touching the Friar, Mr Secretary said he would they were all at the devil!' A pleasant example of self-reporting, direct and indirect, is the Vicar of Bishop's Waltham's rebuke to an obstreperous curate:

'Sir Thomas, this at night, and ye be not well-advised!' and thereupon willed him to go to bed and speak with me again the next morning (26 January 1534).

The clear way in which most of these writers can pass without confusion from direct speech to *oratio obliqua* gives us confidence in the accuracy of both, and the following extracts from a very long letter show how Thomas Wriothesley, a vigorous and fluent writer, so soon to become a Secretary of State, passes to and fro with ease between dialogue and narrative when sending Cromwell an account of his interview with a suspected traitor. He dramatizes the scene vividly, but the particular interest of his account lies in the illustration it gives of the practical use of their rhetorical training made by men in the affairs of public life. His method with the traitor is that of the oration in little—to win his end by eloquence, reasoning, persuasion and every kind of personal appeal. 'I have used him very gently,' he begins:

I caused him to be brought up to my chamber and had there one or two with me in honest sort to wait upon me. When he came within the door, sitting in my chair, made towards me as though he would have taken me by the hand. 'No Sir', quoth I, 'I shake no hands with such fellows as you be till I hear further'....

He then outlines his opening attack, while the man kneels before him, and concludes, 'therefore I shake no hands with you till I hear of your own mouth how you be disposed and whether you do submit yourself to the King's Majesty or no'. Phillips having duly 'submitted' himself, Wriothesley then continues:

'Arise,' quoth I, 'and hear me Phillips. Forasmuch as I see thee, as far as I can judge, repentant, I shall say unto thee that whatsoever any knaves abroad report, thou shall, I hope, assuredly find the King's

Highness a most merciful Prince.... But one thing I shall say unto thee: beware how thou goest about to colour, cloak or excuse thyself. His Majesty is wise and of great experience. He hath been a King these thirty years and was a man before he was crowned. I tell thee plainly, he hath eyes and ears in the bottom of their bellies and in the very lining of their hearts that be of that sort that thou has been.

Finally, professing himself satisfied that Phillips is now truly repentant, he brings the scene to a triumphant climax.

'Well,' quoth I, 'now that I see that thou wilt rather abide whatsoever may come than to continue an unkind person to thy Prince and Country, I shall not stick to give thee that hand that within little more than these xxiiij hours would either have taken thee or have thrust my dagger in thee, wheresoever I should have met thee.' And so to comfort him I was content to take him by the hand.... He said after to others that my hand, with my words, pulled a thousand pound weight out of his heart (7 February 1539).

Unfortunately, Phillips escaped overnight, and the changed style in which Wriothesley then expresses his chagrin is most revealing by contrast. Instead of the sustained, hortatory eloquence, he reports the facts in crisp, short, sharp sentences, building up to his climax:

Phillips came as I writ in th'other letters. I used him as I writ. I talked again with him after supper in such wise (the same having supped at mine own table) that I am sure I put him in manner out of all fear...I put my trust in them to keep him in their chamber. Leighton promised that he should lie with himself. Joye should lie by, in another bed in the same chamber. Leighton's man should watch without the door, and I had two others of my men that watched beneath for all the night and morning till they were up. And yet, as soon as my watchers were gone to bed, which was between vj and vij of the clock in the morning, they being all then up, they suffered him to depart (9 February 1539).

Except for a few phrases, the natural, terse vigorous writing speaks his exasperation as we might speak it today. It has a drive that reminds one not a little of Prince Hal's exposure of the Gadshill episode, beginning, 'We two saw you four set on four', and of Falstaff's earlier speech describing it—good, sinewy prose, bristling with dramatic attack.

The significant point driven home by Wriothesley's account of his interview is that to his generation rhetoric was part of one's mental equipment for the practical business of life that men took for granted. It is easy to find examples of rhetorical address in the grand manner in Henry VIII's letters—some of them drafted by Wriothesley—to be read and heeded by their recipients. It is much rarer to find a personal report, made by a speaker, of what he actually said when suddenly called upon to put *eloquentia* to the test in a situation—when what he wants to do is to appeal to the emotions and to *move* a man of whom he says, 'The fellow hath a great wit. He is excellent in language'. To us his metaphors seem striking: to men who cared for 'well-saying' such phrasing came naturally.

V

The use of imagery, proverbs, 'sayings', word-play, puns and every kind of figurative language is generally first encountered by Elizabethan students in its most exaggerated form, as in *Euphues*. To meet these elements of popular speech, therefore, in their natural surroundings, before they are developed as formal literary ornament, is to realize how freely and effectively ordinary folk, including men of affairs like Wriothesley or Husee, used proverbial phrasing and lively imagery in normal expression. The way Shakespeare's use of proverbs links his writing with the diction of common life has become a study in itself; and though the imagery in these letters may be simple we see clearly how he could rely on its common appeal when men used it so instinctively in their own speech and writing.

As in Shakespeare, some of this figurative phrasing is drawn from the common stock, some of it may have been invented by the writers; but all these instances from the Letters are either the earliest known or the earliest post-medieval examples. Lady Whethill's 'There is an old saying, Threatened men live long' and Thomas Warley's 'But it is an old saying, Well is spent the penny that getteth the pound' vouch for their own proverbial status; and Husee's 'It hath been an old proverb that there is no worse pestilence than a familiar enemy' is the only example on record. How close Lisle's 'You and I cannot live with fair words' comes to an original form we cannot tell, as its next appearance is in *Euphues* as 'Fair words fill not the belly' (1580). I can find no exact parallel for Husee's 'Time and the good hour must be tarried for', which takes on a more individual flavour as 'I can do no more but tarry his time and gawpe for a good hour'. (When the delays are obviously past human help he adds, 'I trust the Holy Ghost will now work in my Lord Privy Seal to discharge me of your lordship's long suit.') When he quotes the old proverb, 'a shrewd cow hath found short horns', he adds, 'yea, the very stumps!' (cf. *Much Ado*, II, i, 25 'God sends a curst cow short horns': Chaucer and Heywood call the cow 'shrewd'). Accused of 'flitting' from Calais, he refutes the report 'that I should leave the key under the door and come no more there', adding indignantly, 'I would not gladly give the candlesticks I left there for the rent I owe him'. This, and his expression, 'to stop two gaps with one bush' are found later, so were probably already proverbial, but his description of Lisle's useful friend, Sir Francis Bryan, who, 'if he set in his foot with a good mind...hath no fellow now in the Privy Chamber', may be original.

Husee's letters are also full of lively little phrases such as 'This will breed a scab', 'It is hard trusting this wily world'. Whether they would qualify for the proverbial category if found in print I do not know. Perhaps catch-phrases is the proper term, as it seems to be for the description Honor Lisle's niece, Elizabeth Staynings, gives of her distressing plight when keeping her husband company in the debtors' prison and expecting another child: 'I am in the taking that I was in the last year; and if it had pleased God he might a' sent it your ladyship, the which would a' been more gladder than I am' (cf. Mrs Ford in the buckbasket scene, 'What a taking was he in when your husband asked what was in the basket'). Sir John Bonde, a Devon vicar, swears 'I will get my fingers unto the elbow' before he will hand over the keys of the manor house to her ladyship's step-daughter without orders. Lisle is 'ready to make answer and amends to my shirt' (1536)—perhaps an early form of 'putting one's shirt on' a horse or a hunch. Wriothesley, finding that his prisoner has escaped, writes to Cromwell, 'the loss of all I have in this world had been but a trifle to this breakfast!' (cf. *Henry VIII*, III, 202, 'and then to breakfast with what appetite you have'). 'Whereat the Frenchmen hangeth the lip' is Husee's colloquialism for looking vexed or put out, (cf. *Troilus & Cressida*, III, i, 152, 'he hangs the lip at something'). The favourite expression for imparting a confidence is 'he told me in mine ear', which Shakespeare uses in this way seven times. To be 'God's prisoner' is a common image for sickness, and Lisle's Hampshire cousin, Antony Wayte, uses the pleasant Old English phrase 'the fall of the leaf' for autumn. The instinctive liking found in this colloquial letter-writing for the homely vigour and the picturesque—or grotesque—visual quality of proverbial phrasing suggests that the genuine, popular, proverb-making mentality was as characteristic of the early as of the late decades. If medieval sources do not yield early forms of the expressions used by Shakespeare and the Elizabethans, the chances are that a considerable proportion will be found in the manuscript collections of the years between the two literatures, medieval and modern, which may ultimately prove to have been one of the most fruitful proverb-eras of this prolific century.

Puns are by nature a delight of speech, but some mild punning appears now and again in these Letters. 'Can sick men play so nicely with their names?' asks Richard II when John of Gaunt puns on his own name for ten lines. The interruption is at once dramatic and critical—ten lines 'o'er steps the modesty of nature'. Just how nicely they could and did play with words in this manner can be seen from the fun they have with one of Lisle's gentlemen who belonged to the Devonshire family of Speccot, which naturally invited the pun of 'spigot'. John Kite, bishop of Carlisle, in his seventies and a sick man, plays the game delicately, simply changing the spelling when he sends Lisle a tun of March beer by 'my friend Spygott'. So light is the touch that one might perhaps query his intention; but there is no mistaking the cruder relish Mr Speccot's fellows took in this joke when Husee sends commendations from one of them to Lisle and her Ladyship,

and to Jack his brother and to all other, saving Mr Spygott, whom in nowise he will not have named. He saith the sounding of that name maketh him more than half drunk (12 June 1537).

A delight in double, triple and even quadruple assemblages of nouns, verbs and adjectives was not a late characteristic of Tudor writing, resulting from the scholars' admonitions to seek more 'copie'. It was native to the language and contributed to its rhythmic effects and was encouraged by the normal education in rhetoric. The popular use of synonyms, coupled words and balanced phrases is so prevalent in the Lisle Letters as to leave no doubt that, far from being a trick of style derived from the 1549 Prayer Book, it was an established feature of the writing of educated men in the 1530's; and comparison with late medieval correspondence shows that there was no similar richness in the average letter of the preceding period. It may have been encouraged at the time by Lord Berners' preface to his Froissart (1523-5), in which he apologizes for not having turned his original into the 'fresh, ornate, polished English' which he illustrates by furnishing most words with one to three synonyms and nouns with as many adjectives.

One guesses that it was more a trick of writing and was used with moderation in speech, as indeed, on the whole, it is in the familiar letter, but men were accustomed to this particular form of amplification from their schooldays, and the pairs and phrases chimed naturally with the simple three-four-five speech rhythms. 'Loss and hindrance', 'bawdy and unthrifty rule', 'proud, presumptuous and opprobrious words', 'the augmentation and amendment of my poor living' slide from the tongue with an easy music and also say more, give greater expressiveness in their contexts. The third example conveys a more vivid impression of the character and behaviour of the rascally curate (cf. p. 235, above): 'grunted and grudged at', applied to an unwanted guest, says more than either verb alone. 'High and importunate suit' is as expressive as it is rhythmically pleasing in the context of competition at Court to obtain the conveyance of the King's New Year's gift to Lisle, who had the reputation for tipping liberally, 'high' referring to the influential suit made and 'importunate' to the vigour with which the requests were urged. This form of 'copie' may not as yet do much to enrich ordinary writing with shades of meaning and the subtle distinctions we shall enjoy when we come to Sir Thomas Browne; but its free indulgence in ordinary writing in the thirties illustrates the native and natural tendency in our speech which eventually produces such 'household' words as 'the expectancy and rose of the fair state' or 'to grunt and sweat under a weary life', with which the poet will enrich and raise to its highest power this ordinary and old-established habit of the diction of common life.

There is, finally, one more personal argument which, for me, reinforces an inner certainty rather than the reasoned belief I have been outlining, that it is in these early manuscript sources instead of contemporary printed ones that we must soak ourselves in order to hear the sixteenth century talking. Out of a common stock of words, phrases and normal modes and devices of expression these people fashion for themselves individual, recognizable styles. And this is equally true of dozens of others encountered among these State Papers of Henry VIII who have no connection with this particular correspondence, who may write only a single letter and of whom we may 'know' literally nothing from any other source. There is a transparency in this writing: simple as it generally is, the style is the man, or the woman. Just as the dramatist gives us the characters of his personages by the manner of their speech and what they say about each other and the business in hand, so these personages who play their parts in the Lisle story characterize themselves for us as vividly as if they were created by an artist, and, like characters on the stage, speak in the first person directly to us of their fellows and their concerns. When Husee writes, 'As for Warley, I assure your ladyship there is no such malice in him as you do think, for it was only his lack of wit, that which he did' (15 September 1538), we learn something of the characters of all three, of their relationships to each other and of the situation and may find ourselves recalling such things as Costard's excuse for Nathaniel—'a marvellous good neighbour, faith, and a very good bowler; but for Alisander—alas, you see how it is—a little o'er-parted'.

Shakespeare the dramatist by-passes the formal elaboration, the cultivated boisterousness, the journalistic extravagance, the exaggeration and the fashionable affectations of contemporary style, unless he needs any of them for his dramatic purposes. With Husee or Lisle he will use the learned word when he feels like it; but Husee will 'gawpe' for his good hour, and Sicinius will declare 'This is clean kam'. We know, 'by instinct', that in Shakespeare we are listening to the real language of men, as well as ascending the brightest heaven of invention with his muse of fire. When, therefore, we are continually reminded of Shakespearian phrasing and rhythm as we read these early letters, it is reasonable to infer that the link, the common factor, is Tudor speech as it was spoken throughout the century, except in so far as new colloquialisms, turns of phrase and fresh words replace what had become old-fashioned. The letters obviously cannot give the whole background of Shakespearian speech, but I believe they can and do provide us more effectively than any other source material with a genuine view of the foundations of the goodly current speech which was the language of that amazing century.

NOTES

Much which would normally be included in the first chapter is dealt with in special chapters such as those covering apprenticeship, hospitals, gaols, religion and learning.

PAGE 3

1 *A Journey into England by Paul Hentzner in ...1598,* ed. Horace Walpole (1757), II, 242, 244.

PAGE 4

1 27 Elizabeth I, c. 31.

2 In city of Westminster record office (no MS. number). Pages 1–52 covering part of 1610 give clear light on their work.

3 John Stow, *Survey of London* (1598); *The annales of England...* (1592).

4 Spelt with a capital, the word is used in this chapter for the court of aldermen, the court of common council, and their officers. With a small 'c' it denotes the city of London. 'London' denotes the city, Westminster, Southwark and the out parishes, i.e. the whole built-up area.

5 Throughout this chapter the materials for the City's actions have mainly been drawn from the manuscript records of the courts of aldermen (repertories) and common council (journals) in the record office of the corporation of the city of London. These have excellent subject indexes, and economy of space has therefore entailed the omission here of most of the page or folio references.

PAGE 5

1 *Acts of the Privy Council,* n.s. XIX (1899), 278–80.

2 Journal 22, ff. 434^b–435^a.

PAGE 6

1 City of London, corporation record office, Remembrancia V, no. 54.

2 City of Westminster, record office, E. 154 and C. T. Onions (ed.), *Shakespeare's England* (Oxford, 1916), p. 319.

3 5 Elizabeth I, c. VIII.

PAGE 7

1 See F. N. L. Poynter, chapter 11 below.

2 Hentzner, *op. cit.* p. 271.

3 Journal 23, ff. 206^b–209^a.

4 Repertory 23, f. 89^b.

PAGE 8

1 Repertory 23, f. 110^b.

2 Journal 22, ff. 417^b–422^a.

PAGE 9

1 Journal 23, f. 164^b.

PAGE 10

1 Repertory 23, f. 77^a.

2 J. C. Jeaffreson (ed.), *Middlesex County Records I* (1886), pp. xxxviii–xlii, 249. This invaluable calendar is well indexed, and page references have therefore been omitted here.

3 For this and the next two sentences see Acts of the Privy Council, n.s. XXVIII (1904), 115, 588; XXIX (1905), 128–9, 140–2, 391, 640–1, 727.

PAGE 11

1 Wallace T. MacCaffrey, *Place and Patronage in Elizabethan Politics,* in S. T. Bindoff, J. Hurstfield and C. H. Williams (eds.), *Elizabethan Government and Society* (1961), p. 98.

2 Wallace T. MacCaffrey, *op. cit.* p. 101.

3 F. Peck, *Desiderata Curiosa* (1779), IV, 142.

4 Journal 22, f. 313^b.

5 Fynes Moryson, *An Itinerary...* (Glasgow, 1907), I, 428.

6 *Ibid.* IV, 170.

7 *The Staple of News,* Act I, scene v in *Works,* ed. Herford and Simpson, vol. VI.

PAGE 12

1 *The Devil is an Ass,* III, 4, *op. cit.*

2 See Sir John Neale, *Essays in Elizabethan History* (1958), p. 61.

PAGE 13

1 A survey of Stratford-upon-Avon made in 1590 gave a total of 217 burgages then, which would represent a town of about 200 houses in 1564.

PAGE 14

1 He first appears in the Stratford records in April 1552.

PAGE 17

1 'By great' means to work by quantity (piece-work) instead of by the day. Hence this very early start.

PAGE 20

1 Philip Stubbes, 'The Anatomie of Abuses', in *Shakspere's England*, New Shakspere Society, series 6, vol. 4, pp. 147, 148.

PAGE 21

1 A report of 1582 showed that of 1495 merchantmen and coasters only 235 were over 80 tons (Sir William Monson, *Tracts*, ed. M. Oppenheim, III (Navy Rec. Soc. 1919), 188–92; see D. W. Waters, *The Art of Navigation in England* (1955), p. 111). Of the 160 or so vessels mobilized against the Armada, of which the tonnage is known, half were of 80 tons or under, and only six were of 300 tons or more (*Defeat of the Spanish Armada*, ed. J. K. Laughton (Navy Rec. Soc. 1894), II, 326–31), while two-thirds of the known vessels which went privateering, 1589–91, were of 80 tons or less, and scarcely more than 10 % of 200 tons or more (K. R. Andrews, *Elizabethan Privateering* (1963), Appendix, which I was privileged to see before publication).

PAGE 22

1 For the Queen's ships, see J. S. Corbett, *Drake and the Tudor Navy*, 2 vols. (1898), *The Successors of Drake* (1900), both invaluable if in need of correction; Michael Lewis, *The Navy of Britain* (1948), *A History of the British Navy* (1957), *Armada Guns* (1961); Garrett Mattingly, *The Defeat of the Spanish Armada* (1959); G. J. Marcus, *A Naval History of England*, vol. 1 (1961). Little of a systematic character has been published on the merchant navy, 1558–1625. D. Burwash, *English Merchant Shipping, 1450–1550* (Toronto, 1947), and G. V. Scammell, 'Shipowning in England 1450–1550', *Trans. Roy. Hist. Soc.* 5th ser. XII, 105–22, provide the background. For privateering vessels Andrews, *Elizabethan Privateering* is invaluable.

2 'The travels of Sir Jerome Horsey', *Russia at the Close of the Sixteenth Century*, ed. E. A. Bond (Hakluyt Soc. 1856), pp. 185–6.

3 Cp. Laughton, *Spanish Armada*, II, 324–31, for the names of the Armada ships, and T. D. Manning and C. F. Walker, *British Warship Names* (1959).

PAGE 23

1 For the English seaman see H. H. Sparling, 'Mariners of England before the Armada', *English Illustrated Magazine*, VIII (1891), 647–54; C. S. Goldingham, 'The personnel of the Tudor navy', *United Services Magazine*, CLXXXVII (1918), 427–51; F. E. Dyer,

'The Elizabethan sailorman', *Mariner's Mirror*, X (1924), 133–46; K. R. Andrews, *English Privateering Voyages, 1588–95* (Hakluyt Soc. 1959), pp. 22–8; *Elizabethan Privateering* (1963), ch. III.

PAGE 24

1 *North-west Fox*. B. Alsop and T. Fawcet, 1635 (*S.T.C.* 11221), sig. A2ʳ.

2 'Observations on the Navy and Sea-service', in *Works*, ed. T. Birch (1751), II, 96.

PAGE 25

1 J. J. Keevil, *Medicine and the Navy*, I (1957), 44–148, is the best authority.

2 F. K[ingston] for H. L[ownes], 1598 (*S.T.C.* 25106).

3 Hugh Plat, *Sundrie new and artificiall remedies against famine*. P. S[hort], 1596 (*S.T.C.* 19996), and *Certaine philosophical preparations of food and beuerage for sea-men in their long voyages* (1607) (Wellcome Historical Medical Library. Not in *S.T.C.*); Keevil, *Medicine and the Navy*, I (1957), 108–9; D. W. Waters, 'Limes, lemons and scurvy in Elizabethan and early Stuart times', *Mariner's Mirror*, XLI (1955), 167–9; C. F. Mullett, 'Hugh Plat: Elizabethan virtuoso', in C. T. Prouty (ed.), *Studies in Honor of A. H. R. Fairchild* (Columbia, Miss., 1946), pp. 93–118.

PAGE 26

1 See Andrews, *English Privateering Voyages, passim*.

2 Richard Hakluyt, *The principall navigations* (G. Bishop and R. Newberie, deputies to C. Barker, 1589 (*S.T.C.* 12625)), pp. 771–3 (repr. D. B. Quinn, *The Roanoke Voyages* (Hakluyt Soc. 1955), II, 562–9).

3 G. D. Ramsay, *English Overseas Trade during the Centuries of Emergence* (1957), p. 45.

4 *The kings prophecie*. T. Creed for S. Waterson, 1603 (*S.T.C.* 12678), repr. Hall, *Poems*, ed. A. Davenport (1949), p. 117.

PAGE 27

1 Peter Hill's (or Hills') career has not been dealt with in print. His brass in St Mary's Rotherhithe (*Surrey Archaeological Collections* XXXII, 80–1) gives some details, including his establishment of a free school at Rotherhithe. His trading activities can be followed in Public Record Office, High Court of Admiralty, H.C.A. 3/19, 14, 20 January 1586, H.C.A. 13/25, 19 October 1585, 15, 17, 21 January, 18 February 1586; H.C.A. 13/28, ff. 39ᵛ, 75ʳ; Hakluyt, *Principal*

Navigations, VIII (1904), 150–83 (mentioned pp. 157–61). He was given a bounty for building ships (P.R.O., S.P. 38/4, 6 April 1594), and contracted to convey troops from France to Ireland in 1598 (*Calendar of Cecil MSS.*, VIII, 28).

2 D. B. Quinn, 'Christopher Newport in 1590', *North Carolina Hist. Rev.* XXIV (1953), 305–16; K. R. Andrews, 'Christopher Newport, mariner', *William and Mary Quarterly*, 4th ser., XI (1954), 28–41, *English Privateering Voyages, passim.*

3 D.N.B.; D. W. Waters, *The Art of Navigation in England in Tudor and Stuart Times* (1955), *passim*; E. G. R. Taylor, *The Haven-finding Art* (1956), pp. 196, 204–6, 'Instructions to a colonial surveyor in 1582', *Mariner's Mirror*, XXXVII (1951), 48–62, with M. W. Richey, *The Geometrical Seaman* (1962); A. H. W. Robinson, *Marine Cartography in Britain* (1962), pp. 29–31.

PAGE 28

1 *Mariner's Mirror*, XXXVII, 49.

2 *The Art of Navigation in England in Elizabethan and Early Stuart Times* (1955); see also E. G. R. Taylor, *The Haven-finding Art* (1956).

3 See his *The new attractive*. J. Kyngston for R. Ballard, 1581 (*S.T.C.* 18647), and W. Borough, *A discours of the variation of the cumpas.* [J. Kyngston] for R. Ballard (*S.T.C.* 3389).

4 L. J. Wagenaer, *Mariners mirrour*, tr. A. Ashley. [J. Charlewood, 1588] (*S.T.C.* 24931).

5 See '"The doctrine of nauticall triangles compendious"'. I, 'Thomas Hariot's manuscript', by E. G. R. Taylor, II, 'Calculating the meridional parts', by D. H. Sadler, *Journal of the Institute of Navigation*, VI, 131–47; Taylor, *Haven-finding Art*, pp. 184, 218–25.

6 V. Sims (*S.T.C.* 26019 and 26019*a*).

7 Taylor, *Haven-finding Art*, pp. 223–7; Waters, *Art of Navigation*, pp. 219–29.

8 Vol. II. G. Bishop, R. Newberie and R. Barker, 1599 (*S.T.C.* 12626).

9 *in aed.* T. Dawson (*S.T.C.* 13906).

10 See Helen M. Wallis, 'The first English globe', *Geographical Journal*, CXVII (1951), 275–90; 'Further light on the Molyneux globes', *ibid.* CXXI (1955), 304–11; 'Globes in England up to 1660', *Geographical Magazine*, XXXV (September 1962), 267–79.

11 G. Gilberti *de magnete*, P. Short, 1600 (*S.T.C.* 11883); English translation, *Gilbert on the Magnet* (1900, Gilbert Club). A useful short account of *De magnete* is in G. Sarton, *Six Wings* (1957), pp. 94–8.

PAGE 29

1 For Drake see H. R. Wagner, *Drake's Voyage Round the World* (San Francisco, 1926); for Hawkins, J. A. Williamson, *Sir John Hawkins* (Oxford, 1927) and *Hawkins of Plymouth* (1949); for Frobisher, V. Stefansson (ed.), *The Three Voyages of Martin Frobisher*, 2 vols. (1938) (though he is not treated with sufficient detachment); for Cumberland, G. C. Williamson, *George, Third Earl of Cumberland* (Cambridge, 1920) (uncritical). Cavendish has not found a biographer.

2 Waters, *Art of Navigation*, p. 162.

3 Birch (ed.), *Works*, II (1751), 104.

4 *English Privateering Voyages*, pp. 22–8.

5 F. Beaumont and J. Fletcher, 'The Scornful Lady', *Works*, ed. Arnold Glover, I (Cambridge, 1905), 255. Compare:

 Trinculo '...A fish: he smells like a fish; a very ancient and fish-like smell; a kind of not of the newest Poor-John' (*The Tempest*, II, ii, 26–8).

6 Pl. III: correspondence with Mr Martin R. Holmes, London Museum. See G. E. Manwaring, 'The dress of the British seamen', *Mariner's Mirror*, VIII (1922), 324–33; IX (1923), 162–73, 322–32.

7 This occurs in a case relating to the voyage of the *William* to Newfoundland in 1536 (P.R.O., H.C.A. 13/2, ff. 51–153ᵛ).

PAGE 30

1 Thomas Churchyard, *A generall rehearsall of warres* (1579), sig. 2B4ʳ. 'A gables end' has been altered to 'A cables end'.

2 Hakluyt, *Principall navigations* (1589), p. 735 (VIII (1904), 314).

3 *Ibid.* p. 666 (XI (1904), 191–2).

PAGE 31

1 For an example, printed as it was composed, see John Davis's 'Traverse-Booke' for his 1587 voyage in Hakluyt, *Principal Navigations*, VII (1904), 424–39.

2 Peter Martyr Anglerius, *The decades of the newe world or West India.* tr. R. Eden, 1555 (*S.T.C.* 645–8, various imprints).

3 No copy of this edition seems to have survived. Hakluyt reprinted it in *Principall navigations* (1589), pp. 270–9.

4 Hakluyt reprinted the Guinea verses in *Principall navigations* (1589), pp. 130–42. For a collection, probably published though without a copy surviving, see E. Arber (ed.), *Transcript of the Stationers' Register*, I, 363.

5 *A true declaration of the troublesome voyage of M. J. Haukins.* T. Purfoote for L. Harrison, 1569 (*S.T.C.* 12961).

6 A. Jeffs (*S.T.C.* 24330).

7 Newly corrected. H. Denham (*S.T.C.* 24327).

8 *A true reporte of the laste voyage by Capteine Frobisher.* H. Middleton, 1577 (*S.T.C.* 22265–6).

9 *A true discourse of the late voyages of discoverie.* H. Bynneman, 1578 (*S.T.C.* 1972).

10 T. Dawson (*S.T.C.* 7607, Huntington Library only).

11 Printed by Hakluyt in *Principall navigations* (1589), pp. 557–62, though no copy is known to survive. For evidence of its publication see W. A. Jackson, 'Humphrey Dyson's library', American Bibliographical Society, *Papers*, XLIII (1949), 285.

PAGE 32

1 He tried his hand at the description of a storm in the Gilbert tract *A discourse of the Queenes majesties entertainement in Suffolk and Norffolk...whereunto is adioyned a commendation of Sir Humfrey Gilberts ventrous iourney.* H. Bynneman, [1578] (*S.T.C.* 5226), and in *A prayse, and reporte of Maister M. Forboishers voyage to Meta Incognita.* [J. Kingston] for A. Maunsell, 1578 (*S.T.C.* 5251), he put in a word for the common mariner, the chief sufferer in difficult voyages, who was liable to be forgotten in tales about his commanders. He attempted a general record of English land and sea exploits in *A generall rehearsall of warres, wherein is five hundred severall services of land and sea.* E. White [1579]. (*S.T.C.* 5235).

2 F. P. Wilson 'An Ironicall Letter', *Modern Language Review*, XV (1920), 79–80 ([*c*. December 1584] Jack Roberts to Roger Williams, Bodleian Library, Tanner MS. 169, ff. 69ᵛ–70).

3 *The travailes of an Englishman.* [T. Scarlet] for W. Wright, 1591 (*S.T.C.* 13828).

4 Printed by Hakluyt in 1589: see D. B. Quinn, *The Roanoke Voyages*, I, 11, 15–17, 91–116.

5 By Walter Bigges and others (*S.T.C.* 3056–7). For the sequence of the published editions see D. B. Quinn, *The Roanoke Voyages*, I, 294.

6 *A report of the truth of the fight about the iles of Açores.* For W. Ponsonbie, 1591 (*S.T.C.* 20651), *The discoverie of the large rich, and bewtifull empire of Guiana.* R. Robinson, 1596 (*S.T.C.* 20634); Lawrence Keymis, *A relation of the second voyage to Guiana.* T Dawson, 1596 (*S.T.C.* 14947).

7 G. Bishop and R. Newberie, deputies to C. Barker.

(*S.T.C.* 12625); facsimile, with an introduction by D. B. Quinn and R. A. Skelton (Hakluyt Society, 1964).

8 G. Bishop, R. Newberie and R. Barker, 1598–1600 (*S.T.C.* 12626).

9 Imprinted for T. Thorpe, sold by W. Aspley (the first two, *S.T.C.* 7459, 7448); T. P[urfoot] for W. Burre (*S.T.C.* 7456).

PAGE 33

1 *Impensis* Geor. Bishop (*S.T.C.* 21322).

2 Imprinted for J. Tappe, sold by W. W[elby] (*S.T.C.* 22795); Oxford, J. Barnes (*S.T.C.* 22791).

3 [E. Allde] for N. Butter (*S.T.C.* 18532).

4 J. Windet, sold by R. Barnes (*S.T.C.* 14816).

5 There is a large literature on the sources of *The Tempest*. R. R. Cawley, 'Shakspere's use of the voyages in *The Tempest*', *Proceedings of the Modern Language Association*, XLI (1926), pp. 688–726, is probably still the best study. See also G. L. Kitteredge (ed.), *The Tempest* [1939] and Frank Kermode (ed.), *The Tempest* (The Arden Shakespeare, 1954).

6 Not published until 1625 (*Purchas his pilgrimes*, IV, 1735–57 (*S.T.C.* 20509), XIX (Glasgow, 1906), 5–72).

7 Imprinted for J. Stepneth (*S.T.C.* 24832); Imprinted for W. Barret (*S.T.C.* 24833).

8 J. Beale for W. Welby (*S.T.C.* 12754).

9 *S.T.C.* 20505–7.

10 Imprinted for T. Nelson (*S.T.C.* 18211).

PAGE 34

1 *Middle Class Culture in Elizabethan England* (1935, repr. 1958), pp. 517–18. His first surviving effort was the verse *A most friendly farewell...to...Sir Francis Drake.* N. Mantel and T. Lawe, [1585] (*S.T.C.* 21084); his verses on Cavendish's return, 1588, are not known to be extant (Wright, p. 517).

2 R. B[lore] for W. Barley, 1592 (*S.T.C.* 22140).

3 A. I. for W. Barley (not in *S.T.C.*: in Huntington Library only).

4 A. J[effes] for W. Barley, 1591 (*S.T.C.* 11921); printed for William Wright, 1594 (*S.T.C.* 20572), the latter attempting to justify Glenham's actions. They had already been denounced as piratical by the privy council (*Acts of the privy council, 1592*, p. 180). See Wright, p. 518 n. 1.

5 A. J[effes] for W. Barley, [1595] (*S.T.C.* 21083).

6 W. How for H. Haslop, sold by E. White (*S.T.C.* 12926).

7 J. Windet, 1588 (*S.T.C.* 17489). He attacked dissension amongst captains: 'For while one saith:

I have beene longer in the warres…An other; I have traveled furder upon the Sea, and have doone greater exploits…What is this, but to teare in sunder the Common weale' (sig. D1ʳ). He exhorted men to care for the navy—'Looke to the amending and new buildinge of ships. Make them strong, light, and nimble for the battaile' (sig. D4ʳ).

8 T. Vautrollier for R. Field (*S.T.C.* 14257). Two issues (B.M. G. 6512/4 and G. 6512/2) followed closely on one another.

9 *A packe….* Deputies of C. Barker, 1588 (*S.T.C.* 23011); Richard Leigh, *The copie…* T. Vautrollier for R. Field, 1588 (*S.T.C.* 15412–13). Medina Sidonia's instructions too were published as *Orders set down by the Duke of Medina.* T. Orwin for T. Gilbert, 1588 (*S.T.C.* 19625).

10 Tr. [R. Adams]. A Hatfield, sold by H. Ryther, 1590 (*S.T.C.* 24481).

11 T. Woodcocke (*S.T.C.* 6790).

12 T. Creede, sold by W. Barley, 1595 (*S.T.C.* 21088).

13 J. Windet (*S.T.C.* 6551). A broadside, *In memoriam celeberrimi viri Domini Francisci Drake militis*, appeared in 1596 (copy in Library of the Society of Antiquaries, London); while Charles Fitz-Geffrey's *Sir Francis Drake his honorable lifes commendation.* Oxford, J. Barnes, 1596 (*S.T.C.* 10943–4) (repr. A. B. Grosart, *Poems* (1881)) .was reprinted in the same year.

14 *A declaration of the causes moving the Queenes Majestie to send a navy to the seas.* Deputies of C. Barker, 1596 (*S.T.C.* 9203, with Latin, Dutch, French, Italian and Spanish versions. *S.T.C.* 9204–8).

15 Though an official account was prepared (J. S. Corbett, *Successors of Drake* (1900), pp. 129, 439–40), its publication was withheld. Hakluyt's appeared in *Principal navigations*, I (1598), pp. 607–19, and was announced on the title-page. On its suppression a cancel title-page was printed (C. E. Armstrong, 'The "Voyage to Cadiz" in the second edition of Hakluyt's "Voyages"', Bibliographical Society of America, *Papers*, XLIX (1955), 254–62). An engraving of Lord Howard of Effingham appeared in 1596 with an inscription beginning *Si domitos Bello Hispanos, Gadiumque; ruinam* (repr. A. M. Hind, *Engraving in England*, I (Cambridge, 1952), pl. 150).

16 E. A[llde] for W. Burre, [1600] (*S.T.C.* 20891).

17 F. Kyngston, sold by J. Newbery (*S.T.C.* 17259).

18 Thomas Panyer (not in *S.T.C.*). See R. A. Skelton, 'An Elizabethan naval tract', *British Museum Quarterly*, XXXII (1960), 51–3, which has an account of the unique copy

19 *S.T.C.* 8267; R. R. Steele, ed., *Tudor and Stuart Proclamations, 1485–1714*, I (1910), no. 900.

PAGE 35

1 *S.T.C.* 8290 ; Steele, *Tudor and Stuart Proclamations*, I, no. 925.

2 *S.T.C.* 8321; Steele, *Tudor and Stuart Proclamations*, I, no. 956.

3 W. W[hite] for T. Archer (*S.T.C.* 22998). Further proclamations, 1603–5 (*S.T.C.* 8334, 8363, 8369), attempted to deal with piracy and the reversion of mariners to civil employment.

4 W. G. Perrin (ed.), *Boteler's Dialogues* (Navy Records Soc. 1929), p. 35.

5 R. R. Cawley, *Unpathed Waters* (Princeton, N.J., 1940), pp. 210–11.

PAGE 36

1 The *Tiger* at Aleppo (*Macbeth*, I, ii, 7–8) is certainly from Hakluyt, *Principall navigations* (1589), p. 209 (*Principal navigations*, II (1598), pt. 1, 251; V (1904), 465).

2 *Unpathed Waters*, p. 239. Cawley's emphasis on the lack of *close reading* is probably justified. His own detailed analysis of Shakespeare's references to overseas and maritime occurrences (*The Voyagers and Elizabethan Drama* (1938), p. 425) is, however, an impressive indication of the range of Shakespeare's interests.

3 The most drastic criticisms are contained in C. L'Estrange Ewen's pamphlets, *A Criticism of the Tempest Wreck Scene* (1937) and *Shakespeare No Seaman* (1938).

4 3rd ed. (1953), pp. 266, 218.

PAGE 37

1 The Levant Company was established in 1579.

2 The Russia Company had its first privileges confirmed in 1569.

3 See Sidney Lee, 'Caliban's visits to England', *Cornhill Magazine*, n.s. XXXIV (1913), 333–45.

4 Prologue, A. 51–9.

5 *Ibid.* A. 463–6.

PAGE 38

1 Cf. C. R. Beazley, *The Dawn of Modern Geography* (1897–1901): 'Devotional travel was as little in sympathy with exploration for the sake of knowledge as the theological doctrines of a scriptural geography

...were in sympathy with the formation of a scientific theory of the world's shape' (I, 13).

2 B. Penrose, *Travel and Discovery in the Renaissance, 1420–1620* (Cambridge, Mass., 1952), p. 7.

3 Translated in Hakluyt Society, vol. XCVII (1897).

4 Beazley, *op. cit.* I, 32.

5 *Ibid.* p. 252.

6 Gilbert de Nogent (Migne, *Patrologia Latina*, CLVI, 25) quoted in Caplan, 'The four senses', *Speculum*, IV (1929), 283.

7 See, for example, the 'Beatus' maps, whose radical purpose was 'the delineation of the twelve apostles, their dioceses and their distribution over the habitable world as "sowers of the word"' (Beazley, *op. cit.* II, 563).

8 R. R. Cawley, *Unpathed Waters* (Princeton, 1940), pp. 75 ff., traces the prevalence of this idea in English literature up to 1641.

9 Denys Hay, *Europe, the Emergence of an Idea* (Edinburgh, 1957), pp. 54 f.

PAGE 39

1 See Pl. VII. John Cayworth's Christmas masque of 1636, *Enchiridion Christiados* (B.M. Add. MS. 10311), is the latest use that I have found. The masque is illustrated by a T–O type map, showing Christ's descent through the world from Heaven (at the top of the map), his descent into Hell, and his re-ascension into Heaven. As Cawley remarks, 'Cayworth would have gone far to seek a design which would suit his purposes quite so perfectly' (*Unpathed Waters*, p. 76). It is clear that Cayworth intends his map-form to be spiritually effective, and this implies (what is more interesting there) that he expected it to be intelligible as a world-shape to his patron and to his generation. Another interesting volume, pointing to the late diffusion of these medieval notions is *S.T.C.* 17297—*Mappa Mundi: otherwyse called the Compasse and Cyrcuet of the worlde, and also the Compasse of every Ilande, comprehendyd in the same* [R. Wyer, 1535]. This is advertised in the colophon as *Very necessary for all Marchauntes and Maryners. And for all such, as wyll labour and traveyle in the countres of the worlde.* But in spite of much invocation of the name of Ptolemy, the image of the world provided is the medieval one, centred on Jerusalem (sig. A3ᵛ), with the Terrestrial Paradise in the East, and Hell 'in the myddes of Affryke under the earth'. Africa is the land 'of dyvers shape of people, and many great wonders' (sig. A4ᵛ), and America has no mention at all.

2 See M. C. Andrews, 'The study and classification of medieval mappae mundi', *Archaeologia*, LXXV (1924–5), 64.

3 'None of [the early printed world maps] is influenced by the advances in geographical knowledge.... There is thus no group of printed maps based on Spanish, Portuguese or Italian portolans, notwithstanding their proximity in time' (Erich Woldan, 'A circular, copper-engraved medieval world map', *Imago Mundi*, XI (1954), 13).

4 On Dee's gifts to Geography see E G. R. Taylor, *Tudor Geography, 1485–1583* (1930).

5 'The discovery of Guiana', in Hakluyt, *Principal Navigations* (Glasgow, 1903–5 edition), X, 406.

6 Josephine Waters Bennett, *The Rediscovery of Sir John Mandeville* (New York, 1954).

7 Quoted in M. Letts, *Sir John Mandeville* (1949), p. 13.

8 See especially Bk XVIII, cap. 48, 'De Faunis et Satiris'.

9 Geoffroy Atkinson, *Les nouveaux horizons de la Renaissance française* (Paris, 1935), p. 14.

10 See, for example, Gilbert Chinard, *L'Exotisme américain dans la littérature française au XVIe siècle* (Paris, 1911), p. 10.

PAGE 40

1 R. Wittkower, 'Marvels of the East', *Journal of the Warburg and Courtauld Institutes*, V (1942), 195.

2 Penrose, *op. cit.* pp. 78, 86, 90.

3 See G. B. Parks, *Richard Hakluyt* (New York, 1928).

4 *De Sphaera*, I, 182, quoted by C. S. Lewis, *English Literature in the Sixteenth Century* (Oxford, 1954), p. 16. Cf. Atkinson, *op. cit.*, 'L'idée maîtresse des voyageurs de la Renaissance fut sans doute l'ambition de faire fortune' (p. 135).

5 *Ibid.* pp. 9 ff.

6 The Renaissance period was fascinated by the Turkish Empire as combining the features of a diabolical portent, with those of a remarkably efficient politico-military organization. Knolles' great *Generall Historie of the Turkes* (1603) nicely catches this ambivalence in his opening phrase about 'the glorious Empire of the Turkes, the present terrour of the World'.

7 See (on Spain) Angel Franco, *El tema de América en los autores españoles del siglo de oro* (Madrid, 1954), and M. A. Moringo, *América en el teatro de Lope de Vega* (Buenos Aires, 1946); on Italy see Rosario Romeo, *Le scoperte americane nella conscienza italiana del Cinquecento* (Milan and Naples, 1954).

NOTES

PAGE 41

1 See S. L. Bethell, *The Winter's Tale* (1947), p. 33.
2 *All's Well that Ends Well*, III, iv, 4 and III, v, 34.
3 *Two Gentlemen of Verona*, II, iii, 30.
4 *The straunge and wonderfull adventures of Don Simonides* (1581), sig. M 3ᵛ.
5 See Cranfill and Bruce, *Barnaby Rich* (Austin, Texas, 1953).
6 See L. B. Wright, 'Henry Robarts', *Studies in Philology*, XXIX (1932), 176–99.
7 Sig. E4.
8 Sig. C2.
9 C. S. Lewis, *op. cit.* p. 424.
10 M. E. Seaton, 'Marlowe's map', *Essays and Studies*, X (1924), 13–35.
11 *Ibid.* p. 28.
12 *Ibid.* pp. 27 f.
13 See G. Boas, *Essays on Primitivism and Related Ideas in the Middle Ages* (Baltimore, 1948); Luis Weckmann, 'The Middle Ages in the conquest of America', *Speculum*, XXVI (1951), 130–41.
14 Hakluyt (ed. cit.), VIII, 305.
15 Peter Martyr [Anglerius], *The decades of the newe world or West India*, tr. R. Eden (1555), sig. E 1ᵛ.

PAGE 42

1 Fulke Greville, *Life of Sir Philip Sidney* (1652), ed. Nowell Smith (Oxford, 1907), pp. 116 f.
2 Gilbert Chinard, *op. cit.* pp. 123 f.
3 The word *foreigners* is not at all common in the sixteenth century; *strangers* is the normal expression. Indeed the first three examples of the former word in *O.E.D.* (that is, up to 1637) are all qualified by the latter word, as if to provide a clue to the meaning.
4 Mark Pattison, *Isaac Casaubon* (1892).

PAGE 43

1 J. O. Thomson, *History of Ancient Geography* (Cambridge, 1948), pp. 106 ff. Charron, *Of Wisdom* (tr. Samson Lennard; ent. *S.R.* 1606), has an interesting discussion of this (Book I, cap. xlii).
2 John Davies of Hereford, *Microcosmos* (ed. Grosart, 1878), p. 32.
3 *The Merchant of Venice*, I, ii, 32 ff.
4 Fynes Moryson, *An itinerary, containing his ten yeeres travell* (1617), III (Glasgow, 1907), 448 ff.
5 (1585) (ed. G. H. Mair (Oxford, 1909), pp. 178 f.
6 *De Peregrinatione* (Strassburg, 1574); *The Traveiler of Jerome Turler* (1575).

7 John Marston, *The Malcontent* (1604), v, ii, 1–4.
8 It is worth while noticing that this 'Portingale' seems to be a Jew, in fact, though the word 'Jew' is never used. He is called 'Signior Bottle-nose' (Hazlitt's Dodsley, X, 522) and elsewhere he is said to have 'a snout / Able to shadow Paul's, it is so great' (p. 481).

PAGE 44

1 Hazlitt's Dodsley, VI, 279.
2 *Ibid.* pp. 438 f., 499.
3 *Two Gentlemen of Verona*, I, i, 2.
4 Foster Watson, *The Beginnings of the Teaching of Modern Subjects in England* (1909), p. 91. F. de Dainville, S. J., *La géographie des humanistes* (Paris, 1940).
5 S. C. Chew, *The Crescent and the Rose* (New York, 1937), p. 29.
6 Foster Watson has a useful survey of attitudes to travel in the period (*op. cit.* pp. 128–35).
7 See Plate IX. Cf. the MORS written round the Hereford *Mappa Mundi*.

PAGE 45

1 *Dutch* simply meant (in this period) 'German-speaking' (distinguished when necessary into 'High-Dutch' and 'Low-Dutch'). Most of the refugees were, however, from the nearest area of Teutonic-speaking population, i.e. were 'Dutch' in the modern sense. But Elizabethan vagueness in these matters defies simple explanation. Thus in Dekker and Webster's *Northward Ho* the 'Hollander' has his home in Augsburg.
2 Huguenot Society Publications, vol. X, part i (1900), p. 365.
3 *Social England*, ed. Traill and Mann (1903), III, 500.
4 E. Eckhardt, *Die dialekt- und ausländertypen des älteren Englischen dramas*, Teil II (Materialien zur Kunde des älteren Englischen dramas, vol. XXXII) (Louvain, 1911), p. 48.
5 In Dekker and Webster's *Northward Ho* (1605).
6 I cannot even guess why Marston represented Franceschina as Dutch. It is entirely proper to her part that she should be foreign, a stranger to the bourgeois comforts of the Subboys and Freevills, but I do not know why Holland should be the foreign country chosen.
7 Huguenot Soc. X (i), 365.
8 W. Besant, *London in the time of the Tudors* (1904), p. 80.

NOTES

PAGE 46

1 *M.S.R.* ll. 250 ff. Cf. the petition against Aliens printed in Besant, *op. cit.*, Appendix III, which lists those by whom the realm is pestered as 'Frenchmen, galymen [? = allemandes], pycardis, flemings, keteryckis [? = Cateians (Highlanders)], Spaynyars, Scottis, Lombards'.

2 G. K. Hunter, 'English folly and Italian vice', *Jacobean theatre*, ed. Brown and Harris (1960), pp. 85–110.

3 In his *King Johan*.

PAGE 47

1 Hazlitt's Dodsley, VI, 268 f.

2 *Macbeth*, IV, i, 26.

PAGE 48

1 *Liturgical Services of the reign of Queen Elizabeth*, ed. W. K. Clay (Parker Society (1847)), pp. 519–23.

2 *C.S.P.* (*Spanish 1568–1579*), p. 359.

3 Holinshed's Chronicle (1808 edn.), IV, 262.

4 *Ibid.*

PAGE 49

1 *A new letter of notable contents* (1593) (*Works*, ed. Grosart, I, 262).

2 *The muses looking glass* (Oxford, 1638), Act III, scene iv (*Works*, ed. Hazlitt, II, 232).

3 *The double dealer*, Act IV, scene, iv. Cf. Brandt/Barclay in the *Ship of Fools*, where in the section 'Of straunge Folys and infydels as sarasyns, paynems, turkes and suche lyke' we may read the following:

> The cursed Iewes despysynge christis lore
> For theyr obstynate, and unrightwyse cruelte
> Of all these folys must nede be set before
> The nacion of Turkes next to them shall be
> The sarrazyns next…
> The Scithians and also they of Sarmatyke
> And they of Boeme, by fendes fraudolent
> Ar led and blynded with an errour lyke…
> The owgly Mauryans ar also of this sect etc.
>   (1874 edn., II, 188 f.)

4 Hazlitt's Dodsley, VI, 345.

5 Ed. Tucker Brooke, II, 979 f.

6 Besant, *op. cit.* p. 239.

7 H. Michelson, *The Jew in Early English Literature* (Amsterdam, 1926), pp. 4 f.

8 John viii. 44. Cf. Thomas Ingelend, *The Disobedient Child* (*c.* 1560) in which the Devil says:

> All the Jews and all the Turks,
> Yea, and a great part of Christendom,
> When they have done my will and my works,
> In the end they fly thither, all and some.
>   (Hazlitt's Dodsley, II, 310)

PAGE 50

1 See G. B. Harrison, *Second Elizabethan Journal* (1931), p. 289.

2 *Ibid.* p. 304.

3 'Of Usury'.

4 C text. Passus V, I, 194.

5 'Lenten Stuffe' (1599), in *Works*, ed. McKerrow, III, 211.

6 IV, ii, 32 f.; *Works* ed. Waller and Glover, III, 283.

7 It is worth noting a correction in Jonson's *Every man in his humour*, where the Quarto text (1601) reads *I am a Jew* (III, i, 40) where the Folio (1616) reads *I am a knave* (III, iii, 48).

8 Hazlitt's Dodsley, VI, 330.

9 'The theology of Marlowe's *Jew*', *Journal of the Warburg and Courtauld Institutes*, (1964).

10 (1648); Wing, S. 545.

PAGE 51

1 It is sometimes supposed that the Elizabethans made a regular distinction between a blackamoor and a tawny moor. Morocco in *The Merchant of Venice* is called a tawny moor, and the New Arden editor glosses this 'in contrast to a black one'. Portia, however, says that he has 'the complexion of a devil' and in any normal usage this would mean 'black' (see text below). The word *tawny* often seems to mean little more than dark. Thus in *King Leir*:

> As easy is it for the Blackamoore
> To wash the tawny colour from his skin.
>   (*M.S.R.* 1271 f.t)

Eleazer, in *Lust's Dominion* is clearly black; yet he is called *tawny* (ed. Brereton (Louvain, 1931), l. 231); he comes from Barbary (229), but is said to be an *Indian* (1819, 2316).

2 *Faerie Queene*, VI, vii, 43.

3 Hakluyt (ed. cit.), VI, 399.

4 Peter Martyr [Anglerius], tr. R. Eden, *The History of travayle* (1577), fol. 348ᵛ.

5 *Works* (Hunterian Society), II, 52.

6 Hakluyt, VI, 321 (where it is quite clear that 'Moorish' means 'Mahommedan').

7 *Doctor Faustus* (in *Works*, ed. Tucker Brooke), p. 150 (cf. the 'black Indians' in Brewer's *The lovesick king* (Bang's Materialien (1907), 952 f.), in Googe's translation of Kirchmeyer's *The popish kingdom*

(1570) (1880 edn.), p. 39, and the African Indians in *Sir Thomas Stukely* (T.F.T. 2169)).

8 *Henslowe Papers*, ed. W. W. Greg (1907), p. 148. Cf. the 'Negro-Tartars in *Gesta Grayorum*' (M.S.R. 46) —'Negarian Tartars' on p. 52.

9 *Volpone*, I, v, 44 f.

10 R. Withington, *English Pageantry* (1918), I, 74. Cf. the collocation of ideas in Wilson's *Three Ladies*, where Mercatore proposes to travel in search of profit:

me dare go to de Turks, Moors, Pagans, and more too:
What do me care, and me go to da great devil for you? (Hazlitt's Dodsley, VI, 306)

11 E. K. Chambers, *The English Folk Play* (1933), p. 28.

12 Ben Jonson, *Sejanus*, V, i, 712; Shakespeare, *Titus Andronicus*, V, iii, 121. See Pl. VIII for iconographical evidence.

13 *Jew of Malta* (ed. Tucker Brooke), 1229.

PAGE 52

1 *The Fair Maid of the West* (Part II) (Pearson Rept. p. 350).

2 *The Discovery of Witchcraft* (1584), p. 535.

3 *Ibid.* p. 89.

4 E.E.T.S. o.s. 178 (1929), 43. I owe this reference to Mr B. F. Nellist.

5 Reginald Scott, *op. cit.* p. 456.

6 Samuel Harsnet, *A declaration of egregious popish impostures* (1603), p. 177.

7 *Ibid.* p. 178.

8 *Hudibras*, II, i, 399 f.

9 Hakluyt (1903–5), V, 122.

PAGE 54

1 Thomas Becon, 'Preface', *The Seconde Part of the Bokes which Thomas Beacon hath made* (1560), fol. ii.

2 Hugh Latimer, 'First Sermon preached before King Edward, March 8, 1549', *Sermons*, ed. George Elwes Corrie (Cambridge, 1844), p. 179.

PAGE 55

1 William Kempe, *The Education of Children in Learning* (1588), sig. D4ᵛ.

2 Martin Bucer, *A treatise how...christian mens almose ought to be distributed* (n.p., 1557?), sig. B4; quoted in W. K. Jordan, *Philanthropy in England, 1480–1660* (1959), p. 160.

3 *John Howes' MS. 1582*, ed. Septimus Vaughan Morgan (1904), pp. 11–12. The rest of this paragraph is based on this same source.

PAGE 56

1 5 Eliz. I, c. 4; *Statutes of the Realm*, IV, i, 415.

2 Richard Mulcaster, *Positions* (1581), p. 134.

3 Sir Francis Bacon, 'On Sutton's Estate', *Works* (1841), I, 495–6.

PAGE 57

1 For development of this point, see my article 'The Alienated Intellectuals of Early Stuart England', *Past and Present*, no. 23 (November 1962).

2 The works upon which the foregoing section is chiefly based are Fritz Caspari, *Humanism and the Social Order in Tudor England* (Chicago, 1954); M. H. Curtis, *Oxford and Cambridge in Transition, 1558–1642* (Oxford, 1959); and W. K. Jordan, *Philanthropy in England, 1480–1660* (1959).

3 John Venn, vol. I, *Admissions, 1349–1713* (Cambridge, 1897), pp. 173–89.

PAGE 58

1 W. K. Jordan, *op. cit.* pp. 279–97, but esp. pp. 287–91.

2 'Canons of Convocation of Canterbury, 1529', A. F. Leach, *Educational Charters and Documents, 598 to 1909*, p. 447.

PAGE 59

1 William Lily, *Introduction of the Eyght Partes of Speche* (1542), verso of title-page.

2 'Royal Injunctions, 1559', A. F. Leach, *op. cit.* p. 494.

3 'Canon LXXIX', *Constitutions and Canons Ecclesiastical*, ed. H. A. Wilson (Oxford, 1923).

4 William Lily, *A Shorte Introduction of Grammar, generallie to be vsed* (1584), sig. Aiiiᵛ.

5 T. W. Baldwin, *William Shakspere's Small Latine and Lesse Greeke* (Urbana, Ill., 1944), I, 435.

6 The description of the grammar school curriculum is based on the exhaustive discussions of the topic in T. W. Baldwin's study, especially vol. I. A good brief summary of the grammar school curriculum can be found in Craig R. Thompson, *Schools in Tudor England*, Folger Booklets on Tudor and Stuart Civilization (Washington, 1958).

PAGE 62

1 Margaret G. Davies, *The Enforcement of English Apprenticeship* (Cambridge, Mass.), 1956, p. 165.

2 John Brinsley, *Consolation for our Grammar Schools* (1622), pp. 10–11; cf. Brinsley, *Ludus Literarius*, p. 307.

3 W. K. Jordan, *op. cit.* p. 281.

NOTES

PAGE 63

1 This section is based on M. H. Curtis, *Oxford and Cambridge in Transition, 1558–1642* (Oxford, 1959), esp. chaps. III–VI.

2 *The Two Gentlemen of Verona*, I, iii, 4–10.

3 *Ibid.* 19–21.

PAGE 65

1 George Dyer, *The Privileges of the University of Cambridge* (1824), I, 289.

2 Gabriel Harvey to Arthur Capel, undated, *Letter-book of Gabriel Harvey, A.D. 1573–1580*, ed. Edward J. L. Scott, Camden Society, n.s. XXXIII (1874), 168.

PAGE 66

1 John Wallis to Thomas Smith, 29 January 1697, *Peter Langtoft's Chronicle*, ed. Thomas Hearne (Oxford, 1735), I, cl. Wallis was here describing his experiences at Cambridge in the 1630's.

PAGE 67

1 Davies, *op. cit.* p. 266.

2 5 Eliz. I, c. 4, secs. 19, 24.

3 *Ibid.* secs. 20–3, 25.

4 *Records of the Worshipful Company of Carpenters:* vol. I, *Apprentices' Entry Books, 1654–1694*, ed. Bower Marsh (Oxford, 1913), pp. x–xi; Douglas Knoop and G. P. Jones, *The London Mason in the Seventeenth Century* (Manchester, 1935), p. 63.

PAGE 68

1 This estimate is based on data extracted from D. F. McKenzie, *Stationers' Company Apprentices, 1605–1640* (Charlottesville, Virginia, 1961), part I: 'Printers' Apprentices'.

2 Edward Arber, *A Transcript of the Stationers' Register, 1554–1640* (1875), II, 807–12. See also Cyprian Blagden, *The Stationers' London Company: A History, 1403–1959* (1960), p. 71.

3 This estimate is based on data contained in D. F. McKenzie, 'Apprenticeship in the Stationers' Company, 1555–1640', *The Library*, 5th ser. XIII (1958), Table I, p. 295.

4 Edmund Bolton, *Cities Advocate, in this case or question of Honor and Armes; Whether Apprenticeship extinguisheth Gentry?* (1629), p. 28.

5 Edmund Coote, *The English Schoolemaister* (1596), sig. A3.

6 Thomas Masterson, *The Second Booke of Arithmeticke* (1592), sig. Eii.

PAGE 69

1 Peele, *Patheway to Perfectnes* (1569), sig. Aiiii^v.

2 C. R. B. Barrett, *The History of the Society of Apothecaries of London* (1905), pp. xxxii–xxxiii.

3 R. H[ayman], *Quodlibets Lately Come Over from New Britaniola, old Newfoundland* (1628). I am indebted to Mr John Crow of King's College, London, for this reference.

4 Edmund Bolton, *Cities Advocate*, p. 39.

PAGE 70

1 Thomas Girton, *The Golden Ram: A Narrative History of the Cloth-workers Company, 1528–1958* (1958), p. 16.

2 Edmund Bolton, *Cities Advocate*, p. 51.

3 Sir George Buck, *The Third Vniversitie of England, or A Treatise of the Foundations of all the Colledges, Auncient Schooles of Priviledge, and of Houses of Learning and Liberall Arts, within and about the most Famous Cittie of London*; appended to John Stow, *Annals* (1615), p. 961.

PAGE 71

1 *Ibid.* 983.

2 A good account of London lectures in the medical sciences can be found in Phyllis Allen, 'Medical education in 17th century England', *Journal of the History of Medicine and Allied Sciences*, I (1946), 137–9.

3 John Ward, *Lives of the Professors of Gresham College* (1740), pp. 34–8.

4 *D.N.B.*

PAGE 72

1 *Ibid.*; John Ward, *Lives of the Professors of Gresham College*, pp. 120–9.

2 The question here referred to is, of course, an old one. For generations the universities have been considered intellectual backwaters in which little was done to advance learning in England. In *Oxford and Cambridge in Transition, 1558–1642*, I tried to show that the universities as well as other educational institutions and learned societies played a role in the development of the new philosophy of the seventeenth century. Recently Mr Christopher Hill, Fellow of Balliol College, has given a rather different and more traditional treatment of this question in the Ford Lectures. A broadcast version of the first of these, all that is in print at the moment, appeared in *The Listener*, LXVII, no. 1731 (31 May 1962), 943–6.

NOTES

PAGE 73

1 William Harrison, *Description of England* (1577, 1587), ed. F. J. Furnivall, New Shakspere Society, series VI, no. 1 (1877), 206.

2 M. E. Finch, *The Wealth of Five Northamptonshire Families, 1540–1640*, Northamptonshire Record Society, XIX (1956), 82.

3 L. Hotson, *Shakespeare versus Shallow* (1931).

4 E. G. Henderson, *Foundations of English Administrative Law* (1963), pp. 9–45.

5 *Ben Jonson*, ed. C. H. Herford and Percy Simpson (1925–52), I, 220–3; XI, 579–80.

6 As in the affair of the bishops' ban on satire, 1599.

PAGE 74

1 Humphrey Gilbert, *Queene Elizabethes Achademy, A Booke of Precedence*, etc., ed. F. J. Furnivall, Early English Text Society, Extra Series VIII (1869), 7.

2 William Fulbecke, *A direction or preparative to the study of the Lawe* (1600).

PAGE 75

1 Richard Robinson, 'Briefe Collection of the Queenes Majesties Most High and Most Honourable Courtes of Records', ed. R. L. Rickard, *Camden Miscellany*, XX, Camden Society, 3rd series, LXXXIII (1953), 2.

2 The description of Westminster is based upon Robinson, and John Stow, *A Survey of London* (1603), ed. C. L. Kingsford (Oxford, 1908), II, 117–20.

3 Thomas Smith, *De Republica Anglorum* (1583), ed. L. Alston (Cambridge, 1906), p. 68.

4 Edward Hake, *Epieikeia*, ed. D. E. C. Yale, Yale Law Library Publications, 13 (1953), pp. v–xii.

5 W. J. Jones, 'Chancery attitudes in the reign of Elizabeth I', *American Journal of Legal History*, 5 (1961), 12 ff.

PAGE 76

1 Stow, *Survay*, II, 120.

2 Smith, *De Republica*, p. 69.

PAGE 77

1 Smith, *De Republica*, pp. 95 ff.

2 A. L. Rowse, *The England of Elizabeth* (1950), pp. 358–9.

3 C. I. A. Ritchie, *The Ecclesiastical Courts of York* (Arbroath, 1956), appendix 1, 'An Abstract of All Causes Belonginge to the Ecclesiasticall Court'.

4 F. D. Price, 'The abuse of excommunication and the decline of ecclesiastical discipline under Queen Elizabeth', *English Historical Review*, LVII (1942), 106–15.

5 From 20 October 1585 to 13 January 1586, the Consistory court at York handled 243 cases. Ritchie, *Ecclesiastical Courts*, p. 17. From 27 November 1638 to 28 November 1640, the court of the Archdeacon of London sat on thirty occasions and dealt with 1800 offenders. W. Holdsworth, *History of English Law* (7th ed. 1956), I, 620.

PAGE 78

1 'There are of them some 24 belonging to the arches which gayne well, and every Bishop hath a Chancellor that liveth in some good creditt.' Thomas Wilson, 'The State of England, Anno Dom. 1600', ed. F. J. Fisher, *Camden Miscellany*, XVI, Camden Society, 3rd series, LII (1936), 25. Civilians who practised below diocesan level had, according to Wilson, a different tale to tell.

2 Public Record Office, State Papers Domestic, S.P. 1/18, XCV, 91; British Museum, Lansdowne MSS. 47, f. 114.

3 P.R.O., S.P. 1/18, XCV, 91; B.M. Lans. 106, f. 95.

4 Wilson, 'State of England', p. 25.

5 *Hatfield MSS.*, Historical Manuscripts Commission, series 9 (1883–), I, 146.

6 P.R.O., S.P. 1/18, XCV, 91.

7 E. W. Ives, 'The reputation of the common lawyer in English society, 1450–1550', *Birmingham Historical Journal*, VII (1960), 146 n. 113.

8 K. Charlton, 'Liberal education and the Inns of Court in the sixteenth century', *British Journal of Educational Studies*, IX (1960–61), 25–38.

PAGE 79

1 F. J. Fisher, 'The development of London as a centre of conspicuous consumption', *Transactions of the Royal Historical Society*, 4th series, XXX (1948), 42.

2 A. Nicoll, *Stuart Masques* (1937), p. 216 and *passim*.

3 *2 Henry IV*, III, ii. Cf. A. Nicoll, *The Elizabethans* (1957), p. 63.

4 The Middle Temple was the first, 22 November, 1555. *Middle Temple Records*, ed. C. H. Hopwood (1904–5), I, 104.

5 *Acts of the Privy Council*, ed. J. R. Dasent (1890–1907), VIII (1571–5), 246.

6 *The Black Books of Lincoln's Inn*, ed. J. D. Walker (1897–1902), II, 441.

7 *Calendar of State Papers Domestic, Charles I*, ed. J. Bruce, etc. (1858–97), VI (1633–4), 251.

8 Robinson lists three each for Star Chamber and Requests and two each for the Wards and the Duchy of Lancaster. The Exchequer and the City of London laid down similar limits.

PAGE 80

1 3 James I, c. 8.
2 Wilson, 'State of England', p. 24.
3 *Black Books of Lincoln's Inn*, II, 81.
4 Sir George Buck, *The Third Vniversitie of England*, in John Stow, *Annals* (1615), pp. 968-9.
5 Smith, *De Republica*, pp. 39-40.
6 P.R.O., SP. 1/18, cxi, 27.
7 James Whitelocke, *Liber Famelicus*, ed. J. Bruce, Camden Society, LXX (1858), xiv.
8 Finch, *Five Northamptonshire Families*, p. 156.
9 Whitelocke, *Liber Famelicus*, p. 106.

PAGE 81

1 Wilson, 'State of England', p. 25.
2 J. Spedding, *Letters and Life of Francis Bacon* (1862-74), V, 242.
3 H. R. Trevor-Roper, 'The Gentry 1540-1660', *Economic History Review, Supplement* (1953), pp. 54-5.
4 Sir Thomas Egerton, Bridgewater, Sir Edward Coke, Leicester, and Sir Henry Hobart, Buckinghamshire.
5 This description of the courts is based upon Pl. X, the series of fifteenth-century illustrations of the royal courts in the Inner Temple library, *Archaeologia*, XXXIX (1863) and Smith, *De Republica*, p. 96.
6 This account of criminal procedure is principally derived from Smith, *De Republica*, pp. 90-104.
7 *Much Ado*, IV, ii; *Measure for Measure*, II, i.
8 Refusal to plead resulted in being pressed to death, the *peine forte et dure*. Cf. *Measure for Measure*, V, 528; *Much Ado*, III, i, 76, etc.

PAGE 82

1 18 Eliz. I, c. 7.
2 Cf. *2 Henry VI*, IV, vii, 45-50, 'Thou hast appointed justices of peace, to call poor men before them about matters they were not able to answer...and because they could not read, thou hast hanged them'.

PAGE 83

1 9 George I, c. 22, 1722; cf. L. Radzinowicz, *History of English Criminal Law* (1948-56), I, 49-79. The act created 350 capital offences.
2 Edward Coke, *Third Part of the Institutes of the Laws of England* (1797), f. 210.
3 'Sometimes it commeth to passe by reason of (will doe all) otherwise called mony, and sometimes by freends, or both...if a Gentleman commit a greeuous offence, and a poore man commit the like, the poore shal be sure of his *Sursum collum?* But the

other shall be pardoned.' Philip Stubbes, *Second part of the Anatomie of Abuses* (1583), ed. F. J. Furnivall, New Shakspere Society, series VI, no. 12 (1882), 13-14.
4 *Measure for Measure*, IV, ii, 140. The mention in this scene of a warrant for execution (l. 159 and also I, iv, 74; IV, iii, 45; V, i, 459) refers to Tudor practice with regard to important prisoners, especially those in the Tower; the execution of humbler offenders was not dignified with any such formality.
5 Coke, *Third Inst.* f. 243.
6 A. H. A. Hamilton, *Quarter Sessions from Queen Elizabeth to Queen Anne* (1878), pp. 30-2.
7 J. C. Jeaffreson, *Middlesex County Records* (1886-92), II, xvii.
8 This figure may well be too low; in 1596 a Somerset J.P. reported that 40 executions had taken place in the county that year. F. Aydelotte, *Elizabethan Rogues and Vagabonds* (1913), pp. 73, 168-73.
9 Radzinowicz, *Criminal Law*, I, 3-8, 138-64. Furthermore, the population of England had doubled.
10 *Ibid.* I, 108.

PAGE 84

1 M. Blatcher, Touching the writ of *latitat*, *Elizabethan Government and Society*, ed. S. T. Bindoff *et al.* (1961), pp. 188-212.
2 For this account of civil litigation at common law, see Smith, *De Republica*, pp. 73-5, 78-80.

PAGE 85

1 Holdsworth, *History of English Law*, V (1924), 233.
2 John Harington, *Letters and Epigrams*, ed. N. E. McClure (1930), p. 204.
3 Edward Hake, *Newes out of Powles Churchyarde* (1575), sig. B 5 ff.
4 J. E. C. Hill, *Puritanism and Revolution* (1958), p. 76.
5 Holdsworth, *History of English Law*, I (1956), 432.

PAGE 86

1 Hake, *Epieikeia*, pp. xi, 3, 10, 79.
2 John Selden, *Table Talk* (1689), ed. F. Pollock (1927), p. 43.

PAGE 87

ABBREVIATIONS EMPLOYED

I. *Manuscript sources*

Corporation of London Records Office

R. Repertories of the Court of Aldermen of the City of London. Roman numerals indicate the volume, arabic numerals the folio number, '*a*' and '*b*' recto and verso.

J. Journals of the Court of Common Council of the City of London. References shown as above.

Orders for Newgate (1574): Ratified by the Court of Aldermen 11 May 1574. Set out in *R.* xviij, 208–210*b*.

Orders for the Counters (1606): 'Bill for the orderinge of prisoners in the severall Compters.' Court of Common Council, 20 May 1606; *J.* xxvij, 41–42*b*.

Orders for Ludgate (1606): 'Bill for the orderinge of prisoners in Ludgate.' Court of Common Council, 20 May 1606; *J.* xxvij, 43–44*b*.

Proclamation concerning Newgate (1617): 'By the Maior / A Proclamation for Reformation of abuses in the Gaole of Newgate.' Entered in the Journals: *J.* xxx, 249*a–b*.

Public Record Office

A.P.C. *Acts of the Privy Council,* i.e. the printed volumes of the Privy Council Registers. The period covered by the printed volume is incorporated in the reference. Unprinted volumes are referred to thus: 'P.C. Reg. Chas. I.'

S.P. Dom. Eliz., Jas. I, Chas. I. State Papers Domestic of Elizabeth, James I or Charles I.

2. *Printed sources*

Œconomy: The Œconomy of the Fleete: or, an apologeticall answeare of Alexander Harris (late Warden there), edited, from the original MS., by A. Jessopp. Camden Society, n.s. xxv (1879).

Judges: *The Elizabethan Underworld: A Collection of Tudor and Early Stuart Tracts and Ballads,* ed. A. V. Judges (1930).

PAGE 88

1 B3^v–B5^r. In the folio edition of Taylor's *Workes* (1630), Mm 1^v–Mm 2^r; the Spenser Society reprint (1869), pp. 292–3.

2 *Christopher Marlowe in London* (1934), p. 39. It must have been late in the day by the time they were examined and the inquest took place at Finsbury next day. See Eccles, pp. 10–11 *passim.* Cf. *The famous Historye of the life and death of Captain Thomas Stukeley* (1605; performed 1596?), C3^v.

3 *Henslowe's Diary,* ed. R. A. Foakes and R. T. Rickert (1961), p. 86.

4 *Ben Jonson,* ed. C. H. Herford and P. Simpson (1925), I, 15–16, 217–18; 18–19, 139, 219–20; 38–9, 140, 190–200.

PAGE 89

1 Margery Bassett, 'The Fleet Prison in the Middle Ages', *University of Toronto Law Journal,* v (no. 2, 1944), 383.

2 See J. Dover Wilson, *The Fortunes of Falstaff* (1943), pp. 118–20.

3 At least three copies of this document exist: S.P. Dom. Eliz. vol. 105, nos. 48 and 49, and B.M. Lansdowne MS. 74, no. 35. All are undated; the first two are placed amongst papers for July–December 1575, the third amongst papers almost all dating from 1593. They are largely identical and must have been made at the same time and sent to persons whose favour the Marshal hoped to gain.

4 John Stow, *A Survey of London* (1603), ed. C. L. Kingsford, II (1908), 59.

5 Ed. cit. II, 122. At this period the word 'convict' seems to have had a markedly ecclesiastical connotation, which it was later to lose. See under meaning 1 in the *Oxford English Dictionary.*

6 *A.P.C. 1613–14,* pp. 331, 350, 464, 540.

PAGE 90

1 John Howard, *State of the prisons* (1777), p. 195.

2 See *A.P.C. 1581–2,* pp. 275–6.

3 The 32 extant bills can be found in B.M. Egerton MS. 806, ff. 30–5 (2), B.M. Add. MS. 41257 (19; printed in Publications of the Catholic Record Society, vol. 53, *Miscellanea: Recusant Records,* ed. C. Talbot (1961), pp. 245–75) and P.R.O., E407/56 (11; printed by the Catholic Record Society in *Miscellanea,* IV (1907), 224–38). It is advisable to consult the originals if strict accuracy is required. The series has suffered heavily from dispersal and injury.

4 London County Council Survey of London, XXII, *Bankside* (1950), 55.

5 John Selden, *Table-talk* (1689), ed. E. Arber (1869), p. 74.

6 William Warmington, *A Modest Defence of the Oath of Allegiance* (1612), ¶2. B.M. Harleian MS. 161, ff. 93–4. I hope to print the latter in full sometime.

7 S.P. Dom. Eliz. vol. 108, no. 4, is the draft of a commission intended for prisoners in Her Majesty's Bench, dated 16 April 1576.

PAGE 91

1 G. W. Prothero (ed.), *Select Statutes and other Constitutional Documents Illustrative of the Reigns of Elizabeth and James I,* 4th ed. (1913), pp. 447–8. The absolute power of the Crown in this respect was destroyed by section VI of 17 Car. I, c. 10.

2 See A. Griffiths, *The Chronicles of Newgate* (1884), pp. 158–9 and Giles Jacob, *A New Law-dictionary,* 9th ed. by O. Ruffhead and J. Morgan (1772), 'Pain Fort & Dure'. For a full definition of the method employed, see E. Chamberlayne, *Angliae Notitia,* 2nd ed. (1669), p. 73, or Samuel Chidley, *A Cry against a crying sin* (1652), B2^r.

3 William Harrison, 'Description of Britain', prefixed to Holinshed's *Chronicle*; 2nd ed. (1587), Bk II, ch. 11, p. 185. The process is illustrated on the title-page of *The Life and death of Griffin Flood informer* (1623).

4 *Abuses stript and whipt* (1613: S.T.C. 25893), H7^{r-v}.

5 *Middlesex County Records*, ed. J. C. Jeaffreson, II (1887), 287–307, xvii–xviii.

PAGE 92

1 Quotations from the quartos or the First Folio as indicated by dates given. There are also four possible metaphorical references: *Merchant of Venice*, IV, i, 425; *King Lear*, IV, iii, 27–8; *Venus and Adonis*, 429–30; *Othello*, III, iv, 177.

2 K. B. Danks, 'Shakespeare and "peine forte et dure"', *Notes and Queries*, CXCIX (September 1954), 377–9, gives a melodramatic account of Elizabethan and early Stuart practice, representing pressing to death as a torture. It was a legal sentence, brutal in execution but no more so than the bungling hanging of the time and a good deal less than the mode of execution for treason. It had nothing to do with the activities of Topcliffe and Young. Danks gives two most dubious Shakespearian allusions: *Romeo and Juliet*, I, i, 192–4 and *Two Gentlemen of Verona*, III, i, 19–21. He cuts short Lucio's exclamation and thereby destroys most of its meaning.

3 *A.P.C.* 1592–3, p. 121; P.C. Reg. Chas. I, vol. VI, 282, 299.

4 Codified into a set of orders in 1634: R. xlviij, 306b–319b. For stories about sergeants, see William Fennor, *The Compters common-wealth* (1617). F4^v–H1^r; Judges, pp. 456–62.

5 See Thomas Dekker, *English villanies* (1632), I4^{r-v}.

PAGE 93

1 Thomas Savile, *The Prisoners conference* (1605), B4^v. Dekker, however, took the opposite view: *Villanies discovered by lanthorne and candle-light* (1616), I4^{r-v}.

2 *Strange newes* (1592); I1^{r-v}: *The Works of Thomas Nashe*, ed. R. B. McKerrow, reprinted; ed. F. P. Wilson (1958), I, 310.

3 1595: Richard Hatchman; R. xxiij, 374b–375. 1636: John Layton; R. l, 114–115b, 216b–217.

PAGE 94

1 R. liij, 278–9; R. lv, 226b.

2 Dekker and Webster, *Northward Ho* (1607), C1^r [signed 'D'].

3 *A.P.C.* 1615–16, pp. 295–6.

4 They can be most readily consulted in the table inserted between pp. 152–3 of *Œconomy*, but this contains some errors. Bodleian MS. Tanner 168, f. 174, has a more accurate version.

5 Orders for Newgate (1574). Apparently these remained in force into the 1640's.

6 Orders for the Counters (1606) and Orders for Ludgate (1606); confirmed in 1621, R. xxxv, 268b–270.

7 See note 3, p. 90 above.

PAGE 95

1 The earliest example quoted in the *Dictionary* dates from 1592. Orders for the Counters of 1547 mention 'garnysshe': J. xv, 314–15.

2 Orders for the Counters 1547 and (1606); Orders for Ludgate (1606) and 1621.

3 Proclamation concerning Newgate (1617). In Newgate the custom survived into the eighteenth century and appears in the *Tale of a tub* and the *Beggars' opera*.

4 *The Compters Common-Wealth* (1617). Modernized reprint in Judges, pp. 423–87.

5 B3^{r-v}; Judges, p. 431. This charge was still being made in 1637. See William Bagwell, *The Distressed Merchant* (1645), P2^v.

6 B4^v; Judges, p. 433. C1^r; Judges, pp. 433–4.

7 *A Quip for an upstart courtier* (1592), E2^v. Fennor, K1^v; Judges, p. 474.

8 Article 12, Bodleian MS. Tanner 168, f. 175^r. But of course the sharing of beds was much more frequent in all ranks of society at that time. See, for example, Iago's account of sleeping with Cassio: *Othello*, III, iii, 413–26.

9 *Essayes and characters of a prison and prisoners*, 2nd ed. (1618), B3^r, G3^r; 1821 reprint, pp. 18, 85.

10 *Villanies discovered* (1616), K4^v.

11 Orders for the Counters (1606). Orders for Ludgate (1606).

12 Luke Hutton, *The Black Dog of Newgate* [1596?], C4^r; Judges, p. 276. 'Chenell' probably means cannel, a hard bituminous coal, see *Oxford English Dictionary*.

PAGE 96

1 Humphrey Giffard, *A Second accompt of what progress hath been hitherto made, etc.* (1670), A3^r. Giffard had long been Keeper of the Poultry Counter and this pamphlet was part of his campaign to have the Counter rebuilt more spaciously after the Fire.

2 *Villanies discovered* (1616), H4^v–I1^r. Brewis: 'Bread soaked in boiling fat pottage, made of salted meat'— Johnson's *Dictionary*.

3 *A.P.C. 1619–21*, p. 270.

4 *Essayes and characters* (1618), G2ʳ, E1ʳ⁻ᵛ, G3ᵛ; 1821 reprint, pp. 51–2, 82, 88.

5 S.P. Dom. Jas. I, vol. 128, nos. 71, 72.

6 Article 2 of the Orders. *The Life, apprehension, arraignement, and execution of Charles Courtney, etc.* (1612), C2ᵛ.

PAGE 97

1 Orders for the Counters (1606), article 9.

2 *A.P.C. 1592*, pp. 109–10: Broughton and Ely; pp. 306–7: Wisbech. The Wisbech orders also include (pp. 307–8) a list of charges to be made for buying and cooking food on the prisoners' behalf, e.g. 'for everie service of fish for boyling onlie jd'.

PAGE 98

1 The cry is quoted from *The Knave in Graine, new vampt. By J. D.* (1640), H1ʳ. This was written *c.* 1625, revised *c.* 1632—see the Malone Society reprint (1961). For references to early sets of Cries including the basketman, see F. P. Wilson's article, 'Illustrations of social life. III: street-cries', in *Shakespeare Survey 13* (1960), pp. 108–10.

2 I1ᵛ, I2ᵛ. *A Select Collection of Old English Plays*, 4th ed. by W. C. Hazlitt, II, 258, 260.

3 *A Rod for run-awayes*, B3ʳ; *The Plague pamphlets of Thomas Dekker*, ed. F. P. Wilson (1925), pp. 148–9.

4 See particularly the report of a committee in July 1618, *R.* xxxiij, 373–4: 'the said Ruins are most noysome against the health of the poore prisoners'; 'The leades over the house are soe faultie that it generally raynethe throughe all the roomes even into the lowest limboes [dungeons]'.

5 Report submitted to the Court of Aldermen by the Visitors of Newgate in 1633, *R.* xlvij, 182*b*–186. Severe punishments recommended for those who misbehaved in divine service or indulged in 'such excerations...not to be named among Christians (as God dame me, and ye like)'.

6 Orders for Newgate (1574): strong beer or ale, articles 7 and 15; gambling, article 10. Orders for the Counters (1606): female visitors, article 5 (repeated in Orders for Ludgate). Proclamation concerning Newgate (1617): keepers accused of 'suffering their Prisoners to become drunke and disordered, permitting them wine, Tobacco, excessive strong drinke, gaming and resort to women of lewd behaviour'.

PAGE 99

1 *Villanies discovered* (1616), I1ʳ.

2 *A.P.C. 1581–2*, p. 198; *A.P.C. 1596–7*, p. 437.

3 *Essayes and characters*, D4ᵛ; 1821 reprint, p. 51.

4 S.P. Dom. Chas. I, vol. 424, no. 65.

5 See the opening quotation by John Taylor and *Œconomy*, p. 14. In *Looke about you* (1600), an anonymous play written near the turn of the century, there is a scene in the Fleet in which a game of bowls is played (D1ᵛ. Malone Society reprint; ed. W. W. Greg (1913)).

6 *Amanda: or, the reformed whore* (1635), a mine of information on the privileges of Fleet prisoners at that period.

7 *Œconomy*, pp. 112–13, 157–9.

8 Mynshul, *Essayes and characters*, E2ʳ; 1821 reprint, p. 58.

PAGE 100

1 S.P. Dom. Eliz., vol. 165, no. 5.

2 *The History of the troubles and tryal of...William Laud* (1694), p. 309.

3 *A.P.C. 1618–19*, p. 309. This was a result of overlaxity in Newgate and the Clink.

4 A good example of the regulations enforced appears in *A.P.C. 1616–17*, p. 255.

5 E.g. George Wither's *The Shepherd's hunting* (1615), written in the Marshalsea.

6 See *The Dictionary of Welsh biography down to 1940* (1951), p. 472; article by Sir William Llewelyn Davies.

PAGE 103

1 The sword is described in *Catalogue of Corporation Plate of England and Wales exhibited at Goldsmiths' Hall, 1952*, p. 50. For the text of the inscription (based on the Geneva version) I am indebted to the City Archivist, Miss Elizabeth Ralph.

2 *Institutes of Religion* (ed. Beveridge, 1863), II, 670.

PAGE 104

1 *Laws of Ecclesiastical Polity*, Bk VIII, ch. ii, §§ 5, 6.

2 'Homily of Obedience', 1547, in *Book of Homilies* (1844 edn.), p. 105.

PAGE 105

1 Robert Crowley, *Select Works* (ed. J. M. Cowper. E.E.T.S., 1872), pp. 132, 134, 143.

2 *Sermons of Bishop Latimer* (ed. Corrie, Parker Soc., Cambridge, 1844), p. 160.

3 *Ibid.* p. 371.

NOTES

PAGE 106

1 *Obedience of a Christian Man* (Christian Classics Series, ed. Lovett, n.d.), pp. 91, 92, 93.
2 *Later Writings of Bishop Hooper* (ed. Nevinson, Parker Soc., 1852), p. 104.
3 *Works of Bishop Jewel* (ed. Ayre, Parker Soc., 1848), III, p. 75.
4 Bilson, *True Difference*, p. 475.

PAGE 107

1 *Book of Homilies*, p. 528.

PAGE 108

1 *Ibid.* pp. 489–533.
2 *Ibid.* pp. 494, 507, 509.

PAGE 109

1 *Utopia* (Everyman edn.), p. 112.
2 Thomas Starkey, *Dialogue between Reginald Pole and Thomas Lupset* (ed. K. M. Burton, 1948), p. 155.
3 It was reprinted, significantly, in 1639 and again in 1642.
4 Ralph Robynson's translation of the 'Utopia' was reprinted in 1597, in the depth of the depression which produced the Elizabethan Poor Law, when More's attacks on the evils of inclosure must have given it a special topical interest.
5 Conyers Read, *Mr Secretary Walsingham* (Oxford, 1925), II, 218.
6 See above, p. 104.

PAGE 110

1 *Book of Homilies*, p. 510.
2 John Foxe, *The Acts and Monuments of the Church* (ed. Seymour, 1838), p. 5.

PAGE 111

1 Louis B. Wright, *Religion and Empire* (University of North Carolina Press, 1943), pp. 15, 71.
2 *Ecclesiastical Polity*, Bk I, ch. x, § 10.
3 5 Eliz. c. 4 (*S.R.* 4 [i]), p. 414.
4 14 Eliz. c. 5 (*ibid.* p. 590).

PAGE 112

1 *Parliamentary Debates in 1610* (ed. S. R. Gardiner, Camden Soc. LXXXI, 1862), p. 23.
2 Chief Baron Fleming in Bate's Case, 1606 (J. R. Tanner, *Constitutional Documents of the Reign of James I*, Cambridge, 1930, p. 341).
3 *Ecclesiastical Polity*, Bk VIII, ch. ii, § 3.

PAGE 113

1 Bilson, *op. cit.* pp. 520–1.
2 Cf. also the imprisonment of Sir John Hayward in 1599, at the Queen's insistence, for publishing his *First Part of the Life and Raigne of Henrie IV* with a dedication to Essex, and the omission of the deposition scene from the two 1597 quartos of Shakespeare's *Richard II*.
3 Christopher Morris, *Political Thought in England: Tyndale to Hooker* (H.U.L., Oxford, 1953), p. 121.
4 On the use of the word 'State' in Elizabethan times see G. N. Clark, 'The birth of the Dutch Republic', *Proceedings of the British Academy*, XXXII (1946), pp. 195, 213–17.
5 *De Republica Anglorum* (ed. L. Alston, Cambridge, 1906), p. 20.
6 *Ibid.* pp. 46–7.

PAGE 114

1 Morris, *op. cit.* p. 77.
2 Smith, *op. cit.* p. 33.

PAGE 115

1 *Two Cantos of Mutabilitie*, VI, 6.
2 Lever, *Sermons* (English Reprints, ed. Arber, 1870), p. 50.

PAGE 116

1 Hist. MSS. Comm., Hatfield (parts 1 and 2), pp. 162–5.
2 Cf. F. J. Fisher, 'Commercial trends and policy in sixteenth century England', *Econ. Hist. Review*, X (1940), pp. 95–117; Lawrence Stone, 'State control in sixteenth century England', *ibid.* XVII (1947), pp. 3–20.

PAGE 117

1 *Visitation of Shropshire, 1623*, part 1 (Harl. Soc. XXVIII, 1889), pp. 1–3.
2 Smith, *op. cit.* 39–40.
3 E. J. Fripp, *Shakespeare, Man and Artist*, 1 (Oxford, 1938), p. 75 n.
4 Cf. P. Styles, 'The Heralds' Visitations of Warwickshire, 1682–3', *Transactions of the Birmingham Archaeological Soc.* LXXI, pp. 123–31.

PAGE 118

1 D. H. Willson, *Privy Councillors in the House of Commons, 1604–29* (University of Minnesota Press, 1940), p. 118.
2 Bodleian Library, MS. English Letters, b. 1, fol. 70. Dineley, writing to Sir Simon Archer on 24 March 1632, speaks of himself as '79 yeares olde within few

weekes' and refers to the time 'when I went to scoole at Stratford'. He would therefore have been about ten years senior to Shakespeare.

PAGE 119

1 *Bishop Andrewes' Works; Sermons* (1843), v, p. 139.

PAGE 120

1 *Essays in Elizabethan History* (1958), p. 44.

PAGE 121

1 See A. C. Southern, *Elizabethan Recusant Prose* (1951), particularly chapter II, 'The Movement and the Men'.

PAGE 123

1 Quoted in Southern, *op. cit.* p. 118.

PAGE 124

1 P. Janelle, *Robert Southwell the Writer* (1935), has a valuable account of this work, pp. 238–48.
2 *Puritan Discipline Tracts* (1844) prints the *Admonition* conveniently, this quotation being on p. 25 of the reprint.

PAGE 125

1 *Essays Presented to Sir John Neale on Elizabethan Government and Society*, Patrick Collinson, 'John Field and Elizabethan Puritanism', pp. 127–62.
2 Quoted in A. F. Scott-Pearson's *Thomas Cartwright and Elizabethan Puritanism* (1925), p. 189.

PAGE 126

1 See the useful collection of data in Mark Eccles's *Shakespeare in Warwickshire* (1961).

PAGE 127

1 *Tudor England* (1961 edn.), pp. 295–6.
2 *Essays in Elizabethan History* (1958), p. 79.
3 'Vertve the best monvment', in *Poems of Sir Walter Ralegh* (ed. A. Latham), p. 53.
4 Joel Hurstfield, *Elizabeth I and the Unity of England*.
5 See a discussion of Persons's book in *Recusant History* (vol. 4, no. 3, 1957): L. Hicks, S.J., 'Father Robert Persons and *The Book of Succession*', pp. 104–37.

PAGE 128

1 For fresh evidence and evaluation see Joel Hurstfield, 'The Succession Struggle in Late Elizabethan England', printed in *Essays Presented to Sir John Neale*, pp. 369–96.

2 Sig. E4ᵛ.
3 *Anatomy of Abuses*, reprinted in *New Shakspere Society transactions* (series 6, nos. 4, 6 and 12), pp. 2–3 of reprint.
4 John Norden, *A Christian Familiar Comfort* (1596), quoted in his *Vicissitudo Rerum* (Shakespeare Association Facsimiles. no. 4), p. xvii.

PAGE 129

1 Joel Hurstfield, *Elizabeth I and the Unity of England*.
2 For this and related material see L. C. Knights, *Drama and Society in the Age of Jonson*, appendix B.

PAGE 130

1 A full discussion of contemporary dedicatory styles is in E. H. Miller, *The Professional Writer in Elizabethan England* (1959).
2 See J. B. Leishman, *The Three Parnassus Plays* (1949) for comment on the relationships of satire and homily.
3 In the Presentation copy of Harington's epigrams made for Prince Henry, Harington reverses the 'Live' and 'dy'.

PAGE 135

1 See C. J. Sisson, *Lost Plays of Shakespeare's Age* (1936), p. 187.

PAGE 136

1 R. Burton, *Anatomy of Melancholy*, 'Democritus to the Reader' (1931 reprint), p. 42.

PAGE 138

1 *King John*, III, i, 77–80.
2 *Ibid.* 72.
3 *Troilus and Cressida*, III, ii, 184–6.

PAGE 139

1 *Othello*, v, ii, 145.
2 *All's Well That Ends Well*, I, i, 96–100.
3 *Merchant of Venice*, v, i, 58–65.

PAGE 140

1 *Twelfth Night*, III, i, 121.
2 The best survey of English works on astronomy in this period remains F. R. Johnson, *Astronomical Thought in Renaissance England* (Baltimore, 1937).
3 See, for example, *Midsummer Night's Dream*, III, i, 52–6.
4 Cf. *Titus Andronicus*, II, i, 5–7 and *Measure for Measure*, I, ii, 172.

NOTES

PAGE 141

1 Quoted at length in Johnson, *op. cit.* pp. 127–8.

PAGE 144

1 In *Certaine Errors in Navigation, Arising either of the ordinarie erroneous making of the Sea Chart, Compasse, Crosse staff, and Tables of declination of the Sunne, and fixed Starres detected and Corrected* (London, 1599): the tables were used by Hondius some years earlier.

2 Cf. John Dee's remark in the preface to the first English edition of Euclid (1570, itself a tribute to the belief that readers unacquainted with Latin should be provided with mathematical texts): 'Some, to beautify their Halls, Parlers, Chambers, Galeries, Studies, or Libraries with; other some, for things past, as battles fought, earthquakes, heavenly firings, and such occurrences, in histories mentioned:… some other, presently to view the large dominion of the Turk: the wide Empire of the Muscovite:… some other for their own journeys directing into far lands, or to understand other men's travels…liketh, loveth, getteth and useth, Maps, Charts, and Geographical Globes.'

3 *Twelfth Night*, III, ii, 84–6. The 'new map' cannot be precisely identified: most maps displayed a multitude of rhumb-lines and many featured the Indies.

4 Cf. *Much Ado about Nothing*, III, iv, 57–8, 'an you be not turned Turk, there's no more sailing by the star'.

PAGE 145

1 *King Lear*, IV, iii, 34–5.
2 *2 Henry IV*, II, iv, 287.
3 *King Lear*, I, ii, 112.
4 *Learned Tico Brahe His Astronomicall Coniectur of the New and Much Admired Star Which Appeared in the Year 1572* (London, 1632), p. 8.
5 *1 Henry VI*, I, i, 2.
6 *Julius Caesar*, II, ii, 30–1.
7 *Othello*, V, ii, 99–101.

PAGE 146

1 *1 Henry IV*, III, iii, 45.
2 Cf. *King Lear*, I, ii, 129 ff. and *Julius Caesar*, I, ii, 140.
3 *1 Henry IV*, V, i, 14–21.
4 *All's Well That Ends Well*, V, iii, 101–3.

PAGE 147

1 *King Lear*, II, iv, 58–9.
2 *Othello*, II, iii, 347–8.

3 *Twelfth Night*, II, iii, 9–10.
4 *Richard II*, I, i, 152–7.

PAGE 149

1 Cf. *All's Well That Ends Well*, II, iii, 10–20.
2 Cf. *2 Henry IV*, I, ii, 122–36.
3 *All's Well That Ends Well*, II, i, 117–127.

PAGE 151

1 Cf. *Julius Caesar*, II, i, 203–5.
2 Cf. Lear's 'pelican daughters' (III, iv, 77) and 'the kind life-rendering pelican' in *Hamlet*, IV, v, 146.
3 Cf. *The Tempest*, IV, i, 249.
4 Sylvester Jourdain, *A discovery of the Barmudas, otherwise called the Ile of Divels* (London, 1610).

PAGE 152

In addition to the references mentioned in the notes to Chapter 11 the following may also be consulted, with the caution that numerous articles published in specialist journals in recent years suggest that a definitive account is yet to be written.

Lawrence Babb, *The Elizabethan Malady. A Study of Melancholia in English Literature from 1580 to 1642* (East Lansing, Michigan, 1951).

J. C. Bucknill, *The Medical Knowledge of Shakespeare* (1860). This discusses the medical references in each play separately. The medical explanations are obsolete and should be ignored.

W. S. C. Copeman, *Doctors and Disease in Tudor Times* (1960).

Charles Creighton. *A History of Epidemics in Britain from A.D. 664 to the Extinction of Plague* (Cambridge, 1891).

R. R. Simpson, *Shakespeare and Medicine* (Edinburgh and London, 1959).

Macleod Yearsley, *Doctors in Elizabethan Drama* (1933).

1 Many sixteenth-century medical books which have survived were preserved in such libraries until recent times. The Lumley library has a number and there are even some in the library of Eton College.

2 A good example is the *Kederminster Pharmacopolium*, a volume of over 500 pages of prescriptions collected by Sir John and Lady Kederminster for use in their own household and among their tenants and friends. It may still be seen in the ancient parish church of St Mary, Langley Marish, near Slough, and a transcript is in the Wellcome Library, which has a number of original MSS. of the same type.

NOTES

3 For the extent of the medical knowledge and skill expected in a 'good housewife' see Gervase Markham, *The English Huswife* (1615).

4 See C. J. Sisson, 'Shakespeare's Helena and Dr William Harvey', *Essays and Studies* (1960), pp. 1–20.

PAGE 153

1 This was an Act to amend the first Medical Act of 1511/12 which restricted practice to the qualified, whose fees the poor were quite unable to afford.

PAGE 154

1 William Clowes, *A Briefe and necessarie Treatise touching the cure of the disease called Morbus Gallicus* (1585), f. 8a.

PAGE 155

1 John H. Raach, *A Directory of English Country Physicians, 1603–43* (1962), and R. S. Roberts, 'The personnel and practice of medicine in Tudor and Stuart England', *Medical History*, VI (October 1962), 363–82. Their findings would imply that the number of doctors to the population resembled modern figures, i.e. one to about 2500; but with the low level of medical knowledge and longer illnesses much more time would be spent on each patient than would be today.

PAGE 157

1 Sisson, *op. cit.* p. 11, suggests that the original of Dr Caius may have been the French-born Dr Peter Chamberlain.

2 *De humani corporis fabrica libri septem* (Basle, 1543). The Geminus version is entitled *Compendiosa totius anatomiae delineatio aere exarata*; the plates were republished with an English text in 1553 and 1559.

PAGE 158

1 For examples of this use of 'tent' and 'search' see *Troilus and Cressida*, II, ii, 14; *Cymbeline*, III, iv, 118; *Lear*, I, iv, 299; *Coriolanus*, I, ix, 31; III, i, 235.

PAGE 160

1 The influence of the same author's *Treatise on Melancholy* (1586) on certain passages in *Hamlet* has been traced by J. Dover Wilson; parallels are listed in the appendix of his book *What Happens in Hamlet* (1935).

PAGE 161

1 Sir Raymond Crawfurd, *The Last Days of Charles II* (Oxford, 1909).

PAGE 162

1 It is described in his *A New Discourse of a stale subject, called the Metamorphosis of Aiax* (1596).

PAGE 163

1 From his 'Description of England' in Holinshed's *Chronicle*, quoted by Sir Walter Raleigh, 'The Age of Elizabeth', *Shakespeare's England*, I (1916), 11.

PAGE 164

1 Girolamo Fracastoro, *Syphilis, sive Morbus Gallicus* (Verona, 1530).

2 W. Clowes, *op. cit.* f. 1b.

PAGE 165

1 F. P. Wilson, *The Plague of Shakespeare's London* (Oxford, 1927; reprinted 1963). See also his recent article 'The Plague', *Shakespeare Survey 15* (1962), pp. 125–9.

2 London, City, *Remembrancia* (1878), pp. 330–1.

3 G. Fracastoro, *De Sympathia at Antipathia...De Contagione...* (Venice, 1546).

4 K. F. Meyer, *Disinfected Mail* (Holton, Kansas, 1962), where it is stated (p. 11) that 'in 1493 the Supreme Magistrate of Public Health in Venice began to extend health precautions to mail and letters'.

PAGE 166

1 *Remembrancia* (1878), pp. 336–7.

PAGE 167

1 E. K. Chambers, *The Elizabethan Stage*, I (Oxford, 1923), 333. It is also quoted in *A Life of Shakespeare*, by J. Q. Adams, pp. 46–7.

PAGE 168

1 R. Willis, *Mount Tabor* (1639), pp. 110–12.

2 J. T. Murray, *English Dramatic Companies 1558–1642*, I, 26; II, 279 and 402.

3 *The Arch-Cheate, or the Cheate of Cheats* (1644), p. 5.

4 *Mount Tabor* (ed. cit.), pp. 92–3.

PAGE 169

1 *Cymbeline*, II, i, 9.

2 *Robin Goodfellow; his mad prankes and Merry feats* (1626). Reprinted in Carew Hazlitt's *Fairy Mythology of Shakespeare* (1875), p. 204.

PAGE 170

1 It is hoped that this will shortly be published in *Somerset Folklore* by R. L. Tongue.

2 *As You Like It*, IV, i, 11–19.

PAGE 171

1 *Twelfth Night*, III, iv, 114.
2 *A Comedy of Errors*, IV, iii, 72–8.
3 J. Jacobs' *English Fairy Tales* (1890).
4 *Ibid.*
5 *Much Ado About Nothing*, I, i, 18–20.
6 E. Spenser, *The Faerie Queene*, Bk III, canto xi, *v.* 54.
7 R. Graves, *The White Goddess* (1948), p. 113.
8 J. Jacobs, *English Fairy Tales*.

PAGE 172

1 *Ibid.*
2 *The Chronicle History of King Leir* (Licensed 1594).
3 *Gesta Romanorum* (trans. Swan and Hooper, 1905), tale CLIII.
4 J. Jacobs, *More English Fairy Tales* (1894).
5 From a chapbook, *The Three Kings of Colchester*, retold in Halliwell-Phillipps' *Nursery Rhymes and Tales*.
6 See G. H. Gerould, *The Grateful Dead* (1908).

PAGE 173

1 *The Knight of the Burning Pestle*, *The Works of Beaumont and Fletcher*, vol. VI (Cambridge, 1908), III, i, 205.
2 Preserved in the archives of the School of Scottish Studies, Edinburgh.
3 *The Knight of the Burning Pestle* (ed. cit.), I, i, 173.
4 R. Scot, *The Discoverie of Witchcraft* (ed. Montague Summers, 1930), p. 86.
5 *The Winter's Tale*, II, i, 24–9.
6 J. Jacobs, *English Fairy Tales* (ed. cit.).
7 Patrick Kennedy, *Legendary Fictions of the Irish Celts* (1891), p. 213.

PAGE 174

1 S. Rowland, *The Letting of Humor's Blood in the Head-Vaine* (1600), pp. 64–5.
2 Rowland has it 'halfe-pottes'.
3 John Brand, *Popular Antiquities* (1894), p. 390.
4 Alice Gomme, *The Dictionary of Folk-Lore, Part I, Games*, I, 21.

PAGE 175

1 Philip Sidney, *The Last Part of the Countesse of Pembroke's Arcadia* (1593); *The Complete Works of Sir Philip Sidney* (Cambridge, 1922), II, 219–20.
2 *The Works of Sir John Suckling* (ed. A. H. Thompson, 1910), p. 20.
3 *The Poetical Works of Robert Herrick* (Oxford, 1915), p. 33.

4 *The Complete Works of Sir Philip Sidney* (ed. cit.), II, 323.
5 *Kemps Nine Daies Wonder* (1600), reprinted Camden Society (1840), pp. 7 and 9–10.
6 Beaumont and Fletcher, *The Two Noble Kinsmen* (ed. cit.), IX, III, v.
7 Rowley, Dekker and Ford, *The Witch of Edmonton* (1658), III, iv.
8 *Twelfth Night*, I, iii, 43.

PAGE 176

1 Shirley and Chapman, *The Ball*, IV, i.
2 F. Quarles, *Emblems* (1635), 30–3.
3 John Bunyan, *A Book for Boys and Girles* (1686, facs. 1890), p. 47.
4 *Two Noble Kinsmen* (ed. cit.), V, i, 361.
5 *The Knight of the Burning Pestle* (ed. cit.), I, i, 178.
6 J. O. Halliwell-Phillipps, *Nursery Rhymes and Nursery Tales of England* (5th edn.), p. 204.
7 *Twelfth Night*, III, iv, 29, 30.
8 *King Lear*, IV, vi, 57–8.
9 *Hamlet*, IV, ii, 32.
10 Anne Halkett, *Autobiography*, Camden Society (1875), p. 21.
11 *The Dramatic Works of Thomas Dekker*, I (1873), 257.

PAGE 177

1 *The Poetical Works of Robert Herrick* (ed. cit.), pp. 230–1.
2 Martin Lluellyn, *Men-Miracles* (Oxford, 1646), pp. 61–2.
3 Ben Jonson, *Christmas his Masque*, VIII (Herford and Simpson, Oxford, 1947), 438–9.

PAGE 178

1 In *Hobsons Horse-load of Letters*, by Gervase Markham, there is *A Merry Letter from an Officer of the twelve days to a Lord of Christmas* (no. III), which well illustrates the festivities of the time.
2 J. Stubbes, *The Anatomie of Abuses* (1st edn. 1585; ed. by F. J. Furnivall, 1879), pt. I, p. 149.

PAGE 179

1 *Ibid.* p. 147.

PAGE 180

1 See Roy C. Strong, *Portraits of Queen Elizabeth*, I (1963), 66, 68 and plate x for the Pinacoteca di Siena 'sieve' portrait (which Strong calls 'One of the finest and most tantalizing portraits of the Queen'). The

NOTES

sieve appears on p. 68 of Whitney's *Emblems* (illustrated in Strong, plate XX); the explanatory verse below the emblem could itself serve as a motto, not only for the difficulties of a monarch, but for one of Shakespeare's chief preoccupations:

The fruictefull feilde amid the goodlie croppe,
The hurtfull tares, and dernell ofte doe growe,
And many times, doe mounte aboue the toppe
Of highest corne: But skilfull man doth knowe,
When graine is ripe, with siue to purge the seedes,
From chaffe, and duste, and all the other weedes.

By which is ment, sith wicked men abounde,
That harde it is, the good from bad to trie:
The prudent sorte, shoulde haue suche iudgement
  sounde,
  And sifte the good, and to discerne their deedes,
  And weye the bad, noe better then the weedes.

For the pillars of Hercules, see Strong, p. 113 (E. 23) and plate XX; for the emblems used in the portraits of the Queen, see p. 22.

2 *The Queenes Maiesties Passage through the Citie of London to Westminster the Day before her Coronacion,* facsimile published by Yale U.P. (1960), ed. James M. Osborn, pp. 33–4.

PAGE 181

1 *Dialogues Moral and Political,* quoted Nichols, *The Progresses of Queen Elizabeth,* I, p. xvi.
2 In this connection see Sir Thomas Browne's *Religio Medici*; according to him Nature is nothing but a 'Universal Manuscript', written in hieroglyphics. To quote an important passage: 'The Finger of God hath left an inscription upon all his works, not graphical or composed of Letters, but of their several forms, constitutions, parts and operations which, aptly joined together, do make one word that doth express their natures. By these Letters God calls the Stars by their names; and by this Alphabet Adam assigned to every creature a name peculiar to its Nature' (*Religio Medici* (Keynes ed., 1928), I, 75).
3 Mario Praz, *Studies in Seventeenth Century Imagery,* I (1939), 20.

PAGE 182

1 Eric Mercer, *English Art, 1553–1625* (1962), pp. 126–7; Rosemary Freeman, *English Emblem Books* (1948), p. 95. For a full account of the tapestries, see an article by A. F. Kendrick in the *Walpole Society Annual,* II (1912–13), 89–97.

PAGE 184

1 The device of the bear appears in other collections as well, but the source cited in the text seems the most likely.
2 Giuliano Pellegrini, 'Coelum Britanicum: A Masque at White Hell. Studio sulle fonti iconologiche italiane', *Rivista di Letterature Moderne e Comparate,* XV (April–June 1962), 85–107.

PAGE 185

1 See Allan Gilbert, *The Principles and Practice of Criticism* (1959), p. 134.

PAGE 191

1 *The Medieval Stage* (Oxford, 1903), II, 358.
2 'The Reputation of Herod in Early English Literature', *Speculum,* VIII (October 1933), 59–61, 67.
3 Hardin Craig (ed.), *Two Coventry Corpus Christi Plays* (Oxford, 1957), p. 27.

PAGE 192

1 *Ibid.* pp. 82–6.
2 *From Mankind to Marlowe* (Cambridge, Mass., 1962).
3 *Ibid.* pp. 15, 68, 80–1.
4 *The Foot out of the Snare* (1624), p. 68.
5 Dedication to *Volpone* in *Ben Jonson,* ed. C. H. Herford and Percy and Evelyn Simpson (Oxford, 1925–52), V, 19. This edition is hereafter referred to as 'Herford and Simpson'.
6 *Twelfth Night* in *The Works of William Shakespeare,* ed. W. G. Clark and A. Wright, IV, ii, 134–8. References throughout are to this edition.
7 Bevington, *op. cit.* p. 82.
8 II, iv, 422–39.
9 I, ii, 42.
10 Bevington, *op. cit.* pp. 14, 19, 20, 21, 25, 54, 71, 74, 75, 92, 110.
11 IV, ii, 21–2.

PAGE 193

1 I, ii, 51–2, 95–8.
2 I, ii, 70–1.
3 I, ii, 6, 108, 4, 102, 69; III, i, 5, 78; I, ii, 43, 32.
4 V, i, 214–16.
5 *Virgidemiarum* (1597), satires i, iii.

PAGE 194

1 III, ii, 47.
2 *Tarltons Jests* (1638), C2ᵛ–C3ʳ.
3 *The Antipodes* (1640), D3ʳ.

4 *The Works of Christopher Marlowe*, ed. C. F. Tucker Brooke (Oxford, 1941), p. 9.

5 *Ibid.* p. 7.

PAGE 195

1 *Quips upon Questions* (1600), C1ᵛ.

2 *Modern Language Review*, LVII (October, 1962), 558.

3 *Brief Lives*, ed. A. Clark (Oxford, 1898), II, 226.

4 *The Roman Actor* (1629), F3ᵛ.

PAGE 196

1 'A Short Discourse of the English Stage' in *Critical Essays of the Seventeenth Century*, ed. J. E. Spingarn (Oxford, 1908–9), II, 94–5.

2 In the preface (dated 1613) to *Speculum Aistheticum*, a German tr. of Thomas Tomkis' *Lingua* (1607); tr. and quoted by Klein, *op. cit.* p. 556.

3 Brome, *op. cit.* L4ʳ.

4 Herford and Simpson, VIII, 587.

5 *The Poetical Works of Robert Herrick*, ed. F. W. Moorman (Oxford, 1921), p. 150.

6 Herford and Simpson, VI, 280.

PAGE 197

1 T. Palmer in F. Beaumont and J. Fletcher, *Comedies and Tragedies* (1647), F2ᵛ.

2 *Roscius Anglicanus* (1708), pp. 21, 24. Though Joseph Taylor did not join the King's Men until 1619, i.e. three years after the death of Shakespeare, he may have received 'instruction' from him earlier.

3 *An Apology for Actors* (1612), C3ᵛ. The italics are mine.

4 *The Three Parnassus Plays*, ed. J. B. Leishman (1949), pp. 336–7.

5 Letoy, *The Antipodes*, E1ᵛ, D3ʳ.

PAGE 198

1 Massinger, *op. cit.* C2ᵛ.

2 Complimentary verses in Sir William Davenant's *The Just Italian* (1630), A4ʳ.

3 *The Doubtful Heir* (1652), A4ʳ.

4 Brome, *op. cit.* D3ʳ.

5 Flecknoe, *op. cit.* p. 95.

PAGE 199

1 *Histrio-Mastix* (1610), F4ʳ, F4ᵛ.

2 See Allardyce Nicoll, *The Development of the Theatre* (1927), pp. 131–3.

3 *Hannibal and Scipio* (1637), A3ᵛ.

4 *The Unfortunate Mother* (1640), A2ᵛ–A4ʳ.

PAGE 200

1 John Webster, *The Duchess of Malfi*, ed. F. L. Lucas (1958), V, iii, 1–4.

2 See *Chief Pre-Shakespearean Dramas*, ed. J. Q. Adams (1924), p. 400.

PAGE 201

1 *Ibid.* pp. 657–8.

2 *Jacob and Esau* (1658), Ciiiᵛ.

3 *The Famous Chronicle of King Edward the First* (1593), F4ʳ.

4 *Ibid.* G1ʳ, G2ᵛ, H4ʳ.

5 *Ibid.* H3ᵛ–H4ʳ.

PAGE 202

1 *The Love of King David and Fair Bethsabe* (1599), B1ᵛ.

2 George R. Kernodle, *From Art to Theatre* (Chicago, 1944), p. 120.

3 *The Faithful Shepherdesse* (1634), A3ᵛ, A4ʳ.

4 Kernodle, *op. cit.* p. 74.

5 IV, iv: item 8 in 'The Order of the Coronation'.

6 *Sophonisba* (1606), F1ᵛ.

7 *The Fatal Contract* (1661), H3ʳ.

8 *The Cuck-Queanes, The Faery Pastorall* (1824), pp. 184, 187.

9 *The Elizabethan Stage*, III (Oxford, 1923), 138.

10 Kernodle, *op. cit.* pp. 82–3.

11 *Queen Anne's New World of Words* (1611), p. 473.

12 *Henslowe Papers*, ed. W. W. Greg (1907), p. 116, l. 65.

PAGE 203

1 George Chapman, Ben Jonson, John Marston, *Eastward Ho!* (1605), A2ʳ.

2 Philip Massinger, *The Renegado* (1630), E3ʳ, E3ᵛ, E4ʳ.

3 *The Plays of George Chapman: The Tragedies*, ed. T. M. Parrott (New York, 1961), I, 405–6, 464.

4 Randle Cotgrave, *A Dictionary of the French and English Tongues* (1611). See entry under 'Eschafaut'.

5 Florio, *op. cit.* p. 351.

6 *The Divils Charter* (1607), F4ᵛ, G1ʳ.

7 *The Plays and Poems of Robert Green*, ed. J. C. Collins, (1905), II, 112.

8 Barnes, *op. cit.* L3ʳ.

PAGE 204

1 *The Workes of Beniamin Jonson* (1616), p. 305.

PAGE 205

1 The ensuing extracts are taken from prefaces printed in Sir Walter Greg, *Bibliography of the English Printed Drama to the Restoration*, III (1957), 1191–1260.

PAGE 207

1 Greg, *Bibliography of the English Printed Drama*, IV (1959), clxii. The matter is more fully discussed in the same author's *Some Aspects and Problems of London Publishing between 1550 and 1650* (Oxford, 1956). For a different interpretation of the evidence see Leo Kirschbaum, *Shakespeare and the Stationers* (Columbus, Ohio, 1955). A more recent, important article is C. J. Sisson's 'The Laws of Elizabethan Copyright: The Stationers' View', *The Library*, 5th series, XV (March 1960), 8–20, which discusses the rival claims to copyright in Rider's *Dictionary*.

2 Greg, *London Publishing*, pp. 75–6.

3 Now that Greg's edition of Henslowe's *Diary* is difficult to obtain, the material may most conveniently be studied in the edition by R. A. Foakes and R. T. Rickert (Cambridge, 1961). See also R. A. Foakes, 'The significance of Henslowe's *Diary*', *Philologica Pragensia*, III (1960), 214–22.

4 E. K. Chambers, *The Elizabethan Stage* (1923), III, 182.

PAGE 208

1 Chambers, *op. cit.* III, 183.

2 Chambers, *op. cit.* III, 184.

3 Chambers, *op. cit.* III, 184. See also Greg, *The Shakespeare First Folio* (1955), pp. 90–1, who quotes Chambers' reasoning with approval, and also includes A. W. Pollard's earlier arguments from the facts and figures.

4 Fredson T. Bowers, *On Editing Shakespeare and the Elizabethan Dramatists* (Pennsylvania, 1955), pp. 17–18. Bowers adds that 'Dekker seems often to have been eager to print his popular plays, doubtless because he needed the extra profit...'.

5 John Russell Brown, 'The printing of John Webster's plays (I)', *Studies in Bibliography*, VI (1954), 118–19.

6 Bowers, *op. cit.* pp. 11–12.

7 Greg, *The Shakespeare First Folio*, pp. 176–425.

PAGE 209

1 Bowers, *op. cit.* p. 13.

2 British Museum MS. Egerton 1994. For a full study see the edition published by the Malone Society (1953).

3 British Museum Additional MS. 36758. For a full study see the edition published by the Malone Society (1951).

4 The Brogyntyn manuscript in the possession of Lord Harlech. For a full study see the edition published by the Malone Society (1951).

PAGE 210

1 Studies in this field are perhaps too numerous to list here in detail. In addition to the works by Greg and Bowers already mentioned, however, attention may be drawn to R. B. McKerrow's *An Introduction to Bibliography* (1927), which was something of a pioneer work and still of great value, Alice Walker's *Textual Problems of the First Folio* (1953), and the many articles by Bowers, Charlton Hinman and others in *Studies in Bibliography*, *Shakespeare Quarterly*, etc. There will possibly have to be some rethinking of the whole subject after the publication of Hinman's *The Printing and Proof-Reading of the First Folio of Shakespeare* which is expected shortly from the Oxford University Press.

2 Charlton Hinman, 'Cast-off copy for the First Folio of Shakespeare', *Shakespeare Quarterly*, VI (1955), 257–73; George Walton Williams, 'Setting by Formes in Quarto Printing', *Studies in Bibliography*, XI (1958), 39–53.

3 Robert K. Turner, Jr., 'Printing methods and textual problems in *A Midsummer Night's Dream* Q1', *Studies in Bibliography*, XV (1962), 33–55; John Russell Brown, 'The printing of John Webster's plays (III): *The Duchess of Malfi*', *Studies in Bibliography*, XV (1962), 57–69.

4 Studies in compositor determination are again very numerous. A good deal of material will be found in the books and articles mentioned in note 1, p. 210 above. For studies of the practical applications of this particular technique attention may be drawn to Alice Walker's 'Some editorial principles (with special reference to *Henry V*)', *Studies in Bibliography*, VIII (1956), 95–111 (the last sentence of which reads 'In accidentals, as in substantive readings, we need to be chary of supposing that compositors reproduced copy with the conservatism that has sometimes been assumed'), and to the textual introductions to the plays in Bowers' four-volume edition of *The Dramatic Works of Thomas Dekker* (Cambridge, 1953–61).

5 John Crow, 'Editing and emending', *Essays and Studies* (1955), pp. 1–20.

NOTES

PAGE 212

1 McKerrow, *An Introduction to Bibliography*, p. 205, remarks that 'it was usual, or at any rate not uncommon, for an author to attend in person at the printing-house in order to revise proofs', and he quotes a number of examples of this practice. Not many of these, however, seem to involve plays. McKerrow himself said a little earlier, 'Of all matters connected with the book-trade in the Elizabethan times, the one of which we know least is probably the relation of the author to the publisher or printer', and I have the impression that a good many authors seem to have been only too ready to find good excuses for their absence from the house at the crucial time—and ready enough to blame the printer for the consequences!

2 Most of what we know about proof-reading at this time is to be found in Percy Simpson's *Proof-reading in the Sixteenth, Seventeenth, and Eighteenth Centuries* (1935). The question as it affects the First Folio is discussed in Hinman's recent study (see note 1, p. 210).

3 Baldwin Maxwell, *Studies in the Shakespeare Apocrypha* (New York, 1956).

PAGE 213

1 *The Times Literary Supplement*, 15 January 1960, p. 40.

2 A useful start was made in William Miller's 'A London Ornament Stock: 1598–1683', *Studies in Bibliography*, VII (1955), 125–51.

PAGE 214

1 1st edn. 1597; 2nd edn. 1608; 3rd edn. 1771; ed. R. A. Harman, in modernized spelling (1952); here quoted from Harman's edn. Cf. also *Shakespeare's England*, edd. C. T. Onions *et al.* (1916), II, 22.

2 J. A. Westrup, 'Domestic music under the Stuarts', *Proceedings of the Royal Musical Association*, LXVIII (1941–2), 19–53, particularly p. 20.

3 Cf. the comments of J. C. Maxwell, with references to previous literature in the *New Shakespeare* edn., p. 191.

PAGE 215

1 Cf. K. D. McRae's facsimile edition of *Bodin: The Six Books of a Commonweal* (Cambridge, Mass., 1962), which makes the Jacobean translation of 1606 conveniently available.

PAGE 216

1 D. P. Walker, 'Musical Humanism in the 16th and early 17th centuries', *Music Review*, II–III (1941–2); F. A. Yates, 'Dramatic religious processions in Paris in the late 16th century', *Annales Musicologiques*, II, (1954).

PAGE 218

1 The first Quarto reads 'viole', the fourth quarto 'viall'. The Globe edition and most modern editors read 'viol'.

PAGE 219

1 W. Chappell, *Popular Music of the Olden Time* (1859), I, 241; *Roxburghe Ballads* (1871–99), II, 460; *Lute Society Journal*, III (1961), 15; Jonson and Marston, *Eastward Ho!* Act II, sc. 1.

2 Chappell, *op. cit.* I, 72: Marston, *Works*, ed. Harvey-Wood, I, 42 and 226; Robinson, *Handful of Pleasant Delights*, ed. Arber, pp. 24–7, ed. Rollins, pp. 29 and 96; J. Ward (ed.), *Dublin Virginal Manuscript* (Wellesley, Mass., 1954), p. 27.

PAGE 220

1 F. S. Boas, *Songs and Lyrics from the English Playbooks* (1945), pp. 29, 44.

2 H. E. Rollins, *Old English Ballads* (1920), pp. 47–53; Nashe, *Works*, ed. McKerrow, III, 104; Chappell, *op. cit.* I, 199; Richard Johnson, *Golden Garland of Princely Roses* (1620), sig. A. ii. 5; G. Bontoux, *La Chanson en Angleterre* (1936), p. 49.

The longer extracts from the Lisle Letters and the State Papers are given date-references, by which they can be located in *Letters and Papers of Henry VIII* (cf. note 1, p. 226), from which latter reference the number of the manuscript can then be traced in the P.R.O. key.

PAGE 223

1 H. C. Wyld, *History of Modern Colloquial English* (1920) (latest edn. 1953).

2 Rose Macaulay, *Letters to a Friend* (1950).

PAGE 224

1 *Cambridge History of English Literature*, III, ch. 22 (1909).

2 F. P. Wilson, *Shakespeare and the Diction of Common Life*, British Academy Annual Shakespeare Lecture (1941).

3 *Shakespeare's Pronunciation* (New Haven, 1953).

4 *Shakespeare as Critic of Language* (Shakespeare Assoc., 1934); *Shakespeare and Rhetoric* (English Assoc., *Essays and Studies*, XXIX, 1943). And *Endeavors of Art* (Univ. of Wisconsin Press, 1954).

5 E.g. the women talking about Old Cole's murder, and Mistress Winchcomb the second discussing with her gossip household catering problems and her new finery of French hood and silken gown.

PAGE 225

1 *English Literature in the Sixteenth Century, Excluding Drama*, Bk II, III, 277, Oxford History of English Literature (1954).

PAGE 226

1 In the P.R.O., in Lisle Papers, 18 vols. (S.P. 3) and State Papers, Henry VIII (S.P. 1): calendared in *Letters and Papers of Henry VIII*, ed. Brewer and Gairdner.

2 *The Enchanted Glass* (New York, 1936).

PAGE 227

1 *The Correspondence of Lady Katharine Paston, 1603–27*, ed. R. Hughey (Norfolk Record Soc. vol. 14, 1941).

2 Cf. Lady Granville (1810): 'My month nurse, a treasure, and the most respectable of dames' (*O.E.D.*).

PAGE 229

1 For easily accessible specimens see the present writer's *Letters of King Henry VIII* (1936), especially pt. III, chs. I, II.

PAGE 231

1 On 12 November 1535, in which he says, 'We have no news but that it is preached here [i.e. London] that priests must have wives'.

PAGE 233

1 *Letters of John Chamberlain* (Camden Soc., 1861).

2 Ralph Winwood, *Memorials of State* (1725).

INDEX

INDEX

INDEX

INDEX

INDEX

INDEX

INDEX

Tresham, Sir Thomas, 73
Trevisa, 39
Trevor-Roper, H. R., 81 n.
Trial of Treasure, 219–20
Trinity House, Deptford, 27–8
*A true credible report of a great fight at sea between...
England and...Spain* (1600), 34
Truth brought to light (1651), 203–4 and Plate XXVII C
Tuke, Sir Brian, 227
Turberville, George, 31
Turks, 40, 40 n. 6, 144 n. 2
 see foreigners
Turler, Jerome, 43
Turner, Robert K., 210 n. 3
Tyndale, William, 105–6, 107

Ubaldini, Petruccio, 34
Udall, John, 126
Udall, Nicholas, 195
Underhill, William, 126
Uniformity, Bill of, 121
universities, 57, 63–6, 115–16, 121–2, 200
 acting at Cambridge, 197
 curriculum, 64–5
 'the third university' (London), 70–2, 72 n. 2
University Wits, 129–30
Unwin, George, 6
urinoscopy, 156

vagrants, 8, 111, 115
Venice, 46–7
Venn, John, 57
Vesalius, Andreas, 148, 157
Vesterian controversy, 124–5
Vicary, Thomas, 157
Vice, the, 191–2
Virgil, 61, 64
Virginia Company, 12, 27, 33
voyage literature, 31–4, 39–42

Wagenaer, L. J., *The mariners mirrour*, 28, 28 n.
wages, 18, 19
Wagner, Alice, 210 nn. 1 and 3
Wagner, H. R., 29 n.
Walker, C. F., 22 n.
Walker, D. P., 216 n.
Walker, J. D. (ed.), 79 n.
Walkley, Thomas, 212
Wallis, Helen M., 28 n.
Wallis, John, 66 n.
Walsingham, Sir Francis, 31, 109, 127
Walter of Henley, 19
Waltham Black Act, 83
Ward, J. (ed.), 219 n.
Ward, John, 71 n., 72 n.
Warde, Luke, 30, 32

Warley, Thomas, 237, 239
Warmington, William, 90 n.
Warwickshire, 14–15
 Saxton's map of, 15
Waters, D. W., 21 n., 25 n., 27 n., 28, 28 n., 29 n.
Wateson, George, 25
Watson, Foster, 44 n.
Watson, Thomas, 88
Waymouth, George, 32–3
Wayte, Antony, 231, 238
Webster, 207, 208, 210, 212
 Duchess of Malfi, 199–200 (staging)
Weckmann, Luis, 41 n.
Westcote, Sebastian, 195
Westminster Hall, 75–7, 75 n. 2, 81, 85–6, Plate X A
Westrup, J. A., 214 n.
Whetstone, George, 206
Whitelock, James, 80 n.
Whitgift, John, 109, 125
Whitney, Geffrey, 180 n. 1, 182, 185–6, 187
Wilcox, Thomas, 125
Willcock, G. D., 224
Willes, Richard, 51
Willett, Andrew, 183
Williams, George Walton, 210 n. 2
Williams, Roger, 32 n.
Williamson, G. C., 29 n.
Williamson, J. A., 29 n.
Willis, Richard, 51, 167–8, 169
Willoughby, Sir Hugh, 32
Willson, D. H., 118 n.
Wilson, F. P., 32 n., 98 n. 1, 165, 165 n., 224
Wilson, H. A. (ed.), 59 n.
Wilson, J. Dover, 89 n., 160 n.
Wilson, Robert, *Three Ladies of London*, 44, 46–7, 49, 50, 51 n. 10, 52
Wilson, Robert, actor, 193
Wilson, Thomas, 43, 78, 78 n. 1, 80, 80 n. 3, 81 n., 225
Winwood, Ralph, 233 n.
Witch of Edmonton, 175
Wither, George, 91, 100 n. 5, 175, 207
Withington, R., 51
Wittkower, R., 39–40, 40 n.
Witton (Chester), grammar school, 53
Woldan, Erich, 39 n. 3
Worcester, Earl of, 10, 168
working-class, 17–19, 115–16
 working day, 17–18
Wright, Edward, 28, 144
Wright, Louis B., 34, 41 n., 111 n.
Wright, Thomas, 216
Wriothesley, Thomas, 235–7
Wyld, H. C., 223–4

Yates, F. A., 216 n.
Yearsley, Macleod, 258 n.